Emerging Issues in Sustainable Development: International Law and Policy

Emerging Issues in Sustainable Development: International Law and Policy

Weston Abernathy

STATES
ACADEMIC PRESS
www.statesacademicpress.com

Published by States Academic Press,
109 South 5th Street,
Brooklyn, NY 11249, USA

ISBN: 978-1-63989-176-4

Cataloging-in-Publication Data

Emerging issues in sustainable development : international law
and policy / Weston Abernathy.
p. cm.
Includes bibliographical references and index.
ISBN 978-1-63989-176-4
1. Sustainable development--Law and legislation. 2. Sustainable development--
Government policy. 3. Environmental law, International. 4. Environmental law.
I. Abernathy, Weston.

K3585 .E44 2022
344.046--dc23

For information on all States Academic Press publications
visit our website at www.statesacademicpress.com

STATES
ACADEMIC PRESS

Contents

Preface

The idea which focuses on meeting human development goals without exhausting the availability of resources for future generations is referred to as sustainable development. It is a way of organizing society and its interaction with the environment so that it can exist in the long term. Sustainable development requires understanding the issues from various angles such as environmentalist and economical. It is essential in tackling a number of inter-related global issues such as poverty, inequality, hunger, and environmental degradation. There has been rapid progress in this area and the environmental reforms are finding their way across multiple industries. This book unravels the recent studies on international laws and policies related to sustainable development. It will provide comprehensive knowledge to the readers.

After months of intensive research and writing, this book is the end result of all who devoted their time and efforts in the initiation and progress of this book. It will surely be a source of reference in enhancing the required knowledge of the new developments in the area. During the course of developing this book, certain measures such as accuracy, authenticity and research focused analytical studies were given preference in order to produce a comprehensive book in the area of study.

This book would not have been possible without the efforts of the authors and the publisher. I extend my sincere thanks to them. Secondly, I express my gratitude to my family and well-wishers. And most importantly, I thank my students for constantly expressing their willingness and curiosity in enhancing their knowledge in the field, which encourages me to take up further research projects for the advancement of the area.

Weston Abernathy

1

Introduction

1. Background

The current state of the world is characterised by two undeniable facts. First, there is ongoing and massive environmental degradation.[1] The global environmental problems attracting the attention of the world include, but are not limited to, the depletion of the ozone layer, high rates of destruction of the earth's biodiversity, including fauna and flora, and increased emissions of anthropogenic greenhouse gases which threaten to destabilise the earth's climate system.

Second, there is a development gap between the North and the South.[2] While the developed North is wealthy, the developing South is characterised by widespread poverty and underdevelopment.[3] While globalisation has led to greater wealth and higher standards of living in industrialised societies, the same is not true in non-industrialised societies.[4] The gap between rich and poor continues to increase. This is true not only for the gap between rich and poor countries, but also for the gap between rich and poor people within these countries.

What is more, the current environmental and developmental crises are not unrelated.[5] The link between environmental degradation, on the one hand, and development and lack of develop-

1 There is much literature and official documentation detailing the ever worsening state of the environment. See, eg, VP Nanda & G Pring *International environmental law and policy for the 21st century* (2003) 3 *et seq*; P Sands *Principles of international environmental law: volume I: Frameworks, standards and implementation* (1995) 9 *et seq*. See especially M Strong *Where on earth are we going?* (2000), in particular 11 - 20. See also B Ward 'Only one earth, Stockholm 1972' in N Cross (ed) *Evidence for hope: The search for sustainable development* (2003) 4. See also World Bank *World development report* (2003) 2 *et seq*.

2 In this study, the term North is used to denote developed countries and South is used to refer to developing countries.

3 For example, according to the 2003 World Bank (n 1 above) the average income of the 20 richest countries in the world is 37 times that of the 20 poorest countries in the world. World Bank *World Development Report* (2003) 3. See also N Schrijver 'De verankering en betekenis van duurzame ontwikkeling in het internationale recht' 2003 *Mededelinge van de Nederlandse Vereniging voor Internationaal Recht: Volkenrecht en Duurzame Ontwikkeling* 1 7

4 The then president of the World Bank, James Wolfensohn, remarked as follows in 2003: 'In our world of 6 billion, one billion owns 80% of the global GDP, while another struggles to survive on less than a dollar a day. This is a world out of balance'. J Wolfensohn 'A new global balance: The challenge of leadership' speech delivered to the Board of Governors of the World Bank, September 2003, Dubai (on file with author).

5 See generally World Commission on Environment Development *Our common future* (1987).

ment, on the other, is well established.[6] Wealthy nations have acquired their prosperity as a result of rapid industrialisation. Rapid industrialisation has, in turn, lead to the degradation of the environment. For example, as a result of a variety of human activities flowing from industrialisation, atmospheric concentrations of greenhouse gases have increased to the extent that they threaten to change the earth's climate with drastic consequences.[7] Developing countries, also seeking development, are now embarking on the same road to industrialisation, which poses a severe danger to the environment.

The process of industrialisation is not the only link between development concerns and environmental degradation. Poverty, a result of underdevelopment, is itself a major cause of environmental degradation.[8] Poor people destroy their immediate environment in order to survive. This overexploitation of natural resources for short-term survival can only be countered through the upliftment of the world's poor to standards that accord with humanity.

The environmental and social crises described above are largely due to a paradigm in which economic growth concerns have triumphed over every other concern.[9] This paradigm has encouraged the economic optimalisation of natural resource consumption, resulting in environ-mental degradation. Further, this economic growth paradigm has been responsible for the promotion of economic policies based on the Washington Consensus, which have had the effect of hurting the poorest people in poor countries.[10]

It is against this background that the concept of sustainable development was conceived. The concept, having its origins at the 1972 United Nations Conference on the Human Environment, continues to evolve. This study is about the conceptualisation of sustainable development.

6 WCED (n 5 above) 28.

7 See in general D Bodansky 'The United Nations Framework Convention on Climate Change: A commentary' (1993) 18 *Yale Law Journal of International Law* 451. See also L Thoms 'A comparative analysis of international regimes on ozone and climate change with implications for regime design' (2003) 41 *Columbia Journal of Transnational Law* 795. See further discussion in ch 5 below.

8 See WCED (n 5 above) 28. See also A Hurrel and B Kingsbury 'The international politics of the environment: An introduction' in A Hurrel and B Kingsbury (eds) *The international politics of the environment* (1993) 3.

9 HD Johnson 'Whose earth is it anyway?' (2002) 39 *UN Chronicle* 8 8. See also RA Malviya 'Sustainable development and environment: emerging trends and issues' (1996) 32 *Indian Journal of International Law* 57 58. See also Ward (n 1 above) 5.

10 The Washington Consensus is an approach to development endorsed by the international financing institutions in Washington, namely the World Bank and the IMF and is based on three pillars, namely, privatisation, liberalisation and macrostability. J Stiglitz *Globalization and its discontents* (2003) 67. On the effects of the Washington Consensus on the poor see also M Chossudovsky *The globalization of poverty: The impacts of IMF and World Bank reforms* (1997). See also World Bank *Adjustment lending: An evaluation of ten years experience* (1988) 30.

2. Study objectives and methodology

The World Commission on Environment and Development defined sustainable development as 'development that meets needs of the present generation without compromising the ability of future generations to meet their own needs'.[11] While this definition is fashionable it is open to various and conflicting interpretations and can thus lead to indeterminacy. The first objective of this study is, therefore, to move beyond this indeterminacy in the conceptualisation of sustainable development in order to make the concept a useful legal tool. To do this requires a nuanced conceptualisation that takes into account the intricacies involved in sustainable development discourse. The conceptualisation offered in this study is influenced largely by ethical considerations surrounding the evolution of sustainable development as a policy and legal concept.

While I am of the view that such a conceptualisation of sustainable development is useful in and of itself, this study has a secondary objective. The secondary objective of the study is to determine what influence, if at all, sustainable development has had on international law and whether this influence is consistent with the rationale underlying the evolution of sustainable development.

The study will thus be approached in two stages. The first stage, in Part A, is to conceptualise sustainable development and suggest a role for sustainable development in international law. This is largely done through a study and analysis of existing literature on sustainable development. The vast majority of the literature analysed is taken from legal writings. However, given the nature of sustainable development, and in particular the fact that it impacts on a variety of disciplines, literature from politics, economics and ethics studies is also included. In addition to literature studies and analysis, the conceptualisation of sustainable development is done with the aid of the key instruments adopted by the international community and related to sustainable development. Further, the historical evolution of sustainable development, and objections to sustainable development from various quarters are used to suggest a nuanced conceptualisation of sustainable development that can be used as a framework to analyse various instruments, as well as aiding policy and law-making. In this respect the three sets of values of sustainable development, namely, social, economic and environmental, play a

11 WCED (n 5 above) 43.

central role in the development of a nuanced conceptualisation of sustainable development.

The second stage of the study, Part B, involves testing the conceptualisation of sustainable development against regimes of international law adopted pursuant to sustainable development. This is undertaken, again, with the aid of literature, primarily legal literature, pertaining to the specific regimes analysed. In addition, the texts of legal regimes such as official documentation adopted under the said regimes, are used as analytical aids.

3. Parameters

A project such as this has the potential to become unmanageable. There are countless instruments, environmental[12] and economic,[13] that can be studied under this topic. In order to make the task manageable I set a few parameters which were adhered to relatively strictly in determining which instruments were to be analysed in the second part of the study, and also from which perspective they were to be studied. The first parameter is that the study is to be limited to normative aspects of sustainable development as opposed to the institutional aspects. The concept of sustainable development carries with it many institutional implications. At the same time, any understanding of sustainable development is impacted upon by many

12 Examples here include, amongst others, the Basel Convention on the Control of Transboundary Movement of Hazardous Wastes and their Disposal, the United Nations Convention to Combat Desertification in those Countries Experiencing Serious Drought and/or Desertification, Particularly in Africa, the Agreement for the Implementation of the Provisions of the United Nations Convention on the Law of the Sea Relating to the Conservation and Management of Straddling and Highly Migratory Fish Stocks, the Convention Against the Illegal Trade in Endangered Species of Wild Fauna and Flora, the Vienna Convention for the Protection of the Ozone, the Montreal Protocol on Substances that Deplete the Ozone Layer, the United Nations Framework Convention on Climate Change and the Kyoto Protocol to the United Nations Convention on Climate Change. All these instruments are reproduced in P Cullet & A Gowlland-Gualtieri (eds) *Key materials in international environmental law* (2004).

13 These would include, amongst others, the World Bank, the IMF, the Word Trade Organisation, the various regional multilateral Banks, the EU, the AU and NAFTA.

factors pertaining to institutional legitimacy.[14] Institutional questions pertaining to the Conference of Parties established under multilateral environmental agreements (MEAs) and the legitimacy of decision-making in international economic institutions are topics worthy of study.[15] However, these questions, while interesting and important, are not addressed in this study. While institutional structures are described, this is done merely to set the background against which normative questions are analysed. This is true especially with respect to the chapter on the Global Environment Facility (GEF).

The second parameter pertains to geographical limitations. Only global regimes are considered in the study. Thus, while institutions of Europe have, in many innovative ways, provided fertile ground for the analysis of practices relating to sustainable development,[16] regional regimes such as the European Union are not considered in the study. As well, perhaps the concept of sustainable development will have the

14 In the context of 'fairness', Franck shows that while the normative aspect of fairness, distributive justice, is distinct from the institutional (or procedural), there is a relationship between the two. See TM Franck *Fairness in international law and institutions* (1995) 7 who states as follows: 'These two aspects of fairness – the substantive (distributive justice) and the procedural (right process) – may not always pull in the same direction'. Elsewhere, Franck asserts that the notion of 'fairness' encompasses two different and potentially adversary components: legitimacy and distributive justice' (at 23). However, on the interplay between the normative and institutional issues, Franck referring to the law of the biosphere for illustration states as follows: 'It is readily apparent that if national quotas for noxious emissions were to be established by the General Assembly, where each state has one vote, they would be rather different than if they were set by the World Bank, where voting power is established by the size of each member's contribution to the Bank's reserve'. Similarly, the second report of the ILA Committee on Sustainable Development, while making the distinction between 'legal mandate underpinning institutional integration' and 'the integration of legal norms' notes that 'it would be incorrect to separate too neatly norms from their institutional setting'. ILA Committee on the International Law on Sustainable Development, Second Report (2006) (on file with author).

15 For interesting and accessible literature on the role of institutional questions in relation to sustainable development see E Hey 'Sustainable development, normative development and the legitimacy of decision making' (2003) 34 *Netherlands Yearbook of International Law* 3. See also, more generally on institutional aspects of multilateral environmental agreements R Churchill and G Ulfstein 'Autonomous institutional arrangements in multilateral environmental agreements: A little noticed phenomenon in international law' (2000) 94 *American Journal of International Law* 623.

16 It is worth noting, in this respect, that it is policy of the European Union to foster 'the sustainable economic and social development of the developing countries ...' (art 130u of the Treaty Establishing the European Community (as Amended by the Treaty on the European Union), reproduced in Berman *et al European Community law (Including European Union materials): Selected documents, 1998 Edition* (1997)).

greatest impact on the African continent. Nevertheless, innovations from Africa, such as the African Union and the New Partnership for African Development are not analysed here.[17]

A third parameter is that instruments covered in the study are those created and driven by a traditional inter-state process. Again, this entails the exclusion of interesting innovations such as the Prototype Carbon Fund, which will also impact on sustainable development.[18] The Prototype Carbon Fund is an initiative established by the World Bank. The purpose of the Fund is to enhance efforts towards carbon dioxide emission reduction through public-private-partnerships. Under the initiative, private sector institutions (principally multinationals) and public sector institutions (states from the North) make contributions to the Fund. The Fund, in turn, invests the money contributed in this way in carbon emissions reduction projects in developing countries.

Although these three parameters limit the breadth of the study somewhat, the project still has the potential to be unmanageable. Against the backdrop of these parameters I decided to cover environmental agreements and international financial institutions responsible for transferring finances from developed to developing countries. Due to the large number of international environmental agreements currently in force, the study focuses, symbolically, on environmental regimes which originated at the United Nations Conference on Environment and Development held in Rio de Janeiro. In particular, I limit the study to the climate change and biodiversity regimes which had their genesis at the Rio Conference, the event that propelled sustainable development onto the agenda of international law.[19] In analysing these regimes, I focus more specifically, although not exclusively, on the protocols adopted under the regimes, such as

17 The New Partnership for African Development (NEPAD) is an instrument adopted by the African Union to drive development on the African continent. Under this instrument, Africa has to own its development initiative but must do so in partnership with the developed world. See for discussion T Maluwa 'The African Union, the Southern African Development Community, and the New Partnership for Africa's Development: Some observations on South Africa's contribution to international law-making and institution building in Africa, 1994 - 2004' (2004) 29 *South African Yearbook of International Law* 5. See also AMB Mangu 'What future for human and peoples' rights under the African Union, New Partnership for Africa's Development, the African Peer-Review Mechanism and the African Court?' (2004) 29 *South African Yearbook of International Law* 136.

18 For more information on the Prototype Carbon Fund see the Fund's website at http://www.prototypecarbonfund.org (accessed 20 November 2004).

19 The United Nations Framework Convention on Climate Change was adopted at the Rio Conference on 9 May 1992. The Convention on Biological Diversity was adopted on 5 June 1992 at the Rio Conference. The texts of both Conventions are reproduced in Cullet & Gowlland-Gualtieri (n 12 above).

the Kyoto Protocol and the Cartagena Protocol.[20] In addition to the climate change and biodiversity regimes, the GEF is also considered in Part B of the study.

The climate change and biodiversity regimes are chosen as the focus of Part B of the study for three reasons (in addition to the symbolic reason given above). The first reason is that, as the instruments launched at the conference most synonymous with sustainable development, the Rio Conference, they provide a critical insight into the international community's understanding of sustainable development. Second, the loss of biodiversity and climate change arguably represent the two most serious contemporary global environmental problems. Third, to varying degrees, biodiversity and climate change problems as well as their solutions affect and are affected by all three values of sustainable development.

I considered the GEF appropriate for study for various reasons. In the first place, in the study of the climate change and biodiversity regimes it will become apparent that a critical issue is 'who pays'. It was, therefore, imperative to consider the instrument aimed at governing financing activities under both regimes. Furthermore, as the financing mechanism for both regimes the GEF provides a meeting point for the climate change and biodiversity regimes as instruments towards sustainable development. The GEF provides an opportunity for analysing various intragenerational equity dimensions of sustainable development in the context of both regimes. Finally, the GEF, independent of the two regimes, is an interesting mechanism for analysing sustainable development. With the GEF you have the use of an economic instrument (transfer of funding) aimed at protecting the global environment and grappling with the role of social concerns in its mandate. In a sense, all these reasons suggest that the GEF represents fertile ground where the values of sustainable development interact. Through financial transfers for global environmental benefits, questions are posed relating to balancing values of sustainable development. This study is precisely about the kind of balance that sustainable development requires.

A final parameter is that of time. The law relating to sustainable development is very dynamic. Given that this field of study is relatively new and evolving rapidly, new materials are published thick and fast. Modern multilateral environmental agreements have created mechanisms, often referred to as a Conference of the Parties (COPs) or a Meeting of Parties (MOPs), through which they meet on a regular basis to facilitate the evolution and development of regimes.

20 The Kyoto Protocol to the United Nations Framework Convention on Climate Change (1997) and the Cartagena Protocol on Biosafety to the Convention on Biological Diversity (2000) are reproduced in Cullet & Gowlland-Gualtieri (n 12 above).

This practice adds to the pace and sheer quantity of development. For that reason it is imperative to set a clearly defined time limit for the study. With that in mind the research contained in this study traces development up to and including October 2006.

I mention these limitations because, in a project such as this, there are endless instruments that could be analysed. Similarly, different approaches could have been taken. However, for this study I have chosen a particular approach and particular instruments, as outlined above.

3. Synopsis

I begin with Part A, consisting of chapters 2, 3 and 4, and I develop a framework in terms of which the instruments will be analysed. This framework consists of a brief historical sketch as well as the aims of sustainable development in chapter 2. In chapter 3 the historical sketch and purpose are used to develop and present a nuanced conceptualisation of sustainable development. The nuanced conceptualisation is developed on the basis of literature and instruments on sustainable development, and specifically by analysing various objections to sustainable development. Chapter 4 consists of investigating the place and role of sustainable development in international law.

Part B of the study analyses two environmental regimes which owe their genesis to the Rio Conference as well as the GEF. These instruments are considered in light of the framework developed in Part A. The climate change regime is considered in chapter 5 while the biodiversity regime is considered in chapter 6. The GEF is considered in chapter 7. The GEF is considered, primarily, in the context of its role as the entity operating the financial mechanism of the multilateral environmental agreements discussed in Part B.

Parts A and B are introduced by brief preliminary remarks. The analysis in Parts A and B are followed by a brief chapter offering conclusions and recommendations.

PART A: FRAMEWORK FOR SUSTAINABLE DEVELOPMENT

Introductory remarks to Part A

Uncertainty surrounds the concept of sustainable development in at least two ways. First, sustainable development is often characterised as indeterminate and therefore of little practical value. Second, the status and role of sustainable development in international law is not much clearer. The purpose of Part A of this study is to rid sustainable development of some the uncertainties surrounding it. I begin, in chapter 2, by tracing and sketching the brief history of sustainable development. Using the brief history I suggest a purpose of sustainable development.

However, neither the history nor the purpose of sustainable development tells us what sustainable development is. The history and purpose of sustainable development are used as a means to conceptualise sustainable development. The approach taken in chapter 3 is to use a variety of tools to come up with a nuanced conceptualisation of sustainable development. In particular, I use existing literature on sustainable development, landmark instruments on sustainable development such as the Rio Declaration on Environment and Development and the Johannesburg Instrument as well as the history and purpose of sustainable development to develop the conceptualisation of sustainable development.

In chapter 4 the role of sustainable development in international law is considered. First, a few words are said about the status of sustainable development in international law. Second, the role that sustainable development is supposed to play in giving effect to sustainable development is considered. While chapter 3 is concerned with the policy changes required, chapter 4 is concerned with the legal environment forming the framework for the operation of sustainable development.

2

A Historical Perspective: History and Purpose

1. Introduction

As described in chapter 1, environmental and development concerns are fundamentally related. This relationship is expressed in a variety of ways, both conflicting and synergic. In chapter 1 it was suggested that this relationship is predominately regarded as conflicting with economic considerations. In this paradigm, where economic concerns are of central importance, it is the environment and the poor that suffer. Sustainable development is advanced as the answer to achieving a more equitable balance and synergic relationship between social, environmental and economic needs.

While sustainable development may be helpful as a starting point in attaining this balance, the uncertainty surrounding the concept has been used to call its usefulness into question.[1] In embarking on a search towards an equitable balance between the environment and development, I will of necessity have to grapple with uncertainties surrounding the concept of sustainable development. The central thesis developed in this study will take sustainable development as its point of departure. Unravelling the uncertainties surrounding sustainable development is a step in developing a conceptualisation of sustainable development. Such a conceptualisation, in turn, can indicate the way in which international law is to develop if it is to contribute to making developmental needs consistent with environmental needs.

To the extent that the next two chapters, and this study in general, are about a search for the content of sustainable development, it must be emphasised that the study is primarily about the normative content of sustainable development. It is concerned with questions relating to the right thing to do in the face of global problems. What does sustainable development require us to do? What are its implications for the various options for solving global problems. The study is about the law in the sense that it considers legal frameworks in which sustainable development is operationalised as well as the role of sustainable development in international law. However, the study is also fundamentally about morality and ethics.

1 See G Handl 'Sustainable development: General rules versus specific obligations' in W Lang (ed) *Sustainable development and international law* (1995), 37 who submits that 'the concept's latent ambiguities ... undermine its policy guidance function'.

In considering the normative content of sustainable development, moral questions about (re)distributive justice as an element of sustainable development come to the fore: how must the benefits derived from the use of natural resources be allocated? Who must pay the cost of efforts towards environmental protection and on what basis are these questions of allocation decided? These moral and ethical questions are considered within the context of various legal frameworks in international law.

The search for the normative content of sustainable development must necessarily begin with a historical sketch of the evolution of sustainable development. This historical exposition is undertaken, not for the sake of historical exposition, but because it sheds light on aspects that are important for the conceptualisation of sustainable development. The historical analysis utilises historical landmarks as a structure for the analysis.

These landmarks are the three main UN conferences on environment and development: the Stockholm Conference on the Human Environment (Stockholm Conference), the Rio Conference on Environment and Development (Rio Conference or UNCED) and the Johannesburg World Summit on Sustainable Development (WSSD or Johannesburg Summit). To these can be added other events that took place between the conferences, which either served as an impetus for the conferences or contributed to the outcomes of the conferences. On the basis of this historical sketch I offer some remarks about the purpose of sustainable development. The purpose of sustainable development will not only be important for the conceptualisation of sustainable development offered in chapter 3, but will also contribute towards an understanding of what role sustainable development is supposed to play in international law.

2. Sustainable development: A historical sketch

2.1 General

The history of sustainable development is closely tied to the history of international environmental law.[2] For that reason a brief commentary on the evolution of international environmental law as it

2 WM Adams *Green development: Environment and sustainability in the third world* (1990) 14.

relates to sustainable development is necessary. It is clear that international environmental law did not begin at Rio or even Stockholm. Sands[3] traces international efforts to protect the environment 'at least as far back as the 1880s' in the *Behring Sea Fur Seals* dispute between the United States and Great Britain.[4] While the development of international environmental law was significant for sustainable development, retracing the steps of international environmental law does not take us very far in the exploration of the concept sustainable development.[5] Certainly, very early on, the development of international environmental law was in very obvious ways linked to economic activity and in that sense international environmental law has always been concerned with a relationship between economic activity and the environment. For example, the *Behring Sea Fur Seals Arbitration* between the United States and Great Britain concerned the United States' alleged interest in preserving the common natural resources outside its area of jurisdiction and, on the other hand, the United Kingdom's pursuit of economic interests.[6] Even the early treaties considered in both Sands' and Kiss and Shelton's historical account of the evolution of international environmental law demonstrate the link between economic activity and environmental concerns.[7]

3 P Sands 'Environmental protection in the twenty-first century: Sustainable development and international law' in RL Revesz *et al* (eds) *Environmental law, the economy and sustainable development: The United States, the European Union and the international community* (2000) 369.

4 Sands (n 3 above) 370. For a fuller discussion of the legal, political and historical issues of the dispute see P Sands *Lawless world: America and the making and breaking of global rules, from FDR's Atlantic Charter to George W Bush's illegal war* (2005) 71.

5 For an interesting account of the internal legal history of international environmental law see P Sands *Principles of international environmental law vol I: Frameworks, standards and implementation* (1995) 25 *et seq* who distinguishes four time-frames in the development of international environmental law. According to the story he tells the first frame began with bilateral treaties and ended with the creation of the United Nations. The second stage takes us from 1945 and ends with the Stockholm Process in 1972. The third period lasted from the Stockholm Conference on the Human Environment until the Rio Conference on Environment and Development. Finally, the fourth stage began at the Rio Conference and is still evolving. A Kiss & D Shelton *International environmental law* 2nd Edition (2000) adopt a three-phrased time-frame, namely pre-Stockholm, post-Stockholm and post-Rio. VP Nanda & G Pring *International environmental law and policy for the 21st century* (2003) adopt a not too dissimilar approach with the early years lasting until Stockholm, followed by the period until the Rio Conference. The next period in Nanda and Pring's analysis is the period from the Rio Conference until the Johannesburg Summit on Sustainable Development. In each of the historical accounts the three UN Conferences relating to sustainable development are key in the evolution of international environmental law and sustainable development.

6 Reported as *Behring Sea Fur Seals Arbitration (Great Britain v United States)* JB Moore *History and digest of the international arbitrations to which the United States has been a party* (1898) 755. A similar link between economic activity can be made with reference to the much celebrated *Trail Smelter case (United States v Canada)*, 1941 reprinted in MW Janis & JE Noyes *International law: Cases and materials* (1997) 584.

7 See Kiss & Shelton (n 5 above) 56. See also Sands (n 5 above) 26.

Thus most, if not all, of international environmental law bears some relation to economic activity. To uncover the content of sustainable development, however, what I am looking for is the point at which this relationship between the environment and economic activity was transformed into a recognition that the solution to environmental problems not only had to be global but, more importantly, that such solutions must be accompanied by solutions to social problems. In that sense, while the history of international environmental law illustrates a focus on typically Eurocentric environmental issues, the history of sustainable development must begin from the point at which these typically Eurocentric issues were linked to the concerns of poor countries and peoples of the world. In this regard, Mickelson points out, the historical dimension of literature on environmental law 'reveals that the discussion tends to be limited to ... issues such as species conservation and various forms of pollution'.[8]

A typical example of a principle developed in the context of pure Eurocentric international environmental law is the polluter pays principle. The polluter pays principle can probably be traced back to the treaties on civil liability.[9] The polluter pays principle refers to the idea that the costs of pollution should be borne by those responsible for the environmental degradation.[10] Principle 16 of the Rio Declaration provides that:

> National Authorities should endeavour to promote the internalisation of environmental costs and the use of economic instruments, taking into account the approach that the polluter should, in principle, pay for the costs of pollution ...

The polluter pays principle is essentially an extension to the environmental sphere of private law remedies. It is an example of the use of market mechanisms to deal with environmental problems.[11] Emissions trading programmes and environmental taxes, both of which are quintessential market mechanisms, reflect the polluter pays principle.[12] Environmental taxes, as an example of a price instrument, are intended to 'force the source to internalise the global

8 K Mickelson 'South, North, international environmental law and international environmental lawyers' 11 (2000) *Yearbook of International Environmental Law* 52 55. Mickelson, at 56 *et seq*, suggests that the history of international environmental law would look very different from a Southern perspective. She suggests that from a Southern perspective, the history of international environmental law would include the appropriation of territories in the context of colonialism for the purposes of economic development.

9 Sands (n 5 above) 653. See, eg 1960 Paris OECD Convention on Third Party Liability in the Field of Nuclear Energy, 956 *UNTS* 251; 1963 Convention on Civil Liability for Nuclear Damage, reprinted in P Cullet & A Gowlland-Gualtieri (eds) *Key materials in international environmental law* (2004) 557.

10 Sands (n 5 above) 213.

11 See eg TM Franck *Fairness in international law and institutions* (1995) 361.

12 See for discussion, JB Wiener 'Global environmental regulation: instrument choice in legal context' (1999) 108 *Yale Law Journal* 677.

environmental costs of their activities'.[13] Emissions trading programmes are no different. In essence, emissions trading programmes allow those able to pay to buy the right to pollute, and in this sense reflect the polluter pays principle.[14]

Unlike the precautionary principle, the polluter pays principle did not find its way into the Climate Change Convention or the Biodiversity Convention. This may be indicative of a lack of support for the principle.[15] According to Sands, however, it may be possible to read the polluter pays principle into those provisions of the two Conventions that refer to the historic responsibility of developed countries for the problems of climate change and biodiversity (the common but differentiated responsibilities provisions).[16] Further, as Sands notes, the polluter pays principle is well-established in the law of the European Union.[17]

The early attempts at environmental regulation, including the polluter pays principle, sowed the seeds for the emergence of sustainable development as an international policy and legal concept, but did not sufficiently integrate developmental concerns to qualify as sustainable development. I am here more interested in those international efforts that resulted in a policy requiring the integration of environmental and developmental concerns.

13 Wiener (n 12 above) 706.

14 For more discussion of emission trading, see chapter 5 in Part B of the study.

15 See also the declaration of the Australian government when signing the Protocol on the Liability and Compensation Resulting from Transboundary Movement of Hazardous Wastes, reprinted in Cullet & Gowlland-Gualtieri (n 9 above), to the effect that art 4 of that Protocol which channels liability to the notifier, exporter, generator and State of Export (all of which will most often be in developed states in trade between developing and developed states) does not reflect the polluter-pays principle. Basel Convention Conference of the Parties (COP) 5 UNEP/CHW. 5.29. See further D Tladi 'The liability protocol to the Basel Convention on Transboundary Movement of Hazardous Wastes: An overview' (2000) 7 *South African Journal of Environmental Law and Policy* 203 208.

16 Sands (n 5 above) 213. See, eg art 3(1) of the Climate Change Convention which provides that the parties 'should protect the climate system ... on the basis of equity and in accordance with their common but differentiated responsibilities'. As will become evident in the discussion of intragenerational equity below, the principle of intragenerational equity is premised on the understanding, in part, that the developed world contributed significantly more to environmental degradation (in this case climate change). See also CD Stone 'Common but differentiated responsibilities in international law' (2004) 98 *American Journal of International Law* 276 291. See, however, Y Matsui 'Some aspects of the principle of "common but differentiated responsibilities"' (2002) 2 *International Agreements: Politics, Law and Economics* 151 155 who, while accepting Sands' argument, notes that the context 'appears to be different'.

17 Sands (n 5 above) 215. He cites, for authority, various instruments including various EC Council Recommendations, and the 1986 amendment of the EEC treaty which provided the EC policy on the environment should be based on, *inter alia*, the notion that 'the polluter should pay'. In terms of the same amendment (art 30(r)), EC policy should be based on various other principles including the precautionary principle and the preventative policy.

The World Commission on Environment and Development (hereinafter the Brundtland Commission)[18] is credited with coining the concept of sustainable development.[19] While it was the Brundtland Commission Report that gave sustainable development an international platform, the Rio instruments[20] gave it prominence in international environmental law. However it was the Stockholm process that laid the foundation for the evolution of sustainable development as an international policy and legal concept. By the Stockholm process I mean not only the conference and its outcomes but also the events that led to and affected the conference and its outcomes.

The 1972 Stockholm Declaration[21] 'secured its place in history' as the 'first global action plan for the environment'.[22] The Stockholm

18 The World Commission on Environment and Development *Our common future* (1987).

19 Given the numerous and often inconsistent accounts of the origins of the concept of sustainable development, it is appropriate to say a few words about the origins of the concept and the reasons for some of the inconsistencies. See Sands 'International law in the field of sustainable development: Emerging legal principles' in Lang (n 1 above) 58 where he states that 'the term 'sustainable development' is widely thought to have been coined and given wide usage by the Brundtland Report'. See, however, Weeramantry in the separate opinion of the *Gabcikovo-Nagymaros (Hungary v Slovakia)* 1997 *ICJ* 3 reprinted in 1998 *ILM* 168 at 206 who states that 'the concept of sustainable development can be traced back, beyond the Stockholm Conference of 1972, to such events as the Founex meeting of experts in Switzerland in June 1971' (footnotes omitted). For this comment the judge relies on AS Timoshenko 'From Stockholm to Rio: The institutionalisation of sustainable development' in Lang (n 1 above) 143. However, a careful reading of Timoshenko's chapter makes it clear that Judge Weeramantry's comments cannot be supported by the text referred to. In light of the text, it is submitted that Judge Weeramantry refers here not to the concept of sustainable development as such, but rather to international endeavours at integrating environmental concerns and development. However, it is clear that sustainable development as a concept itself pre-dates the 1987 Report. See IUCN *World conservation strategy* (1980) which made several references to sustainable development.

20 The 'Rio instruments' refers to the 1992 Rio Declaration on the Environment and Development (1992) 31 *ILM* 876; Agenda 21: A Programme of Action for Sustainable Development, reprinted in N Robinson (ed) *Agenda 21: Earth's action plan*; The Forest Principles (1992) 31 *ILM* 882; The United Nations Framework Convention on Climate Change (1992) 31 *ILM* 851; and the Convention on Biodiversity (1992) 31 *ILM* 822. The first three of these instruments (non-binding instruments) were adopted at the United Nations Conference on the Environment and Development (UNCED) held in Rio de Janeiro in 1992. The last two Conventions were opened for signature at the same Conference.

21 The United Nations Declaration on the Human Environment, adopted in 1972, Stockholm (1972) 11 *ILM* 874.

22 RA Malviya 'Sustainable development and environment: Emerging trends and issues' (1996) 32 *Indian Journal of International Law* 57 57.

Declaration recognised the link between the environment and development.[23] Recent as the birth of the concept of sustainable development may be, it is clear that the ideas underlying the concept pre-date the 1972 Stockholm Declaration.[24] Judge Weeramantry, in his oft-cited separate opinion in the *Gabcíkovo-Nagymaros case,*[25] traced these ideas back to several ancient civilizations.[26] However, for the evolution of the concept of sustainable development itself the starting point has to be Stockholm.

2.2 Towards Stockholm

The Stockholm Conference can be traced back to an inter-governmental conference convened by the United Nations Educational, Scientific and Cultural Organisation (UNESCO) on the Scientific Basis for Rational Use and Conservation of the Resources of the Biosphere in 1968.[27] The UNESCO conference dealt with the effect of human activity on the biosphere.[28]

Although the Stockholm Conference is considered to be of historical significance as the first global conference that recognised the need to alleviate poverty in the developing world as a prerequisite for protecting the environment,[29] the plight of the developing world was not the motivating factor behind the conference. The primary rationale behind the conference 'came from the developed world, and the initial focus was on the environmental problems of industrialisation'.[30] The conference was supposed to be about Eurocentric environmental concerns or what Adams refers to as 'the classic concerns of First World environmentalism', most notably

23 As above. See also para 4 of the preamble to the Stockholm Declaration that, for example, recognises that in 'the developing countries most of the environmental problems are caused by under-development' while in 'industrialised countries, environmental problems are generally related to industrialisation and technological development'. Principle 4 of the same declaration provides that '[n]ature conservation ... must therefore receive importance in planning for economic development' while principle 9 provides that '[e]nvironmental deficiencies generated by the conditions of under-development and natural disasters ... can be best remedied by accelerated development ...'

24 Sands (n 19 above) 57.

25 *Gabcíkovo-Nagymaros* case (n 19 above).

26 *Gabcíkovo-Nagymaros* case (n 19 above) 207 *et seq* Judge Weeramantry, for example, describes (in great detail) the ancient irrigation-based civilization of Sri-Lanka, two ancient cultures of two Tanzanian tribes (the Sonjo and the Chagga), the *qanats* system of irrigation developed in Iran, irrigation sites in China (some of which he asserts are still in use over two millennia after their construction). He adds that there are many more examples that he could have cited.

27 Sands (n 5 above) 33. See also Adams (n 2 above) 32 *et seq* and Kiss & Shelton (n 5 above) 60.

28 Adams (n 2 above) 32.

29 Principle 9, for example, declares that 'environmental deficiencies generated by the conditions of under-development and natural disasters pose grave problems ...'

30 Adams (n 2 above) 36.

pollution.[31] As initially conceived, therefore, Stockholm was intended to be yet another link in the development of international environmental law focusing on typically Eurocentric environmental issues.

Because of its focus on typically First World environmental problems the conference did not, at first, receive support from the developing world. If developing countries did not support the conference then the Stockholm Conference would fail in its endeavour to be truly global. To alleviate the fears of the developing world, a preparatory conference of experts was arranged at Founex, Switzerland, to forge consensus on the issues to be discussed.[32] It was this preparatory conference that secured the success of the Stockholm Conference.[33] While the various instruments adopted at Stockholm were important for the conception of sustainable development as international policy, the report of the Founex Committee was crucial, not only because it ensured the success of Stockholm, but also because it was in the Founex report that the crucial link between environmental protection and developmental concerns (in the broad sense) was forged.[34]

The report recognised that the 'current concern with environmental issues has emerged out of the problems experienced by the industrially developed countries'.[35] The report further recognised that developing countries, on the other hand, face a different set of environmental challenges. The environmental challenges faced by developing countries 'reflect the poverty and the very lack of development of their societies'.[36] It was further emphasised in the report that these problems were no less important than those associated with industrial pollution.[37] Important also is the report's recognition that the kind of environmental challenges facing developing countries are in fact faced by the majority of the earth's inhabitants.[38] At the same time the report recognised that while the environmental problems of developing countries are those caused by lack of development, there was a different relationship between development and the environment, namely, that the process of development that the developing countries are immersed in and that the developed countries have experienced also causes environmental

31 As above. The evolution of the Stockholm process is similarly discussed in Mickelson (n 8 above) 61 *et seq*.
32 Adams (n 2 above) 37.
33 As above. See also Sands (n 5 above) 35.
34 See The Founex Report on Development and Environment (1971) available at http://wwwsouthcentre.org/publications/conundrum/conundrum-o4.htm (accessed 20 July 2006).
35 Founex Report (n 34 above) para 1.2.
36 Founex Report (n 34 above) para 1.4.
37 As above.
38 As above.

problems.[39] Therefore, while lack of development causes environmental problems, the process of development itself can generate environmental problems.

2.3 The Stockholm Conference

The Stockholm Conference was held from 5 to 16 June 1972. Three legally non-binding instruments were adopted at Stockholm.[40] For the conceptualisation of sustainable development the Stockholm Declaration on the Human Environment is the most important one. This document, as was to be expected, was a document of political compromise as can be seen in the wide-ranging issues covered by the 26 principles of the Declaration.[41] However, the importance of the Declaration in the context of the evolution of the concept of sustainable development was the emphasis it placed on the link between development and environmental protection. More fundamentally, the Declaration provides a basis for the idea that development and environmental protection are not, of necessity, in conflict.[42]

The positive synergy between development and environmental protection is illustrated at several places in the Declaration. Principle 1, for example, links 'adequate conditions of life' with 'an environment of quality that permits a life of dignity'. Similarly, Principle 9 recognises that environmental deficiencies 'can best be remedied by accelerated development'. Principle 8, for its part, links development to 'favourable living conditions' and 'working environment'. In addition to recognising the positive synergies between development and environmental protection, the Declaration also recognises that the development process can harm the environment – a relationship of conflict. Principle 5, for example, requires that development processes should not over-exploit non-renewable resources to the point of exhaustion.[43] The same idea of

39 Founex Report (n 34 above) para 1.8.

40 The Stockholm Declaration on the Human Environment (1972) 11 *ILM* 874; the Action Plan for the Human Environment (1972) 11 *International Legal Materials* 1421; the Recommendations for Action at the International Level (1972) 11 *ILM* 1416.

41 For example, Principle 1 declares, *inter alia*, that man 'has the fundamental right to freedom, equality and adequate conditions of life ... [policies that promote] apartheid, racial segregation, discrimination, colonial and other forms of oppression ... must be eliminated'. Principle 3 provides that the 'capacity of the earth to produce vital renewable resources must be maintained'. Principle 9 notes that environmental 'deficiencies generated by the conditions of under-development ... pose grave problems ... and can best be remedied by financial and technological assistance ...'

42 See eg Principle 8 and Principle 11 of the Stockholm Declaration.

43 Principle 5 provides: 'The non-renewable resources of the earth must be employed in such a way as to guard against the danger of their future exhaustion and to ensure that benefits from such employment are shared by all mankind'.

constraint on the development processes for environmental purposes can be found in Principle 6 in relation to pollution.[44]

In addition to the link between development and the environment emerging from the Stockholm Declaration, two important principles of sustainable development can be discerned, namely, the principles of inter- and intragenerational equity. The principle of intergenerational equity – the idea that the environment must be safeguarded for present and future generations – is reflected at several places in the Declaration. Principle 1, for example, provides that humans 'bear[s] a solemn responsibility to protect and improve the environment for present and future generations'. Principal 2 similarly requires us to safeguard natural resources of the earth 'for the benefit of present and future generations'. The principle of intragenerational equity – requiring equity within the present generation and recognising the special position of developing countries – is also reflected at various places in the Declaration. The clearest example of the invocation of intragenerational equity is Principle 11 which states that the 'environmental policies of all States should enhance and not adversely affect the present or future development potential of developing countries'. Principle 12 also provides that resources 'should be made available to preserve and improve the environment, taking into account the circumstances and particular requirements of developing countries'. Similarly, Principle 5 requires that the benefits from the exploitation of natural resources should be 'shared by all mankind'.

While Stockholm recognised the need to reconcile developmental and environmental concerns, it did not provide guidelines on how this should be done. For Adams 'the suggested solution', 'rational planning' or 'integrated development' were words without substance.[45]

Institutionally an important consequence of the Stockholm Conference was the establishment of the United Nations Environment Program (UNEP).[46] UNEP is not a UN Specialised Agency but rather a program of the General Assembly developed to act as a catalyst for environmental programs.[47] UNEP is credited with the establishment and implementation of several environmental regimes, including the

44 Principle 6 provides: 'The discharge of toxic substances or of other substances and the release of heat, in such quantities or concentrations as to exceed the capacity of the environment to render them harmless, must be halted in order to ensure that serious or irreversible damage is not inflicted upon ecosystems. The just struggle of the peoples of all countries against pollution should be supported'.

45 Adams (n 2 above) 39.

46 UNEP was established by UN General Assembly Resolution 2997 (1972).

47 Adams (n 2 above) 39; See also Sands (n 5 above) 72.

Regional Seas Programme,[48] and other environmental treaties adopted subsequent to the period in question such as the Convention on the International Trade in Endangered Species (CITES),[49] and the Basel Convention on Hazardous Wastes.[50] Many of these instruments and programmes regulate activities which, although economically beneficial, cause harm to the environment. For example, the Basel Convention was concluded to curb trade in hazardous wastes. The negotiation of the Basel Convention (and subsequent developments at the Conference of Parties) revealed not only economic/environmental problems but also North/South problems.[51] But perhaps more importantly for sustainable development, UNEP plays an important role in the transfer of funds to developing countries for the incremental costs of projects with global environmental benefits. UNEP is involved in such projects in the context of the Global Environment Facility (GEF).[52]

Stockholm is regarded as the forerunner to the Rio Conference. The institutional and conceptual milestones achieved at and after the Stockholm process paved the way for the Rio Conference. In the next section I consider some of the important post-Stockholm events that paved the way for the Rio Conference. Many events relating to international environmental law occurred during this period. Obviously a restatement of all these is not helpful. For that reason the focus in the next section falls on the Brundtland Commission Report which was, arguably, the single most important event in the period between the two major conferences as far as the conceptualisation and reception of sustainable development concerned.

48 Treaties concluded in this programme include the 1976 Barcelona Convention for the Protection of the Mediterranean Sea Against Pollution (1976) 1974 *ILM* 352; the Protocol for the Prevention of Pollution of the Mediterranean Sea by Dumping from Ships and Aircraft (1976) 1976 *ILM* 300; Athens Protocol for the Protection of the Mediterranean Sea Against Pollution from Land Based Sources (1980) 1980 *ILM* 869; 1978 Kuwait Regional Convention for Co-operation on the Protection of the Marine Environment from Pollution (1978) 1978 *ILM* 511; Kuwait Protocol Concerning Co-operation in Combating Pollution by Oil and Other Harmful Substances in Cases of Emergency (1978) 1978 *ILM 526;* Abidjan Convention for Co-operation in the Protection and Development of the Marine and Coastal Environment of the West and Central African Region (1981), 1981 *ILM* 746; Abidjan Protocol Concerning Co-Operation in Combating Pollution in Cases of Emergency (1981) 1981 *ILM* 756.

49 Convention on the International Trade in Endangered Species of Wild Fauna and Flora (1973) 1973 *ILM* 1085.

50 Basel Convention on the Control of Transboundary Movements of Hazardous Wastes and Their Disposal (1989) 1989 *ILM* 657.

51 See generally on the Basel Convention, D Tladi 'The quest to ban hazardous wastes import into Africa: First Bamako and now Basel' (2000) 33 *Comparative and International Law Journal of Southern Africa* 210; Mickelson (n 8 above) 66 *et seq.*

52 The Global Environment Facility (GEF) is the subject of more detailed study in chapter 7. At this stage it is sufficient to mention that the GEF is responsible for the provision of funding to developing countries in connection with multilateral environmental agreements.

2.4 The Road to Rio

The Rio Conference was held 20 years after the Stockholm Conference. Between the conferences several events and documents would contribute to a better understanding of the ideas underlying the concept of sustainable development. Notable events and documents include the UNEP Draft Principles on Conduct in the Conservation of Natural Resources,[53] the UNEP Montevideo Programme,[54] the World Charter for Nature,[55] *Caring for the Earth*,[56] The Brundtland Commission Report,[57] and the establishment of the GEF in 1991 by the World Bank (restructured in 1994 by the World Bank, UNEP and United Nations Development Programme).

Also of importance for sustainable development in the period between the Stockholm Conference and UNCED was the development of what Schrijver calls 'Noord-Zuidrecht'[58] in the context of the New International Economic Order (NIEO) debate.[59] Proponents of the NIEO, mainly developing countries, argued the need to change the existing 'rules of the game' relating to international economic relations from those that favoured rich states to those that took into account the needs of the poor and were more equitable.[60] Article 9 of the UN Charter of Economic Rights, for example, provides that all states 'have the responsibility to cooperate ... for the economic and social progress ... of developing countries'.[61] More to the point, article 19 of the Charter provides as follows:[62]

> With a view to accelerating the economic growth of developing countries and bridging the gap between developed and developing countries, developed countries should grant generalised preferential, non-reciprocal and non-discriminatory treatment to developing countries in

53 UNEP Principles of Conduct in the Field of the Environment for the Guidance of States in the Conservation and Harmonious Utilisation of Natural Resources Shared by Two or More States (1978) 1978 *ILM* 1097.

54 Programme for the Development and Periodic Review of Environmental Law, Report UNEP/ GC.10/5/Add.2 (1981).

55 1983 *ILM* 455.

56 IUCN, UNEP, WWF *Caring for the Earth: A strategy for sustainability* (1990).

57 WCED *Our common future* (1987).

58 Translated as 'North-South law'.

59 See generally N Schrijver 'De verankering en betekenis van duurzame ontwikkeling in het internationale recht' 2003 *Mededelingen van de Nederlandse vereniging voor internationaal recht: volkenrecht en duurzame ontwikkeling* 1 19.

60 As above, 16.

61 United Nations Charter of Economic Rights and Duties of States (15 January 1975) UN GA Res/3281 (1975) 14 *ILM* 251. Similarly, art 11 of the Charter requires the efficiency of international organisations 'in implementing measures to stimulate the general economic progress of all countries, particularly of developing countries'. Art 13 provides that every state 'has the right to benefit from the advances and developments in science and technology for the acceleration of its economic and social development'. Art 17 provides that 'co-operation for development is the shared goal and common duty of all states'.

62 As above.

those fields of international economic co-operation where it may be feasible.

Although the NIEO itself, as a movement in international law, did not take hold, it did act as a stimulus for inclusion, in multilateral treaties, of provisions recognising the special position of developing countries (North-South law). As examples of this North-South law, Schrijver, for example, refers to the first Lomé Convention between the EU, on the one hand, and African, Caribbean and Pacific states, on the other.[63] In the context of sustainable development this North-South law is reflected in various international instruments adopted at or after the Rio Conference, for example, instruments relating to climate change[64] and biodiversity.[65] Importantly, in the sustainable development discourse, NIEO principles are reflected in the principle of intragenerational equity, in particular, and sustainable development in general.[66]

Between the Rio and Stockholm conferences, perhaps the most influential event towards the mainstreaming of sustainable development was the 'Brundtland Commission Report'. The Commission was established by the UN General Assembly in 1983.[67] It was chaired by the then Norwegian Prime Minister, Gro Harlem Brundtland. The task of the Commission was four-fold:[68]

(i) to propose long-term environmental strategies for achieving sustainable development by the year 2000 and beyond;
(ii) to recommend ways in which concern for the environment may be translated into greater co-operation among developing countries and between countries at different stages of economic and social development and lead to the achievement of common and mutually supportive objectives that take

63 Schrijver (n 59 above) 19. See generally on the Lomé Convention, K Arts *Integrating human rights into development co-operation: The case of the Lomé Convention* (2000). See for further development in ACP-EU relations K Arts 'ACP-EU relations in a new era: The Cotonou Agreement' (2003) 40 *Common Market Law Review* 95.

64 Both the Climate Change Convention and the Kyoto Protocol to the Climate Change Convention incorporate preferential treatment for developing countries in a variety of ways, including the 'North first' approach and the requirement for transfer of financial and technological resources. Both these aspects of the climate change regime form the backbone of the analysis conducted in chapter 5 below.

65 The Biodiversity Convention and the Cartagena Protocol also contain provisions on the transfer of resources in addition to other provisions meant for the protection of developing countries. These aspects are explored further in chapter 6 of this study.

66 French, for example, suggests that sustainable development is the successor of the NIEO. See D French 'The role of the state and international organisations in reconciling sustainable development and globalisation' (2002) 2 *International Environmental Agreements: Politics, Law and Economics* 135 139.

67 UN General Assembly Resolution 38/1161 (1983).

68 WCED (n 57 above) ix.

account of the interrelationships between people, resources, environment and development;

(iii) to consider ways and means by which the international community can deal more effectively with environmental concerns; and

(iv) to help define shared perceptions of long term environmental issues and the appropriate efforts needed to deal successfully with the problems of protecting the environment.

The Report is perhaps best known for the definition it gives to the concept of sustainable development. In the Report sustainable development is defined as 'development that meets the needs of the present generation without compromising the ability of future generations to meet their own needs.[69]

For the Commission this definition contains two elements:

(i) the essential needs of the world's poor must be given priority; and

(ii) the idea of limitations imposed by the state of technology and social organisation on the environment's ability to meet present and future needs.

However, the Commission's contribution to the understanding of sustainable development goes beyond this famous definition of the concept. The Report identifies the major problem areas and the causes of the problems.[70] The Commission focused on population,[71] food security,[72] species and ecosystems,[73] energy,[74] industry,[75] and human urban settlements.[76] It is this integrated approach to socio-economic and environmental issues that makes the Report so important. Crucial to the overall message of the Report is the assumption that the crises we often identify as separate – environmental, energy and development – represent in fact one interlocking crisis.[77] The Report recognises that environment and development issues are interwoven 'into a seamless net of cause and effect'.[78] If the world is, in fact, faced with one interlocking crisis, then what we need is an integrated approach to solving such a crisis. An important theme running through the Commission's report is the need for poverty alleviation in this integrated approach.[79] As will

69 WCED (n 57 above) 43.
70 WCED (n 57 above) 95 *et seq.*
71 As above.
72 WCED (n 57 above) 118 *et seq.*
73 WCED (n 57 above) 147 *et seq.*
74 WCED (n 57 above) 168 *et seq.*
75 WCED (n 57 above) 206 *et seq.*
76 WCED (n 57 above) 235 *et seq.*
77 As above, 4.
78 As above.
79 As above. See especially 29 *et seq.*

become evident in the course of the next chapter, this call for integration is a crucial element in my attempt at developing a nuanced conceptualisation of sustainable development.

The Commission made several proposals which turned out to be key in the Rio process. First the Commission called upon the international community at all levels (national, regional and global) to integrate environmental concerns into developmental activities.[80] Secondly, the Commission emphasised the need to strengthen agencies charged with the protection of the environment such as UNEP.[81] Thirdly, it called for an increase in the co-operation between non-governmental organisations (NGOs), scientific bodies and other members of the international community that could lead to an increased capacity to identify and assess environmental hazards.[82] Fourthly, the Commission recognised the need to include in decision-making and implementation, NGOs, scientific bodies and industries.[83] The fifth recommendation of the Commission was to prepare a UN declaration on the environment and sustainable development with a view to the adoption of a convention.[84] In the sixth place the Report calls for the involvement of multilateral financial institutions in the process towards sustainable development.[85]

The proposals and recommendations of the Brundtland Commission were informed by proposals formulated by the Experts Group on Environmental Law of the World Commission on Environment and Development, a group of legal experts advising the Commission.[86] The Brundtland Commission Report called for and served as impetus for the Rio Conference.

2.5 UNCED 1992

After the Brundtland Commission Report the UN General Assembly called for a UN Conference on the Environment and Development (UNCED).[87] The Conference was convened in Rio de Janeiro in 1992. UNCED resulted in the adoption of five documents, known as the Rio instruments.[88] Three of the documents were legally non-binding while the other two were Conventions with binding force of law once they

80 WCED (n 57 above) 314 *et seq.*
81 WCED (n 57 above) 319 *et seq.*
82 WCED (n 57 above) 323 *et seq.*
83 WCED (n 57 above) 326 *et seq.*
84 WCED (n 57 above) 330 *et seq.*
85 WCED (n 57 above) 334 *et seq.*
86 WCED Expert Group on Environmental Law 'Proposed legal principles for environmental protection and sustainable development'. Summarised in WCED (n 57 above) 348. For full text see RD Munro & JG Lammers (eds) *Environmental protection and sustainable development: Legal principles and recommendations* (1987) 7.
87 UN General Assembly Resolution 43/196 (1988).
88 n 20 above.

entered into force. Non-binding instruments were the Rio Declaration, Agenda 21 and the Forest Principles. Binding instruments opened for signature at Rio are the United Nations Framework Convention on Climate Change and the Convention on Biodiversity, which form the basis of the analysis in Part B.

If the Brundtland Commission gave the concept of sustainable development currency in international policy, it was the Rio Conference and instruments that pushed it into the mainstream thought of international law. The Rio Conference and instruments are so important in the evolution of the concept of sustainable development that it has even been argued that Rio ushered in a new phase of 'international law in the field of sustainable development' of which international environmental law is a part.[89]

The Rio Declaration, as was the case with the Stockholm Declaration, seeks to balance environmental concerns with development concerns. Several key principles enunciated in the Stockholm Declaration are repeated in the Rio Declaration. The most important example of these is the notion that states have the sovereign right to exploit their natural resources, subject to the proviso that such rights are not to be exercised in a manner that causes harm in territories beyond the states' jurisdiction.[90] However, there are differences between the two declarations that may have an impact on the conceptualisation of sustainable development.

A typical example is the exploitation of natural resources principle cited above. In the Stockholm Declaration, states are said to have the 'right to exploit their own resources pursuant to their own environmental policies' while in the Rio Declaration this right is to be exercised 'pursuant to their environmental and developmental policies'. The inclusion of 'developmental' as a qualifier is a subtle difference but has important consequences for the balancing process of the three values of sustainable development.

89 See Sands (n 5 above) 49; Sands (n 19 above) 66; A Boyle & D Freestone 'Introduction' in A Boyle & D Freestone *International law and sustainable development* (1999) 3.

90 See Principle 2 of the Rio Declaration. See also Principle 21 of the Stockholm Declaration. This notion, of course, can be traced back to the *Trail Smelter arbitration* (n 6 above).

Further, while the Stockholm Declaration in Principle 1 recognised, albeit tentatively, some conceptual link between human rights and environmental protection, there seems to be a clear intention to avoid human rights language in relation to the environment in the Rio Declaration.[91] Principle 1 of the Rio Declaration, for example, provides that human beings are 'entitled to' as opposed to having 'rights to' a healthy and productive life. I would suggest that the term 'entitled to' gives rise to weaker entitlements in terms of law than the phrase 'right to'.[92] Although Principle 2 does refer to 'a right', this right to exploit natural resources is, first of all, not a human right but a right of the state. Second, the right, rather than serving to enhance the protection of the environment, in fact allows the state to exploit natural resources. This means that the 'right' in Principle 2, flowing from the fact that the right is the right to 'exploit natural resources', may have the effect of limiting the protection afforded to the environment. Principle 3 also refers to 'a right'. The right referred to in Principle 3 is a right to development rather than a right to the environment. Moreover Pallemaerts argues that the right as phrased appears to be a right of states, rather than of individuals.[93] I certainly agree that the right, as phrased, is not an individual right and that it is more of a third generation or group right. However, by virtue of the references to present and future generations it seems to me that the right is reserved for those groups in general (present and future generations) rather than particular states. In other words, in my view a proper construction of the right in Principle 3 would suggest that the beneficiary of the right to development is humanity as a whole and not individual states.

The difference between the two Declarations in the context of 'rights' is paradoxically heightened by another difference. With regards to the *use* of environmental resources, the Stockholm Declaration appears to emphasise 'duties' or 'responsibilities'.

91 See for discussion D Shelton 'What happened in Rio to human rights?' (1992) 2 *Yearbook of International Environmental Law* 75. See also M Pallemaerts 'International environmental law from Stockholm to Rio: back to the future?' in P Sands (ed) *Greening international law* (1993). See A Boyle 'The role of international human rights law in the protection of the environment' in A Boyle and M Anderson (eds) *Human rights approaches to environmental protection* (1996) 43 who suggests that this avoidance may be due to the uncertain status of environmental rights in international law. Generally on environmental rights and sustainable development see LA Feris & D Tladi 'Environmental rights' in D Brand & C Heyns (eds) *Socio-economic rights in South Africa* (2005).

92 See, for a discussion of the relative strength of rights over other forms of entitlements, X Fuentes 'International law-making in the field of sustainable development: The unequal competition between development and the environment' (2002) 2 *International Environmental Agreements: Politics, law and economics* 105 125.

93 Pallemaerts (n 92 above) 9. It is plausible that the right to development, as formulated in the Rio Declaration, is a right of states but that the enjoyment of this right by states will benefit peoples (present and future generations).

Principle 1, for example, declares that human beings bear 'a solemn responsibility' to protect the environment. Principle 2 places a duty on humans to protect the environment for present and future generations. Principle 4 again reminds us that we have 'a special responsibility to safeguard' the environment. These are but examples of a theme that runs through the Stockholm Declaration. There is no equal emphasis on duties or responsibility towards the environment in the Rio Declaration. It is, in this respect, useful to contrast Principle 1 of the Stockholm Declaration with its counterpart in the Rio Declaration.

Principle 1 of Rio proclaims that humans 'are at the centre' of sustainable development but makes no mention of duties or responsibilities. That is not to say that the Rio Declaration makes no mention of duties, but only that such references are few and not as strongly stated.[94] From the above analysis of the Rio and Stockholm Declarations, several points can be highlighted. First, Stockholm is more receptive to the link between environmental protection and human rights. Second, Stockholm emphasises the responsibility to protect the environment while Rio emphasises the right to utilise environmental resources. Given the nature of the environment debate, these points may suggest an inclination towards economic concerns in the case of Rio and an inclination towards environmental concerns in the case of Stockholm.

The tentative conclusion about the inclination of the Rio and Stockholm declarations can further be tested with reference to other Principles in the Rio Declaration. With reference to Principle 1 of the Rio Declaration, Pallemaerts notes that the entitlement to a 'healthy life in a harmony with nature' is placed 'explicitly within the perspective of a production-oriented logic'.[95] The text of the Rio Declaration is (more so than the Stockholm Declaration) filled with economic growth-orientated language. Principle 12, for example, warns that:

> Trade policy measures for environmental purposes should not constitute a means of arbitrary or unjustifiable discrimination or a disguised restriction on trade.

94 See eg Principle 2 and 7.

95 To be fair Principle 1 does state that the humans 'are at the centre of concerns for sustainable development'. Nevertheles,s a contextual and holistic reading of Principle 1 and the Rio Declaration in general appears to support the conclusion reached by Pallemaerts.

This provision is reminiscent of the *chapeau* of article XX of the General Agreement on Trade and Tariffs. More to the point, since the introduction of the 'two-tiered test' in the environment trade jurisprudence of the WTO it is the arbitrary/unjustifiable discrimination requirement, (the second tier of the test), represented in Principle 12, that has proved to be a stumbling block for environmental policies.[96] Prior to the Appellate Body decision in the *Reformulated Gasoline dispute*,[97] GATT dispute resolution bodies, in applying article XX, first asked whether the measure in question was justifiable under the *chapeau* of article XX and then determined whether the measure fell under one of the specific exceptions listed in article XX(a) - (j).[98] The decision of the Appellate Body in the *Reformulated Gasoline dispute* which has since been followed in subsequent cases before WTO tribunals, to reverse this logical sequence, has been widely hailed as progress in WTO.[99] However, while this new sequence may have introduced a more logical approach, it has not led to a significant impact on environmental measures' chances of success in the article XX analysis. While, prior to *Reformulated Gasoline* dispute, environmental measures failed to meet article XX on account of not being 'necessary to protect' the environment under article XX(b) or not being 'related to' the protection of the environment under article XX(g), under the new test environmental measures fail to meet the test on account of being arbitrary and discriminatory under the *chapeau* of article XX.[100]

The similarity between the language of Principle 12 and the *chapeau* of article XX, which has been proven to be a stumbling block for environmental measures in trade and environment disputes, may suggest that in the environment trade debate Principle 12 leans towards trade (economic concern) rather than environmental concerns. That the promotion of global free trade is central to economic growth is, at this point, trite. The Director-General of the World Trade Organisation, Michael Moore, has for example stated 'poor countries need to grow their way out of poverty' and that trade

96 See further D Tladi 'Can the wolf protect the lamb? Free trade regimes as instruments towards sustainable development' (2002) 27 *South African Yearbook of International Law* 149 157.

97 United States – Standards for Reformulated and Conventional Gasoline AB-1996-1 reprinted in 35 (1996) *ILM* 274.

98 See especially United States – Restrictions on Imports of Tuna Panel Decision reprinted in (1991) 30 *ILM* 1594 and United States – Restrictions on Imports of Tuna Panel Decision reprinted in (1994) 33 *ILM* 839 which both rejected the argument advanced by the United States that a US Tuna embargo was 'necessary' for the purposes of Art XX(b).

99 NL Wallace-Bruce 'Global trade and sustainable development: Two steps forward in the WTO?' (2002) 35 *Comparative and International Law Journal of Southern Africa* 236. See also E Schlemmer 'Compliance with WTO obligations: Trade and the environment revisited' (2002) 27 *South African Yearbook of International Law* 272. See especially M Matsushita, TJ Schoenbaum & PC Mavroidis *The World Trade Organization: Law, practice and policy* (2002) 453 *et seq.*

100 Tladi 'Can the wolf protect the lamb' (n 96 above).

'is a key engine for growth'.[101] In emphasising the point, Moore states:

> One study by the Tinbergen Institute estimates that developing countries would gain $155 billion a year from further trade liberalisation. That is over three times the $43 billion they get annually in overseas aid.[102]

The Rio process and instruments, particularly the Rio Declaration had the effect of pushing sustainable development into mainstream international law. Regardless of whether sustainable development was accepted as a principle of international law or just a concept used in international law, it became difficult after Rio for international lawyers, especially international environmental lawyers and international economic lawyers, to ignore sustainable development. Ten years after Rio the United Nations convened yet another conference, the World Summit on Sustainable Development, in Johannesburg (WSSD or the Johannesburg Summit). The Johannesburg Summit was yet another step in the normative development of the principle of sustainable development.

2.6 WSSD 2002

The Johannesburg Summit was not intended to produce any new ideas or concepts relating to sustainable development.[103] Rather the Summit was intended to be about the implementation of the ideas that had been agreed upon over the years spanning the normative development of sustainable development.[104] However, although the Johannesburg Declaration on Sustainable Development explicitly reaffirms the principles adopted at Rio, the declaration does, whether by design or not, leave its own footprint on the normative content of sustainable development. It is for this reason that a few words must be said about the Johannesburg Declaration.

101 M Moore 'The multilateral trading system in support of Africa-led and Africa-owned development' paper presented at ECOSOC, High-Level Policy Dialogue, United Nations on 16 July 2001, available at http://www.wto.org/english/news_s/spmm_e/spmm68_e.htm (accessed 20 July 2006). See also M Moore 'A grand bargain: A new international deal' paper presented at the United Nations Financing for Development Conference – Summit Level Open Session on 21 March 2002 (accessed 20 July 2006).

102 Elsewhere, during the same ECOSOC meeting mentioned above, Moore is quoted as saying: 'According to the World Bank, complete liberalisation of merchandise trade and elimination of subsidies could add US$1.5 trillion to developing country incomes'. Wallace-Bruce (n 99 above) 237.

103 See M Pallemaerts 'Is multilateralism the future? Sustainable development or globalisation as a "comprehensive vision" of the future of humanity' (2003) 5 *Environment, Development and Sustainability* 275 286.

104 See 'The Johannesburg Summit test: what will change?' available at http://www.johannesburgsummit.org/html/whats_new/feature_story41.html (accessed 11 November 2002). See also Pallemaerts (n 103 above) 277. See further Schrijver (n 59 above) 38.

If the emphasis in the Rio Declaration is on economic growth imperatives, the emphasis in the Johannesburg Declaration appears to be on bridging the gap between 'the deep fault line that divides human society between the rich and the poor'.[105] The declaration urges the bridging of the gap between rich and poor on two levels. First, and more expectedly, the declaration speaks of bridging the gap between the 'developed and the developing worlds' or countries.[106] However, the declaration also appears to imply bridging the gap between rich and poor generally, which includes bridging the rich-poor divide within societies. Thus, the theme of the Johannesburg Declaration appears to be poverty eradication.

The focus on poverty eradication in Johannesburg should not be surprising given that the Summit took place only two years after the adoption of the Millennium Development Goals (MDGs).[107] The MDGs are based on 'collective responsibility to uphold the principles of dignity, equality and equity at the global level'.[108] In particular the MDGs commit states to free the more than 1 billion members of human society 'from abject and dehumanising conditions of extreme poverty'.[109] The MDGs propose to meet these lofty goals by, for example, halving by 2015, the number of the world's poor, ensuring that children have access to basic education and improving the health services available to the world's poor.[110] The MDGs also place a strong premium on the protection of the environment for the benefit of present and future generations.[111] Indeed, the Johannesburg Plan of Implementation expressly invokes the MDGs in the chapter on poverty eradication.[112]

Interestingly, in the Johannesburg Declaration poverty eradication is presented as both an 'objective' and 'an essential requirement for sustainable development'.[113] The environment does get a mention in paragraphs 11 and 13, but the very references to environmental protection imply that environmental protection is important primarily in the context of social and economic problems.

105 Para 12 Johannesburg Declaration on Sustainable Development, available at http://www.johannesburgsummit.org/html/documents/summit_docs/1009wssd_pol_declaration.doc (accessed 4 September 2002).

106 As above.

107 See United Nations Millennium Declaration, UN GA Res/55/2 (2000), available at http://www.un.org/millenniumgoals/ (accessed 22 July 2006).

108 Principle 2 Millennium Development Goals.

109 Principle 11 Millennium Development Goals.

110 Principle 19 Millennium Development Goals.

111 See Principle 21 Millennium Development Goals which provides as follows: 'We must spare no effort to free all of humanity, and above all our children and grandchildren, from the threat of living on a planet irredeemably spoilt by human activities ...'

112 See Plan of Implementation of the World Summit on Sustainable Development available at http://www.un.org/esa/sustdev/documents/WSSD_POI_PD/English/POIToc.htm (accessed 11 November 2004).

113 See para 11 Johannesburg Declaration.

Paragraph 11, for example, provides that 'protecting and managing the natural resource base *for economic and social development*' is an objective and requirement for sustainable development.[114] In the context of sustainable development this link raises very interesting questions that will need consideration in any development of a nuanced conceptualisation of sustainable development. For example, what does this link mean in terms of conflicts and synergies with regards to the values of sustainable development? According to the Johannesburg Declaration 'priority attention' must be given to, *inter alia,* chronic hunger, malnutrition, racial hatred, and communicable and chronic diseases, in particular HIV/AIDS and tuberculosis.[115] These are typically issues of importance to poor societies and relate to underdevelopment.

These social ills facing poor societies are described in the Declaration as posing severe threats to sustainable development. Protecting the natural environment as an issue warranting 'priority attention' is, however, conspicuous by its absence.

The focus in the Johannesburg instruments and the MDGs on social issues such as poverty alleviation is often impeded by, or at least perceived to be impeded by a focus on privatisation.[116] Even the World Bank has conceded that conditionalities imposed by it and the IMF requiring privatisation of state assets have hurt welfare.[117] Gumede uses Telkom, South Africa's fixed-line communication company, to illustrate the negative social effect of privatisation.[118] The privatisation of Telkom began in 1997 and by 2004 Telkom had

114 Emphasis added.

115 Para 19 Johannesburg Declaration.

116 See for discussion D Tladi 'International monetary fund conditionality, debt and poverty: Towards a strong "anthropocentric" model of sustainability' (2004) 16 *South African Mercantile Law Journal* 31. See generally M Chossudovsky *The globalization of poverty: The impacts of IMF and World Bank reforms* (1997) 34 where the author criticises IMF and World Bank conditionalities that require privatisation as being responsible for the impoverishment of 'hundreds of millions of people'. See also for an interesting discussion in the context of the South African transformation from apartheid to a democratic society, WM Gumede *Thabo Mbeki and the battle for the soul of the ANC* (2005). See especially ch 5 titled 'Economics for the poor'. In this hard-hitting and controversial book, Gumede accuses the South African President, Thabo Mbeki, of pursuing economic policies based on the IMF and World Bank prescriptions such as privatisation at the expense of the poor masses of South Africa. See for example, at 106 where he states the following: 'Mbeki is determined to ram through his privatisation efforts, even in the face of widespread popular resistance because of the inherent threat of job losses ... [and] rising cost of basic services'.

117 World Bank *Adjustment lending: An evaluation of ten years' experience* (1988) 30. See also M Todaro *Economic development in the third world* 4th Edition (1989) 420. See also J Stiglitz *Globalization and its discontents* (2002) 75.

118 Gumede (n 116 above) 109.

reportedly reduced its workforce by more than a third and raised its tariffs significantly.[119]

There have been several studies undertaken to test these claims.[120] These studies have generally indicated that, at best, structural adjustment programmes (conditionalities) have had no impact (negative or positive) and at worst have had disastrous consequences for the poor.[121] The worst case-view appears to be confirmed by the IMF's own internal review. In 1991 the IMF felt the need to identify policy and legal 'measures that can cushion the possible adverse effects of certain policies on vulnerable groups ... in ways that are consistent with the program's macroeconomic reforms'.[122] Several points can be made about this statement.[123] First, the need to 'cushion' suggests that the primary objective is economic growth and that in the pursuit of the objective the impacts (necessary evil) need only be cushioned, not prevented. Second, it is interesting to note that this need to cushion negative social effects is further made subject to the program's macroeconomic reforms.

The various events described as landmarks in the history of sustainable development were discussed not only for the sake of providing a historical exposition. They were discussed with a view to uncovering the normative content of sustainable development. A crucial element for uncovering the normative content of sustainable development is to determine the purpose of sustainable development: to ask what led to the evolution of the concept. It can only be through its history that the purpose of sustainable development can be determined. In the next section, relying principally on the historical exposition above, I offer a few remarks about the purpose of sustainable development. It is ideas about the purpose of sustainable development that will inform the conceptualisation of sustainable development in chapter 3.

119 As above. He also gives, as examples, Eskom (the national electricity provider) where, due to privatisation, the electricity tariffs are expected to increase by between 22% and 50%. Similarly, after privatisation, Spoornet (the railway company), increased tariffs for transport of foodstuffs resulting in increase in the prices of some foodstuffs by between 12% and 67%.

120 See eg P Mosley, J Harrington and J Toye *Aid and power: The World Bank and policy-based lending Volume I: Analysis and policy proposals* (1991) and DE Sahn, PA Dorosh and SD Younger *Structural adjustment reconsidered: Economic policy and poverty in Africa* (1997).

121 For more recent literature on the negative effects of IMF structural adjustments see Stiglitz (n 117 above) 36. See A Pinzani 'Global justice as moral issue: Interviewing Thomas Pogge' (2005) 4 no 1 4 and TW Pogge 'Severe poverty as a human rights violation' (2003) both available at http://www.etikk.no/globaljustice/ (accessed 20 July 2006). See also, Tladi 'IMF conditionality' (n 116 above) 45.

122 IMF *Annual report* (1991) 51.

123 Tladi (n 116 above) 46.

3. The purpose of sustainable development: Paradigm shift

In the previous section I considered the historical evolution of sustainable development. In this section, relying principally on the historical evolution sketched, I consider the purpose of sustainable development. Thus, I ask what it is that sustainable development requires of the international community.

Sustainable development grew out of the recognition by humanity (represented by the various states and groups of civil society) that the current[124] global pattern of development is detrimental for the environment and social needs of the poor.[125] The purpose of sustainable development is, therefore, to make (or attempt to make) development processes consistent with environmental and social considerations. As stated in chapter 1, under the current mode of development, economic considerations trump environmental and social considerations.[126] Recognising that humanity is at a precipice, sustainable development requires a change from the 'business-as-usual' paradigm to make more effective provision for the integration of social and environmental values.[127] However, where must this paradigm shift take us?

If, as suggested earlier in the chapter, the Stockholm process is the birth place of the evolution of sustainable development, then it is there that one must begin in the search for a new paradigm. The Founex report essentially calls for greater consideration to be paid to environmental and social issues (in particular concern for the

124 I use current here to refer to the situation without sustainable development.

125 In chapter 1 I describe the environmental and social crisis that can be regarded as the rationale for sustainable development.

126 See eg, para 11 of the Johannesburg Declaration on Sustainable Development, recognising a need for change as an 'objective' and 'essential requirement' for sustainable development. See also HD Johnson 'Whose Earth is it anyway?' (2002) 39 *UN Chronicle* 8 8 who argues that economic considerations have 'overwhelmed' environmental and social issues.

127 In sustainable development discourse, the phrase 'business-as-usual' normally refers to unsustainable practices. See, generally K Bosselmann 'Strong and weak sustainable development: Making the difference in the design of law' paper presented at the World Summit 2002: Environmental Law Foundations for Sustainable Development, Pietermaritzburg, South Africa, 20 - 22 August 2002 (on file with author). See also P Taylor 'Heads in the sand as the tide rises: Environmental ethics and the law on climate change' (2000/2001) 19 *Journal of Environmental Law* 247 who says of the climate change regime: '... the prevalent value is one of preserving current forms of economic prosperity, maintaining the economic *status quo* — 'business-as-usual'. GP Glasby 'Sustainable development and the need for a new paradigm' (2002) 4 *Environment, Development and Sustainability* 333 341 states that 'creating a truly sustainable society should be contrasted with the business-as-usual scenario which will inevitably result in a seriously degraded planet by the end of the 21st century'. In the context of climate change see E Hey 'The climate change regime: An enviro-economic problem and international administrative law in the making' (2001) 1 *International Environmental Agreements: Politics, Law and Economics* 75 78.

poor).[128] In the Stockholm Declaration itself the emphasis seems to fall on environmental considerations and humanity's duty to protect the environment.[129] While the emphasis in the Stockholm Declaration appears to be on the environment, there is, nonetheless, serious concern to improve the 'quality of life' of the poor.[130] The underlying emphasis of the Declaration seems to be on constraining economic activity for environmental and social considerations as well as making development and environmental protection socially beneficial.

This emphasis on economic growth is continued in the Brundtland Commission report.[131] However, as noted by Glasby, the Brundtland Commission report does not only call for economic growth,[132] it also calls for a change in the quality of growth.[133] More importantly, unlike the business-as-usual scenario, economic growth is under the Brundtland conception of sustainable development undertaken not for the sake of economic growth but rather to improve social and environmental considerations. That must mean that economic growth must be made subject to both environmental and social needs.

Throughout the report, the Brundtland Commission stresses the needs of the poor.[134] The emphasis on the needs of the poor also takes centre-stage in the Johannesburg Declaration.[135] Although the *means* of poverty reduction, according to Francine Menstrum,[136] are not adequately spelt out in the Johannesburg instrument, poverty eradication as both 'an objective' and an 'essential requirement' of sustainable development is a theme of the Johannesburg Declaration.[137] The focus on poverty was carried forward from Millennium Development Goals.[138]

128 See generally Founex Report (n 34 above).

129 See eg Principle 1 Stockholm Declaration.

130 See eg emphasis on life of dignity in Principle 1, prevention of pollution which creates 'hazards to human life' in Principle 7, and Principle 8 which emphasises that development should be 'for the improvement of the quality of life'. Principle 5 also reminds us that benefits from natural resources should be shared 'by all mankind'.

131 WCED *Our Common Future* (1997) 8 31.

132 Glasby (n 127 above) 335 says of the Report: 'There are many inconsistencies in these objectives. For example, rapid economic growth was considered essential in both industrial and developing countries if economic, social and environmental collapses are to be averted'.

133 As above, 334.

134 The oft-cited notion from the report that sustainable development is concerned with the 'concept of needs, in particular the essential needs of the world's poor' emphasises this very point. See WCED (n 57 above) 43.

135 See for discussion above, especially para 2.6.

136 F Menstrum 'Poverty reduction and sustainable development' (2003) 4 *Environment, Development and Sustainability* 41.

137 See especially para 11 Johannesburg Declaration. See generally discussion in para 2.6 of this chapter.

138 See United Nations Millennium Declaration, UN GA Res/55/2 (2000) available at http://www.un.org/milleniumgoals/ (accessed 5 June 2004).

The Rio Declaration is slightly different. Rio seems, on the whole, to equally promote the three values of sustainable development. In this sense, the compromise element is more apparent in the Rio Declaration.[139] The analysis in paragraph 2.5 of this chapter may suggest that the Rio Declaration leans towards the economic growth value. That is not to say that social and environmental considerations are not reflected, but that economic growth concerns play a much greater role than in other key instruments of sustainable development that are analysed. Consider further, for example, the main Principle on poverty eradication in the Rio Declaration, Principle 5. In that principle, the eradication of poverty, while considered 'an indispensable requirement' of sustainable development, is not said to be an objective.[140] Furthermore, the manner in which Principle 12 of the Rio Declaration deals with the trade environment debate is also indicative of the relative strength of economic concerns in the Rio Declaration.[141]

Instruments from civil society, although not definitive, should not be ignored.[142] Two instruments are particularly instructive in this case. The first is the ILA New Delhi Principles.[143] A cursory glance at this instrument illustrates that the central concerns are poverty eradication and environmental protection.[144] While economic concerns are reflected, they are not given primacy.[145] A similar point can be made about the Earth Charter, another civil society document.[146] Elsewhere I have said the following of the Earth Charter:

> It is perhaps not by accident that the Earth Charter, while containing principles calling for respect for the ecology and recognition of the intrinsic value of nature and eradication of poverty as an ethical, social,

139 That is not to say the other instruments are not instruments of compromise. See also the ILA Committee on International Law First Report, prepared for the ILA Conference in 2004, Berlin, in ILA *Report of the seventy-first conference – Berlin* (2004) 580 *et seq* discussing the compromise concerning Common but Differentiated Responsibilities.

140 Compare this with the discussion of Johannesburg Declaration and the Brundtland Commission report above.

141 See discussion above, para 2.5.

142 See Judge van der Wyngaert's dissenting opinion in *The Case Concerning the Arrest Warrant of 11 April 2000* 2000 *ICJ* 182 available at http://www.icj-cij.org (accessed November 2003) para 27, endorsing the use of opinions from non-state actors in the determination of rules of international law.

143 ILA New Delhi Declaration of Principles of International Law Relating to Sustainable Development adopted by the International Law Association in 2002, reprinted in Schrijver (n 59 above) 86.

144 See eg Principles 1 (The Duty of States to Ensure Sustainable Use of Natural Resources), 2 (The Principle of Equity and Poverty Eradication), 3 (The Principle of Common but Differentiated Responsibilities) and 4 (The Precautionary Approach to Human Health, Natural Resources and Ecosystems).

145 The New Delhi Declaration, for example, reflects economic concerns in Principle 7 (The Principle of Integration and Interrelationship, in Particular in relation to human rights and social, economic, environmental objectives).

146 The Earth Charter was adopted by the Earth Charter Commission in 2000 and is available at www.earthcharter.org (accessed 20 August 2006).

> and environmental imperative, does not, similarly call for the further growth of economies. More importantly, the Earth Charter does not seek to limit its ecological and social aims by economic growth.[147]

What the Earth Charter does do is to require respect for nature in all its diversity, care for the poor of the world and a commitment to human rights.[148] It requires that the Earth's ecological integrity be respected and protected.[149] The Earth Charter also requires the eradication of poverty as an ethical, social and environmental imperative.[150] Under the Earth Charter economic activity has to promote environmental and social development and is, therefore, subject to both.[151]

On the whole, taking into account the history of sustainable development and the key instruments on sustainable development, it would seem that sustainable development is intended to be a vehicle for a paradigm shift from a situation where economic growth concerns are paramount, to one where social and environmental considerations are of paramount importance.

4. Conclusion

The modern history of sustainable development can be traced from the Stockholm process. The Stockholm, Rio and Johannesburg declarations, along with other significant instruments such as the Brundtland Commission Report, the Millennium Development Goals, the ILA Declaration and the Earth Charter were all important milestones in the evolution of sustainable development. While these instruments are important for their own sake, they also serve an additional purpose in this study. An analysis of these milestone instruments contributes towards uncovering the purpose of sustainable development.

Based on the overview of the history of sustainable development, I argue in this chapter that sustainable development requires a paradigm shift from the ruling economic growth paradigm to a paradigm where social and environmental considerations are prioritised. The idea that sustainable development requires a paradigm shift has implications for both the conceptualisation of sustainable development and for determining the role of sustainable development in international law. In chapter 3, I offer a conceptualisation of sustainable development based on various factors including the purpose of sustainable development. Chapter 4, will consider the place of sustainable development in international law.

147 D Tladi 'Strong sustainable development, weak sustainable development and the Earth Charter: Towards a more nuanced framework of analysis' (2004) 11 *South African Journal of Environmental Law and Policy* 17 28.
148 As above.
149 See Principle II of the Earth Charter.
150 Principle III of the Earth Charter.
151 See especially Principle III art 10 (a).

3

Processes of Conceptualization

'Does globalisation only benefit the powerful and the financiers, speculators and traders! Does it offer nothing to men, women and children who are ravaged by the violence of poverty?'[1]

1. Introduction

In this chapter I provide a conceptualisation of sustainable development. The chapter enquires as to the definition of sustainable development and further asks whether sustainable development have a definite content. Put another way, whether sustainable development is an indeterminate notion incapable of acquiring fixed meaning. An equally important question is whether sustainable development, as a principle of law and/or policy, favours development over the environment or *vice versa*. These questions are crucial to uncovering the normative content of the concept, and both questions tend to raise similar issues. For example, both the indeterminacy and hierarchy questions raise (and respond to) the anthropocentric/ecocentric debate. Similarly, both questions raise (and respond to) to the question of what is meant by the popular characterisation of sustainable development as balancing environmental and developmental needs. These are questions that I analyse in an attempt to provide a coherent and nuanced conceptualisation of sustainable development.

I begin the process of uncovering the content of the concept of sustainable development by analysing its early conceptualisation. I consider the various criticisms levelled at this early conceptualisation. Drawing from the critique of the early conceptualisation of sustainable development I suggest a more nuanced approach to sustainable development. A nuanced conceptualisation of sus-tainable development, I suggest, recognises that there are different variations of sustainable development.

1 Nelson Mandela, address to World Economic Forum, January 1999, available at www.anc.org.za/ancdocs/history/mandela/1999/nm0129.htm (accessed 17 August 2005).

2. Early conceptualisation of sustainable development

The definition often given to the concept of sustainable development is that found in the Brundtland Report.[2] The report itself notes that the definition contains within it two key concepts. In the first place, the definition contains recognition of the 'essential needs of the poor, to which overriding priority should be given'.[3] Second, it recognises the 'idea of limitations ... on the environment's ability to meet present and future needs'.[4] The first concept implies equity within generations.[5] The second concept implies that there should be equity between generations.[6] Along with integration, the principles of inter- and intragenerational equity are, therefore, under the Brundtland definition of sustainable development, key concepts in the conceptualisation of sustainable development. These principles have formed the basis of the early conceptualisation of sustainable development.[7]

2.1 Principle of Intergenerational Equity

Perhaps nothing else has come to symbolise the principle of intergenerational equity like the definition of sustainable development in the Brundtland report as 'development that meets the needs of the present generation without compromising the ability of future generations to meet their own needs.'[8] Thus, sustainable development, as a concept, requires intergenerational equity.[9]

2 WCED *Our common future* (1987) 43.

3 As above.

4 As above.

5 See N Schrijver 'De verankering en betekenis van duurzame ontwikkeling in het internationale recht' 2003 *Mededelingen van de Nederlandse Vereniging voor Internationaal Recht: Volkenrecht en duurzame ontwikkeling* 1 5 who says that implicit in the Brundtland definition is the idea that the 'natuurlike hulpbronne mogen niet door een kleine groep mensen (in industrielanden) worden opgesoupeerd' ('natural resources must not be consumed by a small group of people (in industrialised countries)').

6 Schrijver (n 5 above) 6 where the author says that the definition further implies that 'de huidige generatie toekomstige generaties van mensen niet mag opschepen met onherstelbare schade aan milieu, gezondheid of economie ...' ('the present generation may not disadvantage future generations with irreversible damage to the environment, state of the economy ...').

7 See for conceptualisation of sustainable development along these lines A Boyle & D Freestone 'Introduction' in A Boyle & D Freestone (eds) *International law and sustainable development* (1999). See also G Handl 'Sustainable development: General rules versus specific obligations' in W Lang (ed) *Sustainable development and international law* (1995) 37.

8 WCED (n 2 above) 43.

9 See L Gundling 'Our responsibility to future generations' (1990) 84 *American Journal of International Law* 207 208.

The principle of intergenerational equity implies that the present generation owes a duty to future generations to leave the earth and its environment in no worse a condition than they received it.[10] Although generally accepted as a key element of a sustainable development, this has been questioned on ethical grounds. While the emergence of the theory or principle of intergenerational equity has generated academic debate about the legitimacy and ethics of such a theory, it is clear that the principle has crossed into the domain of international law.[11] Already in 1990 Professor D'Amato, an opponent of the concept, conceded the influence that the concept has had on the development of international environmental law.[12]

The 1972 Stockholm Declaration recognised the need to safeguard the environment against degradation 'for the benefit of present and future generations through careful planning or management'.[13] Thus, we seek to protect the environment not only for our own sakes, but

10 See E Brown Weiss *In fairness to future generations: International law, common patrimony and intergenerational equity* (1989). Although some of the ideas expressed in the work were earlier developed in E Brown Weiss 'The planetary trust: Conservation and intergenerational equity' (1984) 11 *Ecology Law Quarterly* 494 (E Brown Weiss 'The planetary trust') this study remains a must for intergenerational equity. The main thrust of the book is found at page 2 where the author states: 'The thesis of this study is that each generation receives a natural and cultural legacy in trust from previous generations and holds it in trust for future generations. This relationship imposes upon each generation certain planetary obligations to conserve the natural and cultural resource base for future generations ...' See also the judgment in *Minors Oposa v Secretary of Department of Environment and Natural Resources*, judgment of Judge Davide in the Supreme Court of Philippines in which the petitioners claimed a right to a balanced ecology not only for themselves and Filipinos in their generation but also for future generations. Reproduced in 1994 *ILM* 173. The Court found that the petitioners may sue on behalf of future generations.

11 See for example Brown Weiss 'The planetary trust' (n 10 above) who argues at 540 *et seq* that the principle is an *obligatio erga omnes*. The principle has also found its way into several international environmental agreements and policy-setting documents, either expressly or implicitly. Examples include the Brundtland Commission Report and the Rio instruments. See for international instruments supporting the principle of intergenerational equity, Principle 2 of the Stockholm Declaration, Principle 3 of the Rio Declaration and art 3 (1) of the United Nations Framework Convention on Climate Change (1992) 31 *ILM* 851 discussed below.

12 See A D'Amato 'Do we owe a duty to future generations to preserve the global environment?' 1990 *American Journal of International Law* 190 190 where he says: 'A common assumption underlying nearly every book or essay on the global environment is that the present generation owes a duty to generations yet unborn to preserve the diversity and quality of our planet's life-sustaining environmental resources'.

13 Principle 2, Stockholm Declaration. Of course the principle of intergenerational equity predates the Stockholm conference. It appears in the preamble of the 1946 International Convention on the Regulation of Whaling in H Homann (ed) *Basic documents of international environmental law, volume 3* (1992) 1291 which recognises the 'interests of the states of the world in safeguarding for *future generations* the great nature resources represented by the whale stocks'. (Emphasis added). See also preamble the of the 1968 African Nature Conservation Convention and the 1972 World Heritage Convention, both cited in P Sands 'International law in the field of sustainable development: emerging legal principles' in Lang (n 7 above) 59.

for the sakes of those to come. The principle of intergenerational equity recognises that our present-day activities, particularly our economic activities, may disadvantage future generations.

Intergenerational equity is based on a realisation that developmental activities put strain on natural resources at a rate greater than that at which the resources can renew themselves. If this continues unabated future generations will be left without these same life-sustaining resources.[14] The Brundtland Commission report recognised that while 'nature is bountiful ... it is also fragile' such that 'there are thresholds that cannot be crossed without endangering the basic integrity of the system' and 'the survival of life on earth'.[15] It was to this end that the Commission adopted the legal principles proposed by the World Commission on Environment and Development (WCED) Experts Group on Environmental Law which proposed, *inter alia,* that 'states shall conserve and use the environment and natural resources for the benefit of present and future generations'.[16]

The Rio instruments also contain references to intergenerational equity. The Rio Declaration requires the 'right to development' to be fulfilled 'so as to equitably meet developmental and environmental needs of present and future generations'.[17] This formulation, while containing the essential character of intergenerational equity – requiring the present generation to consider future generations in developmental activities – is a little different from previous formulations. Principle 3, as formulated, may be interpreted as placing the 'the right to development' as the central concern, and not the environment, as in previous formulations. Nevertheless, the principle further illustrates the centrality of the principle of intergenerational equity in sustainable development discourse.

The principle of intergenerational equity has also been invoked in numerous multilateral environmental agreements. The Climate Change Convention, adopted at Rio, for example, invokes the principle of intergenerational equity. Article 3 of the Convention is entitled 'Principles'. The article provides that the 'Parties should protect the climate system for the benefit of present and future generations of humankind'.[18] The Convention on Biodiversity makes a similar reference to the principle of intergenerational equity in the preamble. Indeed, the vast majority of environmental agreements are premised, even when they do not invoke intergenerational equity

14 See WCED (n 2 above) 13.

15 WCED (n 2 above) 33.

16 Principle 2, Proposed Legal Principles for Environmental Protection and Sustainable Development adopted by WCED Experts Group on Environmental Law. See for summary Annex 1 WCED (n 2 above) 348.

17 Principle 3, Rio Declaration.

18 Art 3(1) UN Framework Convention on Climate Change. The Kyoto Protocol, as an agreement that seeks to realise the goals of the UNFCCC, is also based on the principle of intergenerational equity. For further discussion see below ch 5.

expressly in the operative parts of the treaty, on the principle of intergenerational equity.[19]

By seeking to achieve equity for future generations, intergenerational equity infuses a forward-looking approach into sustainable development discourse. In that regard the principle of intergenerational equity is closely related to the precautionary principle which is also forward-looking. The precautionary principle is a principle that is intended to prevent environmental damage.[20] However, the precautionary principle goes further than just preventative action. While preventative action applies to environmental damage that is known or foreseeable, the precautionary principle would require action even before there is full scientific evidence of the environmental harm.[21]

The classic formulation of the precautionary approach is found in Principle 15 of the Rio Declaration which provides as follows:

> In order to protect the environment, the precautionary approach shall be widely applied by states according to their capabilities. Where there are threats of serious or irreversible damage, lack of full scientific certainty shall not be used as a reason for postponing cost-effective measures to prevent environmental degradation.

According to Hey and Freestone, writing in 1999, the precautionary approach has been included in virtually every recent treaty and policy document on the environment.[22] Like sustainable development, the

19 Boyle & Freestone (n 7 above) 12. See also P Sands *Principles of international environmental law vol I: Frameworks, standards and implementation* (1995) 200. See, for example, the preamble of the African Convention on the Conservation of Nature and Natural Resources in L Mashava (ed) *Economic and social rights series vol 7: A compilation of essential documents on the rights to water and environment* (2000); preamble of the Convention on International Trade in Endangered Species of Wild Fauna and Flora, (1973) 12 *ILM* 1085.

20 For a discussion of the history of the precautionary principle, see D Freestone 'The precautionary principle' in R Churchill & D Freestone (eds) *International law and climate change* (1991) 21; D Freestone & E Hey 'Origins and development of the precautionary principle' in D Freestone & E Hey (eds) *The precautionary principle and international law: The challenges of implementation* (1996) 3; J Cameron & J Abouchar 'The status of the precautionary principle in international law' in Freestone & Hey (above) 29; D Freestone 'Implementing precaution cautiously: The precautionary approach in the Straddling and Highly Migratory Fish Stocks Agreement' in E Hey (ed) *Developments in international fisheries law* (1999) 287.

21 For literature on the precautionary principle, see Freestone 'The precautionary principle' (n 20 above); Freestone & Hey (n 20 above); Freestone 'Implementing precaution cautiously' (n 20 above). For an in-depth analysis of the various elements of the precautionary principle in international law, see A Trouwborst *Precautionary rights and duties of states* (2006).

22 Freestone & Hey 'Origins and development' (n 20 above) 3. The authors list as examples Draft Agreement on Straddling and Highly Migratory Fish Stocks; Climate Change Framework Convention; Biodiversity Convention (preamble); the Bamako Convention and a host of other Conventions. See also A Kiss 'The rights and interests of future generations and the precautionary principle' in Freestone & Hey (n 20 above) 27.

status of the precautionary approach or principle has been debated widely.[23]

The relationship between the precautionary approach and sustainable development should not be too difficult to discern. As Freestone puts it, the precautionary principle 'occupies a central place in any realistic strategy' towards sustainable development.[24] Sustainable development requires that we are proactive and not only rehabilitate the environment after it has been harmed, but that we also prevent potential environmental degradation where such degradation would be irreversible. Moreover, as can be seen from the formulation of the precautionary principle in the Rio Declaration, the precautionary principle, like sustainable development, involves balancing environmental concerns with economic concerns.[25] Thus when the potential for environmental harm from a particular activity (economic activity) is high and when such activity may result in long-lasting or irreversible damage to the environment, then the precautionary principle would require the taking of steps even where scientific evidence regarding the environmental damage is not conclusive.[26] In fact, like sustainable development, the precautionary principle seeks to protect the environment for future generations.[27] This of course implies that, in many cases, the application of the precautionary principle is a precondition for sustainable development. To this end the Bergen Ministerial Declaration of 1990 provides as follows:[28]

> In order to achieve sustainable development, policies must be based on the precautionary principle. Environmental measures must anticipate, prevent, and attack the causes of environmental degradation. Where there are threats of serious or irreversible damage, lack of full scientific certainty shall not be used as reason for postponing measures to prevent environmental degradation.

But the balancing act in the precautionary principle, at least as formulated in the Rio Declaration, illustrates something else. Under the Rio formulation, the duty to take precautionary measures is itself limited by cost-effectiveness, an economic rationale. Therefore, here again there is an uncomfortable relationship between environmental imperatives, represented by the duty to take precautionary

23 See Cameron & Abouchar (n 20 above); See also Freestone (n 20 above).
24 Freestone (n 20 above) 25. See for further discussion Trouwborst (n 21 above) 33 *et seq*.
25 See A Nollkaemper '"What you risk reveals what you value" and other dilemmas encountered in the legal assaults on risk' in Freestone & Hey (n 20 above).
26 Kiss (n 22 above) 27.
27 As above.
28 Par 7 Bergen Ministerial Declaration on Sustainable Development in ECE Region reprinted in Churchill and Freestone (n 20 above).

measures, and economic concerns requiring such measures to be cost-effective.[29]

Intergenerational equity is not without its detractors. The main criticism against the principle of intergenerational equity derives from an ecocentric perspective. Ecocentrism is an approach that requires the environment to be protected for its own sake and not solely for its interest to humans.[30] From an ecocentric perspective, intergenerational equity as an anthropocentric approach is ethically flawed and insufficient to ensure meaningful protection of the environment.

The argument for an ecocentric approach to environmental protection is made by several authors.[31] Ecocentrists would suggest that our motive for protecting the environment should not be a duty we owe to future generations but rather that we owe a duty to nature *per se* regardless of its utility to humans.[32] D'Amato and Chopra argue that the right of the whales to be protected exists (in part) because they 'are the most specialised of all mammals ... [T]hey are sentient, they are intelligent, they have their own community, and they can suffer'.[33]

Of course, moving from the premise that the whale indeed possesses all the qualities attributed to it,[34] the argument does not take the ecocentric argument that nature should be protected for its own sake very far. Where does the argument leave other natural resources that do not possess comparable qualities? Are other living organisms less deserving of protection? The authors themselves say that they do not claim 'that the entitlements asserted in [the] article should apply exclusively to whales'.[35] However, they do not show how entities other than whales, especially non-sentient creatures, can benefit from their exposition.

29 Trouwborst (n 21 above) 229 *et seq* where he discusses the implications of cost-effectiveness. Discussing the relevance of a cost-benefit analysis, he states that cost effectiveness indicates the cost-benefit analysis where 'economic, social and ecological impacts' are translated into pecuniary equivalents (at 231).

30 R Eckersely *Environmentalism and political theory: Towards an ecocentric approach* (1992); see also S Burchill & A Linklater (eds) *Theories of international relations* (1996) 254 *et seq*.

31 See A D'Amato & SK Chopra 'Whales: Their emerging right to life' (1991) 85 *American Journal of International Law* 21; D'Amato (n 12 above); A Gillespie *International environmental law, policy and ethics* (1997); R Eckersely (n 30 above).

32 D'Amato & Chopra (n 31 above) 23.

33 As above, 22.

34 The contentions regarding the qualities possessed by the whales are well supported by authorities. D'Amato & Chopra (n 31 above) cite, eg, J Lilly *The mind of the dolphin: A non-human intelligence* (1967) for their contention that '[W]hales speak to other whales in a language that appears to include abstruse mathematical poetry'. The authors also assert, citing Morgan 'The whale brain: The anatomical basis of intelligence' in J McIntyre (ed) *Mind in the waters* (1974) that whales have developed interspecies communication with dolphins.

35 D'Amato & Chopra (n 31 above) 27 n 34.

It is submitted that at the heart of every sincere argument for ecocentrism is a fear that *any* anthropocentric approach will necessarily yield less protection for the environment.[36] The assumption here is that intergenerational equity as an anthropocentric approach to environmental protection will countenance the destruction of any species that is not of value to human beings.[37] This assumption is not necessarily true as is clear from a consideration of the standard definition of sustainable development found in the Brundtland Commission Report. The definition refers to the ability of future generations to meet *their* own needs. Inherent in the principle of intergenerational equity, as represented in this definition, is a recognition of the autonomy of future generations to determine for themselves what their needs may be.[38] Unwittingly, D'Amato and Chopra make the point:[39]

> Our moral obligations to others cannot be grounded on our expectation of future help from them. Even so, we cannot now know what *potential future benefit* to persons the continued existence of whales might afford. *Medical science is replete with examples of cures derived from animals and plants, many of which seemed useless* ... (Emphasis added)

The principle of intergenerational equity thus requires the present generation to leave the environment in as good a condition as it was found.[40] The principle of intergenerational equity does not allow or promote the plundering of resources that we may find to be valueless because doing so may limit the options available to future generations to meet their own needs. Thus, a proper understanding of the principle of intergenerational equity would require the protection, and not destruction, of all natural species and not only those that benefit us at present. This would enable future generations to meet their own needs, including those that we may not have foreseen. Brown Weiss observes the following in this regard:[41]

> Reducing the diversity of known reserves of non-renewable resources raises several problems for future generations. It forecloses applications for the resources that the present generation has not yet appreciated, but which could be very valuable for future generations.

36 See generally literature cited in n 31 above.

37 See Gillespie (n 30 above) 22 where he says the protection of nature is only required if it serves man's interest and once 'the interest is gone so too is the reason to preserve the environment'.

38 The argument made here is taken from an earlier article: D Tladi 'Of course for humans: A contextual defence of intergenerational equity' (2002) 9 *South African Journal of Environmental Law and Policy* 177. See also Brown Weiss (n 10 above) 8 where she says: 'Reducing the diversity of known reserves of non-renewable resources ... forecloses application for the resources that the present generation has not yet appreciated'.

39 D'Amato & Chopra (n 31 above) 27.

40 See E Brown Weiss 'Our rights and obligations to future generations for the environment' (1990) 84 *American Journal of International Law* 198 (Brown Weiss 'Our rights and obligations') at 197. See also Brown Weiss (n 10 above).

41 Brown Weiss (n 10 above) 8.

Moreover, I think those who assume that intergenerational equity (as an anthropocentric approach) represents anti-environmental sentiments miss the point. Intergenerational equity is concerned with *our duty* to protect the environment; not *our right* to destroy it. As Brown Weiss argues:[42]

> We alone among all living creatures have the capacity to shape significantly our relationship to the environment. We can use it on a sustainable basis or we can degrade the environment and the natural resource base. As part of the natural system, we have no right to destroy its integrity; nor is it in our interest to do so. Rather, as the most sentient of living creatures, we have a special responsibility to care for the planet.

Of course the preceding discussion does not shed light on the value of intergenerational equity in comparison with any ecocentric approach. Intergenerational equity recognises the need to develop. However, the need for development may not be compatible with an ecocentric approach. To take D'Amato and Chopra's[43] argument for the whale's right to life as an example, sustainable exploitation of natural resources for developmental and/or subsistence purposes would not be permissible.[44] An approach that does not make allowance for development cannot yield an equitable balance between environmental protection and development, as environmental concerns and developmental concerns are inextricably linked.[45]

The ecocentric objection to sustainable development is, of course, much broader than just a concern for whales. As stated, at the heart of the objection lies the fear that anthropocentrism is incapable of effecting adequate protection of the environment because such approaches will countenance the destruction of aspects of nature that are not regarded as useful for humans. A critique of this aspect of ecocentricism plays a crucial role in the development of a more nuanced conceptualisation of sustainable development later in the chapter.

42 Brown Weiss 'Our rights and obligations' (n 40 above) 199. See also the *Minors Oposa* judgment (n 10 above) 108 where Judge Davide says: 'Put a little differently, the minor's assertion of their right to a sound environment constitutes, at the same time, the performance of their obligation to ensure protection of that right for generations to come'.

43 D'Amato & Chopra (n 31 above).

44 Indeed D'Amato & Chopra appear to go that far when they argue that art 1(2) of the International Covenant on Economic Social and Cultural Rights, which provides that no one may be deprived of means of subsistence, 'should be read to imply a caveat: 'so long as other rights are not violated' (at 59 *et seq)*.

45 See discussion para 1 in chapter 1 above.

2.2 Intragenerational Equity

The principle of intragenerational equity requires that there must be equity within generations. Intragenerational equity is concerned with the distribution of the benefits of development activities and the distribution of costs for environmental protection. Much of international environmental law since the Stockholm conference has centred on intragenerational equity. The discourse on intragenerational equity finds expression in the popularly termed 'North-South debate'.[46] Thus, intragenerational equity is really concerned with distributive justice, which, according to Franck, is a prerequisite for a fair system of international law.[47]

The utility of the principle of intragenerational equity lies in that it recognises, on the one hand, the need to protect the environment while also recognising that developing countries have a legitimate right to development. Thus, in the effort towards sustainable development, the precarious developmental situation of non-industrialised countries must be taken into consideration. At the heart of the principle of intragenerational equity lies a two-fold recognition. Firstly, developed states are in a better position to finance efforts towards environmental protection. Secondly, the major environmental problems facing the world arose from activities of industrialisation that benefited the developed world.

The principle may be applied in several ways. First, the principle may imply fewer or different obligations for developing states in the implementation of environmental programmes or policies.[48] Secondly, the principle may be used to 'delay' compliance with obligations.[49] Thirdly, the principle may require the transfer of funds or technology for the purposes of implementing environmental programmes.[50] All these variations of the principle of intergenerational equity have, as a common element, the notion that

46 J Ntambirweki 'The developing countries in the evolution of an international environmental law' (1991) 14 *Hastings International and Comparative Law Review* 906; K Mickelson 'South, North, international environmental law and international environmental lawyers' (2000) 11 *Yearbook of International Environmental Law* 52.

47 See generally TM Franck *Fairness in international law and institutions* (1995). See especially at 8 where he states the following: '... any analysis of fairness must include considerations of the consequential effects of the law: its distributive justice'.

48 The Kyoto Protocol to the United Nations Framework Convention on Climate Change (1997) reprinted in P Cullet & A Gowlland-Gualtieri (eds) *Key materials in international environmental law* (2004) 145, while providing emissions reductions commitments for developing countries, does not contain any such hard commitments for developing countries.

49 See eg art 5 of the Montreal Protocol on Substances that Deplete the Ozone (1987) reprinted in Cullet & Gowlland-Gualtieri (n 48 above) 99.

50 See eg art 20 of Convention on Biological Diversity (1992) reprinted in Cullet & Gowlland-Gualtieri (n 48 above).

developed countries are primarily responsible for the costs associated with efforts for environmental protection. Thus, developed states are required to 'pay' for developing states to implement efforts for environmental protection, especially protection of the global environment.[51]

As stated earlier, the principle of intragenerational equity is the distributional component of the Brundtland commission's definition of sustainable development.[52] In international environmental law the principle of intragenerational equity is encapsulated in the common but differentiated responsibilities principle.[53] The common but differentiated responsibilities principle has found its way into many recent international environmental instruments. The Stockholm Declaration recognised that environmental deficiencies can best be remedied 'by accelerated development through the transfer of substantial quantities of financial and technological assistance'.[54] Several principles in the Rio Declaration invoke the principle of intragenerational equity. Principle 5 requires, *inter alia,* states to co-operate in order to decrease the disparities in standards of living. Principle 6 provides that the 'special situation and needs of developing countries ... shall be given special priority'. The most telling provision in the Rio Declaration invoking intragenerational equity is principle 7 which provides that:[55]

> States shall co-operate in a spirit of global partnership to conserve, protect and restore the health and integrity of the Earth's ecosystem. In view of the different contributions to global environmental degradation *States have common but differentiated responsibilities*. The developed countries acknowledge the responsibility that they bear in the international pursuit of sustainable development in view of the pressures their societies place on the global environment and of the technologies and financial resources they command.

Making the same point, but in a more conversational and forward-looking tone, the Johannesburg Declaration provides:[56]

> The benefits and costs of globalisation are unevenly distributed, with developing countries facing special difficulties in meeting this challenge.

and[57]

51 The modalities and complexities of financial transfers from developed to developing countries for the global environmental benefit are considered in ch 7 on the Global Environment Facility.

52 CS Pearson *Economics and the global environment* (2000) 469.

53 See X Fuentes 'International law-making in the field of sustainable development: The unequal competition between development and the environment' (2002) 2 *International Environmental Agreements: Politics, Law and Economics* 109 122.

54 Principles 9 Stockholm Declaration. See also Principle 5 Stockholm Declaration.

55 Principle 7, Rio Declaration (emphasis added).

56 Para 14 Johannesburg Declaration.

57 Para 15 Johannesburg Declaration.

> We risk the entrenchment of these global disparities and unless we act in a manner that fundamentally changes their lives, the poor of the world may lose confidence in their representatives.

The rationales underlying the common but differentiated responsibilities in these instruments are reminiscent of ancient precepts of justice such as 'to each according to his capacity', 'to each according to his ability' and 'to each according to need'.[58] There is a slight difference between the formulations of these instruments which raises an interesting question. While the Rio Declaration expressly places the *responsibility* on developed countries, the Johannesburg Declaration, by directing the call to action to 'we', may detract from that obligation. While this certainly provides some food for thought, the differences may be explained by the style and overall conversational tone of the Johannesburg Declaration in contrast to the legalistic style of the Rio Declaration, as well as the fact the Johannesburg Declaration was not intended to establish any new principles. In the context of the latter point it is worth remembering that the Johannesburg Declaration expressly recalls and declares itself to be built upon the Rio Declaration.[59] Thus, while the formulation in the Johannesburg Declaration differs from that in the Rio Declaration, the implications remain the same: developed states should bear the lion-share of responsibility for efforts towards sustainable development. Principle 7 of the Rio Declaration reiterates the duality in the rationale underlying the principle of intra-generational equity, namely that developed countries are in a better position to finance efforts towards sustainable development and that the same developed countries contributed (and are still doing so) more than their fair share to the creation of the major environmental problems. Of this duality in the rationale for the principle, Mickelson states the following:[60]

> What is striking about the principle of common but differentiated responsibilities is that depending on the perspective brought to bear on it, it can be seen to reflect totally different ways of thinking about the respective roles of South and North in addressing environmental degradation. On the one hand, it can simply reflect a pragmatic acceptance of, and response to, the fact of differing levels of financial and technological resources available to countries in different economic circumstances. On the other hand, it can be said to reflect an acknowledgment of the historic, moral and legal responsibility of the North to shoulder the burdens of environmental protection, just as it has enjoyed the benefits of economic and industrial development largely unconstrained by environmental constraints.

58 See Franck (n 47 above) 13.

59 See Principle 8 Johannesburg Declaration.

60 Mickelson (n 46 above) 70. See also for detailed discussion Y Matsui 'Some aspects of the principle of "common but differentiated responsibilities"' (2002) 2 *International Environmental Agreements: Politics, Law and Economics* 151 154 *et seq*.

The former view implies that common but differentiated responsibility, as a manifestation of intragenerational equity, is accepted in international environmental law because the North has the '*ability* to pay'.[61] The latter view implies that common but differentiated responsibility is justified because the North has the '*responsibility* to pay' on account of the 'disproportionate share of benefits' received from centuries of unsustainable development.[62] Whatever the underlying rationale put forward for its existence, the principle of common but differentiated responsibility, as a reflection of intragenerational equity, is a firmly-entrenched part of the principle of sustainable development.[63]

Moreover, being premised on distributional justice, the common but differentiated responsibilities principle is consistent with Franck's maximin principle.[64] The unequal burdens placed on the rich *vis-à-vis* the poor is justified as they contribute to 'expectations of the least fortunate group' in the global society.[65] Although the common but differentiated responsibilities principle is intended to benefit poor countries, as an environmental strategy, it also implies benefits for the whole world through an improved environment. In this sense the purpose of the common but differentiated principle, while cognisant of the needs of poor countries, has an environmental dimension. This principle is firmly rooted in international environmental agreements.

The Ozone regime provides a good example for the discussion of the common but differentiated responsibilities principle. The Vienna Convention for the Protection of the Ozone Layer recognises in its preamble the need to take into 'account the circumstances and particular requirements of developing countries.'[66] The Montreal Protocol, which gives substance to the ideals in the Ozone Convention, incorporates the common but differentiated responsibilities principle in two important ways. Firstly, under article 5 of the protocol, developing countries with annual levels of consumption of controlled substances in Annex A[67] of less than 0.3 kg per capita at any time before 1999 may delay for ten years their compliance with the obligations as set out in article 2 of the

61 As above (emphasis original).

62 As above (emphasis original).

63 See, for moral critique of both rationales, CD Stone 'Common but differentiated responsibilities in international law' (2004) 98 *American Journal of International Law* 276 290 *et seq*.

64 Under the maximin principle, inequality in distribution of benefits (burdens) 'is only justifiable if it narrows, or does not widen, the existing inequality'. See Franck (n 47 above) at 18 *et seq*.

65 As above. Although Franck, for his maximin principle, relies heavily on Rawls, he is quick to concede that Rawls himself was hesitant to extend the principle to the global society. He offers, at 18 - 19, reasons why the principle can, notwithstanding Rawls' reluctance, be extended to the global society.

66 Preamble, Vienna Convention for the Protection of the Ozone Layer reprinted in Cullet & Gowlland-Gualtieri (n 48 above).

67 Annex A lists 5 CFC's and three halons.

Protocol.[68] This allowance is made to enable these developing countries to 'meet their domestic needs'.[69] In addition to the delay in obligations the Protocol also provides for the establishment of Financial Mechanisms.[70] This mechanism is intended to provide financial assistance and transfer of technologies so as to meet the 'incremental costs' required for compliance with the Protocol.[71] The concept of incremental costs, found in the financial transfers provisions of various multilateral environmental agreements, refers to costs exceeding those that would in any event have been incurred.[72] The GEF Council has defined incremental costs as in the context of GEF funding as follows:[73]

> The costs of GEF eligible activity should be compared to that of an activity it replaces or makes redundant. The differences between the two costs – the expenditure on the GEF supported activity and the costs saving on the replacement or redundant activity – is the incremental cost.

Similarly, both instruments considered in Part B, namely, the Climate Change regime and the Biosafety regime, give effect to the common but differentiated responsibilities principle. First, the Climate Change Convention provides that in the setting of commitments 'the common but differentiated responsibilities' of states should be considered.[74] This call is taken up in the Kyoto Protocol[75] which imposes differential obligations on state parties. The Protocol lays down limits on emissions of greenhouse gases to be met within certain specified commitment periods. These specific obligations are placed only on developed states (Annex 1 Parties). The Protocol does not impose any hard obligations in terms of emission reductions on developing states, at least not in the first commitment period. Article 10 of the Protocol reiterates that the states have 'common but differentiated responsibilities' towards the environment. Article 10 requires all parties (including developing countries) to formulate programmes 'to the extent possible' aimed at the improvement of the quality of emissions and mitigation of climate change, to co-operate in the attainment of the ideals in the climate change regime. The article 10 obligations are the only obligations imposed upon developing countries by the Kyoto Protocol. The Climate Change regime also has

68 Art 5(1) Montreal Protocol on Substances that Deplete the Ozone Layer in Cullet & Gowlland-Gualtieri (n 48 above) 99.

69 As above.

70 Art 10 Montreal Protocol on Substances that Deplete the Ozone Layer.

71 Art 10(1) Montreal Protocol. Transfer of Technologies is regulated under art 10A.

72 The notion is considered in greater detail in para 3.2.1 of ch 7 concerning the Global Environment Facility.

73 GEF *Incremental costs* GEF/C.7/Inf.5 at para 10.

74 Art 4(1) United Nations Framework Convention on Climate Change.

75 Kyoto Protocol to the United Nations Framework Convention on Climate Change.

financial mechanisms intended to help developing countries with their obligations.[76] It is further worth noting that, in both the Climate Change and the Biodiversity Conventions, the fulfillment of the obligations of developing countries is made dependent on the developed countries meeting their financial transfer commitment. Article 4(7) of the Climate Change Convention, for example, provides that the extent to which developing states 'will effectively implement their commitments under the Convention will depend on the effective implementation' of financial transfers by developed states.[77]

In the Biodiversity Convention the common but differentiated responsibilities principle is invoked in the preamble. The Cartagena Protocol includes provisions that are designed, specifically, with the recognition of the special position of developing countries in mind. These provisions include the advanced informed agreement procedure[78] and the risk management procedures allowing recourse to socio-economic considerations.[79] In addition, both the Biodiversity Convention and Cartagena Protocol on Biosafety require transfer of financial resources under much the same terms as the climate change agreements.[80]

In all these instruments state parties recognise the common but differentiated responsibilities principle by imposing less or different obligations on developing states, delaying compliance with obligations and requiring the transfer of both funds and technologies required for cleaner environment. By so doing these instruments contribute to the implementation of intragenerational equity.

The United Nations Convention on the Law of the Sea, particularly Part XI, provides yet another example of how intragenerational equity can be operationalised.[81] Part XI of the Convention provides, in part, that the deep sea-bed and its resources are 'the common heritage of mankind.'[82] In terms of the Convention the exploitation and utilisation of mineral resources from the seabed in areas beyond national jurisdiction have to be 'for the benefit of mankind as a whole

76 See art 11 Framework Convention and art 11 Kyoto Protocol.
77 See also art 20(4) Convention on Biological Diversity, which contains identical language.
78 See art 7 Cartagena Protocol on Biosafety to the Convention on Biological Diversity, reprinted in Cullet & Gowlland-Gualtieri (n 48 above) 188.
79 See arts 16 and 26 Cartagena Protocol.
80 See ch 6 below.
81 United Nations Convention on the Law of the Sea (UNCLOS) (1982) 21 *ILM* 1261.
82 Art 136 UNCLOS.

... taking into particular consideration the interests and needs of developing countries'.[83] Thus, because developing countries do not have the technologies to mine for mineral resources in the deep seabed, any mining activities for mineral resources that take place in the deep seabed beyond areas of national jurisdiction have to benefit humankind as a whole. For this purpose the International Seabed authority has been created to manage aspects of the deep sea-bed mining, including the sharing of proceeds from commercial activities.[84] The whole regime of benefit sharing in respect of exploitation and utilisation of mineral resources is itself an application of intragenerational equity, where developed countries are required to 'share' benefits derived from the use of resources with developing countries.[85] It is, perhaps, worth noting that developing countries have advocated an extension of the principles of Part XI to genetic resources on the seabed.[86]

Pearson has argued that 'the sustainable development debate has lost its intragenerational equity dimension'.[87] He suggests, incorrectly, that sustainable development is analysed 'almost exclusively from an efficiency perspective or an intergenerational equity perspective'.[88] However, as Brown Weiss points out, the principle of intergenerational equity carries with it an intragenerational dimension.[89] If intergenerational equity did not carry an intragenerational dimension, then a generation could allocate the resources to some communities and the burdens of caring for such resources to different communities and still claim, on a balance, to have met their intergenerational obligations.[90] Further, as is clear from the preceding discussion, intragenerational equity concerns are finding recognition in international environmental regimes.

One of the problems with the intragenerational equity debate is that it often creates the impression that the international environmental arena is made up of two opposing camps, namely, the

83 Art 140 UNCLOS. In a typology of different types of equity, Franck distinguishes the common heritage of mankind principle from 'corrective equity' and 'broadly conceived equity'. The common heritage of mankind type equity is different from the other two types in that it does 'not share the assumption that resources belong *ab initio* to states'. See Franck (n 47 above) 75

84 Art 156. Importantly Part XI of UNCLOS must be read together with the 1994 New York Agreement Relating to the Implementation of Part XI of the United Nations Convention on the Law of the Sea (1994) 33 *ILM* 1309, which has the effect reducing the equity aspects of Part IX. On the sharing of economic benefits from exploitative activities carried out on the seabed see arts 140 and 160.

85 See Franck (n 47 above) 75 who has described the equitable principles reflected in the Part IX of the Convention 'broadly conceived equity'.

86 See generally Report of the Ad Hoc Open-ended Informal Working Group to Study Issues Relating to the Conservation and Sustainable Use of Marine Biological Diversity in Areas Beyond National Jurisdiction (March 2006) UN Doc A/61/65.

87 Pearson (n 52 above) 470.

88 As above, 471.

89 Brown Weiss 'Our rights and obligations' (n 40 above) 201.

90 As above.

developed world, which is pro-environmental protection, and the developing countries reflecting anti-environment sentiments.[91] As Mickelson points out, this viewpoint is deceptive. As an example she highlights the development of the Basel Convention on Transboundary Movement of Hazardous Wastes, where it was the developing countries that were seeking a more stringent regime, totally banning hazardous wastes import from developed to developing countries while developed countries argued for less stringent outcomes. As will be seen in chapter 6, a similar point can be made with respect to the evolution of the Biosafety Protocol. Of course those who endorse the view that international environmental diplomacy is represented by the pro-environmental North and the anti-environmental South would argue that examples such as the waste trade where developing states were seeking stringent obligations are few and far between.

However, it appears that this view ignores the reality and complexity of international environmental diplomacy. States' conduct, in their relations with one another, cannot be explained only with reference to their interests in the preservation of the environment. The reality is that political and economic factors play an important role in the position that states (developed and developing alike) adopt in environmental negotiations.[92] Miller convincingly argues that 'competing, self-interested states can find it in their interest' to co-operate in environmental agreements.[93]

Why were developed states adverse to the idea of a total ban on the transboundary movement of hazardous wastes from developed to developing states? Because it was not in their economic interest to have a total ban. Why has the United States repudiated the Kyoto Protocol? Because, in the words of the US President GW Bush, the 'idea of placing caps does not make economic sense for America'.[94] President Bush added that while he was worried about climate change he was 'also worried about the fact that people may not be finding jobs in America'.[95] Likewise, developing states will be less willing to be involved in environmental arrangements that hamper their development unless the cost and benefits of such environmental arrangements are distributed equitably. If we take climate change as

91 See Mickelson (n 46 above) 54.

92 See generally discussion in A Hurrel & B Kingsbury 'International politics of the environment: An introduction' in A Hurrel & B Kingsbury (eds) *The international politics of the environment* (1991) 5 *et seq*. See also MAL Miller *The third world in global environmental politics* (1995) 2 who says: 'Regardless of their economic status or political perspective, a primary objective of nation-states is growth'.

93 Miller (n 92 above) 11.

94 M Hall 'Bush defends his rejection of pact on global warming' in *USA Today* 1, April 2001 2A.

95 As above. The comment by President Bush also serves to illustrate the existence of the relationship between social and economic values. While the reasons for Bush's suspicious attitude towards the Kyoto Protocol are undoubtedly economic, the reason put forward here, 'jobs', represents a social value. This relationship is explored further in para 3.3 below.

an example, an arrangement designed to curb climate change must take into consideration the fact that developed countries are financially in a better position to finance efforts towards curbing climate change and that the activities of industrialisation (that are responsible for the wealth of the developed states) are at the heart of the climate change problem. It would thus seem unfair or *inequitable* to prevent developing states from also pursuing development objectives, without taking these factors into account.

Thus, to view intragenerational equity as implying that developed states are pro-environmental protection and developing states are contra-environmental protection is naïve. Intra-generational equity is founded on the reality of international relations. Intragenerational equity results from the realisation by developing states of a new 'bargaining chip' that they possess in international environmental politics.[96]

As with intergenerational equity, intragenerational equity is not without its detractors. A recent article by Christopher Stone on the principle of common but differentiated responsibilities illustrates the hostility of some towards intragenerational equity generally, and the common but differentiated responsibilities principle in particular.[97] According to Stone, the principle is 'neither necessary nor helpful'.[98] The common but differentiated responsibilities principle as represented in the Johannesburg instruments, he asserts, would leave the rich countries worse off in 'the interest of 'righting' the inequity of the *status quo ante*'.[99] For Stone, the normative question is whether placing the heavier burden on rich countries is morally persuasive. He suggests that it is not, and offers various reasons for this assertion.

It is not possible here to respond to all of Stone's arguments against the principle of common but differentiated responsibilities.[100] However, it is necessary to respond to some of them. First, he suggests that basing the common but differentiated responsibilities (referred to in his article as 'CDR') on needs would make it difficult to determine 'what kind of measures a needs-regarding equitable CDR would require'.[101] Second, and most disconcerting, he argues that the need to differentiate responsibilities shifts responsibilities from the 'Poor's needs to Rich's wrongs'.[102] This, he argues is not very controversial when understood in terms of current environmental

96 Miller (n 92 above) 10.
97 Stone (n 63 above).
98 Stone (n 63 above) 281. Elsewhere he asserts that 'a moment's' reflection will show that the principle is neither universal nor helpful'.
99 Stone (n 63 above) 284.
100 Some of Stone's arguments appear to be made tongue-in-cheek and thus do not warrant a response.
101 Stone (n 63 above) 291.
102 As above.

degradation by current societies. However, he argues that the principle is untenable when it is understood as referring to historical pressures placed on the environment by societies in rich countries. The latter line of argument, he asserts, is problematic because '[i]t is not clear why a contemporary US citizen should make amends for the overuse of global commons during the stretch before her forebears immigrated'.[103]

None of the issues raised by Stone is convincing. First, Stone is wrong in asserting that the common but differentiated responsibilities principle would leave the richer countries worse off. The common but differentiated responsibilities principle, while certainly incorporating redistributive aims, benefits the world community by facilitating global environmental protection. Such an understanding of the common but differentiated responsibilities principle is consistent with Franck's maximun principle in that the principle contains advantages not only for its main beneficiaries but also for everyone else.[104] As Franck notes, the question of what to do in the face of the massive environmental degradation facing the world is complicated by the level of distributive inequality. Second, it is not clear why, according to Stone, it would be hard to determine what the 'needs-regarding equitable CDR would call for'. After all, just about every modern environmental agreement *already* calls for such differentiation of obligations. Third, Stone's concern about contemporary US citizens having to make amends for the overuse of the global commons prior to the immigration of their ascendants is based on a miscomprehension of international law and how it operates.[105] It is not the individuals that are said to be responsible, nor is it the forefathers of the citizens. It is the state, as a legal subject of international law that is considered to be responsible in terms of the common but differentiated responsibilities principle. The state assumes responsibilities (and rights) that are separate from those assumed by nationals of the state. To be fair, Stone's argument is an ethical and not a legal one. Nevertheless the ethical argument is a critique of a legal principle and, therefore, the characterisation and implications of the legal principle under critique have to be accurate. Moreover, it is further interesting to note that Stone does not question why contemporary US citizens should continue to enjoy the benefits of the overuse of the global commons after the immigration of their forefathers.

103 Stone (n 63 above) 293.

104 See Franck (n 47 above). At 366 Franck states the principle thus: the maximun principle is useful as a means 'to redistribute costs and benefits in such a way as to close the gap between rich and poor without damaging the system's capacity to increase the sum of the goods available for distribution'.

105 To be fair, Stone does not attempt to make an argument based on international *law*. Rather Stone is making an argument based on morality. Nevertheless, to the extent that the Stone's moral argument is directed at international law principles, then such principles have to be accurately characterised.

While the intragenerational equity principle can and has been questioned from many quarters, it has been accepted as a normative principle of modern international environmental law and sustainable development discourse as reflected by its inclusion in just about every modern multilateral environmental agreement, as well as other instruments, such as the Global Environment Facility.

2.3 Integration

At the core of the concept of sustainable development is the recognition that environmental and development issues are inextricably connected. This recognition requires that, in developmental policy-making, environmental concerns should be considered and *vice versa*. The idea of environmental concerns influencing developmental concerns and developmental concerns influencing environmental concerns is what integration is about. In other words, the achievement of sustainable development requires that development and environment be integrated. Such integration would similarly require that institutions concerned with development activities also effectively integrate environmental concerns into their practice. Integration as an element of sustainable development requires that there is a holistic approach to environmental and developmental concerns.[106]

The Stockholm Declaration, as the first global, interstate plan for the environment,[107] contained several references to integration. In the first place the Declaration recognises the relationship between development and environmental protection. To this end Principle 9 recognises that '[e]nvironmental deficiencies [are] generated by the conditions of underdevelopment'. Principle 10 of the Declaration provides that for 'developing countries, stability of prices and adequate earnings for primary commodities and raw materials are essential to environmental management since economic factors as well as ecological processes must be taken into account'.[108] Thus, principle 10 of the Stockholm Declaration acknowledges the need for integrating 'economic factors' and 'ecological processes' in environmental management.

106 The International Law Association Committee on Sustainable Development focused, as the first element of its work, on integration as an element of sustainable development. See generally ILA Committee on International Law on Sustainable Development Second Report (2006) (on file with author).

107 RA Malviya 'Sustainable development and environment: Emerging trends and issues' (1996) 32 *Indian Journal of International Law* 57.

108 See also Principle 8 and Principle 13 Stockholm Declaration.

Integration requires a holistic approach to environmental protection and development. Thus we see that the Stockholm Declaration invokes, as necessities towards sustainable development, the integration of a variety of issues, including science, technology[109] and education.[110]

The Brundtland Commission Report recognised that environmental problems are caused by 'interlocking crises'.[111] According to the report the rapid changes in human population growth, economic growth and the rapid advancement of technology 'have locked the global economy and global ecology together'.[112] Consequently, while the effect of economic growth on the environment is well-documented it is also imperative that we consider 'the impacts of ecological stress – degradation of soils, water regimes, atmosphere, and forests – upon our economic prospects'.[113] According to the Commission 'ecology and economy are becoming ever more interwoven ... into a seamless net of causes and effects'.[114] Recognising the interrelated nature of the problem resulted in the Commission proposing an integrated approach to addressing the problem. Thus, the solution must include the involvement of the scientific community,[115] co-operation with industry,[116] strengthening existing environmental agreements,[117] and focusing on economic development.[118] With respect to the latter the Commission singled out the World Bank, the IMF and regional Developmental Banks for 'special attention' because of the major influence they have on international economic development.[119] As for the World Bank, the Commission commented that while the World Bank had become more sensitive towards environmental concerns this would not be enough until it made 'a fundamental commitment to sustainable development'.[120] With regards to the IMF, the Commission noted the concern that the policies of the IMF may be undermining sustainable development.[121] In short, the Commission recommended that these institutions integrate environmental and developmental concerns in their lending policies.

For its part the World Bank has, since the Brundtland Commission Report, embarked on a series of reforms, both substantive and

109 Principle 18 Stockholm Declaration. See also Principle 20.
110 Principle 19 Stockholm Declaration.
111 See WCED (n 2 above) 4 *et seq.*
112 WCED (n 2 above) 5.
113 As above.
114 As above.
115 WCED (n 2 above) 326.
116 WCED (n 2 above) 329.
117 WCED (n 2 above) 333.
118 WCED (n 2 above) 334 *et seq.*
119 WCED (n 2 above) 337.
120 As above.
121 As above.

institutional, aimed at integrating social and environmental concerns into World Bank economic activities. In attempting to integrate environmental and social concerns, as opposed to narrow economic concerns, (and responding to the criticisms levelled at Bank-supported projects) the World Bank has adopted operational policies. In 2001 the Bank adopted Operational Policy 4.12 on Involuntary Resettlement (OP 4.12) in response to the criticism of the impact of its supported projects on people (particularly indigenous peoples) living in and around project sites. Earlier, in 1999, the Bank had adopted Operational Policy 4.01 on Environmental Assessments (OP 4.01). Both these operational policy documents were successors to previous policy documents.[122]

Under the current World Bank scheme policy instruments can either be legally binding or non-binding.[123] Operational Policies (OPs) such as OP 4.01 and OP 4.12 and Bank Procedures (BPs) are binding World Bank policy instruments while Good Practices (GPs) are not binding.[124] Under the previous World Bank scheme policies were in the Operational Manual Statements (OMSs), which were later replaced by Operational Directives (ODs). OD 4.00, for example, replaced OMS 2.36 as the Bank's main policy instrument on environmental matters.[125] However, while the former General Counsel of the Bank, Ibrahim Shihata, has affirmed that Operational Policies and Bank Procedures are binding, it does appear that by this he means that these policies are internally binding on Bank staff and not that they are binding in the sense the Bank can be compelled to comply with them by an external tribunal.[126] Having said that, the policies are not without legal consequence in the international legal system.[127] One way that the policies infiltrate general international law is through

122 OP 4.01 replaced OMS 2.36 and OD 4.00 while OP 4.12 replaced OD 4.30. There is currently a draft OP 4.10 on indigenous peoples but it has come under some criticism.

123 For an in-depth analysis of these instruments and their legal nature, see L Boisson de Chazournes 'Policy guidance and compliance: The World Bank operational standards' in D Shelton (ed) *Commitment and compliance: The role of non-binding norms in the international legal system* (2000).

124 See NL Bridgeman 'World Bank reform in the "post policy" era' (2001) 13 *Georgetown International Law Review* 1013 1024. Although, the World Bank definition of these terms makes no reference to whether they are binding or not, Ibrahim Shihata has commented that while OPs would be binding on Bank staff GPs would 'indicate successful examples without being binding'. IFI Shihata *The World Bank Inspection Panel* (1994) 46. I must also add that my reading of the relevant text from Shihata's *World Bank Inspection Panel* seems to indicate that these documents are internally binding and are not legally binding in the sense that the Bank can be legally compelled by an external tribunal to comply with them.

125 For a discussion of these instruments see IFI Shihata *The World Bank in a changing world: Selected essays of Ibrahim F Shihata* (1991) 143.

126 Shihata (n 124 above) 46. See also Boisson de Chazournes (n 123 above) 281 who says of these policies: 'They appear to be quasi-administrative in nature, for internal use by the Bank to guide its staff in their activities'.

127 See generally Boisson de Chazournes (n 123 above).

their incorporation into the loan and credit agreements concluded between the Bank and borrowing states. As Boisson de Chazournes notes, when this occurs, the policies become binding under international law as part of the treaty.[128] What we see with these policies is an attempt on the part of the Bank to integrate social and environmental concerns into World Bank lending practice more effectively.[129]

In addition to several policies that the Bank has introduced to integrate environmental and social concerns, the Bank has established, as an institutional reform, an inspection panel to provide an independent forum for members of the public who may feel that a Bank-financed project could negatively affect their interests.[130] This institution, which has played a significant role in the activities of the Bank by allowing social and environmental interests to influence World Bank lending activities, is also an illustration of integration, albeit from an institutional perspective. The World Bank Inspection Panel was created in 1993 by a resolution of the Executive Directors of the Bank, largely as a result of the infamous Wapenhans report, as well as external demands for greater accountability.[131] The Panel is, under the resolution establishing it, entitled to consider applications from members of the community in a borrower country alleging that their rights or interests are affected (or are likely to be affected) as a result of the Bank's failure to follow its operational policies or procedures.[132] In this sense the Panel serves to contribute to the integration of social and environmental concerns into the mainstream economic activities of the Bank.

Both the adoption of the environmental and social policies and the creation of the Inspection Panel illustrate an attempt by the World Bank, in response to the Brundtland Commission's call to 'make a more fundamental commitment to sustainable development',[133] to integrate environmental and social concerns into the World Bank's lending activities.

128 Boisson de Chazournes (n 123 above) 289. For the characterisation of World Bank loan agreements with borrower states as treaties, see A Broches 'International legal aspects of the operations of the World Bank' (1959III) 98 *Recueil des Cours Academie de Droit International* 297, especially at ch III, 'The Bank's loan and guarantee agreements with members'.

129 For a more detailed discussion of these policies in light of sustainable development, see D Tladi 'International law for sustainable development: Sombre reflections on World Bank efforts' (2004) 29 *South African Yearbook of International Law* 64.

130 See T Roessler 'The World Bank's lending policy and environmental standards' 2000 *North Carolina Journal of Law and Commercial Regulation* 105 119.

131 IFI Shihata *The World Bank in a changing world: Volume III* (2000) 539. See IBRD/IDA Resolution 93-10/93-6 creating the Inspection Panel (1993).

132 Para 12 Resolution Establishing the Inspection Panel.

133 WCED (n 2 above) 337.

Integration also featured prominently at the Rio Conference. In capturing the essence of integration as an element of sustainable development, the Rio Declaration provides that to achieve sustainable development 'environmental protection shall constitute an integral part of the development process and cannot be considered in isolation from it'.[134] Similarly, Principle 8 requires for the achievement of sustainable development sustainable patterns of production and consumption and the promotion of appropriate demographic policies. Principle 9 acknowledges the important role that scientific and technological knowledge must play in the efforts towards sustainable development. There is also a reference to trade measures in Principle 12 which, as suggested in paragraph 2.5 of chapter 2, serve to subordinate environmental concerns to trade concerns.[135]

International agreements have also incorporated into their texts the element of integration. The text of the General Agreement on Trade and Tariffs (GATT) is perhaps the best known attempt at integrating environmental protection and trade (as a means to development). Article XX of the GATT contains exceptions to the GATT rules on free trade. Article XX provides in part as follows:

> Subject to the requirement that such measures are not applied in a manner which would constitute a means of arbitrary or unjustifiable discrimination between countries where the same conditions prevail, or a disguised restriction on international trade, nothing in this Agreement shall be construed to prevent the adoption or enforcement by any contracting party of measures: ...
>
> (b) necessary to protect human, animal, or plant life of health ...
>
> (c) relating to the conservation of exhaustible natural resources if such measures are made effective in conjunction with restrictions on domestic production or consumption.

While the GATT text appears to integrate environmental concerns with trade, there nevertheless appears to be dissatisfaction amongst commentators with the degree to which environmental concerns are *really* integrated into the GATT system by the dispute settlement

134 Principle 4 Rio Declaration. See also Principle 11 Rio Declaration.

135 The implication of this trade reference in Principle 12 appears to be very much pro-trade. Principle 12 reads, in part, as follows: 'Trade policy measures for environmental purposes should not constitute a means of arbitrary or unjustifiable discrimination or a disguised restriction on international trade'. I find it interesting that there is nothing in Principle 12 said about the need to ensure that free trade does not lead to environmental degradation.

mechanisms established under the GATT/World Trade Organisation (WTO) system.[136] As Schoenbaum asserts, the burden placed on the party relying on article XX has not often been met 'largely because of the strictness with which its provisions are interpreted'.[137] Several decisions of the Appellate Body established under the WTO have attracted particular attention in this regard. These include the *Shrimp/Turtle dispute*[138] and the *Beef Hormones dispute.*[139] It appears that while the text of the WTO agreement may be interpreted to give effect to integration, more needs to done in the practice of dispute settlement mechanisms to give effect to the integration of environmental values.[140]

As discussed in the context of Principle 12 of the Rio Declaration in paragraph 2.5 of chapter 2, trade concerns are seen primarily as promoting economic growth concerns. However, at the same time environmentalists see the promotion of free trade as harming environmental concerns. Esty, in summarising the green objections to global free trade notes that, *inter alia,* free trade may cause environmental harm by promoting economic growth resulting in unsustainable patterns of consumption of natural resources.[141] To the normal concerns raised about the impact of free trade on the environment one can add the various pollution effects of increased transport demanded by a growth in trade.[142] Similarly, others have

136 See GW Mugwanya 'Global free trade *vis-à-vis* environmental regulation and sustainable development: Reinvigorating efforts towards a more integrated approach' (1999) 14 *Journal of Environmental Law* 401; D Shelton 'Environmental justice in a postmodern world' in K Bosselmann & B Richardson (eds) *Environmental justice and market mechanism* (1999); JL Dunoff 'Institutional misfits: The GATT, The ICJ and trade-environment disputes' (1993 - 1994) 15 *Michigan Journal of International Law* 1043; R Houseman & D Zaelke 'Trade, environment, and sustainable development' (1992) 15 *Hastings International and Comparative Law Review* 535. See also D Tladi 'Can the wolf protect the lamb? Free trade as instruments towards sustainable development' (2002) 27 *South African Yearbook of International Law* 149.

137 TJ Schoenbaum 'International trade and the protection of the environment: The continuing search for reconciliation' (1997) 91 *American Journal of International Law* 268 274.

138 *US-Measures Concerning Import Prohibition of Certain Shrimp and Shrimp Products* AB-1998-4 (1999) 38 *ILM* 123.

139 *EC-Measures Concerning Meat and Meat Products (Hormones),* available at http://www.wto.org/wto/dispute/distab.htm (accessed on 5 January 2002), concerned the application of the Sanitary and Phytosanitary Agreement.

140 For further discussion, see above para 2.5 of ch 2 where principle 12 Rio Declaration is discussed in the context of WTO decisions.

141 DC Esty *Greening the GATT: Trade, environment and the future* (1994) 42. See also Mugwanya (n 136 above) 401.

142 One delegate at an Ecological Integrity Group meeting in Urbino, Italy, in 2003, asked the following question during a break from the sessions: 'Why must Europeans make biscuits and then ship them all the way to America only to have Americans also bake biscuits and ship them all the to Europe? Why not just exchange recipes?' One could also ask why must grapes from Africa be transported to Europe, and the get shipped back to Africa as wine? Why not just make the wine in Africa and save the massive costs to the environment created by excessive transportation?

suggested that the global free trade system has had a negative effect on the social needs of the poor.[143]

These concerns about the negative impact of the trade system on society and the environment typify criticism against integration. According to Pallemaerts:[144]

> The new discourse of 'integration' suggests that there is no longer any conflict between environmental protection and economic development, and that the latter has become a necessary complement, condition even, of the former. This obfuscates the very real and increasing conflict between [economic development] and [environmental protection]. It ambiguously stands as much for the subordination of environmental policies to economic imperatives ...

In the context of sustainable development, the concept of integration does not deny 'the very real' conflict between development and environmental protection. Indeed, if there were no conflict the concepts of sustainable development and integration would serve no purpose. Integration recognises the conflict and represents an approach towards reconciling that conflict. In other words, integration becomes necessary as a consequence of several recognitions. First, there are two needs (environmental protection and development) which are important. Second, the two needs are connected in a relationship of cause and effect. There are, in turn, two elements to this relationship of cause and effect. The first element is that activities geared towards economic growth have contributed significantly to environmental degradation. The second is that the lack of economic (and social development) contributes towards environmental degradation. Consequently one cannot deal, at least not effectively, with environmental protection without considering development and *vice versa*.

That is not to say that Pallemaerts' concern is without any basis. As an anecdote I may add that the first draft of this chapter of the study was written a few weeks prior to the Johannesburg 2002 World Summit on Sustainable Development. It was interesting to see the difference in the perceptions of what the Summit was about. If you opened a local (Johannesburg or Pretoria) newspaper you read about how the Summit was geared towards alleviating poverty and improving the living conditions of the poor (very little if anything on the environment). If you turned on CNN news you found that discussion on the World Summit focused on the ozone layer and the

143 See generally M Cohn 'The World Trade Organization: Elevating property interests over human rights' (2001) 30 *Georgia Journal of International and Comparative Law* 427. See also UN Sub-Commission on the Promotion and Protection of Human Rights 'The realisation of economic, social and cultural rights: Globalization and its impact on the full enjoyment of human rights' (preliminary report compiled by J Oloka-Onyango and D Udagama) E/CN4/Sub.2/2000/13 (on file with author).

144 M Pallemaerts 'International environmental law from Stockholm to Rio: Back to the future?' in P Sands (ed) *Greening international law* (1994) 17.

rain forests of Brazil with very little attention being paid to issues of poverty alleviation.

This paradox is equally evident in a principle related to sustainable development widely accepted as being a principle of customary international law: the principle of sovereignty over natural resources as limited by responsibility for environmental harm. In the *Advisory Opinion on the Legality of the Threat or Use of Nuclear Weapons*[145] the International Court of Justice confirmed that:[146]

> the existence of the general obligation of States to ensure that activities within their jurisdiction and control do not cause damage to the environment of other States or of areas beyond national control is now part of the corpus of international law relating to the environment.

The principle of sovereignty over natural resources as limited by responsibility for environmental harm accepts, on the one hand, that states are free to do in their territories and with their natural resources what they wish. On the other hand, this freedom is curtailed by responsibility not to cause environmental harm.

This principle is not new to the international lawyer. International law recognises that while states have sovereignty over their territory they may not use or allow their territory to be used to harm other states.[147] In the context of environmental law the leading case in this regard is the *Trail Smelter Arbitration*.[148] In resolving a dispute concerning transboundary pollution, the tribunal held that 'no state has the right to use or permit the use of its territory in such a manner as to cause injury by fumes in or to the territory of another [state]'.[149]

The famous words of the tribunal are echoed in the equally famous Principle 21 of the Stockholm Declaration (some thirty years later), which provides that:

> States have in accordance with the Charter of the United Nations and the principles of international law, the sovereign right to exploit their own resources ... [and] the responsibility to ensure that activities within their jurisdiction or control do not cause damage to the environment of other States ...

145 1996 *ICJ Reports* 226.

146 *Nuclear Weapons case* (n 145 above) para 29.

147 See *Corfu Channel Case (UK v Albania)* 1949 *ICJ* 4 22 where the International Court of Justice stated that a state is under an obligation not to allow its territory knowingly to be used for acts that violate the rights of other States. This principle is also reflected in 1982 United Nations Law of the Sea Convention which provides that states 'shall take all measures necessary to ensure that activities under their jurisdiction and control are so conducted as not to cause damage by pollution to other states and environment'. See art 194 of the Law of the Sea of Convention, (1982) 21 *ILM* 1248.

148 *Trail Smelter case (United States v Canada)*, 1941 reprinted in MW Janis & JE Noyes *International law: Cases and materials* (1997) 584.

149 *Trail Smelter case* (n 148 above) 589.

Principle 2 of the Rio Declaration is substantially similar to Principle 21 of the Stockholm Declaration. The only difference (which may be a significant difference) is that while the Stockholm text grants the right to exploit natural resources 'pursuant to their own *environmental policies*' the Rio text allows for the exploitation of resources 'pursuant to their own environmental and *developmental policies*'. This, it has been said, significantly alters the balancing act in favour of the developing states in the quest for development.[150]

In some sense the principle of sovereignty over natural resources limited by responsibility for environmental harm represents a concrete operationalisation of sustainable development or the integration principle as part of sustainable development. If sustainable development is about 'balancing' environmental concerns with development concerns then the principle aims to perform the quintessential balancing act. On the one hand, the principle allows a state to pursue development goals. On the other hand, the pursuit of development must not impair the extra-territorial environment. Precisely how this balancing act is to be performed and where the boundaries of the freedom to pursue developmental activities *vis-à-vis* the restraint for environmental purposes are to be drawn cannot be an exact science.

So, yes, there is the danger that the principle of integration (and for that matter sustainable development) can result in the 'subordination of environmental to economic imperatives' and for that matter *vice versa*. However, that danger is not inherent in integration or sustainable development, but is rather a result of perception and practice. Like many other flexible legal and political concepts, integration and sustainable development can be misunderstood, misused or even abused to further particular positions. However, a proper understanding and implication of integration will incorporate both developmental and environmental concerns. I will return to the concept of integration and Pallemaerts' concern with it (which is closely related to the ecocentric concern over sustainable development) in the development of an alternative conceptualisation of sustainable development.

2.4 Human Rights and Sustainable Development

Sustainable development law has been described as an intersection between three fields of international law, namely, international environmental law, international economic law and international human rights law. In this section the relationship between human rights and sustainable development is explored. Perhaps, in considering the relationship between sustainable development and

150 See Pallemaerts (n 144 above) 5.

human rights, the best starting position is former Judge Weeramantry's opinion in the *Gabcikovo-Nagymaros case*. There Weeramantry defines sustainable development as the right to development which is limited by the need to preserve the environment.[151] The definition offered by Weeramantry is noteworthy for at least two reasons. First, the definition assumes the existence of a right to development. Further, while development is posited as a right, the need to protect the environment is not awarded the same status in this definition. Instead the 'protection of the environment' is said to be a '*sine qua* non for numerous human rights'. This raises a second point: whether there is space for environmental rights in sustainable development discourse? In exploring the relationship between sustainable development and human rights I will consider the position of both the right to development and environmental rights.

As to the first point, there is certainly support for the view that the right to development exists.[152] Karin Arts, arguing that international law recognises a right to development, notes that there is a 'string of World Conferences and Summits' proclaiming a right to development.[153] While doubts over the existence of a right to development may be waning, there continues to be uncertainty over the content of such a right. One issue remains: whether the right to development is a right of states or whether it is right of individuals. The definition in the 1986 Declaration on the Right to Development would suggest that it is both an individual right and a collective right.[154]

Beyond the question of beneficiaries, an understanding of the right to development can only come about by unpacking the concept of 'development'. In simple terms, does development amount to economic growth? Is it more than just increased economic growth? Is it something less? Here again Weeramantry's conceptualisation of development is instructive. According to Weeramantry, development

151 *Case Concerning Gabcikovo-Nagyramos (Hungary v Slovakia)* 1997 *ICJ* 3 reprinted in 1998 *ILM* 168 206.

152 See K Arts *Integrating human rights into development co-operation: The case of the Lomé Convention* (2000) 40 *et seq*; see also for discussion essays in SR Chowdhury *et al* (eds) *The right to development in international law* (1992).

153 Amongst these she lists the United Nations Declaration on the Right to Development of 1986, UNGA Res 41/128; Vienna Declaration and Programme of Action of 1993, UN Doc A/Conf.157/23; and the Beijing Declaration adopted at the Fourth World Conference on Women in 1995, UN Doc A/Conf.177/20. In addition to these she notes that there are also treaties which either proclaim or imply a right to development. Arts 55 and 56 of the United Nations Charter and art 22 of the African Charter on Human and Peoples' Rights are two prominent examples in this regard.

154 1986 United Nations Declaration on the Right to Development defines the right to development as an 'alienable human right by virtue of which *every human person* and *all peoples* are entitled to participate in, contribute to, and enjoy economic, social, cultural and political development ...'

is more that just 'economic gain'.[155] He suggests, referring to the UN Declaration on the Right to Development, that it fundamentally has to be understood to refer to the 'value in increasing the sum total of human happiness and welfare'.[156] Thus, a right to development aims to improve human well-being. In the same vein Principle 1 of the Millennium Declaration provides for a 'collective responsibility to uphold the principles of human dignity'. The pursuit of the right to development, of course, would serve to give effect to intra generational equity. The inequity that intragenerational equity attempts to address relates to the unequal state of development between developed and developing states and between the rich and poor generally. This inequity can be addressed by providing tools and mechanisms to enable developing countries also to develop. The right to development is one such tool.

A little more needs to be said about environmental rights. Is there space for environmental rights in sustainable development discourse? In what form must such environmental rights be recognised?[157]

There are several forms that the relationship between environmental protection and human rights may take. First, one can perceive a general right to the environment (whether for individuals or for groups or both). The second approach may be to see the environment as being protected under already existing and recognised rights such as the right to life, the right to health or privacy. The third approach, which Boyle asserts is the 'narrowest but strongest argument' for a human rights approach to the environment, is the use of procedural rights, such as access to information, to achieve environmental protection.[158]

Under the first approach there is a distinct and independent right to the environment. This approach is perhaps most famously found in the African Charter on Human and Peoples' Rights.[159] Not only does article 24 recognise a distinct right to the environment, the right is phrased as a peoples' right (collective right). The right, as it is contained in the African Charter, also refers to development, thus invoking considerations of sustainable development. The invocation

155 *Gabcikovo case* (n 151 above) 206.
156 As above.
157 See for discussion LA Feris & D Tladi 'Environmental rights' in D Brand & C Heyns (eds) *Socio-economic rights in South Africa* (2005). D Shelton 'Human rights, environmental rights, and the right to the environment' (1991) 28 *Stanford Journal of International Law* 103; Shelton (n 136 above) 26 *et seq;* J Van der Vyver 'The Criminalisation and prosecution of environmental malpractice in international law' (1998) 23 *South African Yearbook of International Law* 1 8 *et seq*. See also contributions in A Boyle & M Anderson (eds) *Human rights approaches to environmental protection* (1996).
158 A Boyle 'The role of human rights law in the protection of the environment' in Boyle & Anderson (n 157 above) 59.
159 Art 24 of the African Charter provides as follows: 'All peoples shall have the right to a general satisfactory environment favourable to their development'.

of a distinct right to the environment is also found in the Draft Principles on Human Rights and the Environment.[160] The Principles first declare the interdependence and indivisibility of human rights, sustainable development and peace.[161] Principle 2 declares that all persons 'have the right to a secure, healthy and ecologically sound environment'. This approach has not found much support in international legally binding instruments although there are several national constitutions that recognise a right to the environment.[162]

The second approach does not recognise a specific and independent right to the environment, but sees a potential for protecting the environment under already existing and recognised rights such as the right to life, health and privacy (or private life).[163]

In 1987 hazardous wastes were dumped in Koko, Nigeria, pursuant to an agreement between a Nigerian citizen and an Italian waste trader (The Koko incident).[164] As a consequence of the illegal dumping, local Nigerians in Koko started falling ill. This environmental problem could be characterised as a violation of the right to health of the Nigerians living in Koko.[165] This approach has found support in the jurisprudence

160 UN Commission on Human Rights, Sub-Commission on Prevention of Discrimination and the Protection of Minorities, *Human rights and the environment* (1994) UN Doc E/CN.4/Sub.2/1994/9 reproduced in Boyle (n 158 above) 65 *et seq.*

161 UNCHR (n 160 above) Principle 1.

162 See eg s 24 South African Constitution. See also art 86 Constitution of the Ecuador, in GH Flanz (ed) *Constitutions of the countries of the world* (1999); art 23 Constitution of Belgium, in GH Flanz (ed) *Constitution of the countries of the world* (2002); art 39 Constitution of the Azerbaijan, in GH Flanz (ed) *Constitutions of the countries of the world* (2002); art 27 Constitution of Benin, in AP Blaunstein & GH Flanz (eds) *Constitutions of the countries of the world* (1993).

163 Perhaps the most convincing argument in favour of this approach can be found in JG Merrils 'Environmental protection and human rights: Conceptual aspects' in Boyle & Anderson (n 157 above) 30 who argues that there is no need to create new rights to deal with matters that can be dealt with under existing rights. For example, it is unnecessary to create a right to sleep if the problem to be solved can be addressed with reference to the prohibition on torture and also minimum working standards under the ILO instruments.

164 For a discussion of the Koko incident, see SF Liu 'The Koko incident: Developing international norms for the transboundary movement of hazardous wastes' (1992 - 1993) 8 *Journal of Natural Resources and Environmental Law* 121; D Tladi 'The quest to ban hazardous waste import into Africa: First Bamako and now Basel' (2000) 33 *Comparative and International Law Journal of Southern Africa* 210 212.

165 In fact the OAU Ministers did regard the dumping of hazardous wastes on the continent as a human rights abuse, terming it 'a crime against Africa and the African People'. See OAU Council of Ministers Resolution on the Dumping of Nuclear and Industrial Wastes in Africa (1988) reproduced in CH Heyns & M Van der Linde *Human rights law in Africa* (2004).

of the European Court of Human Rights. In *Lopez Ostra v Spain*,[166] the European Court ruled that article 8 of the European Convention which provides for a right to a private family life should be interpreted to imply certain guarantees against pollution. The Stockholm Declaration, in similar vein, provides that:[167]

> Man has the fundamental right to freedom, equality and adequate conditions of life, in an environment of quality that permits a life of dignity and well-being, and he bears a solemn responsibility to protect and improve the environment for present and future generations.

The third approach is based on procedural rights such as access to information and just administrative action. This approach assumes that if the principles of democratic governance such as access to justice, openness, accountability and civic participation are adhered to, then environmental standards will be maintained and improved. This approach is represented in the Arhus Convention on Access to Information.[168] The Convention, for example, provides for a right to access to information[169] as well as public participation[170] in an environmental context. The procedural rights approach seems to be the most favoured approach.[171] It has to be understood that while procedural rights are vital, they can only be effective in conjunction with other rights (or substantive rules). Indeed, substantive rights and procedural rights may serve as an example of how efforts towards substantive fairness and procedural fairness can 'pull in the same direction'.[172]

The favourable position that is occupied by the procedural rights approach in environmental rights discourse is aptly illustrated in the case of the South African legal system. In South African jurisprudence, even with the inclusion of an explicit right to the environment in the

166 1995 ECHR Ser. A, No 303-C. See also *Oneryildiz v Turkey* (2002) European Court of Human Rights case 48939/99 available at http://hudoc.echr.coe.int/hudoc/default.asp?Cm=query (accessed 7 April 2004) where the court found that the failure of the Turkish government to remove a rubbish tip situated near a residential area violated the right to life enshrined in art 2 of the European Convention. See especially para 62 *et seq*. See also *Hatton and Others v The United Kingdom* (2001) European Court of Human Rights case 36022/97. For other cases see *Fredin v Sweden* (1991) ECHR Ser. A 192 and the dissenting opinion of Pettiti in *Balmer-Schrafroth and others v Switzerland* (1998) 25 EHRR 598.

167 Principle 1 Stockholm Declaration.

168 2001 Arhus Convention on Access to Information, Public Participation in Decision-Making and Access to Justice in Environmental Matters, text available in Cullet & Gowlland-Guatieri (n 48 above).

169 See art 4 Arhus Convention.

170 See art 6 Arhus Convention.

171 See generally for discussion K Tomaševski 'Environmental rights' in A Eide *et al* (eds) *Economic, social and cultural rights: A textbook* (1995) 261 *et seq*. See also Boyle (n 158 above) 59.

172 See Franck (n 47 above) 7 who discusses the relationship between substantive and procedural fairness.

Bill of Rights, the courts have tended to rely primarily on procedural rights in environmental matters.[173] An interesting case in point is *Biowatch Trust v The Registrar: Genetic Resources, the Executive Council for Genetically Modified Organisms.*[174] In that case the Court, relying on the right to information as enshrined in the Constitution and prescribed in the National Environmental Management Act, ordered the South African government to provide information on, *inter alia,* all risk assessments and information on all permits to grow GMOs as well permits and permit applications for exports and imports of GMOs. The facts of this case illustrate the interdependence of procedural and substantive rights in the context of the environment. While access to the information required can assist the applicants in showing the possible environmental and health impacts of GMOs, once GMOs are shown to be harmful to the environment, it is only a reliance on the substantive right to the environment or some other substantive rule that can be used to compel the South African government to take any action.

Notwithstanding the lack of certainty on the status of environmental rights in international law, the principle of sustainable development, by embracing intergenerational equity, implicitly incorporates environmental rights. The principle of intergenerational equity has two implications for environmental rights discourse.[175] In the first place, it implies that future generations have a right to a clean environment. Obviously, the idea of future generations (as a group) having rights against the present generation is subject to criticism on practical grounds of standing. How are future generations to claim their intergenerational rights? This concern, however, should not be a bar to the recognition of such rights. After all, there exist in law many fictions to protect rights of entities that, in the absence of the fiction, would seem impractical.[176] The second implication of intergenerational equity for environmental rights discourse is aptly captured in the judgment of Davide J in the *Minors Oposa case:*[177]

> Put a little differently, the minors' assertion of their right to a sound environment constitutes, at the same time, the performance of their obligations to ensure the protection of that environment for generations to come.

173 See eg *Van Huysteen NO and Others v Minister of Environmental Affairs and Tourism and Others* 1995 (9) BCLR 1191 (C) (access to information); *Director: Mineral Development, Gauteng Region, and Another v Save the Vaal Environment and Others* 1999 (2) SA 709 (SCA) (*audi alteram partem).*

174 2005 (4) SA 111 (T).

175 See for discussion, Feris & Tladi (n 157 above) 253.

176 Examples from South African domestic law include the *nasciturus fiction* and the notion that companies can have rights and obligations. See also Brown Weiss (n 10 above) 86 who suggests that the creation of an institution of a guardian *ad litem* could be a solution to the problem of standing in cases of enforcement of intergenerational environmental rights.

177 *Minors Oposa* case (n 10 above) 185.

This means that the enforcement of environmental rights, by members of the present generation, implies, at the same time, the performance of our intergenerational obligations to future generations. In this context the principle of intergenerational equity may answer some questions about the beneficiaries of rights in environmental rights discourse. It appears, from the above, that rights of the present generation *could* be conceived of as both individual and group rights. In other words, the present generation as a group could be entitled to environmental rights without precluding the extension of these rights to individuals. As regards environmental rights of future generations, it would seem that such rights could *only* be for future generations as a group.

In addition to the obvious ecocentric arguments against human rights to the environment, some sustainable development commentators have, however, cautioned against an overzealous acceptance of human rights as a basis of sustainable development. An interesting critique of environmental rights in sustainable development discourse comes from Ximena Fuentes who suggests that the focus on environmental rights can have the effect of undermining the development agenda.[178] Noting that couching environmental protection in human rights terms implies 'a strong claim' or a 'claim to absolute entitlement', Fuentes states the following:[179]

> the notion of environmental rights may contradict the very idea of sustainable development, shifting the balance in favour of the protection of the environment and pushing development aspects into the background.

Of course, in response to this argument it can be argued that the reference to environmental rights would be only one part of the equation. The other part must be, as suggested by Judge Weeramantry in the *Gabcikovo* separate opinion, the right to development. Fuentes pre-empts this counter argument. She suggests two arguments against the right to development as a leveller for the environment. First, she suggests that resorting to rights may make it harder for right holders to accept a compromise. Second, and more important, the content, legal implications and the beneficiaries of the right to development remain unclear. Third, to the extent that some aspects of the right to development are clear, such as 'its clear relation to economic justice between States', the right to development has not been able to establish an obligation to provide financial assistance.

The following can be said in brief response to Fuentes' concerns. Human rights litigation has tended to be more about the limits of rights rather than their actual content. Put another way, rights

178 Fuentes (n 53 above).
179 Fuentes (n 53 above) 125.

litigation has tended to be about the limits of rights in relation to other rights. In many instances one set of rights may be seen as limits to other rights. It was for this reason that Shelton has suggested that one of the benefits of a human rights approach to sustainable development arises from the fact that human rights litigation is about balancing competing interests or competing rights.[180] The facts in the South African Constitutional Court decision in the *Kyalami Ridge case*[181] illustrate the point well. In this case, a series of floods resulted in severe damage to homes in Alexandra township (one of the poorest areas in South Africa). The state, in an effort to alleviate the plight of the inhabitants, accommodated the flood-affected residents of Alexandra on a portion of state-owned land near Kyalami, an affluent neighbourhood. The residents of Kyalami objected to the accommodation on environmental grounds. Although the Court proceeded to decide the case on the basis of the state's compliance with the right to just administrative action under various legislative enactments, notwithstanding the inclusion of sustainable development in the South African Bill of Rights, the case provided an opportunity to develop sustainable development jurisprudence by balancing the socio-economic rights of the displaced residents with the environmental rights of the Kyalami residents.

Second, it is true that there is much uncertainty and debate surrounding the right to development. However, as is clear from preceding paragraphs, the same is true of environmental rights. Thus, this in itself cannot be a bar to accepting the argument that the right to development can serve as a balancing factor against environmental rights. Finally, the last argument by Fuentes ignores the various financial transfer provisions in multilateral environmental agreements as well as development in the Global Environment Facility. To be fair these financial transfer commitments are not *based on* the right to development. Nevertheless, it is postulated that these financial and technology transfer obligations reflect, in the context of the common but differentiated responsibility, principles related to the right to development.

The conceptualisation of sustainable development in terms of human rights can contribute towards the further evolution of sustainable development. Such a conceptualisation illustrates the balancing between two competing rights (interests), namely, the right to an environment of quality and the right to development. Given that more often than not human rights disputes involve the conflict between two or more rights, human rights forums have over

180 See generally Shelton (n 136 above).
181 *Minister of Public Works and Others v Kyalami Ridge Environmental Association and Others* 2001 7 BCLR 652 (CC); Feris and Tladi (n 157 above) 262.

the years developed a wealth of jurisprudence from which sustainable development practitioners can draw.[182]

3. A more nuanced conceptualisation of sustainable development

Early attempts at conceptualising sustainable development, including the Brundtland report and the human rights approaches, have tended to see sustainable development as the balancing of environmental and developmental needs. While this is true, it is an oversimplified conceptualisation. More importantly, such a simplified conceptualisation makes sustainable development vulnerable to attack from different quarters. In this section I consider the various criticisms flowing from the simplified conceptualisation of sustainable development. Using the criticisms as a point of departure I attempt to construct a more nuanced framework within which the concept of sustainable development can be understood.[183] I do not propose that the early conceptualisation of sustainable development as a tool to balance environmental concerns with development concerns is wrong. I merely suggest that to contribute to a better understanding of the normative implications of balancing environmental and development needs, a more nuanced conceptualisation is required.

3.1 Unlocking Sustainable Development: Integration is the key

The definition often given to sustainable development is the Brundtland definition.[184] From that definition, the principles of inter- and intragenerational equity can be extrapolated. The conceptualisation of sustainable development as the balancing of environment and development needs is firmly rooted in this definition. Under this definition the long-term, intergenerational equity concerns have to be balanced against immediate, intragenerational equity concerns.

182 See especially authorities cited (n 157 above). In the wider human rights context reference can also be made to the protection of the right to freedom of expression. See for illustration: *Markt Intern and Beerman v Germany* (1989) 12 EHRR 161 (where right the exercise of the right to freedom of expression was to be exercised with due regard to the privacy rights of others).

183 My thinking about this more nuanced framework within which to analyse and understand development has evolved over a series of publications arising from the study. The most important of these are: Tladi (n 30 above); D Tladi 'Strong sustainability, weak sustainability, intergenerational equity and international law: Using the Earth Charter to redirect the ethics debate' (2003) 28 *South African Yearbook of International Law* 200; D Tladi 'IMF Conditionality, Debt and Poverty: Towards a "Strong anthropocentric" model of sustainability' (2004) 16 *South African Mercantile Law Journal* 31; D Tladi 'Strong sustainable development, weak sustainable development and the Earth Charter: Towards a more nuanced framework analysis' (2004) 29 *South African Journal of Environmental Law and Policy* 17 (Tladi 'Towards a more nuanced framework').

184 WCED (n 2 above) 43.

In the context of conceptualising sustainable development, however, the Brundtland Commission report is perhaps more important for a different reason. At the heart of the Brundtland Commission report lies a call for integration. The Report describes the various economic, social and environmental problems as 'interlocking crises'[185] requiring an integrated solution.[186] As I stated earlier, this call for integration is the essence of sustainable development.[187] At the same time, the centrality of integration to the sustainable development discourse is fundamental to the two main criticisms that can be levelled at the principle of sustainable development.

On the one hand, sustainable development can be criticised as a concept that is so flexible and without fixed content that it can mean different things to different groups (the indeterminacy objection).[188] Moreover, it can be argued that sustainable development undermines (or at least has the potential to undermine) the ability of environmental law and policy to protect the environment (ecocentric objection). Both criticisms, in my view, flow from integration as the central concept in sustainable development discourse.

Arguments around the indeterminacy of sustainable development relate to the numerous interpretations potentially attaching to the concept. The difficulty in defining or describing sustainable development begins with the flexibility of the concept and this, in turn, results from the fact that sustainable development involves the integration of various areas of law and policy. Sustainable development can be used by environmentalists and those pursuing the ends of economic development respectively in support of opposite claims.[189] For those advocating economic growth in defining sustainable development, the emphasis should fall on the economic growth value of sustainable development. Thus, sustainable development should mean 'lasting economic growth' and lasting 'energy development'.[190] In this paradigm it is the economic growth that must

185 WCED (n 2 above) 4.

186 WCED (n 2 above) 40. See also discussion above where the Brundtland Commission report is discussed as an important milestone on the road to the Rio Conference.

187 See also Matsui (n 60 above) 152.

188 See eg P Nelson 'An African dimension to the Clean Development Mechanism: Finding a path to sustainable development in the energy sector' (2004) 32 *Denver Journal of International and Policy* 615 615 who says the following of sustainable development: 'The concept of "sustainable development" is probably suffering from its success as a buzzword. So frequently adopted by so many groups with wildly differing agendas – from the Sierra Club to the coal industry – the term might seem well on its way to becoming meaningless' (footnotes omitted).

189 IM Porras 'The Rio Declaration: A new basis for international co-operation' in Sands (n 144 above) 34. In this respect, the ILA Committee on the International Law on Sustainable Development has noted that integration 'should not necessarily be seen, simplistically, as a rather neutral phenomenon, but rather, as a much more complex process'. See ILA Committee on the International Law on Sustainable Development, Second Report (2006) (on file with author) 22.

190 See eg World Bank *World development report* (1992) 34.

be sustained. Critiquing the discourse of sustainable development, Pallemaerts notes the following:[191]

> Economic growth, trade liberalisation and trade-led globalisation suddenly acquired a sort of newfound environmental legitimacy, as Principle 12 of the Rio Declaration affirmed that 'States should cooperate to promote a supportive and open international economic system that would lead to economic growth and sustainable development in all countries, to better address the problems of environmental degradation'.

Of course, for environmentalists, the emphasis should fall not on development, but on the ecology.[192] Thus it is ecological conditions that should be sustained and not economic development.

More to the point, the flexibility of sustainable development means that a single activity can be described as promoting or undermining sustainable development depending on the vantage point of the analyst.[193] A typical example is free trade. Free trade proponents will, more than likely, argue that by promoting economic growth, free trade enhances sustainable development.[194] Those opposing free trade may argue that free trade is harmful to the environment and therefore contrary to sustainable development.[195] Others, instead, argue that free trade harms the social needs of the

191 M Pallemaerts 'Is multilateralism the future? Sustainable development or globalisation as a "comprehensive vision" of the future of humanity' (2003) 5 *Environment, Development and Sustainability* 275 294.

192 See eg E Brown Weiss 'Introductory note' (1992) 31 *International Legal Materials* 814 814.

193 See Pallemaerts 'Is multilateralism the future?' (n 191 above) 280 who states that the objective of sustainable development remains 'a vague concept without any agreed, unambiguous definition...'

194 See, for example, M Moore (Director-General of the WTO) 'Multilateral trading system in support of Africa-led and Africa-owned development' speech delivered to ECOSOC cited in NL Wallace-Bruce 'Global free trade and sustainable development: Two steps forward in the WTO?' (2002) 35 *Comparative and International Law Journal* 236. See also EU Petersmann 'Time for a United Nations "global compact" for integrating human rights into the law of world wide organisations: Lesson from European integration' (2002) 13 *European Journal of International Law* 621 643 who says that the WTO is 'the most important legal and institutional framework for the worldwide liberalisation of welfare-reducing discriminatory barriers to' free trade. See ILA Committee on International Law on Sustainable Development Second Draft Report, arguing that the reference to mutual supportiveness between trade and sustainable development in WTO law suggests that 'trade is not subsumed within the wider goal of sustainable development' rather that while trade can contribute towards sustainable development, it can do so while pursuing some 'other, equally valid, purpose'.

195 Esty, for example, in summarising the 'green objection' to free trade, notes that free trade may cause environmental harm by promoting economic growth resulting in unsustainable consumption of natural resources. Furthermore, he notes that trade agreements override natural environmental regulation. See DC Esty *Greening the GATT: Trade, environment and the future* (1994) 42. See further on the trade-environment debate, D Brack 'The *Shrimp-Turtle* case: Implications for Multilateral Environmental Agreements – World Trade Agreement Debate' (1999) 10 *Yearbook of International Environmental Law* 13. See also Mugwanya (n 136 above).

poor, which defeats the objectives of sustainable development.[196] To respond to objections of indeterminacy requires asking some questions about the nature and implications of integration. The purpose of this section is to uncover some of these questions in order to develop a nuanced conceptualisation of sustainable development.

The second criticism often levelled at sustainable development, is that sustainable development, as an anthropocentric concept, undermines the ability of environmental law to safeguard the environment.[197] Using this criticism as a springboard, Klaus Bosselmann has proposed a juxtaposition of two forms or models of sustainable development, namely 'strong' and 'weak' sustainable development.[198]

Traditionally, weak sustainable development has been defined as policies leading to the 'maintenance of the aggregate stock of capital'.[199] Thus weak sustainable development implies, on the one hand, that different resources (economic and ecological) can be expressed in common terms, namely money, and, on the other hand, that different resources can serve as substitutes for one another.[200] With weak sustainable development 'it is possible to lose natural capital and replace it with economic capital' (author's translation).[201] With strong sustainable development, on the other hand, 'all capital must be independently preserved' (author's translation).[202] For Bosselmann, however, the basis of the juxtaposition is the ecocentric-anthropocentric dichotomy, where anthropocentric approaches to sustainable development, such as the current paradigm, are dubbed 'weak' sustainable development and variations centred on the environment are dubbed strong sustainable

196 See UN Commission on Human Rights, Sub-Commission on the Promotion and Protection of Human Rights 'The realisation of economic, social and cultural rights: Globalisation and its impact on the full enjoyment of human rights' (preliminary report compiled by J Oloka-Onyango and Deepika Udagama) E/CN4/Sub.2/2000/13 (on file with author). See also Cohn (n 143 above).

197 See Pallemaerts (n 144 above). In the discussion of intergenerational equity in para 2.2 of this chapter I attempted to respond to general ecocentric objections. I do not attempt to do that here.

198 K Bosselmann 'The concept of sustainable development' in K Bosselmann and D Grinlinton (eds) *Environmental law for sustainable societies* (2002); see also K Bosselmann 'Strong and weak sustainable development: Making the difference in the design of law', paper presented at the *World Summit 2002: Environmental Law Foundations for Sustainable Development*, University of Natal, Pietermaritzburg, South Africa (Bosselmann 'Making the difference in the design of law').

199 A Markandya *et al* 'A conceptual framework for analysing climate change in the context of sustainable development' in A Markandya & K Halsnaes *Climate change and sustainable development: Prospects for developing countries* (2002) 30.

200 As above.

201 Schrijver (n 5 above) 58. With weak sustainable development 'kan het zijn dat natuurlijk kapitaal verloren gaat en vervangen wordt door economische kapitaal'.

202 As above. With strong sustainable development '[kan] elke kapitaal afzonderlijk behouden blijft'.

development.[203] Similarly, as mentioned earlier, Pallemaerts objects to sustainable development along with its 'new discourse of integration' because, he argues, it stands for the subordination of environmental imperatives to economic objectives.[204] Again, while I do not agree with the call to move away from an anthropocentric approach, the concerns raised by ecocentrists about sustainable development are not unfounded. Interestingly, just as environmentalists have argued that sustainable development may serve to subordinate environmental objectives to the development agenda, so too, arguing from a development perspective, others have suggested that the current discourse on sustainable development may be skewed in favour of the environment at the expense of development.[205] To respond to such criticism requires a deeper understanding of sustainable development, which, as I have suggested, requires further consideration of the concept of integration.

As a starting point to unlocking the concept of integration, and in so doing better understanding sustainable development, two questions must be posed. First, 'what' is it that sustainable development requires us to integrate? Second, 'how' are we directed to integrate whatever it is that we must integrate? One way of answering the 'what' question could be to say that sustainable development requires the integration of environmental concerns with development concerns. That answer, while true, is not helpful because it begs the question asked earlier in the chapter, namely, what is development? Moreover, such an answer runs the risk of becoming vulnerable to both the ecocentric and indeterminacy objections. Thus, to answer the question as to 'what' we are asked to integrate requires a dissection of the notion of development.

In the recent past there has been a gradual realisation that it is not sufficient to conceptualise sustainable development as the balancing of environment and development. Increasingly, sustainable development is being defined as the integration of social, economic and environmental concerns. The ILA New Delhi Declaration on Principles of International Law Relating to Sustainable Development, for example, defines sustainable development as involving the inte-

203 The literature on environmental ethics does make a distinction between, on the one hand, ecocentrism as an ethical approach to environmentalism which places the natural world at the centre of its concern, and biocentrism as an ethic which makes life in all its diversity the centre of its concern. Nothing turns on this distinction for the purposes of this study. See, however, DA Brown *American heat: Ethical problems with the United States' response to global warming* (2002) 52.

204 Pallemaerts (n 144 above) 17.

205 See Fuentes (n 53 above).

gration of, *inter alia*, environmental, economic and social considerations.[206] Huey D Johnson notes that sustainability is about 'balancing the health of the environment and social considerations with economic efficiency'.[207] The Johannesburg Declaration on Sustainable Development also defines sustainable development in the context of environmental, social and economic concerns.[208] Defining sustainable development in terms of social, economic and environmental concerns more accurately pinpoints what it is that is being integrated.[209] Moreover, implicit in such a conceptualisation is the recognition that, while there is a relationship between economic and social considerations, they are not the same and meeting one does not necessarily imply meeting the other.

Having established that sustainable development requires the integration of environmental, social and economic values cannot be the end of the matter. It is equally important to establish *how* these values (social, economic and environment) are to be integrated. Bosselmann correctly notes that sustainable development involves 'the need for compromises and allows for trade-offs' between the values of sustainable development.[210] Establishing *how* integration takes place thus requires determining how these compromises and trade-offs are to take place. How do international law and the institutions created under international law deal with cases of conflict between these values? Do the compromises and trade-offs made when these values collide suggest some kind of hierarchy of values in sustainable development discourse? Is Pallemaerts correct when he asserts that integration stands for the subordination of

206 ILA New Delhi Declaration of Principles of International Law Relating to Sustainable Development, reprinted in Schrijver (n 5 above) 86; also reprinted in (2002) 2 *International Environmental Agreements: Politics, Law and Economics* 211. See also ILA Committee on International Law and Sustainable First Report prepared for the ILA Conference, Berlin, August 2004 in ILA *Report of the Seventy-First Conference* (2004).

207 HD Johnson 'Whose Earth is it anyway?' (2002) 39 (3) *UN Chronicle* 8. Interestingly in the same issue von Weizsacker refers to the harmonisation of 'environmental and developmental goals'. See E von Weiszacker 'Harmonizing environmental and developmental goals' (2002) 39 (3) *UN Chronicle* 12. See also Fuentes (n 53 above) 109 who describes sustainable development as 'the idea of integration of environmental protection and economic development'.

208 According to the Johannesburg Declaration 'the protection of the environment, and social and economic development are fundamental to sustainable development'.

209 To this day, however, there are those who continue to define sustainable development in terms of environment and development. See eg G Mayeda 'Where should Johannesburg take us? Ethical and legal approaches to sustainable development in the context of international environmental law' (2004) 15 *Colorado Journal of International Environmental Law and Policy* 29.

210 Bosselmann 'Making the difference in the design of law' (n 198 above) 5. The ILA Second report notes that integration is better seen as a 'form of multilateral dialogue, in which the intrinsic conflicts of sustainable development can be played out'. Elsewhere the Second Report states as follows: 'Of course, unfortunately, concurrent attainment of both human development and environmental protection can only ever be at the level of rhetoric. Real life situations almost always involve trade-offs' (at 7).

environmental imperatives to economic objectives?[211] Or does sustainable development stand for the subordination of economic concerns to environmental concerns? Or, further still, does sustainable development stand for the subordination of environmental and economic interests to social interests? It is in answering these questions that we are able to get some idea of how the integration process takes place. More to the point, in thinking about these questions, it seems to me that there must be at least three different ways that the values of sustainable development can be integrated and, consequently, three variations of sustainable development.

3.2 Three Variations of Sustainable Development

On the basis of the question as to *how* integration is to take place, I suggest that there are at least three possible approaches to integration and consequently three variations of sustainable development. These variations are distinguishable on the basis of the values that take pole position in cases of conflict. In the first variation, the economic growth-centred variation, economic growth takes top position. In cases of conflict, economic growth and related values are given priority. In the second variation, the environment-centred variation, the natural environment is more important and in case of conflict it triumphs. Finally, the human needs-centred variation (referred to also as the social well-being or social needs-centred variation), places the social needs and general well-being of humanity at the centre of its concerns.[212]

Immediately I need to make two points against which this conceptualisation of sustainable development is to be understood. First, the variations are based on the process of integration of the *three* values. For that reason, none of these variations reject the relevance of other values in the integration (otherwise it would not

211 Johnson (n 207 above) 8 makes a similar point: 'The problem is that the economic dimensions have overwhelmed the environmental and social aspects, limiting the success of sustainability as a concept'.

212 In discussing these distinctions some development ethicists have suggested that, perhaps, the human needs approach is inadequate and that, perhaps, my focus should be on a capabilities approach entailing that 'development' must serve to empower people rather than merely meeting their needs. For an introductory text on development ethics see DA Crocker 'Development ethics and globalisation' (2003) 30 *Philosophical Topics* 9. For more in-depth studies see A Sen 'Development thinking at the beginning of the 21st century' in Louis Emmereji *Economic and social development in the XXI century* (1997). In this study (and in my previous work) the term human-needs is understood in a broad sense to include anything and everything necessary for a life of dignity. Thus, capabilities necessary for a life of dignity, as will become clear when expanding further upon the distinction between economic growth and human needs centred models, are included in my understanding of human needs. For this reason the distinction made by development ethicists between the human-needs approaches and capabilities is not made here.

be an integration process). Rather, proponents of the variations would argue that placing their preferred value at the centre would have the effect of simultaneously advancing the other values. Thus, proponents of the economic growth-centred variation will argue that placing economic growth at the centre of sustainable development will have the effect of providing much needed resources for poverty alleviation and environmental protection.[213] Proponents of the environment-centred variation would similarly argue that the natural environment, as the basis upon which both social and economic development takes place, must be given priority.[214]

Secondly, and perhaps more importantly, both the economic growth-centred and the human needs-centred variations of sustainable development are anthropocentric, as they both place human-related concerns at the centre of the integration process. In fact, the central values in these two variations can, together, be said to represent 'development'. Fuentes, for example, clearly groups social and economic concerns aspects together by stating that sustainable development is the 'basis for reconciliation between social and economic development, on the one side, and the protection of the environment, on the other.'[215] Nevertheless, in my view, these two variations of sustainable development tend to pull in fundamentally opposite directions.

While the human needs variation has, as its focus, basic human needs required for a life of dignity, under the economic growth variation the focus is on those activities that can lead to the growth of national economies. Thus, in social needs-centred variations the emphasis tends to be on issues such poverty eradication, improved access to health facilities, education and meeting all other needs necessary for a life of dignity. A good indication of the kinds of interests required for a life of dignity can be gleaned from the Millennium Development Goals. The MDGs focus on poverty eradication,[216] provision of safe drinking water,[217] provision

213 See for example the comments of M Moore text accompanying n 191.

214 See Bosselmann 'Making the difference in the design of law' (n 198 above) where he says 'the ecology [must be seen] as the overarching system, society as part of it and the economy as part of both systems'.

215 Fuentes (n 53 above) 111, 110.

216 Principle 19 of the Millennium Development Goals states, as a goal, to 'halve, by the year 2015, the proportion of the world's people whose income is less than a dollar a day and the proportion of people who suffer from hunger'.

217 States also committed themselves in the MDGs to 'halve the proportion of people who are unable to reach or to afford safe drinking water' by 2015.

of education,[218] and improved access to health services.[219] Economic growth-centred variations of sustainable development, on the other hand, would tend to focus on those areas necessary for the expansion of economies, such as increased free trade, investment opportunities, improved (and increased) production and privatisation. Economic growth-centred variations of sustainable development, by focusing on privatisation, would also tend to promote a lesser role for the public sector. Typically, the kinds of policies consistent with an economic growth variation of sustainable development are those typically promoted by the IMF.[220]

That these two variations of sustainable development cannot simply be grouped together under the anthropocentric or development banner is aptly illustrated by a perusal of statistics in the *Human Development Reports*. The 1999 report, for example, indicates that while the global economy grows, the gap between rich and poor continues to widen.[221] These concerns are echoed by the comments of the then President of the World Bank, James Wolfensohn, in a speech delivered to the Bank's Board of Governors in 2003: 'In our world of 6 billion, one billion owns 80% of the global GDP, while another struggles to survive on less than a dollar a day. This is a world out of balance'.[222]

The nuanced conceptualisation of sustainable development is important truly to understand the integration process. It more accurately allows decision-makers to decide which variation best serves the aims of sustainable development. It allows us, as analysts, more accurately to analyse the kinds of balances that are struck between the values represented in the area of international law relating to sustainable development.

3.3 Identifying the Variations of Sustainable Development in Specific Instruments

At the time of writing this study many instruments exist to give effect to sustainable development. One of the questions asked in this study

218 States further committed themselves to ensuring that children everywhere will be able to complete primary schooling.

219 The MDGs specifically focus on maternal mortality rates and the HIV/AIDS pandemic. Another source from which to glean the kinds of interests that this variation of sustainable development would promote is TW Pogge 'Severe poverty as a human rights violation' (8 April 2003) available at http://www.etikk.no/globaljustice (accessed 20 July 2006): 'People living in poverty lack secure access to sufficient quantities of these basic necessities [safe food and water, clothing, shelter and basic medical care]'.

220 See J Stiglitz *Globalization and its discontents* (2002) 54 *et seq.*

221 See UNDP *Human development report* (1999) 3 *et seq.*

222 J Wolfensohn 'A new global balance: The challenge of leadership' speech delivered to the Board of Governors of the World Bank, September 2003, Dubai (on file with author).

is what variation of sustainable development is reflected in the instruments under consideration. At a very basic level the purpose of this classification is for classification's sake — to know and disseminate knowledge about the particular inclination of an instrument. At another level the purpose is to determine if, and the extent to which, anything can be learnt about how the values of sustainable development are integrated and, perhaps, about whether this can tell us anything about the impact that sustainable development has had on international law. In order to determine what kind of variation of sustainable development is reflected in the respective instruments, tools are required to assist in categorising each instrument as reflecting one variation or the other. The purpose of this paragraph is thus to identify tools to assist in determining whether an instrument reflects one variation or another of sustainable development.

I have identified the principle of integration as the key concept in sustainable development. It is from this principle that the various variations of sustainable development are discernable. Analysing international law instruments with a view to classification under the variations requires, therefore, asking the question *how* integration, in those particular instruments, is effected. Thus, we need to ask what kinds of trade-offs and compromises are made in cases where economic growth, environmental and social values collide. Put another way, in cases of conflict between the various values, which value prevails in the documents establishing the regimes as well as the practice of the relevant institutions responsible for the implementation of the regimes. For example, in the analysis of a specific regime we may find that in the drafting history there were various options open to the drafters, favouring social, environmental or economic values respectively. To classify the regime in terms of one of the variations of sustainable development would require a determination of which value in the final analysis, taking into account the regime as a whole, is most favoured in the regime. To answer these questions the following enquiry is proposed:

(i) to what extent do choices made in the regime show a willingness to sacrifice economic growth concerns for the sake of ecological and/or social concerns;
(ii) to what extent do the choices made in the regime show a willingness to sacrifice ecological concerns for the sake of economic and/or social concerns; and
(iii) to what extent do the choices made in the regime show a willingness to sacrifice social concerns for the sake of economic and/or ecological concerns?

This kind of analysis will allow one to determine the central value in the instrument under consideration and thereby determine the variation of sustainable development that best reflects that instrument. I must emphasise that these determinations are not, and cannot be, precise mechanical determinations. The determinations, by their very nature, are dynamic and require some value judgment. Given the fluidity of the analysis, some characteristics of each variation of sustainable development may also be helpful.

Instruments reflecting an economic growth-centred variation of sustainable development would tend to reflect characteristics that advance economic growth imperatives. In the discussion earlier in this chapter it was suggested that free trade promotes economic growth, while at the same time having the tendency or potential to harm environmental and social interests.[223] The promotion of free trade is thus an example of a characteristic that is likely to indicate an economic growth-centred variation of sustainable development.

In negotiations on many modern multilateral environmental agreements there is tension between strict environmental regulation and free trade. Most recently this tension was illustrated in the negotiations of the Biosafety of Protocol[224] as well as the two Conventions related to transboundary movement of hazardous wastes.[225] Another trade-related tool used in environmental regulation is the prohibition of trade used in the Convention on International Trade in Endangered Species.[226] Seen in this light, trade, or rather the prohibition of trade for environmental purposes, would suggest an environment-centred variation of sustainable development.

Other factors to be on the look out for that may suggest an economic growth-centred variation of sustainable development include the use of market mechanisms, including the various manifestations of the polluter pays principle, in lieu of prohibitive environmental regulation.[227] Environmentalists may be suspicious of market mechanisms, including the polluter pays principle, for fear that they imply a 'license to pollute as long as market forces permit the polluter to compensate'.[228] None of the studies I consulted on the

223 See for discussion on the environmental and social objections to free trade above para 2.3.

224 2000 Cartagena Protocol on Biosafety to the Convention on Biological Diversity in Cullet & Gowlland-Gualtieri (n 48 above) 188.

225 1989 Basel Convention on the Control of Transboundary Movement of Hazardous Wastes and Their Disposal in Cullet & Gowlland-Gualtieri (n 48 above) 131 and Bamako Convention on the Ban of the Import into Africa and the Control of Transboundary Movement of Hazardous Wastes within Africa (1991) 30 *ILM* 773.

226 1973 Convention on International Trade in Endangered Species of Wild Fauna and Flora in Cullet & Gowlland-Gualtieri (n 48 above) 222.

227 See for discussion ch 2 above at para 2.1.

228 See Franck (n 47 above) 361.

use of market mechanisms suggested that market mechanisms are the preferred tools for environmental purposes.[229] The literature supporting the use of market mechanisms suggest that market mechanisms are useful for economic reasons.[230] Indeed, market mechanisms go hand in hand with privatisation since the scaling back of government leads to a greater reliance on market forces.[231] Generally, an economic growth-centred variation would tend to promote business opportunities and, more specifically, aggregated economic growth at the expense of human needs.

An economic growth variation of sustainable development would also support a specific approach to fundamental rights. This specific approach to fundamental rights is well captured by Ernst-Ulrich Petersmann.[232] Human rights, in this paradigm, closely resemble economic growth tools listed above. For example, according to Petersmann, the protection of human rights results in 'economic and political market mechanisms' and they render 'market economies more effective'.[233] Some of the human rights recognised in this paradigm include freedom of information, which would protect 'spontaneous information mechanisms (such as market prices)', property rights and freedom of contract (as a human right).[234] Property rights and freedom of contract, for example, 'protect individual rights to buy and to sell goods'.[235] He suggests that the inevitable conflict between the producer's interest in high prices and

229 See eg Atul Kohli 'Introduction' in A Kohli *et al* (eds) *States, markets and just growth: Development in the twenty-first century* (2003). See also JB Wiener 'Global environmental regulation: Instrument choice in legal context' in J Tietenberg (ed) *Emissions trading programs: Vol I* (2001). See in the context of climate change F Missfeldt 'Flexibility mechanisms: Which path to take after Kyoto?' (1998) 7 *Review of European Community and International Environmental Law* 128 130 where the author states: 'The debate preceding Kyoto identified that the main economic benefit of emission trading is that it enables targets to be implemented in a cost efficient or even a least cost way'. See also A Rose & B Stevens 'An economic analysis of flexible permit trading in the Kyoto Protocol' (2001) 1 *International Environmental Agreements: Politics, Law and Economics* 219; P Taylor 'Heads in the sand as the tide rises: Environmental ethics and the law on climate change' (2000/2001) 19 *UCLA Journal of Environmental Law and Policy* 247.

230 As all above.

231 See Kohli (n 229 above) and I Adelman & K Ralston 'Institutions and economic linkages at village level in West Java, Indonesia' in A de Janvry *et al* (eds) *State, market and civil organizations: New theories, new practices and their implications for rural development* (1995), especially 384 *et seq*. See also, in the same volume, DE Sahn & A Sarris 'Political economy of economic decline and reform in Africa: The role of the state, markets and civil institutions' especially 421.

232 Petersmann (n 194 above).

233 Petersmann (n 194 above) 626.

234 As above.

235 As above. On property rights and development see GP O'Driscoll and L Hoskins 'Property rights: The key to economic development' in HB Schäfer and AV Raja (eds) *Law and economic development* (2006).

the consumer's interest in low prices can be 'reconciled best on the basis of equal liberty rights (eg freedom of contract)'.[236] This conception of fundamental rights involves the instrumentalisation of human rights to economic growth promoting values.[237] As implied by Alston, this conception of human rights would tend to benefit industries rather than people.[238]

While an economic growth variation places economic concerns at the centre, it has to be remembered that all these variations are based on an integration of all three values. This raises the question of how social and environmental values may be catered for (or integrated) in an economic growth-centred variation of sustainable development. Put another way, how are social and environmental values trumped by economic growth? One way that social and environmental values in an economic growth-centred variation of sustainable development are trumped, is to pose the achievement of economic concerns as necessary for the achievement of social concerns and/or environmental concerns. The response of US President George W Bush to the Kyoto Protocol referred to in paragraph 2.2 of this chapter illustrates the point well. Bush suggested that the Kyoto Protocol did 'not make economic sense for America' and that he was concerned that 'people may not be finding jobs in America'. The effect of regulation on the ability to 'find jobs' is a social concern used in the context of the promotion of economic concerns. Environmental values may be trumped by economic concerns through the postponing of environmental action or by reducing the impact or effectiveness of environmental regulation or subjecting the environmental regulations to economic concerns. Again showing the interrelated nature of these values, social concerns may even be advanced as the rationale for the trumping of environmental concerns by economic concerns.

236 As above. Elsewhere, in the context of South African domestic law, I have argued against such an assumption. See D Tladi 'One step forward, two steps back in the constitutionalisation of the common law: *Afrox Health Care* case' 2002 *SA Public Law* 473 and D Tladi 'Breathing constitutional values into the law of contract: Freedom of contract and the constitution' 2002 *De Jure* 306.

237 In criticising this suggestion, P Alston makes the following observation: '[The approach is] especially problematic in relation to terms such as 'human rights', 'fundamental rights', 'economic rights', 'economic liberties' and 'economic freedoms', all of which appear at different times in his analysis. For the most part they seem to be used interchangeably, although from both a philosophical and legal perspective there are enormous differences among them'. See P Alston 'Resisting the merger and acquisition of human rights by trade law: A reply to Petersmann' (2002) 13 *European Journal of International Law* 815 823. Alston, further, at 816 describes this approach as an approach that 'at best is difficult to reconcile with international human rights law and at worst [it] would undermine it dramatically'. For further criticism see R Howse 'Human rights in the WTO: Whose rights, what humanity? Comment on Petersmann' (2002) 13 *European Journal of International Law* 651.

238 Alston (n 237 above) 836.

A social well-being-centred variation of sustainable development would, first and foremost, adopt a different approach to human rights than that adopted in the economic growth variation of sustainable development. The social well-being variation focuses on issues relating to the eradication of poverty and the creation of conditions of dignity for those living under inhuman conditions.[239] Human rights approaches reflected in this variation of sustainable development would include traditional human rights found in the International Bill of Human Rights, namely the Universal Declaration of Human Rights and the two International Covenants on Human Rights.[240] In particular, human rights approaches reflecting a social well-being-centred variation of sustainable development would focus on civil and political rights as well as socio-economic rights. In this paradigm human rights typically aim at protecting people (groups or individuals), especially the vulnerable rather than states or corporations.[241] According to this conception important human rights would include the right to dignity, the right to the environment (in its many facets), the right to development as well as various socio-economic rights. Civil and political rights such as, for the example, the right to dignity, would serve to highlight the impact of poverty on the dignity of the majority of people of the world. Socio-economic rights, amongst others, the rights to food, education, housing and adequate health care, implicate those interests most relevant to social needs of the world's poor which are at the centre of a social well-being variation of sustainable development.

Given the emphasis on addressing concerns of the poor, the social needs variation of sustainable development would tend to emphasise a broad concept of intragenerational equity not limited to the common but differentiated responsibilities principle, the operation of which is, in general, limited to the environmental context. Fuentes, for example, laments the fact that financial transfer obligations in terms of multilateral treaties are limited to assistance for environmental programmes and 'have never been extended to assistance for sustainable development of developing countries in general'.[242] Further, given that the argument proposed above is to the effect that this variation of sustainable development tends to pull in the opposite direction to the economic growth variation of sustainable development, the values espoused in the former, including the reliance on market mechanisms, privatisation, a limited role for government and trade instruments, would tend to pull in a

239 See Pogge (n 219 above). To be fair, in this essay Pogge is concerned mainly with moral rights rather than legal rights. Nevertheless he does stress the relationship between the moral and legal basis of human rights.

240 See Alston (n 237 above) 828.

241 See in the context of the right to development, discussion above on Principles 2 and 3 in the Rio Declaration.

242 Fuentes (n 53 above) 161.

direction different to the social well-being variation of sustainable development.

As with the economic growth variation of sustainable development it is worth asking how the other values are trumped in the social well-being variation of sustainable development. In relation to human rights, it is interesting to note what Alston, relying on Sen's conception of human rights, suggests:[243]

> Money is, in many ways and in many contexts, essential to the full enjoyment of human rights. Yet no one has yet suggested that there is a right to money per se. Following philosophers like Amartya Sen, there may well be an 'entitlement' to that amount of money which is necessary in order to purchase the essentials required for a life of dignity.

Thus, in this approach, money (and by extension economic growth) may well be necessary for the achievement of social concern. However, under this variation, the objective is social well-being, while the economic growth values *could* be a means to that end. Howse also provides a glimpse into how economic concerns could be accommodated under the social well-being variation of sustainable development.[244] He suggests that under Petersmann's conception of human rights (which I have argued reflects an economic-centred variation of sustainable development), social well-being concerns may only be pursued to the extent that they are shown to be 'necessary' limits to market imperatives.[245] Howse proposes that the reverse would be more appropriate.[246] Thus, under the social well-being variation of sustainable development, economic growth policies such as free trade rules, privatisation and market mechanisms would only be permissible where they have been shown to be 'necessary' to protect social needs. This kind of approach is also reflected in the practice of the Committee of Economic, Social and Cultural Rights which has, with respect to water, commented that '[w]ater should be treated primarily as a social and cultural good, and not primarily as an economic good'.[247]

As with the social well-being variation of sustainable development, the environment-centred variation of sustainable development would tend to repel economic growth concerns such as the use of market mechanisms and trade instruments.[248] The environment-centred variation, which has the environment at the centre of the integration process, places a high premium on environ-

243 Alston (n 237 above) 828.
244 Howse (n 237 above).
245 Howse (n 237 above) 655.
246 As above.
247 UN Committee on Economic, Social and Cultural Rights *Substantive issues arising in the implementation of the international covenant on economic, social and cultural rights: General comment 15* (2002), E/C.12/202/11.
248 See discussion of trade above in para 2.3 of this chapter.

mental protection and this should be reflected in those instruments that promote an environment-centred variation of sustainable development.

First, it goes without saying that an important characteristic of this variation of sustainable development would be stringent and uncompromised environmental regulation designed to meet the targeted environmental objectives in mind. In this variation, the precautionary principle, with its focus on action for environmental protection even in the face of scientific certainty, takes on a central role. Furthermore, in the environmental rights context, an instrument reflecting an environment-centred variation is likely, implicitly or explicitly, to recognise rights *for* the environment (as opposed to rights *to* the environment) as an integral part of rights discourse.[249] In that context intergenerational equity is likely to be understood in broader terms as including generations of aspects of nature other than humans.[250] The essence of such a claim would imply the promotion of the intrinsic value of nature and an ecocentric approach to environmental law. Moreover, such recognition of rights is also likely to be accompanied by an emphasis on duties towards the environment.

The centrality of economic concerns in the economic growth-centred variation of sustainable development may countenance the destruction of some aspects of the natural environment if the destruction is accompanied by economic and technological advance. Thus, economic and technological advancement can serve as substitutes for natural resources. In this sense an economic growth variation of sustainable development can be described as a 'weak' version of sustainable development.[251] This, as Bosselmann has shown in his various publications, is inconsistent with an environment-centred variation. Thus, an environment-centred variation of sustainable development will be characterised by strict environmental regulation. Moreover, this 'weak' sustainable development would also be inconsistent with a social needs variation of sustainable development. The autonomy, inherent in the principle of intergenerational equity, of future human generations to determine for themselves what their needs may be, precludes the destruction or substitution of natural resources with economic technological advancements.[252] In this way, social concerns would be accommodated in an environment-centred variation of sustainable

249 For a critique of the human rights approach to environmental protection from an ecological perspective see K Bosselmann 'Human rights and the environment: A circular affair – the case for an ecological approach' (Draft manuscript on file with author).

250 See K Bosselmann 'Justice and the environment: Building blocks for a theory on ecological justice' in Bosselmann & Richardson (n 136 above) 43.

251 See discussion on weak and strong sustainable development above.

252 See discussion on ecocentric objection to intergenerational equity. See also Tladi (n 38 above) 184.

development. At the same time this reinforces the idea that, while economic growth variations of sustainable development will reflect 'weak' sustainable development, both the environment and social well-being variation will reflect a 'strong' approach to sustainable development.

However, while the argument advanced here is that both the social well-being and the environment-centred variations of sustainable development represent 'strong' sustainable development, the two variations are different. With the environment-centred variation, the environment is at the centre and, therefore, in case of conflict the environment takes precedence. For the social well-being-centred variation it is the needs of humans, especially the most vulnerable in society, that occupy a place of priority. This means that in some cases where hard choices have to be made, different conclusions could be arrived at under alternative variations. For example, given the impact of HIV/AIDS on the world's poor, the approaches to HIV/AIDS (as part of nature) may be very different.[253] A social well-being-centred variation of sustainable development *may* well require the destruction of the virus, while an environment-centred variation *may not* be in favour of the destruction of the virus. However, the point being made here is that while there may be a tendency to assume a common ground between the economic growth and social well-being variations on account of anthropocentricity, a closer analysis reveals that there is more common ground between the social well-being and environment-centred variations of sustainable development.

4. Conclusion

The principle of sustainable development has elicited severe criticism from some quarters. On the one hand it has been described as an indeterminate concept with no fixed meaning. On the other hand sustainable development has been accused of undermining the value of international environmental law. Neither of these criticisms is without merit. However, both criticisms flow from the lack of an appropriate conceptualisation of sustainable development that moves beyond regarding sustainable development as the balancing of environment and development. Such a definition obviously misses important questions, namely, what kind of balance is struck and what is development?

A more nuanced conceptualisation of sustainable development recognises that sustainable development aims to integrate social, economic and environmental issues. Such a conceptualisation also recognises that there are a variety of ways in which this can be done.

253 See Tladi 'Towards a more nuanced framework' (n 183 above) 27.

In this chapter, three different ways in which these values can be integrated and consequently three different variations of sustainable development are proposed. The aim in this study is to analyse various instruments of international environmental law to determine which model of sustainable development best reflects the particular instrument. On the basis of this analysis we could begin to ponder the question as to the impact of sustainable development on international law.

Before beginning with this process I will, in the next chapter, consider the role of sustainable development in international law. This involves more than just enquiring about its status in international law. Although questions of status invariably come up, questions about the role of sustainable development involve, more importantly, asking where sustainable development fits into the landscape of international law. Is it some kind of modifier of existing rules or principles? Is the principle of sustainable development simply a tool for interpreting other norms of international law? Or does it operate in the same way as other principles of international law?

4

Relationship between International Law and Sustainable Development

> The role of the international *legal* system in promoting sustainable development has been a central, if ambiguous, element of this political process since the notion of sustainable development was first introduced.[1]

1. Introduction

Sustainable development plays an important role in integrating the (potentially) conflicting economic, environmental and social values. As explained in the previous chapter, sustainable development is, in some sense, an amorphous concept. For this reason, I suggested that there are three variations of sustainable development.

But what does this mean for the place of sustainable development in international law? I am concerned in this chapter with that very question. At a very basic level this question involves commenting on the legal status of sustainable development. However, the status of sustainable development in international law is not all there is to questions about its place in international law. Consideration of the place of sustainable development in international law concerns the relationship between the principle of sustainable development and other aspects, principles, rules and/or fields of international law. Put another way, how is sustainable development to function in the body of international law? Is sustainable development a principle that operates within different areas of international law or is there a separate field of international law relating to sustainable development? Does it serve to modify existing international legal rules? Or does sustainable development have a more transformative role in international law?

In thinking about the role(s) that sustainable development can play in international law it is worth bearing in mind the purpose of sustainable development, from a policy perspective. In paragraph 3 of chapter 2 it was argued, based on *inter alia* the key instruments of sustainable development, that sustainable development requires a paradigm shift from the ruling economic-based paradigm where economic concerns trump environmental and social concerns. The role of sustainable development in international law, and law in

1 ILA Committee on International Law on Sustainable Development First Report prepared for the ILA Conference in, 2004, Berlin in ILA *Report of the seventy-first conference Berlin* (2004) 570.

general, has to facilitate this (policy) purpose. Therefore, the purpose of sustainable development has to be kept in mind when determining the role of sustainable development in international law.

I begin the chapter by briefly considering questions around the status of sustainable development under international law. In section 3, sustainable development is placed within the context of international law by considering the place and role of sustainable development in international law. When considering the place of sustainable development I investigate its place in the context of a variety of areas and principles of international law. The role of sustainable development, on the other hand, is concerned with uncovering the effect that sustainable development is supposed to have on general international law. Having considered these questions I offer some concluding remarks, in particular focusing on the meaning of the specific place of sustainable development in international law for the analysis of the various instruments considered in Part B of the study.

2. The status of sustainable development under international law

The content (or meaning) of sustainable development, as discussed in chapter 2, is not the only aspect of the concept suffering from uncertainty. There is, similarly, much debate as to the international legal status of sustainable development.[2] Several authors have, for example, described sustainable development as a principle of international law.[3] However, at least in the past, others have denied that sustainable development is a principle of international law.[4] The majority of contributions remain, largely, non-committal. Mayeda, for example, makes the following observations: 'Though not a treaty, the Johannesburg Declaration is nevertheless indicative of an

2 ILA Committee on International Law (n 1 above) 570 *et seq*. See also A Boyle & D Freestone 'Introduction' in A Boyle & D Freestone (eds) *International law and sustainable development* (1999) 7. See specifically describing the uncertainty, MC Cordonier Segger & A Khalfan 'Sustainable development in policy and in law' in MC Cordonier Segger & A Khalfan (eds) *Sustainable development law* (2004) 46.

3 See, for example, CG Weeramantry *Universalising international law* (2004) 432 where he states that there 'is no room any longer for denying the legal status of the concept of sustainable development'. See also N Schrijver 'De verankering en betekenis van duurzame ontwikelling in het internationale recht' 2003 *Mededelingen van de Nederlandse vereniging voor internationaal recht: Volkenrecht en duurzame ontwikkeling* 1 1 where he states that the concept of sustainable development 'een plaats in het internationale recht verworven' (the concept of sustainable development 'has assumed a place in international law' my own translation).

4 See, generally, G Handl 'Sustainable development: General rules versus specific obligations' in W Lang (ed) *Sustainable development and international law* (1995). See also V Lowe 'Sustainable development and unsustainable arguments' in Boyle & Freestone (n 2 above).

emerging commitment to sustainable development *as a framework for both international law and international environmental law*'[5] (emphasis added).

Similarly, Gunther Handl, writing in 1998, asserts that multilateral development banks 'are already legally obliged to conduct banking activities in [developing countries] consistently with the basic objective and specific normative ramifications of sustainable development'.[6]

Yet it is not clear what, in Handl's view, is the international legal status of the concept of sustainable development. By and large, Handl seems to view sustainable development as 'international public policy', the significance of which is also unclear.[7] Yet it seems equally clear that there is some relationship between this international public policy and 'international normative concepts – including both general international law and general principles of law', and also treaty law.[8] These normative concepts are said to provide dimensions against which the World Bank's Articles of Agreements can be interpreted to allow for the 'change in international public policy epitomised by 'sustainable development'.[9] But Handl does seem to draw a distinction between 'the body of norms of international law' and sustainable development.[10] On the other hand, the general thrust of the argument, that multilateral development banks have obligations flowing from sustainable development, is based, at least in part, on the fact that 'the general reach of the customary international law ... extends' to the banks.[11] The latter proposition may suggest that he views sustainable development as part of customary international law.

Thus, the status of sustainable development in international law remains contested. It is in the context of this uncertainty that the *Gabcikovo-Nagymaros*[12] decision of the International Court of Justice, along with the contribution by Vaughan Lowe commenting thereon

5 Mayeda 'Where should Johannesburg take us? Ethical and legal approaches to sustainable development in the context of international environmental law' (2004) 15 *Colorado Journal of International Environmental Law and Policy* 29 29 *et seq.*

6 G Handl 'The legal mandate of multilateral development banks as agents for change towards sustainable development' (1998) 92 *American Journal of International Law* 642 647.

7 As above.

8 As above.

9 As above.

10 Handl (n 6 above) 662 where he comments that 'there exists today a growing and ever more specific body of norms of international law bearing on "sustainable development"'.

11 As above.

12 *Case Concerning Gabcikovo-Nagymaros (Hungary v Slovakia)* 1997 *ICJ* 3 reprinted in 1998 *ILM* 168.

provide a good starting point for exploring the legal status of sustainable development under international law.[13]

In the majority decision of the *Gabcikovo-Nagymaros* case the 'concept of sustainable development' is referred to only once.[14] The majority, in its only reference to sustainable development, asserts that:[15]

> new norms and standards have been developed, set forth in a great number of instruments during the last two decades. Such new norms have to be taken into consideration, and such new standards given proper weight, not only when states contemplate new activities but also when continuing with activities begun in the past. [The] need to reconcile economic development with protection of the environment is aptly expressed in the concept of sustainable development.

The most obvious point to make about the reference to sustainable development is that the court refers to it as a 'concept' rather than as a rule or principle. Thus, at best, the court is non-committal on the legal significance of sustainable development; at worst the court does not believe that sustainable development has any legal status at all. However, earlier in the extract the court does refer to 'new norms and standards'. Although, as Lowe comments,[16] it is not clear whether sustainable development is one of these norms and standards, the invocation of sustainable development immediately following reference to these norms and standards suggests that sustainable development *could* be one such norm.

It seems to me that the big question is not whether the court includes sustainable development as one of these new norms, but rather whether these new norms are, in fact, norms of international law or just norms of policy. After all, the court asserts, with reference to these new norms, only that they must be considered and taken into account. This wording may imply that they are not binding in a legal sense.[17] Of course this wording also does not conclusively indicate that the court implies the norms and standards not to be binding. In terms of article 31(3)(c) of the Vienna Convention on the Law of Treaties, when interpreting treaties, *binding* customary international law 'shall be taken into account'.[18] Certainly no one would suggest that customary international law is not legally binding under international law. Thus, the fact that the court says these norms and standards must be taken into consideration does not necessarily mean they lack the force of law. Nevertheless, the phrasing does cast some

13 Lowe (n 4 above).
14 See para 140 of the Judgment of the Court.
15 As above.
16 Lowe (n 4 above) 20.
17 As above.
18 See for discussion of the provision P Sands 'Sustainable development: Treaty, custom, and the cross-fertilisation of international law' in Boyle & Freestone (n 2 above) 39.

doubt on the view of the court on the legal status of sustainable development. Indeed the whole extract is rather non-committal. It can be argued, therefore, that the majority opinion adds to the uncertainty surrounding the legal status of sustainable development under international law.

In this regard the majority opinion is in stark contrast to the separate opinion of Judge Weeramantry, who has no doubt in his mind as to the legal status of sustainable development. Very early on in his opinion he states the following to make his position clear:[19]

> The Court referred to [sustainable development] as a concept in paragraph 140 of its judgment. However, I consider it more than a mere concept, but as a principle with normative value ...

Elsewhere in the opinion Judge Weeramantry says that sustainable development is part of modern international law.[20] In particular he asserts that the principle is part of customary international law.[21] For this contention Weeramantry relies on international soft law instruments,[22] multilateral treaties,[23] the practices of international financial institutions,[24] regional declarations and planning documents,[25] and state practice.[26] Judge Weeramantry then asserts that the adoption of these instruments illustrates a 'wide and general acceptance' of the principle of sustainable development by the global community.[27] To the instruments relied upon by Judge Weeramantry

19 *Gabcikovo-Nagymaros* case (Separate opinion of Judge Weeramantry) (n 12 above) 204.

20 As above, 205. See also Weeramantry (n 3 above) 432.

21 As above.

22 Eg the Rio Declaration and the 1995 Copenhagen Declaration on Social Development. To judge Weeramantry's list one can today also add the Johannesburg Declaration on Sustainable Development available at http://www.johannesburgsummit.org/html/documents/summit_docs/1009wssd_pol_declaration.doc (accessed 4 September 2002) and United Nations Millennium Declaration, UN GA Res 55/2 (2000) available at http://www.un.org/millenniumgoals/ (accessed 5 June 2004).

23 Eg the Preamble and art 9(1) of the 1994 United Nations Convention to Combat Desertification; arts 2 and 3 of the 1992 United Nations Framework Convention on Climate Change; Preamble and arts 1 and 10 of the 1992 Convention on Biological Diversity; Preamble of the 1993 North American Free Trade Agreement; Preamble of the 1994 Marrakech Agreement Establishing the World Trade Organization.

24 Eg the World Bank Group, the Asian Development Bank, the African Development Bank, the Inter-American Development Bank and the European Bank for Reconstruction and Development. According to Weeramantry these institutions all subscribe to the principle of sustainable development.

25 Eg the 1989 Langwaki Declaration on the Environment adopted by the Heads of Government of the Commonwealth 'which adopted 'sustainable development' as its central theme'; the 1990 Ministerial Declaration on Environmentally Sound and Sustainable Development in Asia and the Pacific; and the Plan for the Protection and Management of the Marine and Coastal Environment of the South Asian Seas Region.

26 Eg the statements made under the 1990 Dublin Declaration by the European Council on the Environmental Imperative States.

27 *Gabcikovo-Nagymaros* case (Separate opinion of Judge Weeramantry) (n 12 above) 207.

one can add instruments adopted by civil society organisations including, *inter alia*, the Earth Charter of 2000[28] and the ILA Declaration on Sustainable Development, which, while forming part of the opinion of civil society, cannot be 'completely discounted' in the formation of customary international law.[29]

Lowe[30] creatively argues that sustainable development cannot be a principle of international law (at least not in the traditional sense). Moreover, according to Lowe, sustainable development can never (in its current form) acquire the status of customary international law.

On why sustainable development is inherently incapable of having 'the status of customary law' Lowe advances two arguments. The first argument is that while the concept of sustainable development has been referred to often 'there is lack of clear evidence' that the drafters of the many instruments referred to regarded sustainable development as having the force of law.[31] This particular objection would be applicable if Judge Weeramantry sought to show that all of these instruments were a reflection of an already existing principle of customary international law, that these instruments were declaratory of customary international law. But, as I understand Judge Weermantry's reasoning, he asserts that these instruments contributed to the evolution of a principle of customary international law.[32] For such a contention it would not be necessary to show that the authors of *specific* instruments believed the concept already to be a part of customary international law as it is the totality of the instruments together, when seen as a whole, that results in the development of a principle of customary international law. Lowe himself concedes that, given the notorious difficulty of proving the elements of customary international law, and *opinio iuris* in particular, reliance on the lack of *opinio iuris* in Weeramantry's

28 The Earth Charter is available at http://www.earthcharter.org (accessed 20 July 2006). The Earth Charter has been endorsed by, *inter alia*, IUCN at its Third Session at the Annual Congress in Bangkok Thailand in 2004 and UNESCO at the Plenary Session of its Conference in 2003.

29 ILA Declaration on Principles of International Law Relating to Sustainable Development (2004) in N Schrijver 'De verankering en betekenis duurzame ontwikkeling in het internationale recht' 2003 *Mededelingen van de Nederlandse vereniging voor internationaal recht: Volkenrecht en duurzame ontwikkeling* 1 at 86. Statements by non-state actors to support the existence of a customary international law have been relied upon in the dissenting opinion of Judge van den Wyngaert in *The Case Concerning the Arrest Warrant of 11 April 2000 (Democratic Republic of Congo v Belgium)* 2000 *ICJ* 182 available at http://www.icj-cij.org (accessed Nov 2003) para 27.

30 Lowe (n 4 above).

31 Lowe (n 4 above) 24.

32 *The North Sea Continental Shelf Cases (Federal Republic of Germany v Denmark; Federal Republic of Germany v The Netherlands)* 1969 *ICJ* 3 para 61 *et seq* for a discussion on the different roles that treaties (and arguably other instruments) can play in the evolution of customary international law.

opinion to support his argument 'would smack of the meretricious arguments of the Inquisitor'.[33]

This brings me to Lowe's second and main argument. Lowe's main argument can be summed up as an assertion that sustainable development does not meet the requirement of being fundamentally norm-creating as set out in the *North Sea Continental Shelf* cases.[34] For Lowe this requires that sustainable development be capable of being couched in normative terms such as that states have a duty to develop sustainably or states have a right to develop sustainably.[35] Because, he argues, there is no hope of uncovering a norm of 'sustainable development', the concept of sustainable development can never meet the requirement of being fundamentally norm creating. Thus, sustainable development can *never* become part of customary international law.

The fact that, in Lowe's view, sustainable development can *never* become part of customary international law does not mean that it has no normative status whatsoever.[36] He suggests that sustainable development does have a legal normativity in law – a normativity that does 'not depend upon state practice or *opinio iuris* for its status' because, unlike rules of customary international law, sustainable development 'is not *created* by the traditional combination of 'state practice + *opinio iuris*' or some variation thereon'.[37] It is, in the view of Lowe, a rule borne within the process of judicial activity. On the one hand, proponents of sustainable development may well be very drawn to Lowe's thesis, which liberates the legal normativity of sustainable development from the strict purview of customary international law. On the other hand, under Lowe's account, sustainable development becomes:[38]

> a judicial rule, created by judges and under their control. The judges are, of course, free to draw upon the practices of states (and indeed upon any other articulations of the concept): *but they are not bound to do so, and they are not confined by it.*

First, it is factually not true that sustainable development is created by judges. Sustainable development, as was demonstrated in chapter

33 Lowe (n 4 above) 24.
34 See *North Sea Continental Shelf* cases (n 32 above) para 71 *et seq.*
35 Lowe (n 4 above) 24.
36 Lowe (n 4 above) 31.
37 Lowe (n 4 above) 34 *et seq.*
38 Lowe (n 4 above) 35 (emphasis added).

2, was principally developed through an ongoing interstate process, beginning with the Stockholm process (including the Founex Conference). Second, to make sustainable development 'optional' is clearly undesirable given that the concept emerged to solve major environmental and social crises facing the world.[39] While Lowe suggests that it is this kind of legal normativity (or something close to it) that Judge Weeramantry implies in his separate opinion, it seems patently clear that Judge Weeramantry does not view sustainable development as a legal norm that courts are free to ignore. In a recent publication, Weeramantry stated that sustainable development is a substantive part 'of the law in a very real sense – a law which the courts must endeavour to administer in the same way as law they consider to be 'hard' and established law'.[40]

I cannot agree with Lowe's refusal to accept that sustainable development can *ever* become a principle of customary international law. His objection to the *possibility* of sustainable development acquiring the status of customary international law based on the 'norm-creating' requirement expounded in the *North Sea Continental Shelf* cases needs to be dissected. First, leaving aside the fact that the 'norm creating' requirement has not, to my know-ledge, been repeated in any subsequent decision of the Court,[41] the requirement in *North Sea* appears to be set in the context of *a treaty provision*, which, purportedly, reflects a rule of customary international law.[42] It is the *treaty provision* to which the norm creating element is attached and not the rule (or principle) itself. Considering the facts of the case, the equidistance rule could, for example, easily meet the 'norm creating character' test. However, it is the manner in which the equidistance principle was reflected in *that particular treaty provision* (article 6 of the Geneva Continental Shelf Convention) that prevents the Court from finding that *the provision* is not of a fundamentally norm creating character. The suggestion by Judge Weeramantry is not that a *particular provision in a particular treaty*

39 Lowe states eg that 'judges employ these modifying norms because they are judges, and not because the law expressly requires them to do so' (as above, 33).

40 Weeramantry (n 3 above) 432.

41 The reliance on treaty provisions to show the existence of a customary international law rule came up in *The Case Concerning the Military and Paramilitary Activities In and Against Nicaragua (Nicaragua v United States)* 1986 *ICJ* 14. To be fair, the use of the treaty in that case was different in that it was suggested that the treaty provision – art 51 of the UN Charter – was a codification of existing customary international law and not that the provision created or (at least contributed to the creation of) customary international law. However, the Court does note that the content of the customary international law rule on self-defence has been 'influenced' by article 51. Furthermore, of great interest is that the reliance on this leg of the argument is significantly reduced by Lowe himself in a subsequent contribution on the matter. See V Lowe 'The politics of law-making: Are the method and character of norm creation changing?' in M Byers (ed) *The role of law in international politics: Essays in international relations and international law* (2000).

42 *North Sea Continental Shelf* cases (n 32 above).

(or other instrument) reflects customary international law. Rather, it is that the plethora of soft law instruments and treaties invoking sustainable development may be an indication of *opinio iuris* accepting sustainable development as a principle in the general *corpus* of customary international law.[43]

A principal reason, according to Lowe, for his conclusion that sustainable development is not fundamentally norm creating is what he terms the 'lack of meaning'.[44] Lowe argues that one of the problems with sustainable development is that it 'is often exemplified and instantiated but rarely, if ever, defined'.[45] A definition most commonly used (and perhaps over-cited) is that given by the Brundtland Commission. However, if Lowe is referring here to the flexibility or indeterminacy of the concept, then as would be apparent from the previous chapter, I would agree fully.[46] As discussed in chapter 3, sustainable development is a very flexible concept. The definition of the Brundtland Commission, as mentioned at the beginning of that chapter, is not conclusive as to the content of sustainable development. However, that can also not be a bar to the creation of a legal principle. While, for example, the principle that the normal baseline from which the territorial sea is determined is the low-water line along the coast, is firmly established in international law, there remains some uncertainties about its application in some instances.[47] Similarly, while there is great uncertainty about the principle of self-determination and its application, it is indisputably a principle of international law.[48]

However, Lowe's arguments regarding the flexibility of sustainable development may shed light on the *legal* nature of the status of sustainable development. If Lowe's objection to sustainable development as a (traditional) principle of international law hinges on

43 *Military and Paramilitary Activities* case (n 41 above) 188 *et seq.*

44 Lowe (n 4 above) 25.

45 Lowe (n 4 above) 25.

46 Similar arguments often characterised the early debates on the precautionary principle. See for example P Birnie & A Boyle *International law and the environment* (2000) 118 *et seq*. See, however, P Sands *Principles of international law environmental law vol I: Frameworks, standards and implementation* (1995) 208. See J Cameron & J Abouchar 'The status of the precautionary principle in international law' in D Freestone & E Hey (eds) *The precautionary principle and international law: The challenge of implementation* (1996). The indeterminacy of sustainable development is considered above in section 3 of chapter 3.

47 See for discussion I Brownlie *Principles of public international law* (2003) 180 *et seq.*

48 See D Freestone 'International fisheries law since Rio: The continued rise of the precautionary principle' in Boyle & Freestone (n 3 above) who argues, using self-determination as an analogy, that the precautionary principle is a principle of international law. See also OC Okafor 'The status and effect of the right to development in contemporary international law: Towards a South-North *entente* (1995) 7 *African Journal of International and Comparative Law* 865 867 who, arguing for the recognition of a right to development in international law, notes that it is in the nature of international norms to be 'indeterminate and malleable'.

the uncertainty relating to its application, its flexibility or its lack of fixed content (as I think it does), then the objection can be overcome by a distinction made famous by Ronald Dworkin between rules and principles.[49] Certainly, because of its flexibility, sustainable development cannot be a rule. Thus, while sustainable development does not operate in 'an all or nothing fashion' it is a principle that '*must* be taken into account ... as a consideration inclining in one way or another'.[50] Sustainable development does not operate as rules described elsewhere by Lowe that 'mandate or forbid or permit certain activities'.[51] That does not mean, as I think Lowe's contribution may imply, that the application of the principle is elective, whether for states or for tribunals applying international law.[52] All that it means is that the application of sustainable development (which is compulsory when relevant) will not have a pre-determined result. That its application is compulsory when relevant is clear from Lowe's own examples of another principle, which, he argues, has a similar normative value to sustainable development, namely reasonableness in domestic legal systems.[53] Certainly, in the South African law of delicts (torts) reasonableness is the standard that *must* be considered in determining the wrongfulness or otherwise of a damage causing act. By the same token contractual terms that are clearly unreasonable are unenforceable. Thus, in each particular case the elements of sustainable development must be considered together in an integrated fashion to determine the sustainability of a particular action.

The reference by Lowe to reasonableness, a principle from domestic law, to illustrate his point raises the question whether Lowe is referring to principles of law derived from the domestic legal systems and assuming legal relevance in international law. These would be legal principles in the sense of article 38(1)(c) of the ICJ statute. However, to describe sustainable development as a principle of law derived from domestic legal systems in the sense of article 38(1)(c) of the Statute would be erroneous. General principles of law in the sense of article 38(1)(c) are not, unlike other sources of international law, created through the interaction of states.[54] As illustrated in chapters two and three, the concept of sustainable

49 R Dworkin *Taking rights seriously* (1977).

50 As above, 20 *et seq*.

51 See Lowe 'The politics of law-making' (n 41 above) 216.

52 See P Sands 'International law in the field of sustainable development: Emerging legal principles' in Lang (n 4 above) 54 who accepts that some principles may reflect customary international law.

53 See Lowe (n 41 above) 216.

54 See for discussion MN Shaw *International law* 5th Ed (2003) 94 *et seq*. See also W Friedmann 'The uses of 'general principles' in the development of international law' (1963) 57 *American Journal of International Law* 279 282 where the author suggests that general principles of law are 'formed by a comparative study of the relevant principles of different national systems'.

development clearly owes its evolution to a distinct interstate process beginning with the Stockholm process and the Founex meeting in particular. It is also not clear why, if Lowe meant to imply that sustainable development is a principle of law in the sense of article 38(1)(c), he does not say so expressly. More importantly, Lowe's characterisation of sustainable development flows, not from the source or origin of the principle, but rather from its very content (or lack thereof) and operation, thereby excluding the applicability of the distinction between principles of international law proper and principles of law in the sense of article 38(1)(c) of the Court's statute.

It seems, therefore, that Lowe's characterisation of sustainable development as a concept with a specific normative value has to be understood in the light of the principle/rule dichotomy. However, the characterisation of sustainable development as a principle (as opposed to a rule) does not exclude its inclusion in the general corpus of international customary law or the possibility of it having a binding effect outside of treaty law.[55] Proportionality, for example, is, without a doubt, a principle of international law.[56] Self-defence against an armed attack, for example, has to be proportional to the armed attack.[57] WTO decision-making, in determining whether a measure is 'relating to conservation' under article XX relies on, *inter alia,* proportionality.[58] The proportionality principle is, similarly, a requirement for valid reprisals.[59] Like sustainable development, however, proportionality does not function in an all or nothing fashion. Yet this quality on its own cannot prevent the concept becoming part of customary international law.[60]

The view taken in this study is that sustainable development can be a principle of international law. At the very least, the argument advanced here is that nothing prevents sustainable development acquiring the status of a principle of international law. Moreover, the

55 See also D Freestone 'The road from Rio: International environmental law after the Earth Summit' 1994 *Journal of Environmental Law* 193 216 where the author argues that several *principles* have, since Rio, arguably become 'part of customary law binding on all States'.

56 See generally PTK Rakate *The duty to prosecute and the status of amnesties granted for gross and systematic human rights violations in international law: Towards a balanced approach model* (Unpublished Doctoral Thesis, UNISA, 2004).

57 See eg *Military and Paramilitary Activities* case (n 41 above) para 176.

58 See eg US-Import Prohibition of Certain Shrimp and Shrimp Products AB-1998-4 1999 *ILM* 123.

59 Shaw (n 54 above) 1023.

60 *S v Makwanyane and Other* 1995 (6) BCLR 665 (CC) where the South African Constitutional Court, duty bound to consider international law in the interpretation of the rights in South African Bill of Rights, discusses the role of importance of proportionality in international human rights law. With regards to equity, the ILA Committee on Sustainable Development has had this to say: 'The legal notion of equity is neither descriptive nor particularly measurable, but a reasonably clear jurisprudence of what it does or does not involve has evolved'. See ILA Committee on Sustainable Development, Second Draft Report (2006) (on file with author) 26.

plethora of national and international instruments on sustainable development and instruments giving effect to sustainable development along with judge Weeramantry's separate opinion would seem to justify a conclusion that sustainable development is now firmly part of the body of international law.[61]

3. Sustainable development in international law

I suggested, in the last section, that sustainable development is a principle of international law. Moreover, all the instruments considered in this study subscribe to the principle of sustainable development.[62] However, what is more important is the place and role of sustainable development in international law. How is sustainable development to be placed in the midst of various fields and sub-fields of international law? What effect is sustainable development supposed to have on international law in general? It is to these questions that I now turn.

61 See generally instruments cited by Judge Weeramantry such as the Stockholm Declaration on the Human Environment (1972) in P Cullet & A Gowlland-Gualtieri (eds) *Key materials on international environmental law* (2004) 2; the Rio Declaration on Environment and Development (1992) in Cullet and Gowlland-Gualtieri 7. To these one can add other 'soft-law' instruments such as the Johannesburg Declaration on Sustainable Development, the ILA Declaration on Principles Relating to Sustainable Development as well as the Millennium Declaration, all cited previously in this chapter. In addition to the plethora of soft law instruments on sustainable development there are also many international agreements which either explicitly or implicitly proclaim sustainable development such as the climate change agreements and biodiversity agreements. Furthermore, at the 7th UN Open-Ended Informal Consultative Process on Oceans and the Law of the Sea, the G-77 and China countries, through South Africa as 2006 chair of G-77, made a statement implying that sustainable development was a principle of international law, which statement was not challenged from the floor. The statement read, in parts, as follows: 'Thus the norms emanating from sustainable development law, policy and discourse must not be lost on this meeting'. See, indirectly, also the *Advisory Opinion on the Legal Consequences of the Construction of a Wall in the Occupied Palestinian Territory,* 2004 ICJ 131, available at http://www.icj-cij.org (accessed 25 July 2006) para 70 where, in the context of mandates, the court provides that the 'principle that the well-being and development' of peoples is of paramount importance must be borne in mind.

62 The Climate Change and Biodiversity Instruments expressly invoke sustainable development and principles related to sustainable development. See, eg, art 3 Climate Change Convention and art 1 Biodiversity Convention. The GEF was established to support international efforts towards sustainable development. See para 4 of the Instrument for the Establishment of the Restructured GEF (2004). The World Bank has also committed itself towards sustainable development. See for discussion the exchange between Gunther Handl and the then Vice-President and former General Counsel of the Bank, I Shihata 'Correspondence' (1999) 93 *American Journal of International Law* 625.

3.1 The Place of Sustainable Development in International Law

The frequent references to 'international law in the field of sustainable development', 'international law on sustainable development' or even 'international law relating to sustainable development' may suggest that sustainable development may constitute a separate specialised field or subject area of international law in the same way as, for example, international human rights law, international economic law, international humanitarian law or international trade law.[63] Whether sustainable development has developed to that stage is, to say the least, debatable.

To view sustainable development as occupying the position of a specialised subject area of international law would mean that sustainable development becomes 'an umbrella' phrase for a set of principles or norms requiring the integration of environmental, economic and social values. In that sense, sustainable development is more than just a principle, just like human rights and humanitarian law are both more than just principles (to these one can add international trade law, international economic law). There are advantages to treating sustainable development as a separate specialised body of international law. For one thing, as a specialised body of international law, sustainable development law would, arguably, be able to develop its own approaches to the sources where, for example, declarations could acquire a more important role than would be possible in general international law. Although contestable, this seems to be the case with international environmental law.[64]

However, there are doubts as to whether sustainable development can be viewed in this way. Commenting on the name of the ILA Committee on sustainable development, Boyle noted that there really was no 'international law on sustainable development' as sustainable development was not a 'self-contained body of law'.[65] Rather, according to Boyle, what was being studied was the totality

63 See for references to international law in the field of sustainable development, various contributions of P Sands, including Sands (n 18 above) 39. The International Law Association established a committee on 'international law on sustainable development' in 2003.

64 See VP Nanda & G Pring *International environmental law and policy for the 21st century* (2003) 14. Considering this point, D Bodansky *et al* state the following: 'It is suggested that international environmental law has, to a significant degree, become a distinct field – distinct not simply in the sense of addressing a discrete set of problems through a discrete set of substantive rules, - but also in the stronger sense of having its own characteristic structure and processes and its own set of conceptual tools and methodologies'. See D Bodansky *et al* 'Introduction' in D Bodansky *et al* (eds) *Handbook of international environmental law* (forthcoming, 2007).

65 ILA Committee on International Law on Sustainable Development, Working Session Report in ILA *Report of the seventy-first conference* (2004) 608.

of international law in so far as it affected the sustainability of development.[66]

If there is no sustainable development law in international law – that is a separate field of international law relating to sustainable development – could sustainable development be seen as forming part of another field of international law? Sustainable development, seen in this light, could be regarded as a norm or principle (customary or otherwise) of international environmental law.[67] Guruswamy, for instance, suggests that sustainable development has been accepted by the international community as 'the grundnorm' of international environmental law.[68] For that matter, sustainable development may be seen as a principle of international human rights law or international economic law; it may even be regarded as a principle of international development law (if such a field exists). But the point is that sustainable development would not be an autonomous field of international law but a principle within a branch or different branches of international law.

It seems to me that the best approach to understanding the place that sustainable development occupies in international law is to see sustainable development as a principle emanating from the intersection of international human rights law, international economic law and international environmental law.[69] This may mean that sustainable development has to be viewed as a principle of all three fields of international law. Furthermore, to view sustainable development as emanating from the intersection of these three fields of international law would also be consistent with the view of sustainable development as not being bound by any distinct branch or branches of international law, not even the three branches from which sustainable development has developed.

It is the latter view, to which I subscribe, which seems to be supported by the ILA Committee on Sustainable Development. In response to Boyle's comments about sustainable development not being an autonomous branch of international law, Schrijver, the Committee's chair, notes that the name of the ILA Committee on Sustainable Development was chosen purposely to reflect precisely the fact that there was no international sustainable development

66 As above.
67 See, eg Mayeda (n 5 above).
68 LD Guruswamy 'Sustainable agriculture: Do GMOs imperil biosafety?' (2002) 9 *Indiana Journal of Global Legal Studies* 461 463.
69 See eg Principle 27 of the Rio Declaration on Environment and Development. See also M Pallemaerts 'International law and sustainable development: Any progress in Johannesburg' (2003) 12 *Review of European Community and International Environmental Law* 1 6. An argument may even be that international development law (if such a law exists) should also be included in this list. It may, however, be better to view those principles associated with law on development as emanating from human rights law, and in particular the right to development.

law.[70] More to the point, Schrijver suggests that it would not be desirable to have a distinct autonomous branch of international law since sustainable development should be integrated into the *whole of international law*.[71] Over the years sustainable development language has been relied upon in various areas of international law, including water law,[72] treaty law,[73] law relating arms control[74] and trade law[75] amongst many others. Thus, there is support for the view that sustainable development should not be confined to the three branches of international law normally associated with it: international economic law, international environmental law and international human rights law or any other branch of international law.

The accepted view appears to be that, notwithstanding frequent references to 'international law in the field of sustainable development', sustainable development does not constitute a self-standing branch of international law in the same way as, for example, international human rights law or international humanitarian law. It can also, with some confidence, be said that the principle of sustainable development is not confined to any autonomous branch of international law. In the view proposed above, the principle of sustainable development is a principle of general international law in the sense that is intended to apply to and affect all of international law and not just specific areas.[76] Accepting this proposition raises the question, as to the way sustainable development is supposed to affect international law. It is this question to which I turn in the next section.

3.2 The Role of Sustainable Development in International Law

Accepting that sustainable development is a principle of international law not confined to any distinct branch of international law raises the question as to the way in which this principle of law functions (or is

70 ILA Committee on Sustainable Development, Working Session Report (n 60 above) 619.

71 As above (emphasis added).

72 See generally discussion on Helsinki Rules in the ILA Committee on Water Resources Law, Working Session, in ILA *Report of the seventieth conference (New Delhi)* 2002 324 *et seq.*

73 *The Gabcikovo-Nagymaros* case (n 12 above) was essentially a case on a dispute concerning the application of a treaty.

74 See eg *Advisory Opinion on the Legality of the Use or Threat of Use of Nuclear Weapons* 1996 *ICJ* 66. See for discussion Weeramantry (n 3 above) 448.

75 The preamble of the Agreement Establishing the World Trade Organisation refers to sustainable development as an objective.

76 I recognise, of course, that the fields of international law most likely to be affected (and to the greatest extent) by sustainable development will be international human rights law, international economic law and international environmental law. However, sustainable development needs not be confined to these areas and may apply equally to the law of the sea or the law of armed conflict.

supposed to function). Sustainable development could function as a principle of interpretation. On the other hand sustainable development could function as, what is termed by Lowe, an 'interstitial norm'.[77]

Lowe's notion of an interstitial norm is not that dissimilar from Weeramantry's conception of how sustainable development operates, as expounded in the separate opinion in *Gabcikovo-Nagymaros Dam*. According to Judge Weeramantry:[78]

> The problem of steering a course between the needs of development and the necessity to protect the environment is a problem of the law of development and the law of the environment. Both these vital and developing areas of law require, and indeed assume, a principle which harmonises both needs.

This 'principle of reconciliation' is the principle of sustainable development.[79] Thus, sustainable development serves to reconcile the right to development (a principle of international law)[80] with environmental protection (also a principle of international law).[81] According to Vaughan Lowe, sustainable development is a metaphysical principle that acts upon primary rules and principles of international law such as the right to development and environmental protection.[82] Sustainable development, Lowe asserts, is an interstitial norm operating in the interstices of primary norms when they threaten to overlap or conflict.[83] The essence of such interstitial norms is that they 'modify the effect of' primary norms of international law.[84] Weeramantry's position as reflected in the *Gabcikovo-Nagymaros* case is essentially the same, as he suggests that sustainable development operates between environmental protection and development to make them consistent with one another. Mayeda[85] sees Lowe's position as essentially limiting the role of sustainable development to 'simply articulate broader principles in concrete situations'.[86] In other words, according to Mayeda, Lowe regards sustainable development itself not as a principle, but rather as a tool that sets out the boundaries of already existing principles.

A second possibility is to see sustainable development as a principle for the interpretation of treaties. According to Mayeda, this is the role that Sands[87] envisions for sustainable development.[88] The

77 See generally Lowe (n 4 above) and Lowe (n 41 above)
78 *Gabcikovo-Nagymaros* case (Weeramantry's opinion) (n 12 above) 205.
79 As above.
80 As above.
81 *Gabcikovo-Nagymaros* case (Weeramantry's opinion) (n 12 above) 206.
82 See Lowe (n 4 above) 31.
83 As above.
84 Lowe (n 41 above) 213.
85 *Gabcikovo-Nagymaros* case (Weeramantry's opinion) (n 12 above) 205.
86 Mayeda (n 5 above) 37.
87 Sands (n 18 above).
88 Mayeda (n 5 above) 37.

former states that 'sustainable development should not *just* serve to interpret formal treaty obligations', ascribing this minimalist view to Sands.[89] In fairness to Sands, I do not understand this to be his argument. Rather, it seems to me that Sands is concerning himself with a specific problem – the inability or unwillingness of tribunals to use customary international law rules in interpreting treaties. He suggests that one way that principles contained in treaties can be reconciled with customary international law principles (or general principles of law for that matter) would be to use article 31(3)(c) of the Vienna Convention on the Law of Treaties, which requires 'any relevant rules of international law to be taken into account' as a tool for interpreting treaties.[90]

In fact in many ways the two approaches to sustainable development, that sustainable development is an interstitial norm and that it is a principle for interpretation (while not identical) are related. As an interstitial norm, as described by Lowe, sustainable development serves an interpretative function – it (re)interprets the boundaries of the applicable competing primary norms which may emanate from treaties.[91]

While I think that the argument advanced by Sands is not inconsistent with the increased role for sustainable development in international law proposed by Mayeda, I am nevertheless sympathetic to Mayeda's view on the role that sustainable development *should* play in international law. Certainly, sustainable development can function as an interstitial norm.

At the same time sustainable development would be a valuable tool in interpreting treaty law and other norms of international law. It seems that sustainable develop-ment can (and should) play a greater role in international law. If, as suggested in paragraph 3 of chapter 2, sustainable development requires a paradigm shift, then, in terms of international law, it would seem that sustainable development would, in the words of Mayeda, require 'us to rethink the validity of pre-existing' unsustainable principles and, where necessary, 'challenge treaty obligations' that perpetuate unsustainable development.[92]

89 As above (emphasis added).
90 Sands (n 18 above).
91 Lowe (n 4 above) 33.
92 Mayeda (n 5 above) 37.

Very few, I think, would question the desirability of the proposition made above. Some, I think, may question the legal validity of the proposition.[93] However, given the proposition is that sustainable development is a general principle of international law, whether emanating from treaty law, customary international law or general principles in the sense of article 38(1)(c) of the Statute of the International Court of Justice, the notion that sustainable development requires us to 'rethink' and even 'challenge' treaty obligations should not be hard to accept. While the notion that a non-treaty norm can 'challenge' or trump a treaty norm may seem controversial, there is nothing in international law preventing this.[94]

The argument advanced here about the role that sustainable development has to play in international law — that in addition to serving as an interstitial norm and a tool for interpretation it has to force a rethinking and imply a challenging of principles that result in unsustainable practices — has significant implications for the nuanced conceptualisation of sustainable development proposed in chapter 3. It is to this question that I now turn.

3.3 Variations of Sustainable Development, International Law and the Paradigm Shift

Thus far several arguments have been put forward in this study. It was argued in chapter 2 that, as a matter of policy, sustainable development requires a paradigm shift from the business-as-usual approach where economic considerations trump both social and environmental considerations to a paradigm where environmental and social considerations are accorded greater value (both as an objective and as a means). In chapter 3 I suggested that there are at least three

93 I might add that even under the arguments of Lowe, this radical view appears possible, albeit remotely. He states as follows: 'Whether the principle will reach further, time alone will tell. There is certainly scope for it. For example, a tribunal might one day, on the basis of the principle of sustainable development, assume power to modify not only the application of primary norms of customary law but also treaty law'. See Lowe (n 4 above) 36 *et seq*. See also ILA Committee on Sustainable Development stating as follows: 'Though promoting the development of *integration as a judicial reasoning tool* should allow a judicial body to act in a more integrated manner than is currently the case, this should not be taken to require a reductionist approach to problems through the judicial application of some kind of formula or methodology in which rules are modified and misshaped, so that a sustainable outcome is then inevitable'.

94 See for discussion D Tladi & P Dlagnekova 'The will of state, consent and international law: Piercing the veil of positivism' (2006) 21 *SA Public Law* 111. See also Sands (n 18 above) 50 *et seq* commenting on the Institute de Droit's conclusion that while there is 'no *a priori* hierarchy between treaty and custom as sources of international law ... in the application of international law, relevant norms deriving from a treaty will prevail'. Sands comments that *this conclusion* is controversial. He notes further that the statement received support from less than 10 percent of its membership and is therefore 'of dubious authority'. A general reading of Judge Weeramantry's opinion would be consistent with this approach.

variations of sustainable development, namely the environment-centred variation, the economic growth-centred variation and the human needs-centred variation of sustainable development. I must again emphasise that these are variations of *integrating* the three values of sustainable development. In other words, for example, in the economic growth-centred variation of sustainable development, social and environmental concerns are considered, but the primary position is reserved for economic considerations. Finally, it was argued, in this chapter, that sustainable development should, in addition to serving as an interstitial norm and an interpretative tool, facilitate the rethinking and challenging of international law rules (including treaty rules) that perpetuate unsustainable patterns of development.

What do these arguments mean for sustainable development? It seems to me that these arguments, together, would have a significant impact on the understanding of sustainable development in international law. If the purpose of sustainable development is to effect a paradigm shift in international policy and the role of sustainable development in international law is to facilitate the very same paradigm shift, then international law must recognise a variation of sustainable development that is consistent with the paradigm shift argued for.

It would appear that, in the final analysis, the economic growth-centred variation, which places economic considerations at the centre, would pull in the opposite direction of such a paradigm shift. In that sense the economic growth-centred variation of sustainable development would represent the business-as-usual approach, generally seen as unsustainable development.[95] If, in the words of Mayeda, sustainable development (whether as a policy or legal principle) requires us to 'rethink the validity'[96] of the unsustainable business-as-usual approach, in terms of which economic growth trumps environmental and social considerations, then adopting the economic growth-centred variation of sustainable development has the effect of simply dressing the emperor in new clothes. The economic growth variation of sustainable development, by reflecting the *status quo,* is not consistent with the paradigm shift required by sustainable development and can thus not form the basis of an international law principle of sustainable development.

In some sense, the call of sustainable development to 'to rethink' legal principles that allow or promote unsustainable patterns of development requires the variation of sustainable development adopted

95 See generally discussion under para 3.1 in ch 3 above.
96 Mayeda (n 5 above) 37.

to be a variation of 'strong' sustainable development.[97] Both the human needs-centred variation and environment centred variations of sustainable development, in my view, respond to this call for 'strong' sustainable development while the economic growth-centred variation, by hanging on to a paradigm that elevates economic concerns over both environmental and social concerns (the business-as-usual scenario) represents weak sustainable develop-ment. This view of sustainable development is buttressed by an analysis of the key instruments of sustainable development.[98] In the analysis in Chapters two and three above I illustrate how the main concerns in those instruments, with the possible exception of the Rio Declaration, are poverty alleviation and environmental protection.

4. Conclusion

Although both the status and role of sustainable development in international law are hotly contested, it is argued here that sustainable development is a principle of international law with an important role to play in the development of the international legal system. The role of sustainable development in international law is to facilitate the paradigm shift referred to in chapter 2, from a paradigm where economic concerns trump environmental and social concerns to a paradigm where environmental and social concerns are effectively integrated.

If the role of sustainable development is to facilitate the paradigm shift as suggested, then the variation of sustainable development supported by international law has to reflect the values called for in this paradigm shift. Given the similarity between the 'business-as-usual' approach and the economic growth-centred variation of sustainable development, the latter cannot be supported as a basis for international law on sustainable development. This has significant implications for the design of instruments under international law in a framework of sustainable development. It means that, in the design of legal instruments, states should ensure that economic considerations are not given weight greater than social and environmental concerns. The implications of this chapter, when considered in the light of chapters 2 and 3, are also that international legal instruments that perpetuate the dominance of economic values over social and environmental concerns may have to be reconsidered.

97 On the juxtaposition of 'strong' and 'weak' sustainable development see ch 3 above. See also D Tladi 'Strong sustainable development, weak sustainable development and the Earth Charter: Towards a more nuanced framework analysis' (2004) 11 *South African Journal of Environmental Law and Policy* 17.

98 See for discussion, chs 2 and 3 above.

PART B: ANALYTICAL TECHNIQUES IN SUSTAINABLE DEVELOPMENT

Introductory remarks to Part B

Climate change and the alarming rate of biodiversity loss are two of the most serious global environmental problems. The legal regimes designed to combat these environmental problems were given birth to at the Rio Conference, in the form of the United Nations Framework Convention on Climate Change and the Biodiversity Convention. These two conventions, along with their protocols, are considered in chapters 5 and 6 respectively. In addition to the climate change and biodiversity regimes the Global Environment Facility (GEF), the mechanism through which financial and technological resources are transferred under climate change and biodiversity regimes, is considered in chapter 7 of the study.

In Part B, the instruments mentioned above, such as the climate change regime, biodiversity regime and the GEF, are analysed in the context of the conceptualisation of sustainable development proposed in Part A. The primary aim of Part B is, therefore, to determine the variation of sustainable development each of these instruments reflects. To determine which variation of sustainable development best reflects a particular instrument, the key question is which of the three values of sustainable development occupy a priority position. In particular, we seek to establish the kinds of compromises and trade-offs between the values of sustainable development in each of the instruments. In particular we ask how conflicts are resolved in cases of tension between various values and what kinds of compromises and trade-offs are made in the integration process. To assist in the analysis of the kinds of compromises that are made in the respective regimes we ask the following questions posed in chapter three, namely:

(i) to what extent do choices made in these regimes show a willingness to sacrifice economic growth concerns for the sake of environmental and/or social concerns;
(ii) to what extent do the choices made in these regimes show a willingness to sacrifice environmental concerns for the sake of economic and/or social concerns; and
(iii) to what extent do the choices made in there relevant regimes show a willingness to sacrifice social concerns for the sake of economic and/or environmental concerns.

In addition to these questions, I also identify in chapter 3 various characteristics that could be associated with each of these variations of sustainable development. Thus, for example, whether the instruments are characterised by strict environmental regulation that would *suggest* that the particular regime reflects an environment-centred variation of sustainable development. Similarly, a strong reliance on market mechanisms would *possibly* imply that the regime reflects an economic growth centred variation of sustainable development. An emphasis on redistributive policies to effect poverty alleviation *may* suggest that the regime reflects a social well-being-centred variation of sustainable development. What is important to note, however, is that these are but factors that must together be taken into account to arrive at a determination. The presence of one factor will not be conclusive as to the nature of integration or the variation of sustainable development reflected in the particular regimes. Thus, for example, the mere fact that the Kyoto Protocol includes market mechanisms as a means for meeting the obligations under the Protocol does not, in and of itself, justify the conclusion that the regime reflects an economic growth-centred variation. This fact would have to balanced with other factors in the climate change regime, such as the strong emphasis on the common but differentiated principle.

A few words must be said about the structure of the chapters in Part B. The first structural point that must be made is that in some way the chapters are symmetrical. Given that GEF is not aimed at a specific environmental problem the symmetry is less pronounced in that chapter. Nevertheless, all three chapters begin with a general introduction followed by a discussion of the background giving rise to the particular instrument. In the chapter on climate change this background discussion focuses on the problem of climate change as well as the interests and countervailing interests making consensus in regime building difficult. Similarly, the background section in the chapter on biodiversity considers the scientific, environmental and social problems as well the dilemmas facing negotiators. In the chapter on the GEF the background focuses on the problems experienced in the initial attempts at structuring the GEF (pilot phase) as well as the difficulties in restructuring the GEF.

After the background discussion all three chapters move on to consider the relevant provisions to be analysed. In these sections the provisions are only described and are not analysed. Thus, the relevant provisions of the climate change, biodiversity and GEF instruments are recounted without much analysis. In the chapters on climate change and biodiversity regimes the sections recounting the relevant provisions begin with a brief discussion of the provisions of the framework conventions adopted at the Rio Conference, such as the UN Framework Convention on Climate Change (chapter 5) and the Biodiversity Convention (chapter 6). In the GEF chapter, chapter 7, the descriptive section focuses on two key aspects of GEF law, the provisions in the GEF instrument relating to 'incremental costs' and 'global environment benefit'. The aim in these sections, in all three chapters, is simply to elucidate the provisions. In the following section the provisions are then analysed in the light of the framework provided in Part A. It is in these sections where the provisions described in the previous sections are tested against the variations of sustainable development. Finally, some concluding remarks are given.

The second point that must be made about the structure is that, while they are symmetrical, there are also differences in approaches owing to the nature of the instruments. Each chapter focuses on the aspects of the instruments that give the regime their particular character. For climate change the focus falls on the flexible mechanisms while for the biodiversity regime the focus falls on the provisions having an impact on trade, such as the Advance Informed Procedure as well as the decision-making procedures. Further, in both chapters aspects relating intragenerational equity such as the CBD (in climate change) and benefit sharing (in biodiversity), are considered. In the GEF, given the complex institutional structure and the importance of both the climate change and biodiversity regimes in this complex structure, the focus is on the evolution of the funding requirement under the GEF owing to the interplay between the GEF and the Conference of the Parties. More importantly, as mentioned in paragraph 3 of chapter 1, the GEF represents an intersection where all the climate change and biodiversity regimes come together under an institutional framework.

5

Role of Sustainable Development in Fighting Climate Change

'If we do not act soon, it is our children and children's children who will have to pay the price'.[1]

1. Introduction

The Kyoto Protocol to the United Nations Convention on Climate Change (the 'Kyoto Protocol') is the world's response to the climate change problem.[2] In this chapter I consider the climate change regime, and in particular the Kyoto Protocol as the basic text of the regime to combat climate change. Although the emphasis falls on the Kyoto Protocol, attention is also paid to the United Nations Framework Conventions on Climate Change (Climate Change Convention or UNFCCC).[3] Specifically, given that the regime is developed to give effect to sustainable development, I consider the extent to which the regime, and the Kyoto Protocol in particular, gives effect to sustainable development.[4] In undertaking the analysis here, I am mindful of the underlying assumption in this study, namely that sustainable development was developed to affect a paradigm shift. My analysis, thus, must contribute to determining whether, and the extent to which, the climate change regime reflects or contributes towards such a paradigm shift.

The analysis in this chapter draws heavily on the framework developed in Part A of the study. The insights obtained from this analysis will contribute to a better understanding of the role of sustainable development in international law. In this context the main aim of this chapter is to characterise the climate change regime, with

1 Quote from the film on the potential consequences of climate change, *The Day After Tomorrow*, 20th Century Fox (2004).

2 Kyoto Protocol to the United Nations Framework Convention on Climate Change (1998) 37 *ILM* 22 available at http://unfccc.int/resource/docs/convkp/kpeng.pdf (accessed on 19 February 2002) (1997). The text of the Protocol is reproduced in P Cullet & A Gowlland-Gualtieri (eds) *Key materials in international environmental Law* (2004). The Protocol came into force on 16 February 2005.

3 The United Nations Framework Convention on Climate Change (1992) 31 *ILM* 851.

4 The UNFCCC, for example, invokes inter- and intragenerational equity, the precautionary principle and integration in Principle 3. See also the Joint Declaration of the Heads of State and/or Government of Brazil, China, India, Mexico and South Africa participating in the G8 Gleneagles Summit, where the respective states declare in para 12 that the UNFCCC and the Kyoto Protocol 'establish a regime that adequately addresses the economic, social and environmental aspects of sustainable development'. The declaration is available at http://www.indianembassy.org/press_release/2005/July/5.htm (accessed 5 September 2005).

specific reference to the Kyoto Protocol, in terms of the variations of sustainable development identified in chapter 3.

In the next section of the chapter I briefly set out the climate change problem. In particular I look at the science of climate change and the different interests, claims and counter-claims that have influenced the negotiation and design of the climate change regime. In section three of the chapter I describe the various provisions of the climate change instruments with a special focus on the Kyoto Protocol. I also consider documents and decisions adopted under the regime. Then, in section four, I analyse the regime in the light of the text of the Protocol and documents flowing from the regime in order to determine which variation of sustainable development the regime can be said to approximate.

2. The climate change problem

2.1 Background to Climate Change and the Development of the Regime

The problem of climate change is quite complex, especially for a non-natural scientist.[5] A large body of literature has been produced on climate change, most of which gives a brief explanation of the science of climate change.[6] Based on these and other works, I summarise climate change. Climate change is caused by the emission of greenhouse gases that increase the greenhouse effect. One of the complexities of climate change arises from the fact that not only is the greenhouse effect a natural phenomenon but it is also important for life on earth.[7]

5 See TM Franck *Fairness in international law and institutions* (1995) 387 who states as follows: 'Compared to the Ozone depletion problem, the threat of global warming or 'greenhouse effect' is considerably more complex'.

6 See P Hayes & K Smith *The global greenhouse regime: who pays?* (1993); O Kuik, P Peters & N Schrijver (eds) *Joint implementation to curb climate change: Legal and economic aspects* (1994); RS Maya & J Gupta (eds) *Joint implementation: Carbon colonies or business opportunities? Weighing the odds in an information vacuum* (1996); P Taylor *An ecological approach to international law: Responding to challenges of climate change* (1998); E Hey 'The climate change regime: An enviro-economic problem and international administrative law in the making' (2001) 1 *International Environmental Agreements: Politics, Law and Economics* 75; A Markandya & K Halsnaes *Climate change and sustainable development* (2002); M Bothe 'The United Nations Framework Convention on Climate Change – An unprecedented multilevel regulatory challenge' (2003) 63 *Heidelberg Journal of International Law* 239.

7 Bothe (n 6 above) 239; Hey (n 6 above) 77. See also C Breidenich *et al* 'The Kyoto Protocol to the United Nations Framework Convention on Climate Change' (1998) 92 *American Journal of International Law* 315 316

The naturally-occurring greenhouse effect can be described as follows: Small amounts of trace greenhouse gases[8] are present in the earth's atmosphere.[9] These gases allow the sunlight's rays (short wave radiation) through thus warming the earth's surface.[10] However, these gases absorb heat radiated by the earth, acting as a heat trap.[11] This naturally occurring greenhouse effect maintains the earth's climate at a level which makes it possible for life on earth to exist. It is said that in the absence of these gases the mean temperature of the earth's surface would be 33 degrees Celsius lower than it is today.[12]

However, due to certain human activities this phenomenon that makes life on earth possible has been turned into a threat to the existence of the very life it serves to protect.[13] Various human activities related to the combustion of fossil fuels, such as the increase of vehicles on our roads and the reliance on electricity, have resulted in the increased concentration of greenhouse gases in the lower levels of the atmosphere.[14] The main greenhouse gas, carbon dioxide, is emitted principally from the combustion of fossil fuels and industrial processes.[15] The Intergovernmental Panel on Climate Change (IPCC) has concluded that carbon dioxide is 'responsible for over half the *enhanced greenhouse effect*'.[16] According to some estimates, the burning of fossil fuels contributes 73 per cent of total carbon dioxide emissions.[17] Thus, the carbon cycle plays a central role in the science of climate change.[18]

Human activities increasing the concentration of greenhouse gases include the use of energy,[19] industrial activity,[20] agriculture,[21]

8 The most notable greenhouse gases include carbon dioxide, methane, nitrous oxide, halocarbons and chlorofluorocarbons.

9 Taylor (n 6 above) 10.

10 As above. See also N Mabey *et al* (eds) *Argument in the greenhouse: The international economics of controlling global warming* (1997) 4.

11 As above.

12 Mabey *et al* (n 10 above) 5.

13 Breidenich *et al* (n 7 above) 316.

14 Hey (n 6 above) 77.

15 As above.

16 IPCC *Climate change 1995: Impacts, adaptation and mitigation of climate change: Scientific technical analysis — Contribution of Working Group II to the second assessment report of the IPCC* (1995) quoted in Taylor (n 6 above) 12 (emphasis original).

17 Taylor (n 6 above) 12.

18 The carbon cycle refers to the exchange of carbon between various media such as the biosphere, atmosphere, oceans and geosphere. Often this is a two-way process. However, with anthropocentric emissions of greenhouse gases, the movement of carbon is one way, from industries etc to the atmosphere. See for discussion 'Exploring the environment: Earth on fire' available at http://www.cet.edu/ete/modules/carbon/efcarbon.html (accessed 15 July 2006)

19 Coal production results in the emission of carbon dioxide and methane. In addition to the two greenhouse gases emitted during the production of coal, the combustion of coal, oil and gas results in the emission of nitrous oxide.

20 Including cement manufacture, use of CFC's and landfills.

21 Including wet rice cultivation, fertiliser use and biomass combustion.

deforestation and land use change (destruction of 'sinks').[22] The increased concentration of greenhouse gases threatens to change the climate with adverse effects for the environment and our society that is dependent on that environment. It is generally agreed that this global change in climatic patterns will lead to an increase in the frequency and intensity of climate-related natural disasters such as flooding, droughts, loss of biodiversity, desertification where it does not naturally occur, the spread of diseases such as malaria, shortages of water supply and the rising of the sea level which could result in the flooding and subsequent disappearance of small islands.[23] Other possible effects of climate change include harsher winter weather in some regions, reduced soil moisture, and a negative impact on food production.[24] The IPCC has noted that changes in the global climate pattern have already had discernible impacts.[25]

The possibility of carbon dioxide affecting the global climate system was first noted by scientists in the 1970s.[26] The movement towards international regulation of the climate change problem, however, gained momentum in the late 1980s. The first official action towards understanding the climate change problem and, consequently, some international regulation, came in 1988 with the establishment of the IPCC by UNEP and the World Meteorological Organisation (WMO).[27] At the time of the creation of the IPCC there was much scientific uncertainty, not only with respect to the causes and effects of climate change, but also with respect to the very existence of the problem. Throughout its existence the IPCC has produced reports on climate change that have served to strengthen the case for global action to mitigate or reduce the impact of climate change.

22 Mabey *et al* (n 10 above) 6. See also O Kuik & J Gupta 'Perspectives on Africa and the global debate on Joint Implementation' in Maya & Gupta (n 6 above) 2.

23 See Hey (n 6 above); L Thoms 'A comparative analysis of international regimes on ozone and climate change with implications for regime design' (2003) 41 *Columbia Journal of Transnational Law* 795 812. Hurricane Katrina, reportedly the worst natural disaster to hit the United States, has been blamed in various news publications, at least partly, on climate change. See G Barry 'Hurricane Katrina and catastrophic climate change: Deadly storm provides vision of human family's future' available at http://earthmeanders.blogspot.com/2005/08/hurricane-katrina-and-catastrophic.html (accessed on 1 December 2005); See also R Gelbspan 'Katrina's real name' available at http://www.boston.com/news/globe/editorial_opinion/oped/articles/2005/08/30/katrinas_real_name/ (accessed on 1 December 2005).

24 P Schwartz & D Randall *An abrupt climate change scenario and its implications for the United States national security* (2003) (A report prepared for the Pentagon).

25 IPCC *Climate change 2001: Impacts, adaptation, vulnerability* (2001) available at http://www.grida.no/climate/ipcc_tar/wg2/index.htm (accessed 19 February 2004).

26 Thoms (n 23 above) 812.

27 See Mabey *et al* (n 10 above) 9; Thoms (n 23 above) 813; Taylor (n 6 above) 9.

In 1990 the United Nations General Assembly established the Intergovernmental Negotiating Committee for a framework convention.[28] The Committee negotiated and drafted the United Nations Framework Convention on Climate Change which was adopted at the Rio Conference and entered into force in 1994. In 1997 the parties to the Framework Convention adopted the Kyoto Protocol which established legally binding limits for emissions in developed countries and countries with economies in transition. The Kyoto Protocol not only establishes legally binding emissions limits for developed countries, it also creates, as a means of achieving emissions reduction, flexible mechanisms, namely, the so-called bubble,[29] joint implementation (JI),[30] the clean development mechanism (CDM)[31] and emissions trading.[32] It is these flexible mechanisms that give the Protocol its character and, for that reason, form the core of the analysis.[33] More importantly, the flexible mechanisms, by seeking to solve an environmental problem through the use of economic instruments, provide a prism through which the integration of values of sustainable development can be studied. Further, as will be discussed below, these mechanisms also involve developing countries with no reduction commitments and, in this way, North-South questions, which are so central to sustainable development, are implicated.

2.2 Interests and Countervailing Interests: A Note on the Negotiating Hurdles in Climate Change Regime Building

To understand the various arguments put forward for the inclusion of flexible mechanisms in the climate change regime one has to understand the various interests and conflicting interests involved in the attempts at climate change mitigation. The interests in curbing climate change are relatively obvious. The various scenarios forecast

28 Hey (n 6 above) 79.
29 Art 4 Kyoto Protocol.
30 Art 6 Kyoto Protocol.
31 Art 12 Kyoto Protocol.
32 Art 17 Kyoto Protocol.
33 In considering the Kyoto Protocol I chose, for the reasons outlined above, the flexible mechanisms as the focus of analysis. There are different ways that one can choose to analyse this complex instrument designed for an equally complex problem. Hey (n 6 above) eg chose to focus on the institutional aspects of the Protocol while Thoms (n 23 above) chose to juxtapose the Protocol with the Ozone regime. J Brunnée 'The Kyoto Protocol: Testing grounds for compliance theories' (2003) 63 *Heidelberg Journal of International Law* 255 uses compliance theories as a platform for analysis of the regulatory framework established to curb climate change. An equally different and valid used approach to analyse the climate change debate is that of Taylor (n 6 above) who uses traditional state sovereignty based principles of international law to test whether these can be sufficient to avoid climate change.

will have detrimental consequences for the environment and for humanity.[34] In addition to the environmental and social costs, climate change carries with it added economic burdens. As Hey observes, the failure of the world to curb climate change could require numerous countries to make economic investments to counter the impact of climate change.[35] In particular, Hey observes, small island developing states will have to make significant economic investments to protect their territories.[36]

There are, however, countervailing economic and social interests militating against climate change regulation.[37] Human society's economy and lifestyle are driven by the burning of fossil fuels and other processes that produce greenhouse gases.[38] We are a fossil fuel-based society. Think of everyday activities that humans engage in: a large percentage of those activities probably results in the emission of greenhouse gases in some way.[39] Thus, any attempt at regulating the emissions of greenhouse gases has the potential to have negative consequences for multiple sectors of the global economy.[40] As Thoms notes:[41]

> The most problematic characteristic of the climate change problem is that it has implications for multiple sectors of the economy that go to the heart of industrialised society ... required emissions reduction for one greenhouse gas (carbon dioxide) would impose economic loss worldwide on industries involved in the supply of fossil fuels, the production of energy, and the use of energy intensive production processes.

This further implies that any attempt to regulate climate change will involve large costs.[42] The big question in climate change negotiation is how these costs are to be allocated.[43]

34 Bothe (n 6 above) 243.
35 Hey (n 6 above) 79.
36 As above.
37 For a very useful sketch of the operation of these push and pull factors see Hey (n 6 above) 78 *et seq*. See also Franck (n 5 above) 387 *et seq*.
38 Hey (n 6 above) 78.
39 Bothe (n 6 above) 244 adds: '[t] here is also a countervailing social interest: the interest in maintaining a lifestyle based on high energy consumption'.
40 Thoms (n 23 above) 812; Bothe (n 6 above) 244.
41 Thoms (n 23 above) 824.
42 Taylor (n 6 above) 23.
43 Hey (n 6 above) 78.

Invariably North-South issues dominate discussions on climate change regime building.[44] The climate change problem results primarily from the path of industrialisation travelled by the developed world. These countries have in the past contributed, by far, the greatest percentage of greenhouse gas emissions. Truth be told, these countries continue to emit a much larger percentage of greenhouse gases into the earth's atmosphere.[45] Hey asserts that both:[46]

> in absolute terms and in per capita terms industrialised countries are the largest emitters of greenhouse gases ... Furthermore under the business-as-usual scenarios emissions levels were expected to rise in industrialised countries.

Statistically, industrialised countries were since 1800 responsible for over 80 per cent of industrial carbon dioxide emissions.[47] This serious disparity in the global level of pollution of the earth's atmosphere is, furthermore, responsible for the 'heavily skewed distribution of wealth in favour of the' developed nations.[48] Developing countries have thus argued that it would be inequitable to expect them to halt their progress to 'development' now that developed countries have achieved their economic development from environmentally destructive activities.

The essence of the argument from the South is aptly captured by Drumbl:[49]

> Industrialised nations have attained their current level of development largely by imposing externalised costs on the global environment. Now that consensus has emerged that the planet no longer can withstand many of these externalities or has hit some sort of tipping point, considerable Southern skepticism attaches to the Northern suggestion that everyone must mitigate these externalities, including those not responsible for creating the problem in the first place. There is thus an element of moral coherence to the developing world's skepticism.[50]

44 In addition to the literature cited above, see F Yamin *et al* 'Kyoto mechanisms: Key issues for policy makers for COP 6' (2001) 1 *International Environmental Agreements: Politics, Law and Economics* 187; C Kemfert & R Tol 'Equity, international trade and climate policy' (2002) 2 *International Environmental Agreements: Politics, Law and Economics* 23; P Bohm 'Improving cost-effectiveness and facilitating participation of developing countries in international emissions trading' (2002) 2 *International Environmental Agreements: Politics, Law and Economics* 261; J Pan 'Emissions Rights and their transferability: Equity concerns over climate change mitigation' (2003) 3 *International Environmental Agreements: Politics, Law and Economics* 1.

45 Hey (n 6 above) 78. See also Kuik & Gupta (n 22 above) 4.

46 Hey (n 6 above) 78 at endnote 9, citing Oberthur & Ott *The Kyoto Protocol: International climate policy for the 21st century* (1999).

47 As above. See also Taylor (n 6 above) 23.

48 Kuik & Gupta (n 22 above) 2.

49 M Drumbl 'Northern economic obligation, Southern moral entitlement, and international environmental governance' (2002) 27 *Columbia Journal of Environmental Law* 363.

50 As above 366.

This disparity in contribution to the climate change problem leads to calls for developed countries to bear the costs related to the prevention or mitigation of climate change. These calls are further strengthened by the fact that developed countries are, because of the 'skewed distribution of wealth', in a better position to finance costs associated with climate change mitigation.[51] In essence the question that developing countries ask is why they must bear the costs when the benefits accrued only to developed countries? This moral argument encapsulates the rationale underlying the common but differentiated principle, that the rich countries primarily bear the costs for climate change alleviation both because they are primarily responsible for climate change and also because they are more financially and technological capable of doing so.[52]

However, as noted by several authors, this simple illustration of cost allocation is complicated by the fact there are indications that the emissions of developing countries are on the rise.[53] Thoms notes that the 'IPCC expects greenhouse gases from developing countries to exceed those from industrialised nations sometime between 2015 and 2020'.[54] This therefore means that developing nations must also play some role in attempts at preventing or mitigating climate change. As Kuik and Gupta note, to deal with the climate change problem effectively there has to be some co-operation between those who are responsible for the problem and those 'who in fact suffered economic

51 See K Smith *et al* 'Who pays (to solve the problem and how much)?' in Hayes & Smith (n 6 above) 80 showing a table that illustrates a strong correlation between the ability to pay for climate change abatement and the responsibility for the climate change problem.

52 See Principle 7 Rio Declaration. See, however, CD Stone 'Common but differentiated principle in international law' (2004) 98 *American Journal of International Law* 276 who dismisses both rationales. Although Stone's argument is addressed in para 2.2 of ch 3, it is worthwhile briefly to recall the issues here: Stone (292), in setting out his rejection of the rationale based on harm caused – that developed countries historically and presently have been responsible for the majority of greenhouse gas emissions – says the following: 'For one thing, it is not clear why a contemporary US citizen should make amends for the overuse of the global commons during a stretch before her forebears had immigrated'. Of course this reasoning, as is the case with much of Stone's reasoning in the article, is misplaced because it is not the individual nationals of the state (the United States in Stone's example) but the state who is responsible. The common but differentiated responsibilities principle is directed at states and not individual nationals within the state.

53 See Thoms (n 23 above) 822. Hey (n 6 above) 78 who states as follows: 'If greenhouse gas emissions are to be reduced developing countries will not be able to pursue development under the business-as-usual scenarios'.

54 Thoms (n 23 above) 822; Taylor (n 6 above) 24. See also Hey (n 6 above) at endnote 11, citing Oberthur & Ott (n 46 above) stating that carbon dioxide emissions from some developing countries such as India and China were already 'considerable' in 1990. For example, she adds that carbon dioxide emissions from China were expected to double by 2010. Although the literature is quite clear that emissions of developing countries will exceed those of developed countries by 2020, I think it is equally clear (although not expressly discussed in literature) that this refers to overall emissions and not *per capita* emissions.

disadvantage during the era of 'climate pollution'.[55] To curb climate change effectively we must not only seek to reverse the ongoing polluting behaviour in the North but we must also prevent 'new polluting behaviour from emerging' in the developing world.[56] Similarly, Thoms argues that an effective climate regime must include developing countries who are, with reason, 'reluctant to curb economic development for an environmental problem' caused by developed countries. The idea that developing countries must be part of any effective regime designed to curb climate change arises also from the global nature of climate change.[57]

However, the dichotomy between developed and developing countries is not the only one relevant for an analysis of the climate change regime. At the heart of climate change rests an attempt to improve energy efficiency and to switch from fossil-based to non-fossil-based fuels.[58] From an economic standpoint this creates a further dichotomy between those countries that are net importers of fossil fuels such as oil, and those that produce oil and consequently export oil.[59] The former are keen to see a reduction of consumption and reliance on fossil fuel while, for the latter a reduction in the consumption of fossil fuels will mean less revenue.[60]

A further dichotomy, related to the developed-developing world dichotomy, flowing from climate change regime building is that emissions of climate affecting gases and 'vulnerability to [effects of] climate change show a strong negative correlation'.[61] In other words, those primarily responsible for climate change are likely to suffer less than those not responsible. This is due to various reasons, including geographical location, for example in the case of small island states, and the ability to adapt.[62] The IPCC, for example, has made the following observations:[63]

55 Kuik & Gupta (n 22 above) 2.
56 Drumbl (n 49 above) 367.
57 Thoms (n 23 above) 798.
58 Hey (n 6 above) 79. See also generally T Marahun 'A global energy strategy as a viable means for redressing climate change?' (2003) 63 *Heidelberg Journal of International Law* 281.
59 See Hey (n 6 above) 79.
60 As above. See also Taylor (n 6 above) 23.
61 Kemfert & Tol (n 44 above) 23. See also J Gupta 'Contribution to the ILA report on integration in sustainable development through interlinkages with other international treaties' (on file with author). This is borne out by various scientific models on the likely impacts of climate change. These show that the poorer regions are likely to suffer more if climate change is not mitigated. See eg IPCC (n 25 above). See also Schwartz & Randall (n 24 above) although the latter indicate that the negative consequences in poorer regions could affect those not as harshly affected.
62 See generally JB Wiener 'Global environmental regulation: Instrument choice in legal context' in T Tientenberg (ed) *Emissions trading programs: Volume I* 2001 reprinted from 1999 *Yale Law Journal* 677 698. See also Thoms (n 23 above) 824.
63 IPCC (n 25 above) 8.

> The ability of humans to adapt to and cope with climate change depends on such factors as wealth, technology, education, information, skills, infrastructure ... Least developed countries are, generally poorest in this regard. As a result they have lesser capacity to adapt and they are more vulnerable to climate change, just as they are more vulnerable to other stresses.

Others, especially in the past, have also argued that the perception by some states that climate change could be beneficial, could be a complicating factor.[64] But the global nature of climate change requires that efforts towards preventing climate change be global. Another problem, which discourages universal participation in a regime designed to curb climate change is the free rider problem.[65] In explaining the difficulties of such free riding in global regimes Wiener notes that:[66]

> If a thick stratospheric ozone layer or a comfortable climate is provided, no one on the planet can be excluded from its effect; once the ozone thins or the climate changes, everyone is affected to some degree ... As a result the individual is likely to receive only a tiny fraction of the global benefits of her abatement efforts.

All of the above issues indicate the magnitude of the complexities involved in climate change regime building. These interests and countervailing interests further reflect the difficulties in identifying an efficient and fair response to the climate change problem.[67] These complexities should be borne in mind in analysing the instruments developed to deal with climate change policies. In developing the regime the negotiators, while recognising the importance of reducing greenhouse gas emissions, also had to deal with these complexities.

3. The climate change regime: An analysis of Kyoto

3.1 Principles in the UNFCCC: Paving the Way for Kyoto

The United Nations Framework Convention on Climate Change, adopted at the Rio Conference, provides an example of what is meant by a framework convention. While it contains few (and soft) substantive commitments it does contain the basic principles and objectives upon which more and 'harder' obligations can be negotiated. In addition to the basic principles, the UNFCCC lays down the institutional rules of the game.[68] These basic principles form the

64 See Hey (n 6 above) 79 citing Oberthur & Ott (n 46 above). See also Taylor (n 6 above) 23 who notes that a UNEP study indicates that 1.5 degrees Celsius temperature increase in Russia could mean a 30 per cent increase in wheat yield. See further Thoms (n 23 above) 824.

65 See Wiener (n 62 above) 690. See also Thoms (n 23 above) 799.

66 See Wiener (n 62 above) 690 *et seq*. See also Thoms (n 23 above) 799.

67 Franck (n 5 above) 387.

68 Hey (n 6 above) 83.

basis of the climate change regime and, thus, play a significant role in the analysis of the regime.

Article 2 of the Convention sets out the objective of the treaty, namely, the 'stabilisation of greenhouse gas concentrations at a level that would prevent dangerous interference with the climate system'. Article 3 of the UNFCC contains basic principles such as inter-generational equity,[69] intragenerational equity,[70] the pre-cautionary principle[71] and the principle of integration.[72]

The Climate Change Convention was established in the midst of some scientific uncertainty. The uncertainty related to various aspects including the impact of anthropogenic emissions of greenhouse gases on climate change, the long-term effects and even the very existence of climate change. Given this uncertainty the climate change regime is built on precaution. Article 3(3) of the Climate Change Convention, to this end, calls on parties to 'take pre-cautionary measures to anticipate, prevent or minimise the causes of climate change'. The precautionary principle in the climate change regime is considered further below.

Article 4 of the UNFCCC spells out commitments that state parties undertake. Reflecting the developed/developing world debate highlighted above, article 4 provides different commitments for different categories of state parties. First, for all states, article 4 declares general (and very soft) commitments such as, *inter alia,* the commitment to develop and update national inventories of anthropogenic emissions,[73] formulate national programmes con-taining measures to mitigate climate change[74] and the commitment to take climate change considerations into account in social, economic and environmental policies.[75]

The climate change convention creates further obligations for Annex II states (developed countries) and Annex I (developed countries and countries with economies in transition). Annex II states commit themselves, in addition to the general commitments, to provide new and additional financial resources to meet the agreed full costs incurred by non-Annex I parties in complying with their obligations under the Convention[76] and to assist developing countries in meeting costs associated with adaptation to climate change.[77]

69 Art 3(1) UNFCCC.
70 Arts 3(1) and 3(2) UNFCCC.
71 Art 3(3) UNFCCC.
72 Art 3(4) UNFCCC.
73 Art 4(1)(a) UNFCCC.
74 Art 4(1)(b) UNFCCC.
75 Art 4(1)(f) UNFCCC.
76 Art 4(3) UNFCCC.
77 Art 4(4) UNFCCC.

For the purposes of our analysis, article 4(2) of the Convention is perhaps the most important. It provides, in part, that Annex I countries commit themselves to adopt measures and policies 'with the aim of returning individually or jointly to their 1990' levels of greenhouse gas emissions by the year 2000.[78]

Two points are worth emphasising regarding article 4(2) of the Convention. First, by placing the general obligation to reduce greenhouse gas emissions on Annex I countries and not including developing countries, the Convention adopts the so-called 'North-first' approach and responds to the arguments of developing countries outlined above. However, the general (softer) commitments placed on all states make it clear that even though developed states will take the lead in curbing climate change, the solution of the climate change problem requires global action. Second, article 4(2)(b), by adding 'individually or jointly',[79] opened up the possibility of co-operative action as a means of achieving the objectives of the convention.

The second point also has implications for the North-South's roles in curbing climate change. Although initially intended to operate only between developed countries, the Conference of the Parties (COP) decided to sanction the application of joint implementation projects between developed and developing countries.[80] Thus, joint implementation between developed and developing states allows a developed country to seek credit towards its own obligations by investing in greenhouse gas emission reductions in a developing state.[81] It is important when considering joint implementation, and indeed any of the other flexible mechanisms established under the climate change regime, to understand the rationale. The rationale is cost-effectiveness. It has been observed that it is cheaper to reduce greenhouse emissions in developing countries than it is to do so in developed countries, largely because of the disparity in technologies available between developed and developing countries.[82]

In addition to the North-first approach reflected in article 4(2), the UNFCCC contains several other (re)distributive provisions designed to benefit developing countries.[83] The first provision to take note of in this context is article 3. Article 3 provides that in meeting the objectives of the Convention, namely 'the stabilisation of greenhouse gas concentrations' at levels that would prevent

78 Art 4(2)(a) and (b) UNFCCC.

79 Art 4(2)(a) provides that the parties 'may implement such policies and measures jointly with other parties'.

80 Report of COP 1 Decision 5 FCCC/CP/1995/7/Add.1.

81 Maya & Gupta (n 6 above) at ix; Hey (n 6 above).

82 Kuik *et al* (n 6 above) xii. See also Bothe (n 6 above) 245.

83 See generally Franck (n 5 above) 392 who says that while the UNFCCC may not be 'particularly explicit on environmental standards, it does put in place significant fairness-based concepts'. More explicitly, Franck suggests that the Convention 'commits parties to redistributive outcomes'.

dangerous interference with the climate system, the Parties should be guided by, *inter alia*, 'their common but differentiated responsibilities'.[84] Article 3 further provides that the 'specific needs and special circumstances of developing' countries should be taken into account.[85] The Convention provides parties with 'a right to ... sustainable development' taking into account that 'economic development is essential for adopting measures to address climate change'.[86] Moreover, the Convention provides for the needs of specific classes of countries to be taken into account. In this respect, the needs of Small island states, countries with low lying coastal areas, countries with areas prone to natural disasters, amongst others, are to be given special consideration.[87] However, it is noteworthy that the list of countries in article 4(8) of the UNFCCC includes: 'countries whose economies are highly dependent on income generated from the production, processing and export, and/ or on consumption of fossil fuels and associated with energy-intensive products'.[88]

An important aspect of the redistributive elements of the Climate Change Convention relates to the transfer of financial resources.[89] Article 11 of the Climate Change Convention makes provision for the creation of a mechanism for the transfer of financial resources.[90] The financial mechanism adopted by the COP in terms of article 11(1) is the Global Environment Facility and is considered in greater detail in chapter 7. As is stated in paragraph 2.2 of chapter 3, an equally important aspect of the Climate Change Convention in relation to financial transfers is the fact that the obligations of developing states under the Convention are made dependent on the 'effective implementation by developed country Parties' of their commitment related to financial and technological transfers.[91]

The Climate Change Convention takes the needs of developing countries into account in another important way. For many developing countries, especially small island states and those especially vulnerable to the adverse effects of climate change, adaptation measures are more important than mitigation.[92] The UNFCCC recognises that the 'specific needs and special

84 Art 3(1) UNFCCC. See for full discussion of common but differentiated responsibilities, ch 3 above.
85 Art 3(2) UNFCCC.
86 Art 3(4) UNFCCC.
87 Art 4(8) UNFCCC.
88 Art 4(8)(h) UNFCCC. See also art 4(10) UNFCCC.
89 See generally art 11 of the UNFCCC.
90 Art 11(1) UNFCCC. See also art 12(4), which provides that developing countries may propose projects for funding activities that may result in the reduction of greenhouse gas emissions.
91 See art 4(7) UNFCCC.
92 GEF *Overall performance study 3: Progressive toward environmental results (complete report)* (2005) 154 available at http://www.gefweb.org (accessed 9 November 2005).

circumstances' of developing countries, 'especially those that are vulnerable to the adverse effects of climate change', should be given special consideration.[93] To this end the Convention provides that state parties, taking into account common but differentiated responsibilities, shall co-operate 'in preparing for adaptation to the impacts of climate change'.[94] Moreover, the Convention requires the transfer of financial and other resources for adaptation purposes.[95]

The Convention was intended to be a framework convention. The obligations in the convention were soft and broad. It had always been envisaged that a stronger instrument would have to be adopted to give effect to the purposes stated in the UNFCCC. In 1997, at COP 3 the parties adopted the Kyoto Protocol to the UNFCCC with the aim of strengthening the regime.

3.2 Key Provisions of the Kyoto Protocol

The Climate Change Convention gave explicit recognition to some of the interests and conflicts discussed in paragraph two of this chapter. The Kyoto Protocol expands on this by providing more detail. In what follows I briefly set out some of the key provisions of the Protocol.

In keeping with the common but differentiated responsibilities principle, the Kyoto Protocol does not deviate from the 'North first' approach adopted under the UNFCCC. The Protocol establishes legally binding limits for Annex I states on emissions of greenhouse gases. No such limits are set for non-Annex I states. Article 3 of the Protocol provides as follows:[96]

> The Parties included in Annex I shall, individually or jointly, ensure that their aggregate anthropogenic carbon dioxide equivalent emissions of the greenhouse gases listed in Annex A do not exceed their assigned amounts, calculated pursuant to their quantified emissions limitation and reduction commitments inscribed in Annex B and in accordance with the provisions of this article, with a view to reducing their overall emissions of such gases by at least 5 per cent below 1990 levels in the commitment period 2008 to 2012.

Several points relating to the nature of the substantive commitments can be observed from this provision. First and foremost, developing countries are excluded from the application of legally binding emissions reduction commitments. The possibility of developing countries undertaking emissions reduction commitments in sub-

93 Art 3(2) UNFCCC. In addition to small island states, developing countries that are particularly vulnerable to the adverse effects of climate change include African states affected by drought and desertification. See art 4(1)(e) and art 4(2)(8) of the UNFCCC.

94 Art 4(1)(e) UNFCCC.

95 See art 4(8) UNFCCC

96 Art 3(1) Kyoto Protocol.

sequent commitment periods will be the subject of the future negotiations. The second point worth mentioning is that the Protocol establishes the years 2008 to 2012 as the first commitment period. The third point is that, under the Protocol, the aim is to reduce the overall Annex I emissions level to at least 5 per cent below 1990 levels in that commitment period. Fourth, each Annex I state has been assigned a quantity of greenhouse gas emissions that must not be exceeded. The assigned amount is calculated in terms of the quantified emissions reduction and limitations commitment (QELRC) which is expressed in terms of a percentage of 1990 levels.[97] Thus, the QELRC of, for example, Japan, will be 94 per cent of its emissions for 1990.[98] This means that for the commitment period the aggregate emissions of Japan must not exceed 94 per cent of its 1990 emissions level (Assigned Amount Units). Put another way, the Japan must reduce its emissions by 6 per cent from its 1990 levels during the commitment period.

The emissions reduction commitments adopted are, in principle, designed to compel states to reduce their emissions of greenhouse gases. However, for various reasons, this is not necessarily the result of the Protocol in any given case. One such issue which has received significant attention in the literature relates to countries with economies in transition.[99] These countries have been experiencing negative growth in economic activity since the base year and will therefore have large amounts of unused emissions rights.[100] This state of affairs means that these countries can either increase their emissions significantly or trade these excess emissions, a situation termed the 'hot air' problem.[101] In the final analysis this could mean that the total emissions of Annex I countries would be higher during the first commitment period as a result of the hot air than would have been the case had the base year been set after the negative growth in economic activity.

Furthermore, the Protocol provides that, in the determination of whether or not an Annex I party has met its obligations under article 3(1), 'removals by sinks' of greenhouse gases from 'direct human-induced land-use change and forestry activities, limited to afforestation, reforestation and deforestation since 1990' will be taken into

97 It must be noted that some countries with economies in transition chose a year other than 1990 as the year to establish its baseline level. See art 3(5) of the Kyoto Protocol and decision 9 of COP 2. It must be further be noted that Annex I parties may use 1995 as the base year for hydrofluorocarbons, hyperfluorocarbons and sulphur hexafluoride. See art 3(8) Kyoto Protocol.

98 See for list Annex B Kyoto Protocol

99 See Hey (n 6 above) 87 and DA Wirth 'The sixth session (part two) and seventh session of the Conference of the Parties to the Framework Convention on Climate Change' (2002) 96 *American Journal of International Law* 648 652.

100 Wirth (n 99 above) 652.

101 Hey (n 6 above) 87.

account.[102] Thus, although sinks are not considered in the calculation of base year emissions they do play a role in the meeting of the QERLC.[103] The idea behind this provision is that since sinks sequestrate and thereby reduce greenhouse gas concentrations in the atmosphere, an increase in sinks should contribute to meeting a party's commitments. As Bothe notes, the problem with this approach is that as a rule sequestration is not permanent.[104] Moreover, those countries with net emissions from sinks in 1990 are allowed to include such emissions in the calculations of the emissions for the purposes of establishing base year emissions.[105] The effect of this provision is to increase the actual allowable emissions under the Protocol and, therefore, it weakens the environmental strength of the Protocol.[106] Other problems with the use of sinks include uncertainties regarding the capacity to assimilate carbon and accounting rules.[107] However, with respect to the use of sinks, the Protocol does provide that particular rules and guidelines should be decided in the future by the COP.[108]

Perhaps the most important aspect of the Protocol for the purpose of our analysis is the adoption of flexible mechanisms under the Protocol.[109] These flexible mechanisms give the parties to the Protocol a variety of ways to meet their obligations and, in essence, allow the parties to meet their obligations away from home. The first mechanism established under the Protocol is popularly termed 'bubble' or joint fulfilment of commitments and is covered under article 4 of the Protocol.[110] Other flexible mechanisms are joint implementation under article 6, the clean development mechanism under article 12 and emissions trading under article 17 of the Protocol. I now proceed briefly to describe each of the four flexible mechanisms provided for in the Protocol.

Under 'Bubble', Annex I parties may agree to fulfil their commitments jointly.[111] Such parties will be deemed to have met their commitment if 'the total combined aggregate' of greenhouse gas emissions does not exceed their assigned amounts over the commitment period.[112] Where the parties to the said agreement fail to meet their commitments jointly, each party will be responsible for

102 Art 3(3) Kyoto Protocol.
103 Breidenich *et al* (n 7 above) 322.
104 Bothe (n 6 above) 247.
105 Art 3(7) Kyoto Protocol.
106 Breidenich *et al* (n 7 above) 322.
107 Wirth (n 99 above) 653.
108 Art 3(4) Kyoto Protocol. The effects of the decisions relating to the use sinks are discussed below in relation to the Bonn Agreements and Marrakech Accords.
109 For an in-depth and comprehensive analysis of key aspects of these mechanisms see essays in D Freestone & C Streck (eds) *Legal aspects of implementing the Kyoto Protocol mechanisms: Making Kyoto work* (2005).
110 Bothe (n 6 above) 247.
111 Art 4(1) Kyoto Protocol.
112 As above.

their own emissions.[113] 'Bubble' is essentially a pooling of responsibilities with a view to meeting commitments jointly. While this mechanism was initially created specifically for Europe, it is now available to all parties with emissions reduction commitments.

Joint implementation, on the other hand, refers not to the joint achievement of commitments but rather to the joint implementation of greenhouse gas reducing projects. To that end, article 6 provides that as a means of meeting its QELRC, an Annex I party may[114]

> [t]ransfer to, or acquire from, any other such Party emission reduction units resulting from projects aimed at reducing anthropogenic emissions by sources or enhancing anthropogenic removals by sink of greenhouse gases in any of the sectors of the economy ...

Joint implementation under article 6 is subject to the qualification that all parties involved in the project must have consented to the project,[115] the project must create a reduction in emissions that is additional to any that would otherwise occur,[116] that parties not complying with certain reporting obligations under the Protocol may not use this mechanism to acquire emissions reduction units[117] and that the meeting of QELRC by means of acquisition of emissions reduction units from joint implementation projects shall be supplemental to domestic action.[118] Article 6 further allows Annex I parties to authorise (private) legal entities to take part in Joint Implementation projects.[119] Importantly, however, the Protocol makes it clear that the state party authorising private entities to take part in joint implementation remains responsible.[120] Thus, in joint implementation an Annex I country (the investor) invests in a specific project in another Annex I country (host), which project must result in additional reduction of emissions in the host country. For this investment the investor country is then entitled to receive emissions reduction units from the host country.

Under the UNFCCC's activities implemented jointly pilot programme, joint implementation could take place between Annex I and non-Annex I countries. The divisions between the negotiating parties on whether the Joint Implementation should operate between developed and developing countries were very contentious with some delegations, including the United States, adamant that the Protocol should allow joint implementation to take place between developed

113 Art 4(5) Kyoto Protocol.
114 Art 6(1) Kyoto Protocol.
115 Art 6(1)(a) Kyoto Protocol.
116 Art 6(1)(b) Kyoto Protocol.
117 Art 6(1)(c) Kyoto Protocol.
118 Art 6(1)(d) Kyoto Protocol.
119 Art 6(3) Kyoto Protocol.
120 As above.

and developing countries.[121] From an economic point of view this position makes sense. It is much cheaper to effect emissions reductions in poor countries than it is in wealthier countries (including countries with economies in transition).[122] As Kuik and Gupta note, while there may be a narrow gap in the marginal costs of emission reduction among and between Annex I states, this gap is much wider between Annex I and non-Annex I countries.[123] Furthermore, the operation of joint implementation between Annex I and non-Annex I countries would allow the inhabitants of Annex I countries to maintain the comforts provided for by activities dependent on fossil fuels. At the same time the poor (host) countries receive much needed financial and technical resources.[124] Seen in this light joint implementation between developed and developing countries can be presented as 'an international instrument that may simultaneously satisfy the concerns of the people who want to maintain high standards of material comfort with those whose major concern is poverty eradication'.[125]

Developing countries, however, were strongly opposed to joint implementation between Annex I and non-Annex I countries.[126] These countries felt that joint implementation was a way of Annex I countries to shirk their responsibilities in terms of the 'North first' approach adopted under the regime.[127] There was a fear on the part of some that Joint Implementation between Annex I and non-Annex I countries could end up permitting developed countries to continue 'their current wasteful lifestyle'.[128] Moreover, while the argument for joint implementation between Annex I and non-Annex I countries was based on costs, the fear was that this would mean that Annex I countries could 'buy up' all the cost-effective emissions reduction options available in developing countries, leaving developing countries with only expensive options once they take on QELRC.[129]

Although the Kyoto Protocol does not allow joint implementation between Annex I and non-Annex I countries, a separate flexible mechanism was created to operate between Annex I and non-Annex I

121 See Breidenich *et al* (n 7 above) 323.
122 See D Freestone 'The United Nations Convention on Climate Change, the Kyoto Protocol and the Kyoto mechanisms' in Freestone & Streck (n 109 above) 11.
123 Kuik & Gupta (n 22 above) 5.
124 K Arts *et al* 'Legal and institutional aspects' in Kuik *et al* (n 6 above) 31 discussing the benefits of a possible joint implementation project between the Netherlands and Kenya.
125 Maya & Gupta (n 6 above) ix.
126 Breidenich *et al* (n 7 above) 323.
127 See Maya & Gupta (n 6 above) ix.
128 Kuik & Gupta (n 22 above) 6. In this respect the Joint Declaration by Heads of State and/or Government of Brazil, China, India, Mexico and South Africa (above) n 3, reminded the Northern states of the need to change 'unsustainable production and consumption patterns in the industrialized countries'.
129 As above.

countries. This flexible mechanism is called the Clean Development Mechanism (CDM). According to article 12 of the Protocol:[130]

> The purpose of the clean development mechanism shall be to assist Parties not included in Annex I in achieving sustainable development and in contributing to the ultimate objective of the Convention, and to assist Parties included in Annex I in achieving compliance with their [QELRC].

Under the clean development mechanism Annex I countries invest in emission reducing projects in non-Annex I countries and obtain the emission reduction units obtained from such projects (referred to as certified emissions reduction or CERs).[131] As with joint implementation, the CDM can only be used with the consent of all parties involved,[132] must result in 'real, measurable, and long-term benefits related to the mitigation of climate change',[133] and reductions resulting from the CDM project must be additional to any that would have occurred in the absence of the CDM project.[134]

Given that joint implementation takes place between Annex I countries, while the CDM will take place between Annex I and non-Annex I countries, the increases in reduction units of the investing country are offset by an equivalent decrease in the Assigned Amount Units of the host country (in joint implementation) while no such set-off takes place in the CDM as the host country in the CDM does not have QELRC.[135] A further significant difference, which is administrative in nature, is that the CDM is made subject to 'the authority and guidance of the' Conference of the Parties serving as a Meeting of the Parties (COP/MOP) and is to be supervised by 'an executive board'.[136] This is in contrast to Joint Implementation which is to operate on a purely bilateral basis. The need for a central control mechanism in the CDM was necessitated by the fear of the CDM's potential negative impact on the environmental integrity of the Protocol given that both the host and investor states will have an interest in generating high volumes of CER. Beyond these differences there appears to be little difference between the two mechanisms. At the core, both mechanisms involve the transfer of emissions reduction units (called certified emissions reduction under the CDM) to an investing country from a host country for emission reductions achieved at the host country. Moreover, the Protocol makes provision for private entities to take part in both joint implementation and the

130 Art 12(2) Kyoto Protocol.
131 Art 12(3) Kyoto Protocol.
132 Art 12(5)(a) Kyoto Protocol.
133 Art 12(5)(b) Kyoto Protocol.
134 Art 12(5)(c) Kyoto Protocol.
135 Wirth (n 99 above) 652. See also E Meijer & J Werksman 'Keeping it clean — safeguarding the environmental integrity of the Clean Development Mechanism' in Freestone & Streck (n 109 above) 192. In this regard, Freestone (n 122 above) 13 notes that with the CDM 'a far wider pool of possible reductions is possible than would be available through reductions in Annex I countries alone'.
136 Art 12(4) Kyoto Protocol.

CDM. It seems, on the whole, that the CDM is a species of joint implementation programme operating between Annex I and non-Annex I countries.

The third flexible mechanism is emissions trading. Unlike the joint implementation and the CDM which involve the transfer between countries of emission reductions actually achieved from some or other project, international emissions trade involves the sale or acquisition of portions of a party's assigned amount or 'rights to emit greenhouse gases'.[137] Article 17 of the Protocol provides that:

> The Conference of the Parties shall define the relevant principles, modalities, rules and guidelines, in particular for verification, reporting and accountability for emissions trading. The Parties included in Annex B may participate in emissions trading for the purposes of fulfilling their commitments under article 3. Any such trading shall be supplemental to domestic actions for the purposes of meeting [QELRC] ...

Article 17 says nothing further about emissions trading. The Protocol merely provides that Annex B countries (more or less similar to Annex I) may engage in emissions trading. As with the CDM and joint implementation, a party's reliance on article 17 must be 'supplemental to domestic action'. There is no indication of how emissions trading is to operate. The COP is tasked with compiling rules and modalities for international emissions trading.[138]

All three mechanisms involve, in some way or the other, trading. With joint implementation and the CDM it is emission reductions actually achieved that are 'traded'. With international emissions trading it is assigned amount units that are traded. Moreover, emissions reduction, either in the form of emissions reduction units under joint implementation or certified emissions reduction under the CDM, are tradable under the international emissions trading programme.[139]

Like the Framework Convention on Climate Change, the Kyoto Protocol includes redistributive provisions. Again, as with the Convention, the Protocol invokes the principle of 'common but differentiated responsibilities' as a basis for the obligations of the parties to the Protocol.[140] The common but differentiated responsibilities principle is reflected in various aspects. The first one,

137 Brunnée (n 33 above) 269.

138 For various options available for emissions trading see B Haddad & J Palmisano 'Market Darwinism vs. market creationism: Adaptability and fairness in the design of greenhouse gas trading mechanisms' (2001) 1 *International Environmental Agreements: Politics, Law and Economics* 427; JB Wiener 'Global environmental regulation: Instrument choice in legal context' in T Tientenberg (ed) *Emmissions trading programmes*: Vol 1 (2001) reprinted from 1999 Yale Law Journal 677 698.

139 Wirth (n 99 above) 653.

140 Art 10 Kyoto Protocol. Art 10 emphasises that it is not meant to introduce 'any new commitments' for developing countries.

the North-first approach exempting developing countries from emissions reduction targets in the first commitment period, has already been mentioned.[141] Of course the possibility that developing countries can take on reduction commitments in the second commitment period – 2013 to 2017 – remains open.[142] Moreover, the Protocol does make provision for developing countries to take on emissions reduction commitments voluntarily.[143]

A second redistributive aspect of the Kyoto Protocol relates to the transfer of financial and technological resources. Article 10, for example, requires states to 'take all practicable steps to promote, facilitate and finance' the transfer of environmentally sound technologies.[144] Furthermore, the Protocol imposes further obligations on developed countries to provide 'new and additional financial resources to meet the agreed full costs' incurred by developing countries for the purposes of advancing the objectives of the climate change regime.[145]

Finally, the Protocol reiterates the provisions of UNFCCC relating to adaptation. Recalling article 4 of the Convention, article 2(3) of the Protocol provides that developed states are to implement the obligations under the Protocol in such a way as to minimise 'adverse effects of climate change' on other parties, especially developing parties.[146] The Protocol further provides that parties, taking into account common but differentiated responsibilities, should formulate programmes containing 'measures to facilitate adequate adaptation to climate change'.[147]

3.3 Bonn and Marrakech Agreements

Due to a failure to agree on some important points during the negotiations of Kyoto, several provisions relating to the flexible mechanisms and the use of sinks were left up to the COP to resolve. A deal on these and other outstanding issues was supposed to be thrashed out at the COP 5 in Den Haag. Unfortunately the talks in Den Haag disintegrated without any deals having been reached. When the Bush administration in the United States signalled their intention

141 See art 3(1) read with Annex I of the Kyoto Protocol.

142 It may be mentioned that the Parties have already begun discussions on future commitments. See generally Decision 1/CMP.1 (advance unedited version) where the first Conference of the Parties meeting as the Meeting of the Parties (COP/MOP) decided to initiate the process to consider further commitments for Parties for the period beyond 2012' in terms of art 3 (9) of the Protocol.

143 See generally arts 20 and 21 of the Protocol. At the first COP/MOP to the Kyoto Protocol, the COP/MOP approved Belarus' request to assigned emissions reduction commitment. See Decision 32/CMP.1 (advance unedited version).

144 Art 10(c) Kyoto Protocol.

145 Art 11(2)(a) Kyoto Protocol.

146 See also art 3(14) Protocol.

147 Art 10(b) Protocol.

never to ratify Kyoto, it seemed that what was left to say to the Kyoto Protocol was: '*requiescat in pace*'. It seems, however, that the declaration by the United States only served to strengthen the resolve of the world to make Kyoto work.[148]

At COP 6, in Bonn, the parties thrashed out a deal which, in COP 6*bis* in Marrakech was completed, signed and sealed. The agreements, known as the Bonn Accords and the Marrakech Agreements respectively, spelt out agreement on some of the outstanding issues.[149] In particular, COP 6 reached agreement on issues relating to sinks and flexible mechanisms. The Marrakech agreements were adopted by the first COP/MOP in December 2006 in Canada.[150]

One of the burning issues relating to the use of flexible mechanisms was the question of the extent to which Annex I countries can rely on mechanisms in meeting QELRC under article 3. Although all three provisions relating to the use of flexible mechanisms make it clear that their use is to be supplemental to domestic actions, there was still some uncertainty as to the degree.[151] Could, for example, an Annex I country achieve its QELRC relying primarily on joint implementation or would there be some sort of a cap on the use of flexible mechanisms? The issue of whether there would be caps on the use of flexible mechanisms was important in view of the need to achieve domestic reduction of greenhouse gases in Annex I countries discussed above. Furthermore, unrestricted use of the Kyoto mechanisms could undermine the environmental aims of the Kyoto mechanisms.[152] Two provisions agreed upon at COP 6 attempt to shed some light on the issue. First, the parties agreed that Annex I countries will 'implement domestic action ... with a view to reducing emissions in a manner conducive to narrowing per capita differences between developed and developing country Parties'.[153]

Second, the parties agreed that the use of flexible mechanisms 'shall be supplemental to domestic action, and that domestic action

148 Brunnée (n 30 above) 246.

149 See Bothe (n 6 above) 241.

150 See para 5 of Decision 2/CMP 1 FCCP/KP/CMP/2005/8/Add.1 available at http://ifccc.int (accessed 24 October 2006).

151 While arts 6 and 17 on joint implementation and emissions trading respectively provide that such measures must be supplemental, article 12 on the CDM provides for the certified emissions reduction from CDM to 'contribute to compliance with part of' the QERLC.

152 Yamin *et al* (n 44 above) 188.

153 UNFCCC *Report on the Conference of the Parties on the second part of its sixth session* FCCC/CP/2001/5 25 September 2001 Annex: 'The core elements for the implementation of the Buenos Aires Plan of Action' S VI, art 1(4). The provisions were adopted at COP 7 as decision 15/CP.7. See *Report on the Conference of Parties on its seventh session* FCCC/CP/2001/13 21 January 2002.

shall thus constitute a significant element of the effort made by each [Annex I party] to meet its [QELRC]'.[154]

Although these provisions do not set specific caps on the use of flexible mechanisms, they may be taken to suggest that the bulk of actions taken to meet commitments must be taken at home. Meijer and Werksman, for example, note that some delegations in the negotiation forums argued that the 'supplemental' requirement 'strongly suggests that the percentage of the cap' met through the use of the flexible mechanism cannot 'exceed 49%'.[155] All of this, of course, is speculation.

In the context of the CDM, various specific decisions designed to allay the fears of those who were concerned about the impact of the CDM on the environmental integrity of the Protocol were taken. The Marrakech agreements adopted a complex approval and verification procedure to protect the integrity of the Protocol.[156] In addition to the COP/MOP and the Executive Board, which are both provided for in article 12, the modalities for the CDM include Designated Operating Entities, the function of which is to monitor various aspects of the project cycle, including the proposal stage and the implementation stage. The Marrakech agreement also includes rules on the requirement that the emissions reductions which are the subject of the CERs are additional to any which would have occurred without the project.

The parties also had to reach agreement on various aspects pertaining to emissions trading. There had been several fears raised about emissions trading in addition to the fears relating generally to flexible mechanisms. In general these additional fears flow from the fact that, unlike emissions reduction units and certified emissions reductions from joint implementation and CDM projects, the assigned amount of units traded in emissions trading are not from specific projects that result in an actual decrease in emissions. The first fear was in relation to those Annex I countries whose economic activities and consequently emissions of greenhouse gases have been on the decline since the 1990's (states with economies in transition). Because these countries' emissions levels have fallen well below their assigned amounts in terms of the Protocol, the idea that they can trade the excess ('hot air') has been questioned as such emissions will not correspond to any *de facto* reduction of emissions.[157] There were also fears that, without sufficient control, Annex I countries may trade more assigned amount units than they actually had. On the whole, emissions trading could result in *de facto* increase in emissions

154 As above, art 1(5).
155 Meijer & Werksman (n 135 above) 197.
156 See generally Decision 15/CP.7. For discussion see Meijer & Werksman (n 135 above) 197 *et seq*.
157 See Yamin *et al* (n 44 above). See also Wirth (n 99 above) 652.

because, as Yamin *et al* have noted 'emissions trading under article 17 provides an economic incentive for Parties to transfer [assigned amounts] that would not exist in the absence of trading'.[158]

Both of these problems had the potential to put the environmental integrity of the Protocol in (further) doubt. At COP 6*bis* the parties agreed that each party included in Annex I shall maintain a 'commitment period reserve which should not drop below' 90 per cent of the party's assigned amounts or 100 per cent of five times its most recently reviewed inventory, whichever is lower.[159] Thus, states may only 'trade' emissions in such a way that they constantly retain 90 per cent of the assigned amounts or five times the national emissions. This agreement has the effect of limiting the ability of states to oversell. The Agreement further limits the ability of states to sell 'hot-air' as countries whose actual emissions have fallen below their budget can, effectively, only trade 10 per cent of their emissions budget.[160]

A further complex problem relates to the use of sinks as means of meeting the QERLC. The Protocol left open the question of whether agricultural activities – revegetation, cropland management, grazing-land management and forest management – can contribute to the meeting of commitments under article 3.[161] At the Bonn and Marrakech meetings, the parties agreed to expand the use of sinks to meet commitments by extending the application of sinks to forest management, cropland management, grazing land management and revegetation.[162] Further, during the Marrakech negotiations Russia was able to negotiate an increase in its forest management credits to roughly double its ceiling under the Bonn Accord.[163]

In the next section I consider what the provisions of the Kyoto Protocol, along with the various agreements reached at Bonn and Marrakech relating to the flexible mechanisms and sinks mean for the variation of sustainable development promoted by Kyoto.

158 Yamin *et al* (n 44 above) 188.
159 UNFCCC/CP/2001/5 (n 152 above) S VI art 4(1).
160 See Wirth (n 99 above) 653. See C Corino 'The Kyoto Protocol: Tradable emissions credits and compensatory solutions under the Bonn Resolutions' (2001) 18 *European Environmental Law Review* 294 298.
161 Wirth (n 99 above) 654.
162 UNFCCC/CP/2001/5 (n 152 above) S VII art 4.
163 Wirth (n 99 above) 654.

4. Analysis – Determining the Kyoto Protocol variation of sustainable development

4.1 General

In attempting to characterise the Kyoto Protocol in terms of the variations of sustainable development identified in this study we need to enquire about the kind of compromises that are made when the various values of sustainable development collide. To what extent do economic concerns trump environmental and social concerns? Do environmental concerns trump social and economic concerns? What about social concerns? These are some of the issues I consider in attempting to characterise the climate change regime in terms of one of the variations of sustainable development identified in chapter 3 of the study.

The analysis is conducted by scrutinising the provisions of the UNFCCC and the Protocol set out above. In particular I scrutinise the emissions reduction target and the flexible mechanisms. Other aspects of the regime considered include the precautionary principle and the common but differentiated responsibilities principles. These aspects of the climate change regime are critiqued with a view to determining which value is central.

4.2 Kyoto's Emissions Reduction Target

Perhaps the first place to start is the objective of the Protocol. The objective of the Protocol is to reduce the emissions of greenhouse gases of Annex I countries by at least 5 per cent below emission levels in 1990.[164] The Kyoto targets have been described by some as too strict and unachievable.[165] Nevertheless, the targets are generally

164 Corino (n 160 above) 296.

165 See DG Victor *The collapse of Kyoto Protocol and the struggle to slow global warming* (2001) 3-4. Of course the argument of Victor against the Protocol goes much further. However, that the targets of the Protocol are unrealistic is an integral part of the overall argument. In response to Victor, Eileen Clausen says the following: 'If Victor were saying merely that the targets negotiated in Kyoto were too strict, he would surely attract widespread support for his contention'. See E Clausen 'Carping at Kyoto' (2002) 34 *George Washington International Law Review* 247 250 *et seq*. Clausen herself, although defending Kyoto, asserts that 'the specific targets negotiated in Kyoto ask for too much too fast'. See for a consideration of this critique, CC Joyner 'Burning international bridges, fuelling global discontent: The United States and rejection of the Kyoto Protocol' (2002) 33 *Victoria University of Wellington Law Review* 27 at 34 *et seq*. See also KA Baumert 'Participation of developing countries in the international climate change regime: Lessons for the future' (2006) 38 *George Washington International Law Review* 363 374 who states the Kyoto targets are 'highly specific and ambitious (substantively 'deep')'.

viewed as falling short of what is required to curb climate change.[166] Bothe notes that as the targets have not been established (only):[167]

> on the basis of the calculated reduction for the stabilisation of temperature at a specific level, but also, and perhaps *even more so, with the problem of cost and economic feasibility in mind, that means that the goal has been set rather low.* There are few environmental regulations where it is as clear as here that the regulation is inadequate ... (emphasis added).

In 1990 the IPCC estimated that, to stabilise levels of greenhouse gases at 1990 levels, there would need to be an 'immediate reduction in emissions from human activities of over 60%'.[168] Prue Taylor notes two points with regard to the Kyoto Protocol in relation to the IPCC's statement.[169] First, the reduction target is about twelve times less demanding than the reduction recommended by the IPCC. Second, and exacerbating the first problem, the reduction under the Protocol takes place about twenty years later. This means that, in comparison to the reduction requirement set by the IPCC, we are doing too little and we are doing it too late. Thus, according to Lomborg:[170]

> The effect of Kyoto on the climate will be miniscule. All models agree that the Kyoto Protocol will have surprisingly little impact. One model by a lead author of the 1996 IPCC report shows how an expected temperature increase of 2.1°C in 2100 will be diminished to an increase of 1.9°C. Or to put it more clearly, the temperature that we would have experienced in 2094 we have now postponed to 2100. In essence the Kyoto Protocol does not negate global warming but merely buys the world six years.

Thus it appears clear that the target set by the Protocol would be insufficient to protect the integrity of the earth's climate system.[171] One author has gone as far as to refer to the Protocol as 'a weak and potentially impotent document'.[172] This raises the question: why? Why, while knowing what the scientists argued would be required, did the negotiators of the Kyoto Protocol still agree on targets that are

166 Brunnée (n 33 above) 268; Arcas, although seeing the Protocol as a first step in the right direction, describes the Kyoto targets as 'disappointingly unambitious'. See RL Arcas 'Is the Kyoto Protocol an adequate environmental agreement to resolve the climate change problem' (2001) 18 *European Environmental Law Review* 282 285.

167 Bothe (n 6 above) 246. See also Thoms (n 23 above) 821.

168 IPCC/UNEP *Climate change: The IPCC scientific assessment* JT Houghton *et al* (eds) (1990) xi.

169 P Taylor 'Heads in the sand as the tide rises: Environmental ethics and the law on climate change' (2000/2001) 19 *UCLA Journal of Environmental Law and Policy* 247 259.

170 B Lomborg 'Global warming — Are we doing the right thing?' available at http://image.gaurdian.co.uk/sys-files/Gaurdian/document/2001/08/14/warming.pdf (accessed on 15 February 2004).

171 See Arcas (n 166 above) 286 who notes that 'even if we fulfil the Kyoto Protocol's requirement, we do not even come close to solving the problem'.

172 TM Lopez 'A look at climate change and the evolution of the Kyoto Protocol' (2003) 43 *Natural Resources Journal* 285 286.

not nearly sufficient? From the literature it appears that the primary reason for the rather low target is economic.[173] Many observers would argue that it is not only economic reasons that underlie the unambitious targets, but that there are other factors such as convenience for societies dependant on greenhouse emitting sources of energy and the unachievability of any targets set higher than the current Kyoto targets. Political analysts may even argue that the low targets may be explained in terms of game-theoretical analysis.[174] However, a close inspection of all these and other underlying reasons reveal imbeddedness in economic activities and economic growth. As Thoms notes 'the most problematic characteristic of the climate change problem is that it has implications for multiple sectors of the economy that go to the heart industrialised society'.[175]

It seems difficult, if not impossible, to refute that the primary factor dictating the low targets under Kyoto was economic feasibility rather than ecological need. This fact is further underscored by the suggestion that the *actual* reductions that would occur if Kyoto were to be implemented would be less than the 5 per cent proclaimed in the Protocol.[176] As stated in paragraph 3.3 of the chapter 3, the setting of low environmental targets is indicative of the trumping of environmental concerns by economic concerns and would thus suggest, subject to other considerations, an economic growth variation of sustainable development.

4.3 Flexible Mechanisms under the Kyoto Protocol

In analysing questions relating to the hierarchy of values in the Kyoto Protocol we may also consider the options available to contracting parties in meeting their obligations under the Protocol. One of the contentious issues in the various negotiating forums of Kyoto was the issue of sinks as a means to meeting the obligations under the Protocol. Certainly, there is a scientific basis for the use of sinks. Scientifically sinks have the capacity to sequester large amounts of

173 See Taylor (n 169 above) 261.

174 See AI Michaelowa & RSJ Tol 'Outlook for the international climate policy — Revolution or reform?' (2002) 2 *International Environmental Law Agreements: Politics, Law and Economics* 217 217 who notes that 'game theoretical analysis usually comes to the conclusion that it is not possible to have a global agreement to mitigate climate change that leads to a strong deviation from a business-as-usual emission path'. For discussions of game theory see RO Keohane *After hegemony: Co-operation and discord in the world political economy* (1984) 65 *et seq.*

175 Thoms (n 23 above) 824.

176 For example, a US government press release is quoted as saying: 'the 7% target [of the United States under the Protocol] represents at most a 3% real reduction ... the remaining 4% points result from certain changes in the way gases and sinks are calculated and do not reflect any increase in effort'. Quoted from Taylor (n 169 above) 261.

carbon.[177] However, we also know that this sequestration is not permanent and that there is much uncertainty about the storage rate of biospheric sinks.[178] Thus, during the negotiations there was division between those who favoured the generous use of sinks, such as the United States, Japan and Australia, and those who feared that such a reliance on sinks might be a threat to the (already weak) environmental effectiveness of the Protocol.[179] Again the economic 'realities' won out and the Protocol makes it possible to achieve a state's obligations under the Protocol by using sinks. Moreover, the Bonn and Marrakech Agreements expand the parties' ability to rely on sinks.[180] As Corino notes, under the Bonn and Marrakech Agreements Japan could, for example, 'achieve a reduction of 3.5%, hence more than half of its obligatory reduction of 6% by means of' sinks.[181] Thus, once again, it appears that the need to reach agreement on 'achievable' or 'feasible' targets triumphed over the need to reach an agreement on targets sufficient to protect the Earth's climate system.

What gives the Kyoto Protocol its character, perhaps more than anything else, is the flexible mechanisms: bubble, joint implementation, clean development mechanism and emissions trading. These mechanisms have been much analysed in literature ranging from legal to economic.[182] What is clear from the literature is that the primary motivation for the development of these flexible mechanisms was economic, not environmental and certainly not social. These mechanisms are there to cut costs. The golden thread running though all the literature in support of flexible mechanisms is that flexible mechanisms are necessary to ensure cost-effectiveness. Very few, if any, make the argument that flexible mechanisms are *necessary for environmental reasons* relating to climate change. For example, Yamin, Burniaux and Nentjes comment that literature 'consistently demonstrates that the Kyoto Mechanisms could significantly reduce the aggregate economic costs of achieving the Kyoto commitments'.[183] Similarly, Brunnèe notes that the main argument in support of flexible mechanisms is 'that they provide avenues for more

177 See Wirth (n 99 above) 653.

178 As above. For definitions of land use, land-use change and forestry activities under the Kyoto Protocol see Conference of the Parties serving as a Meeting of the Parties, advance unedited version of Annex of Decision 5/CMP.1 (Land use, land-use change forestry).

179 Wirth (n 99 above) 654.

180 As above. According to Wirth, the Bonn agreements 'expanded the range of sink-related activities that operate to fulfil a party's obligations'.

181 Corino (n 160 above) 297. See also Thoms (n 23 above) 816 who notes that under the Marrakech agreements Russia was granted a larger increase of the use of sink credits than those agreed to under the Bonn Accords.

182 See eg in addition to some of the literature cited above, A Rose & B Stevens 'An economic analysis of flexible permit trading in The Kyoto Protocol' (2001) 1 *International Agreements: Politics, Law and Economics* 219.

183 Yamin *et al* (n 44 above) 187.

efficient and cost-effective emissions reductions'.[184] Wiener, in support of flexible mechanisms, argues that[185]

> several studies of policies to limit GHG emissions show that allowing flexibility in the location of GHG emissions abatement would cut the estimated global cost, compared to an equally stringent constraint on emissions without such locational flexibility (e.g. fixed national caps), by roughly fifty to seventy percent.

To get an idea of the role of flexible mechanisms in Kyoto it may be helpful to consider the mechanisms separately. In joint implementation, one Annex I country invests in a project in another Annex I country in exchange for emission reduction units generated by the project. As mentioned above, the idea is that emission reductions be carried at the location where it will be less costly. The Clean Development Mechanism operates in much the same way, except that the host state is a non-Annex I country.

With respect to these two mechanisms it may be argued that there is nothing objectionable as they result in *actual* emissions reduction. However, there is the problem, alluded to above, that joint implementation and the CDM in fact perpetuate the problem by promoting the continued over-reliance on fossil fuels in wealthy countries. In that sense, the Kyoto Protocol encourages a business-as-usual approach to the use of fossil fuels. As already noted above, the inclusion of the CDM also results in equity concerns by creating the impression (whether wrongly or rightly held) that the North are shirking their 'North first' responsibilities and are eager to 'buy up' all the cheap emissions reductions options, leaving the more expensive options for the poor(er) nations. In addition, the CDM suffers from the added problem that the increase in reduction units of the investing state are not offset by a decrease in the assigned amount units of the host state. This is because the host state (non-Annex I state) does not have QELRC. The effect of CDM transactions may therefore be to increase the total amount of allowable emissions and thereby further decrease the already modest target under the Protocol.[186] Moreover, as mentioned above, the effect of this is a win-win situation for participants on both sides of the CDM equation where higher CERs are generated.[187]

Notwithstanding the risks that the CDM pose for the environmental integrity of the Protocol, some have defended its environmental integrity.[188] Meijer and Werksman, while conceding

184 Brunnée (n 33 above) 269.
185 Wiener (n 62 above) 716.
186 See Wirth (n 99 above) 652. See also Meijer & Werksman (n 135 above) 192.
187 See Meijer & Werksman (n 135 above) 193.
188 See generally essays in Freestone & Streck (n 109 above). On the Kyoto mechanisms generally, see M Wemaere & C Streck 'Legal ownership and the nature of Kyoto Units and EU allowances' in Freestone & Streck (n 109 above) 186.

the risk that the CDM poses to the environmental integrity of the Protocol, suggest that the various checks and balances introduced into the CDM project cycle under the Marrakech agreements[189] may, if applied correctly, alleviate some of the concerns raised about the CDM. However, the contributions are filled with many 'ifs and buts' and conclude that some of the 'innovations raise more questions ... than its designers have thus far been able to answer' and that these 'questions may plague the CDM for some time'. Responding directly to the key issues raised above, Freestone states the following in defence of the CDM:[190]

> Despite some initial concern that the [the CDM] might be seen as the 'thin end of the wedge' in the introduction of commitments to developing countries, in fact the basic assumptions on which the CDM is based are sound. Even if the majority of the responsibility for the historical emissions leading to climate change can be laid at the doors of the developed world, a reduction of emissions everywhere in the world has an equally beneficial impact on the global climate system.[191]

Of course, what Freestone says here is true. However, the point that Freestone misses is that emissions reductions in developing countries are, in any event, supposed to be part of the Kyoto regime. In other words, while developing countries are not subjected to specific reduction commitments, the Convention and the Protocol require all Parties to take some action to combat climate change.[192] More to the point, the climate change instruments make it clear that developed countries are to co-operate with developing countries in greenhouse gas emissions mitigation programmes.[193] This is a responsibility additional to their emissions reduction commitments. In essence what the CDM does is to allow developed countries to claim CERs for carrying out their responsibilities under the Protocol. This has a negative impact on the environmental integrity of the Kyoto Protocol. The perpetuation of the over-reliance of those in rich societies on climate changing gases, as well as the effect of the CDM of decreasing the already low target under the Protocol may be a symptom of a more fundamental issue. The Kyoto Protocol was created to curb climate change. Yet, it seems that the same Protocol is designed to change the international community's over-reliance of climate changing gases as little as possible.

The state parties to the Kyoto Protocol recognised the problems relating to emissions trading, namely, emissions trading transactions will not be based on specific projects and therefore will not result in any *actual* emissions reduction and that emissions trading may

189 See, for discussion, para 3.3 above.
190 Freestone (n 122 above) 13.
191 Meijer and Werksman (n 135 above) 203 *et seq*.
192 See art 10 Kyoto Protocol as well as art 4 UNFCCC.
193 As above.

exacerbate the 'hot air' problem by allowing those states with economies in transition to sell emissions units they would, in any event, not have used (the 'hot air'). To some extent the Bonn and Marrakech agreements may be seen to have solved some of these problems. The requirement under the agreements that countries should maintain a commitment period reserve of at least 90 per cent of the country's assigned amounts may go some way in solving some of the issues relating to emissions trading. The decision does imply that states cannot oversell their assigned amounts. Secondly, the consequence of the decision may be to limit the ability of countries with economies in transition to sell 'hot air'.

However, the results of the Bonn and Marrakech agreements must be applauded with caution. First, the agreements do not solve the 'hot air' problem as such. Although these countries' ability to trade in the 'hot air' is limited, they can still effect a significant factual increase in emissions while meeting the obligations to *stabilise* their emissions under the Protocol. The availability of 'hot air' means, for example, that Russia would be able to increase its emissions by 50 per cent while the Ukraine can increase its emissions by 120 per cent and still meet their targets under the Protocol.[194] Even with the limitation to trade 'hot air' under the Marrakech agreements, because of this significant increase in emissions allowed, they will still be entitled to trade a fair portion without compromising the commitment period reserve. In other words, because of this 'hot air' situation, 10 per cent of these countries' assigned amounts is still relatively high.

On the whole it seems likely that the environmental effectiveness of the Kyoto Protocol is further weakened by the Marrakech accords. This resulted, in large part, from concessions made to states with regards to the use of sinks for the purposes of meeting Kyoto obligations. It has been noted that, in essence, 'the Marrakech agreement lowers the overall emissions reduction from the 5.2% reduction negotiated in the Kyoto Protocol to 1.5%'.[195] Wirth, in a tone sympathetic to the Kyoto process and Marrakech accords, concedes that, environmentally, the effect of the Bonn and Marrakech accords was to reduce 'the magnitude of the Kyoto Protocol's already modest reduction commitments'.[196]

194 A Moe 'Russian quota sales: Not just a lot of hot air' available at http://program.forskingradet.no/pretropol.hotair.php3 (accessed on 5 September 2005) notes that between 1990 and 1998 Russian fuel consumption dropped by about 50%. Similarly, D Lashof & J Fiedler 'Hot air – Controlling the flow' available at http://www.climatenetwork.org/eco/4_Cop5_hot.html (accessed on 5 September 2005) suggest that hot air available from Russia, the Ukraine and other Eastern European countries is '370 million metric tons of carbon equivalent.' See also AE Kramer 'In Russia, pollution is good for business' in 15 January 2006 *Sunday Times (South Africa), New York Times* 7.

195 Thoms (n 23 above) 822.

196 Wirth (n 99 above) 660.

It seems fair, therefore, to suggest that the Kyoto Protocol sets rather low environmental standards.[197] These low environmental standards are reflected most obviously in the Kyoto targets of approximately 5 per cent reduction below 1990 levels. These low standards are, however, also reflected in the use of sinks as well as flexible mechanisms as instruments towards meeting individual targets. It also seems equally fair to suggest that these low environmental standards are principally justified on account of economic concerns. Indeed, the latter suggestions are probably irrefutable, even by proponents of the Kyoto Protocol. However, these facts on their own cannot justify a conclusion that the Protocol represents an economic growth-centred variation of sustainable development. Other factors, such as the emphasis on intra-generational equity and the precautionary principle may need to be considered. It may well be that, while the flexible mechanisms incline one towards the view of the Protocol as reflecting an economic growth-centred variation of sustainable development, the influence of the precautionary principle may tilt the balance towards an environment centred variation of sustainable development. Similarly, aspects of intragenerational equity, so central to both the UNFCCC and the Protocol, may have the effect of tilting the balance towards a social well-being-centred variation.

4.4 Intragenerational Equity

It is hard to argue that the climate change regime does not reflect the principle of intragenerational equity.[198] Both the UNFCCC and the Kyoto Protocol contain a variety of principles giving effect to intragenerational equity. The UNFCCC, for example, has fewer and (even) softer obligations for developing countries for purposes of dealing with climate change.[199] What is more, the Kyoto Protocol has been faithful to these principles by imposing differential obligations and obligations relating to financial and technological transfers.[200] The implementation of financial transfers under the climate change regime is done by the Global Environment Facility which is considered in chapter 7 below. Against great opposition (and supported by vociferous arguments from developing nations) the negotiators and drafters of the Protocol maintained the 'North first' approach as an integral part of the regime.

197 In the foreword to Freestone & Streck (n 109 above), the Senior Manager of the Carbon Finance Business at the World Bank, Roberto Dañino, while fully supporting the Protocol, noted that while the Protocol is a step in the right direction, 'the targets it sets can only be seen as a modest beginning'.

198 See Joint Declaration of Heads of State and/or Government of Brazil, China, India, Mexico and South Africa (n 4 above) para 14.

199 See generally art 4(1) UNFCCC. See specifically art 4(2), on differential obligation and arts 4(3) and 11 on obligations to transfer finances and technologies.

200 See arts 3, 10 and 11 Kyoto Protocol.

In chapter 3, I suggested that a strong presence of intra-generational equity concerns is likely to indicate an inclination towards a social well-being variation of sustainable development. The common but differentiated responsibilities principle in the climate change instruments may well serve that purpose – that even though there is a fair amount of attention being paid to economic interests, the social interests of the poor are also taken into account. The common but differentiated responsibilities principle, as understood in modern environmental agreements including both climate change treaties, obviously reflects a more indirect approach to intra-generational equity.

But what effect does the centrality of this principle have on the analysis? First, it seems unlikely that the inclusion of the common but differentiated responsibilities principle is, on its own, sufficient to outweigh the importance of economic concerns reflected generally in the rest of the Protocol. Second, even the inclusion of the principle of common but differentiated responsibilities is somewhat diluted by economic interests. As discussed above, the Clean Development Mechanism has been criticised as encouraging the North to abdicate their responsibilities in terms of the 'North first' approach.[201] Moreover, the very operation of the Clean Development Mechanism will probably represent a very profitable experience for Northern countries and multinational corporations loosely attached to them.

While the Kyoto Protocol only entered into force in 2004, some valuable insights can be obtained from another related endeavour, namely the Prototype Carbon Fund.[202] The Prototype Carbon Fund is an initiative established by the World Bank. The purpose of the Fund is to enhance efforts towards carbon dioxide emission reduction through public-private-partnerships. The basic concept is that private sector institutions (principally multinationals) and public sector institutions (states from the North) make contributions to the Fund. The Fund, in turn, invests the money contributed in carbon emissions reduction projects in developing countries. For these investments the Fund receives emissions reduction units. These reduction units (or proceeds from the trade in reduction units) are then distributed amongst the investors (the Northern governments and multinationals). Assuming that the relevant provisions of the Protocol have been complied with, investors are then able to trade the emissions reductions units under the Kyoto emissions trading programme or use such units against their own emissions reduction

201 See discussion at para 3.2. above.

202 For more information on the Prototype Carbon Fund, see the fund's website at http://www.prototypecarbonfund.org (accessed 20 November 2004). A discussion of the Prototype Carbon Fund, while an interesting innovation, falls outside the scope of this book.

commitment under the Protocol.[203] Indeed, ultimately, reduction units obtained under Fund projects are to be used to meet Kyoto targets.[204]

Two observations impacting on the analysis of the CDM (and also joint implementation) can be made about the operation of the Protype Carbon Fund. First, the purpose of the CDM and joint implementation mechanism is essentially the same as the purposes of the Prototype Carbon Fund.[205] Second, although the amount to be received from the investments remains unknown due to some uncertainty regarding some of the rules pertaining to emissions trading and certification under the Protocol, it is clear that the Fund (and the investors in the Fund) expect to make quite a substantial profit. Citing the Fund's 2002 Annual Report, Ellen Hey observes:[206]

> It is expected that the average cost at which the PCF will be able to generate ERUs will amount to 3 to 4 US$ per ton CO_2 equivalent. The average cost of attaining similar reductions in industrialised states is estimated to be US$15/t$CO_2$, energy efficient states.

The difference between the emissions abatement costs in developing versus developed countries and the huge savings implied by the said difference suggests that the CDM could potentially be very profitable for the investor. The actual profit, of course, will depend on supply and demand in accordance with the market approach reflected in the Kyoto Mechanisms.[207] However, the point here is that there is great potential for profit (a potential which may or not materialise) from investment in CDM projects. Comparing the amount spent by investors in achieving emissions reductions with profits they are likely to make in the selling of emissions units reinforces the notion that profit and economic gain are the primary drivers and rationale of flexible mechanisms. Consider, as an example, an approved PCF project and the potential profit that could be derived from it. In 2003, the PCF agreed to purchase 3.8 million tons of CO_2 equivalent from the Durban

203 See, PCF *Prototype Carbon Fund — Public private partnership: 2004 Annual report* (2004) available at the Prototype Carbon Fund website. According to the PCF Board, by 2002 the 'modalities and procedures that the' PCF had adopted were already in line with the procedures agreed upon at Marrakech. See PCF Board *Fourth report on the implementation of the Prototype Carbon Fund and proposed amendment to the Instrument Establishing the Prototype Carbon Fund* (2002), available at the Fund website.

204 See for discussion Freestone (n 122 above) 17 *et seq.*

205 The Fund actually proclaims itself to operate 'within the framework of Joint Implementation (JI) and the Clean Development Mechanism (CDM)'. See Prototype Carbon Fund website above n 201.

206 E Hey 'Sustainable development, normative development and the legitimacy of decision making' (2003) 34 *Netherlands Yearbook of International Law* 3 37.

207 Baumert (n 165 above) 386. The author notes, in this regard, that given the withdrawal of the United States from the Kyoto Protocol, the demand shrank by about 70%. He further suggests that the current market price of emission credits ranges between US$5.63 and US$7.15.

Landfill Gas Energy Project in Ethekwini Municipality, South Africa.[208] The PCF would purchase the CERs at US$3.75 per ton of CO_2 equivalent. The PCF would thus invest approximately $US15 million and, according to the figures provided, produce a saving of US$57 million. This differential in abatement costs provides significant potential for profit.[209] The profitability of involvement in the CDM for investors has been confirmed by the World Bank based on the experiences from PCF.[210] Given that the Prototype Carbon Fund operates in terms of the modalities approved under the Kyoto Protocol, it can be expected that the CDM produce the same amount of profit for investors. This profit-making by the rich, whether multinational corporations or Northern countries, from investments in poor countries, has the effect of casting doubt on the intra-generational equity benefits of the Kyoto mechanisms.

That is not to say that there are no benefits for developing states. As mentioned above in paragraph 3.2 of this chapter, the CDM will provide much needed financial resources for developing countries. Furthermore, Huq and Reid highlight the benefits arising from six CDM projects, including job creation and refurbishment of local schools,[211] and improved access to electricity.[212] However, in their analysis of the projects, Huq and Reid also identify some obstacles to real transmission of benefit.[213]

However, quite apart from the practical problems of implementation, the projects considered by the Huq and Reid raise another more fundamental issue. They raise the concern considered earlier about whether the CDM would allow developed countries to profit from less onerous emission reduction options in developing

208 The project consists of an enhanced collection of landfill gas at three sites in eThekwini and the use of some of the recovered gas to produce electricity. For more project details see the Project Idea Note, South Africa – Durban landfill gas use available at http://www.carbonfinance.org/Router.cfm?Page=Project&ProjID=9615 (accessed 1 August 2006).

209 For sizes of other projects, see World Bank *Submission on regional distribution of CDM project activities* (April 2006) available at http://www.carbonfinance.org (accessed 1 August 2006). See especially Attachment II. *Further information and observations regarding the regional distribution of CDM project activities* at 8 *et seq*. For a discussion of other projects and the volume of CERs likely to be produced from them, see SL Huq & H Reid 'Benefit sharing under the Clean Development Mechanism' in Freestone & Streck (n 109 above) 232 *et seq* where the authors discuss a variety of projects.

210 See generally World Bank/International Emissions Trading Association *State and trends of the carbon market 2006* (2006) available at http://www.carbonfinance.org (accessed on 1 August 2006).

211 The Jepirachi Wind Power Project, Colombia, Huq & Reid (n 208 above) 235 *et seq*.

212 Solar Home Systems in Bangladesh, Hug & Reid (n 208 above) 239 *et seq*.

213 See eg Electricity Generation from Biogas and Bio-diesel in Brazil, Huq & Reid (n 208 above) 238 where the authors state that the 'provision of local social benefits for some low-income groups therefore remains a challenge'. See also the Plantar Project, Brazil where, amongst other problems, 'concern has been expressed over the integrity of the project developers who are accused of expelling local people from their land ...' Huq & Reid (n 208 above) 243 *et seq*.

countries, leaving the more expensive options for developing countries once they themselves undertake emissions reduction commitments. All the projects considered by Huq and Reid may be characterised as *relatively* inexpensive emissions reduction options involving readily available technology. The projects include a wind power project in Colombia, the installation of solar power in Bangladeshi homes, the introduction of energy-efficient technologies during construction of homes and the replacement of fossil fuels with biomass in Brazil.

Distributive justice in the climate change regime is also reflected in various provisions relating to adaptation.[214] However, a close inspection of these provisions on adaptation reveals that, in addition to fulfilling a distributive justice function, they also serve to protect the economic endeavours dependent on the use of fossil fuels. The provisions on adaptation include, in addition to adaptation to the impact of climate change, the economic impact of responses to climate change. For example, article 4(8) of the UNFCCC provides that some of the impacts to be considered in the implementation of the obligations include the impact 'on countries whose economies are highly dependent on income generated from ... fossil fuels'. Similarly, article 4(10) of the Climate Change Convention provides that the parties should take into account the position of states 'with economies that are *vulnerable to the adverse effects of the implementation of measures to respond to climate change*'.[215]

The subtle inclusion of economic interests related to fossil fuels in provisions directed at adaptation to climate change, as opposed to adaptation to climate change regulation, may again suggest the importance attached to economic concerns in the climate change regime.

The consistent insulation of economic interests from the effects of climate change regulation is apparent also in provisions of the UNFCCC and the Protocol relating to trade. Article 3(5) of the UNFCCC provides that the measures taken in response to climate change 'should not constitute a means of arbitrary or unjustifiable discrimination or a disguised restriction on international trade'. Article 3(5) of the UNFCCC, of course, is reminiscent of the *chapeau* of article XX of the GATT. As argued in chapter 2 of this study in connection with a similar provision in the Rio Declaration, this provision suggests an inclination towards economic growth concerns. Moreover, the Kyoto Protocol provides that in implementing the Protocol, the parties should, *inter alia*, strive to minimise the adverse effects on international trade.[216] In both these provisions the

214 See arts 3(2), 4(1)(e), 4(2)(8) UNFCCC. See also arts 2(3), 3(14) and 10(6) Kyoto Protocol.

215 Art 4(10) UNFCCC (emphasis added).

achievement of the goals pursued under the Protocol is made subject to trade imperatives. There is, thus, even in provisions designed to give effect to distributive justice, such as the provisions on adaptation – which would normally suggest concerns with human well-being – a significant role for economic concerns. Moreover, the CDM, while promoting economic concerns, also serves to reduce the effect of the 'North-first' approach.

The aspects considered above, namely, the CDM and the provisions on adaptation, illustrate another important point: how social and environmental considerations are trumped by economic concerns. As argued above, the CDM impacts negatively on the environmental integrity of the Protocol. However, the CDM is presented as entailing social benefits. In fact, what we see in the discussion is that the CDM has the potential to harm future emissions reduction prospects of developing states by using up cheap options. More importantly, it appears that the economic rationale of the CDM outweighs any social benefits it may produce. In this context then, social concerns are instrumentalised to promote economic concerns.[217]

4.5 The Precautionary Principle

The precautionary principle is another principle that has a central role in the climate change regime. In paragraph 3.3 of chapter 3 I suggested that an emphasis on precaution may suggest an environment-centred variation of sustainable development. Climate change and responses to it can be analysed (and have been analysed) in terms of the precautionary principle.[218] It is therefore necessary for the purposes of this discussion to consider the role of the precautionary principle in the climate change regime.

There is no question that the precautionary principle plays *some* role in the climate change regime. In addition to textual references to the principle,[219] the very existence of conventions relating to climate change suggest a precautionary approach. This is because although there is a high degree of certainty regarding the existence of the climate change problem, uncertainty exists regarding the long-term effects, especially at the time the Convention was adopted.[220] To this effect Lopez notes that while there is a strong consensus in the scientific community that anthropogenic emission of greenhouse

216 Art 3(2) Kyoto Protocol. The provision does also include economic, social and environmental concerns.
217 See, for discussion, para 3.3 of ch 3 where the various ways that the values of sustainable development can trump (and be trumped) is considered.
218 Taylor (n 169 above). For a discussion of the role and significance of the precautionary principle in sustainable development, see ch 2 above.
219 See art 3(3) UNFCCC.

gases exacerbates the greenhouse effect 'much remains unknown about the long-term' effect of such emissions on the Earth's climate system.[221] It is clear, however, that if there is any scientific uncertainty at present, it relates not to the existence of the climate change problem but rather to the details and long-term effects of the problem.

If one accepts that there is still *some* scientific uncertainty in the science relating to climate change,[222] the question becomes what, if any, kind of action must we take to prevent *potential* serious harm? The argument put forward in this study is that a precautionary principle suggests an environment-centred variation of sustainable development. This is because the precautionary principle seeks to protect the environment even in the absence of scientific certainty. Given the economic costs associated with environmental protection such an approach entails, at least at face value, that economic concerns are sacrificed for environmental concerns. Is this true of the precautionary principle in the climate change regime? Consider the precautionary approach upon which the climate change regime is based:[223]

> The Parties should take precautionary measures to anticipate, prevent or minimise the causes of climate change and mitigate its adverse effects. Where there are threats of serious or irreversible damage, lack of full scientific research shall not be used as a reason for postponing such measures, taking into account that the policies and measures to deal with climate should *be cost-effective* so as to ensure global benefits at the *lowest possible cost* (emphasis added).

While the text of the provision may be interpreted in a variety of ways, a cogent argument can be made that the obligation to take action to prevent climate change is limited by its cost-effectiveness. Thus, the precautionary principle in the UNFCCC lacks what Nollkaemper referred to as 'absolutist pretence' – the notion that once a certain risk threshold is crossed action to prevent the environmental harm should be undertaken regardless of the costs.[224]

220 See Taylor (n 6 above) 19 *et seq*. Taylor, for example, notes that there are some specific unanswered questions relating to continued and future emission levels, the effect of increased temperatures on sinks and the impact on feedback mechanisms.

221 Lopez (n 172 above) 286.

222 For literature questioning some or all of the conclusions of the IPCC see, *inter alia*, Wojick 'The UN IPCC's artful bias: Glaring omissions, false confidence and misleading statistics in the summary for policymakers' cited in Joyner (n 156 above) 35 n 31; Green 'Newest IPCC report on global warming fails to deliver policymaking models' cited in Joyner (n 164 above) 35 n 32; Lomborg (n 169 above).

223 Art 3(3) of the Climate Change Convention.

224 A Nollkaemper 'What you risk reveals what you value' and other dilemmas encountered in the legal assault on risks' in D Freestone & E Hey (eds) *The precautionary principle and international law: The challenges of implementation* (1996) 74.

Certainly the interpretation that the obligation to take precautionary actions is limited by cost-effectiveness would be supported, in accordance with article 31(3) of the Vienna Convention on the Law of Treaties, by the texts of the Kyoto Protocol, in particular the aspects discussed above concerning the low environmental targets and the heavy reliance on market mechanisms, and the Marrakech agreements adopted by the first COP/MOP which further reduced the environmental efficacy of the Protocol for economic reasons.[225] Thus, even the precautionary principle, apparently an environmental principle, is coloured by economic concerns to the extent that its aims are conditioned on economic concerns.

4.6 The Malignancy of the Climate Change Problem as a Factor

It seems an unavoidable conclusion that the climate change regime, in particular the Kyoto Protocol, reflects an economic growth-centred variation of sustainable development. The low environmental targets set for economic reasons and the heavy reliance on market mechanisms both seem to point in that direction. This conclusion is further buttressed by an analysis of intragenerational equity and the precautionary principle in the Protocol. These principles, at first glance respectively suggest a social well-being-centred variation and environment-centred variation of sustainable development. However, in the Protocol they are made to serve and are accepted subject to economic growth concerns.

The argument may be that the environmental effectiveness of the Protocol is enhanced by the modest targets, sinks and flexible mechanisms because without them states would be unwilling (perhaps even unable) to meet the obligations under the Protocol. True, such an argument is not without merit. Most of the authors cited in this chapter, although recognising that the Protocol is insufficient as a tool to curb climate change, see the Protocol as an important foundation upon which more stringent and effective obligations can be built. In this sense Brunnèe considers the Protocol, much like the UNFCCC, as a framework treaty. Emphasising the point, Wirth notes that like 'any process involving compromise, the result is[226] less satisfying than some would like. Realistic expectations focus on the Kyoto Protocol's future promise, as to which the forecast, though now brighter, is still clouded in uncertainty'.[227]

225 Art 31(3) of the Vienna Convention on the Law of the Treaties provides, in part, that in the interpretation of a treaty, together with the context, any subsequent agreements and practice by the Parties relating to the agreement shall be taken into account.

226 Brunnée (n 33 above) 266.

227 Wirth (n 99 above) 660.

Essentially such arguments remind us that the malignancy of climate change makes solutions very difficult.[228] Nevertheless, the difficulties of solving the climate change problem cannot excuse us from honestly and critically assessing its contribution to the development of international law on sustainable development. The conclusion that has to be arrived at is that the Kyoto Protocol, while recognising the importance of protecting the earth's climate system, seeks to solve the problem by making minute amendments to the business-as-usual scenario. The reliance on flexible mechanisms, the use of sinks and the low targets set by Kyoto are illustrative of the need to keep things the same as before. Flexible mechanisms, sinks and low targets allow parties to make the assertion that they are contributing to the protection of the climate while maintaining the use of the very agents that threaten to negatively affect our climate. Thus, the response to climate change represented in the Kyoto Protocol has to be described as minimalist. It is this minimalism in the design of the legal framework to combat climate change that leads to the conclusion that the climate change regime represents an economic growth-centred variation of sustainable development.

5. Concluding remarks

The climate change regime, including the UNFCCC and the Kyoto Protocol, integrates environmental, social and economic concerns. The question, in light of the arguments made in Part A, is how these values are integrated. In this chapter I considered which variation of sustainable development is reflected in the climate change regime. Taking into account the compromises and trade-offs made in the creation of the regime and, in particular, taking into account the environmental targets set in the Protocol and the employment of flexible mechanisms to meet the target, I concluded that the Protocol reflects an economic growth-centred variation of sustainable development, which as described in chapter 3, is a weak form of sustainable development.

In the analysis I further considered whether various principles in the climate change regime, which would normally be associated with environment-centred variations and social well-being-centred variations, could affect the analysis. Specifically, I considered the intragenerational equity principle, which I suggested is characteristic of a social well-being-centred variation, as well as the precautionary principle, which I suggested was characteristic of an environment-centred variation. The environmental value reflected in the setting of emissions reduction targets and the employment of the precautionary approach is trumped by economic considerations through the setting

228 See Thoms (n 23 above) 823.

of low emissions targets (low environmental standards), the use of the CDM, as well as subjecting the precautionary approach to economic considerations. The social value, on the other hand, is instrumentalised to serve economic concerns in the CDM. Adaptation measures, also representing concerns, are also made subject to economic concerns. An important aspect of the social value, financial transfers, is outsourced to the GEF which is considered in chapter 7.

Like most other commentators on the climate change regime, I applaud the efforts to create a regime to combat climate change. Like most other commentators, I recognise that the climate change regime is not sufficient for the protection of the earth's climate system. However, the argument advanced is not merely that the climate change regime is weak. The argument goes further. It is argued here that the climate change regime is ineffective because of the variation of sustainable development it reflects. By placing economic interest at the centre, at the expense of both social and environmental concerns, and thus promoting a business-as-usual approach, the climate change regime is ineffective.

6

Role of Sustainable Development in Biosafety

'How can we know whether we'll say in ten years, 'We were right – this was the solution to end world hunger' or 'We were right – these were Frankensteins that have caused major damage to the earth's environment and to our bodies'.[1]

1. Introduction

In this chapter I consider the international regulation of biotechnology under the Biodiversity Convention with specific reference to the Cartagena Protocol. The raging debate surrounding international (and, indeed national and regional) regulation is testimony to the complexities of issues on biotechnology.[2] On the one hand, biotechnology is said to offer great potential for solving, or at least contributing to the solution of major problems facing the world today.[3] On the other hand there are risks associated with the use of modern biotechnology.[4] The instrument developed by states to regulate the use of bioengineering is the Cartagena Protocol on Biosafety to the Convention on Biological Diversity ('Protocol').[5] In addition to the regulation of biotechnology, the chapter will also consider the benefit sharing of genetic resources provisions in the Convention on Biological Diversity ('the Convention' or 'Biodiversity Convention').[6]

The object of this chapter is, as with the previous chapter, to classify the biodiversity regime in terms of one of the variations of sustainable development identified in Part A of the study. Through an analysis of the Convention and the Protocol, I try to determine which of the values of sustainable development is afforded central position

1 RA Leach, Executive Director, Friends of the UN World Food Programme, in a telephonic interview cited in VP Nanda & G Pring *International environmental law and policy for the 21st century* (2003) 351.

2 L Tracy 'Does a genetically modified rose still smell as sweet? Labelling of genetically modified organisms under the Biosafety Protocol' (1999) 6 *Buffalo Environmental Law Journal* 129 130.

3 J Adler 'More sorry than safe: Assessing the precautionary principle and the proposed international Biosafety Protocol' (2000) 35 *Texas International Law Journal* 173.

4 See K Jabara 'The Biosafety Protocol' (2001) 8 *University of Baltimore Journal of Environmental Law* 121.

5 Cartagena Protocol on Biosafety to the Convention on Biodiversity (2000) reprinted in P Cullet & A Gowlland-Gualtieri (eds) *Key materials in international environmental law* (2004) 188.

6 Convention on Biological Diversity (1992) reprinted in Cullet & Gowlland-Gualtieri (n 5 above) 169.

in the Protocol. Thus, does the regime reflect a human-needs-centred variation, an economic growth-centred variation or an environment-centred variation of sustainable development? In engaging in this kind of analysis, I bear in mind the general question posed by the study: Whether the emergence of sustainable development as a central concept in international law and policy has contributed towards the paradigm shift promised by the emergence of the concept.[7]

As in the previous chapter, I undertake the analysis by considering the kinds of choices, compromises and trade-offs made when the values of sustainable development — social, environmental and economic — collide. Do the kinds of choices reflected in the instruments suggest dominance by one value over the others? In other words, do these choices, compromises and trade-offs suggest that environmental, economic or social concerns are accorded a place of priority? Further, to what extent do characteristics associated with one or the other variation of sustainable development dominate in the regime? Thus, is the regime strongly characterised by the precautionary principle, enhancement of trade or intragenerational equity?

The structure of the chapter is, in many respects, similar to the structure of chapter 4. I begin in section 2 by giving a brief description of the science and dilemmas of genetic modification. In section 3 I give a brief description of the content of the Convention and the Protocol.

The latter description is intended merely to provide an overview of the instruments and does not pretend to provide detailed analysis of the Protocol. In section 4 I analyse the content of the instruments described in section 3 in order to determine the variation of sustainable development reflected in the regime. Finally, I offer some concluding remarks.

While reading this chapter the reader will immediately notice that there is a relationship (whether conflictive or supportive) between the Protocol and the free trade regime under the WTO. It is not the purpose of this chapter to try to determine the compatibility of this regime with the WTO, as is done by several publications on the Bio-

7 In ch 2, I suggest that the origin of sustainable development was a reaction to the environmental destruction and widespread poverty described in ch 1.

safety Protocol.[8] Such a determination will not take the analysis any further, since the standards by which all the regimes considered in this study are to be judged relate to sustainable development, and the WTO is not the standard-bearer for sustainable development.[9] Nevertheless, a few words or comments are offered in the course of the chapter on the relationship between the two. In particular, I consider the manner in which the drafters of the Protocol attempt to deal with the potential conflict between WTO agreements and the Biosafety Protocol. This aspect is considered for two reasons. First, it is meant to pre-empt criticism that the failure to consider the relationship makes the chapter incomplete in some way. Second, and more importantly, the solution offered by the Protocol for the potential conflict is the quintessential compromise solution. This compromise offers some insights into the kind of trade-offs made and consequently contributes to the determination of which value is central to the biosafety regime.

2. Background: Science and dilemmas

Biotechnology relates to the scientific efforts of humans to modify living organisms for human use.[10] In particular, biotechnology seeks to modify or manipulate living organisms to enhance favourable traits or reduce unwanted traits in living organisms.[11] Biotech procedures allow scientists to 'move specific genes within an organism or from one organism to another' with the view to improving certain targeted

8 For literature canvassing the issue on the Cartagena Protocol's compatibility with the WTO regime, see MJ Oliva 'The Cartagena Protocol: On biosafety and the Agreement on Sanitary and Phytosanitary Measures: What will decisions on GMOs have to be based on' (2002) 13 *International Legal Perspectives* 22; HD Heavin 'The Biosafety Protocol and the SPS Agreement: Conflicts and dispute resolution' (2003) 12 *Journal of Environmental Law and Practice* 373; O Rivera-Torres 'The Biosafety Protocol and the WTO' (2003) 26 *Boston College International and Comparative Law Review* 263; S Safrin 'Treaties in collision? The Biosafety Protocol and the World Trade Organization agreements' (2002) 96 *American Journal of International Law* 606; PT Stoll 'Controlling the risks of genetically modified organisms: The Cartagena Protocol on Biosafety and the SPS Agreement' (2001) 13 *Yearbook of International Environmental Law* 82; B Grosko 'Genetic engineering and international law: Conflict or harmony? An analysis of the Biosafety Protocol, GATT and the WTO Sanitary and Phytosanitary Agreement' (2001) 20 *Virginia Environmental Law Journal* 295.

9 See for comparison, LD Guruswamy 'Sustainable agriculture: Do GMOs imperil biosafety?' (2002) 9 *Indiana Journal of Global Legal Studies* 461 who remarks the following of the Biosafety Protocol-WTO debate: One issue 'deals with a brewing trade and environmental (*sic*) conflict. What is at issue here is the extent to which the restrictions on trade in GMOs, or living modified organisms (LMOs) ... are consistent with SD'. To present the debate in this way creates the impression that the free trade regime somehow reflects the standards by which sustainable development is to be judged. That is not the approach taken by this study.

10 See Adler (n 3 above) 175.

11 Jabara (n 4 above) 122.

traits.[12] Organisms modified in this way can, therefore, be termed genetically modified organisms (GMO's) or, using the terminology of the Cartagena Protocol, living modified organisms (LMO's).[13] The Biodiversity Convention defines biotechnology as technological applications that use 'biological systems, living organisms, or derivatives thereof, to make or modify products or processes for specific use'.

Biotechnology has been described as the 'Jekyll and Hyde environmental issue of our time'.[14] On the one hand, proponents of biotechnology emphasise that genetically modified organisms have the potential to end global hunger and malnutrition while contributing to the preservation of global biodiversity.[15] On the other hand, there are risks associated with biotechnology, including risks to biodiversity, human health and the livelihood of traditional farmers.[16]

While most proponents of GMOs concede that there are risks associated with the genetic modification of organisms by means of biotechnology, they argue that these risks are no different from risks posed by traditional methods of genetic modification.[17] However, others note that 'modern biotechnology innovations represent a dramatic leap in human capacity' to modify organisms and 'they can carry an appropriately large component of risk.'[18] The difference between the traditional manipulation of organisms and modern biotechnology is that modern biotechnology allows scientists to isolate individual genes for the purposes of manipulation.[19] Once the

12 D Schnier 'Genetically modified organisms and the Cartagena Protocol' (2001) 12 *Fordham Environmental Law Journal* 377 379.

13 The Cartagena Protocol defines living modified organisms as 'any biological entity that possesses a novel combination of genetic material obtained through the use of modern biotechnology'.

14 See Oliva (n 8 above) 22.

15 See eg Adler (n 3 above). See also Nanda & Pring (n 1 above) 349.

16 See Oliva (n 8 above) 22; Tracy (n 2 above) 130; Jabara (n 4 above) 121.

17 See eg Adler (n 3 above) 27 where he quotes the Ecological Society of America as follows: '[g]enetically modified organisms should be evaluated and regulated according to their biological properties (phenotypes), rather than the genetic techniques used to produce them'. See also Schnier (n 12 above) 382 who quotes from a declaration signed by a '400 prominent scientists' which states: '[t]he addition of new or new different genes into an organism by recombinant DNA techniques does not inherently pose new heightened risks relative to the modification of organisms by traditional methods'. In another publication Adler makes a similar argument. See also J Adler 'The Cartagena Protocol and biological diversity: Biosafe or bio-sorry' (2000) 12 *Georgetown International Law Review* 761. See also Jabara (n 4 above) 124.

18 Nanda & Pring (n 1 above) 350. The debate as to whether modern biotechnology is just an extension of traditional of cross breeding or whether it is fundamentally different is too complex for non-experts to even attempt to enter. See for discussion Schnier (n 12 above) 387.

19 Nanda & Pring (n 1 above) 352. Their simplified scientific explanations are based on S Kolehmainen 'Genetically engineered agriculture: Precaution before profits: An overview of issues in genetically engineered food and crops' (2001) 20 *Virginia Environmental Law Journal* 261.

gene is isolated it can be incorporated into a recipient cell's DNA.[20] When this transfer of genes is successful 'an offspring results with the new cellular qualities and a phenotype (the appearance and qualities of the organism) that includes the desired trait'.[21]

Traditional methods of genetic selection were limited to transfers of genetic material between individuals capable of mating and producing offspring, which generally meant those within a single species.[22] In contrast, modern biotechnological advances 'expand the genetic combinations that can be created, as they enable the insertion of a gene from any other, irrespective of sex, their sexual compatibility or genetic relation'.[23]

Modern biotechnology promises more nutritious food products. With modern methods of biotechnology scientists can also create organisms that are resistant to viral and fungal diseases, drought and frost, which are herbicide tolerant and pest resistant.[24] An often cited example of modern bioengineering is the transgenic seed hybrid, *Bacillus thuringiensis* corn (Bt corn).[25] This hybrid is developed by splicing a gene from the naturally toxic soil bacterium *Bacillus thuringienisis* (Bt), a bacterium that when ingested by insects germinates and eventually kills them, into the corn genome.[26] Bt corn produces the insecticide internally making it unnecessary to spray the pesticide Bt.[27] An example of a herbicide tolerant seed is Monsanto's Roundup Ready soybeans, which are resistant to the active chemical found in Roundup Ultra herbicide.[28] Scientists are also working on bioengineering crops that can thrive in lands unsuited for agriculture such as land with a high concentration in salt, acid or iron.[29]

Biotechnology promises to promote sustainable development in several important ways. First, GMOs promise to meet (or at least contribute towards meeting) human needs by increasing food pro-

20 Nanda & Pring (n 1 above). There are various ways that an isolated gene can be transferred into cells. First, there is recombinant DNA (rDNA), being the most common method, in which 'plasmids and viruses are used to carry genetic material into cells' where the recipient cell will introduce the genetic material into its own genes. Second, micro-injection where the 'new genetic material is injected directly into the' the recipient cell. Third, electro and chemical poration involves the creation of pores into the recipient cell membrane to allow new genes to enter. Finally, with bioballistics the target gene is 'shot' into the recipient cell.

21 Nanda & Pring (n 1 above) 353.

22 As above.

23 Adler (n 3 above) 176. See also Schnier (n 12 above) 379; Jabara (n 4 above) 124.

24 See generally Nanda & Pring (n 1 above) 352; Schnier (n 12 above) 386 *et seq;* Jabara (n 4 above) 123; Adler (n 3 above) 175 *et seq.*

25 See Jabara (n 4 above) 123. Another example of Bt crops is Bt cotton.

26 Nanda & Pring (n 1 above) 353 and Schnier (n 12 above) 387.

27 As above.

28 See Jabara (n 4 above) 123. See also Nanda & Pring (n 1 above) 353 *et seq.*

29 Schnier (n 12 above) 387.

duction.[30] Jonathan Adler, arguing for GMOs, notes that 'genetic modification of crops can increase yields' in several ways, including resistance to pests and the elements.[31] Furthermore, biotechnology offers the potential for increased nutritional value of crops.[32] Thus Adler, echoing Guruswamy's concern for the 800 million undernourished people in the world, adds, '[g]enetically modified crops may well make food both more abundant and more nutritious'.[33] Similarly, Nanda and Pring note that with GMOs the opportunity exists to revolutionise the ability to produce crops of maximum nutritional value while making 'food more available to the Earth's growing population, much of which is in a constant state of hunger'.[34]

The promise of GMOs contributing towards meeting human needs promotes social needs or welfare value. Bioengineering not only promises to contribute to the meeting of human concerns, but promises to do so while promoting ecological integrity. As Adler notes there:[35]

> are ways to increase food production other than through the development and use of GMOs. Perhaps the easiest way of producing more food would be to put more acres under plow ... feeding a global population of 10 billion [it is estimated that the world population could reach 10 billion by 2050][36] could readily be achieved by simply doubling the amount of cropland.

According to this argument, the promise of GMOs to increase per-acre yield of crops also reduces the need to convert more natural habitats such as tropical rainforest into farmlands.[37] The use of genetically modified organisms, in terms of the argument, therefore, contributes to the protection of biodiversity. Additionally, by modifying organisms to create crops that are resistant to weeds and pests, bioengineering could contribute to the reduction of herbicides and pesticides and, thereby, contribute towards slowing environmental degradation.[38] In this context Melanie Griffiths notes that GMOs will enable 'developing

30 Schnier (n 12 above) 389 *et seq*. See also Guruswamy (n 9 above) 461 who emphasises this point by noting that there are over 800 million people living on the verge of starvation.

31 Adler (n 3 above) 199. According to Adler, a study by a panel convened by the World Bank found that 'genetic engineering can increase agricultural yields by as much as twenty-five percent'.

32 Adler (n 3 above) 200. Examples of biotechnology research providing more nutritious crops include sweet potato with greater protein, soybean and corn with improved protein and carbohydrates and 'golden rice' with the additional Vitamin A.

33 As above.

34 Nanda & Pring (n 1 above) 355. See also Schnier (n 12 above) 389.

35 Adler (n 3 above) 201.

36 Adler citing D Avery 'Saving the planet with pesticides, in the true state of the planet'.

37 Schnier (n 12 above) 387.

38 Schnier (n 12 above) 386. See also Nanda and Pring (n 1 above) 355.

countries to feed their people while maintaining their biodiversity habitat'.[39]

Opponents of genetically modified organisms point, primarily, to possible risks to human health and the environment posed by the release of GMOs.[40] Potential risks to human health include the introduction of new allergens in foods that people with allergies thought to be safe.[41] An oft-cited study showed that soybeans genetically modified to contain Brazilian-nut protein cause allergic reactions in people who are allergic to Brazilian nuts.[42] The problem with allergens in GMOs is aptly described by Kolehmainen:[43]

> Though an individual with an allergy to certain types of fish can take care to avoid fish in all its forms, they have no weapons against a tomato genetically engineered with a fish gene.

Those seeking strict regulation of biotechnology also view some of the alleged benefits of GMOs as double-edged swords. There is a fear that the use of powerful pesticides produced through genetic modification could 'kill everything else in and around fields, such as wildflowers, insects and birds dependent upon seeds'.[44] Another well-documented example of such a risk is the Cornell University study that suggested that genetically altered corn could kill caterpillars of the monarch butterfly.[45] Similarly, there is a fear that the creation of herbicide-tolerant crops through genetic modification could pose a threat to biodiversity. First, the herbicide-resistant crops could themselves become 'so evasive they are a weed problem themselves or they could spread themselves to wild weeds making them more evasive'.[46] Moreover, the creation of superweeds could induce farmers to apply even more herbicide, knowing that the herbicide will not harm herbicide resistant crops.[47] Therefore, in the end, herbicide-tolerant and pest-resistant crops could result in the need for more pesticides

39 M Griffiths 'Biosafety Protocol' (1998) *Colorado Journal of International Environmental Law and Policy* 113 114.

40 S McCaffrey 'Biotechnology: Some issues of general international law' (2001) 14 *Transnational Lawyer* 91 91.

41 Kolehmainen (n 19 above) 275, who cites a study in which rats were fed potatoes. One group of rats was fed genetically modified potatoes while another group was fed non-genetically modified potatoes. According the findings of the research, the group fed genetically modified potatoes showed stunted growth and suppressed immune systems.

42 Schnier (n 12 above) 392; Jabara (n 4 above) 125; Nanda & Pring (n 1 above) 356. See also Kolehmainen (n 19 above) 278.

43 Kolehmainen (n 19 above) 278.

44 Jabara (n 4 above) 125.

45 As above; Nanda & Pring (n 1 above) 354. Other lab studies have shown the lives of ladybugs are shortened when they are fed aphids living on GM crops and that lacewings (natural predators of insect pests) are killed when they are fed corn borer raised on genetically modified corn plants. See Nanda & Pring (n 1 above) 355 citing RC Cowen 'New findings say genetically altered corn poison the soil' 1999 *Christian Science Monitor.*

46 Schnier (n 12 above) 396, quoting from the Greenpeace website. See also Kolehmainen (n 19 above).

47 Schnier (n 12 above) 397.

and herbicides.[48] Guruswamy notes that critics of GMOs argue, therefore, that using GMOs without further information regarding their long-term effects may be of a more serious threat to biodiversity.[49]

Proponents of GMOs offer rebuttals to these criticisms. First, as to the threat of unknown allergies, GMO proponents argue that the risks of introducing new allergies are the 'same for both biotech and traditional breeding varieties'.[50] Second, regarding the fear that the benefits of GMOs could act as a double edged sword, GMO proponents point out that the 'Cornell study' mentioned earlier, which is held as support for the claim, has been largely discredited as the findings were found to have been overstated.[51] Nevertheless, the risk still exists. None of these responses address the existence of the long-term risk of the modification of organisms through modern biotechnology. While scientists can tell us about the short term effects of this biotechnology, the long-term (side) effects or risks are still largely unknown.[52]

It is really here where the complexity of biotechnology regulation lies. In the climate change debate (considered in chapter 5), unlike the biotech debate, there is relative scientific certainty with regards the risks (and the benefits) of the use of fossil fuels. The need to act is clear and most commentators agree on the need to act. In biotechnology, only one side of the equation is known, the benefits, although, in truth even the question of benefits is highly disputed.[53] However, very little is known about the risks. As Nanda and Pring note:

> the possibilities of the unintended consequences of biotechnology in agriculture are indeed overwhelming. The stakes are almost unacceptably high on both sides of the debate – the well-being of

48 As above. See also Friends of the Earth International *Who benefits from GM crops? Monsato and the corporate-driven genetically modified revolution* (2006) (on file with the author) para 8.2 where the report states that by '2005, six different weeds had reportedly become resistant to Roundup in many countries, not to mention a growing list of weeds that have developed a degree of tolerance sufficient to require application of other, toxic, herbicides.'

49 Guruswamy (n 9 above) 476.

50 Schnier (n 12 above) 394.

51 Guruswamy (n 9 above) 477 referring to studies published by the National Academy of the Sciences.

52 Nanda & Pring (n 1 above) 357. With regards to the 'Cornell Study', while the authors concede that the results were 'somewhat overstated' largely because the insects were 'not likely to consume such great quantities' of corn in the wild, they note that the study 'did not consider the long-term risks and potential for harm'.

53 See especially Kolehmainen (n 19 above). I am prepared to accept for the purposes of the study that biotechnology does offer some benefits because, at the very least, biotechnology offers indisputable benefits for the biotech industries. Whether or not there are benefits for humanity as a whole is questionable.

> countless poor people and the future of viability of the earth's ecosystem.[54]

William Rees, known for developing the eco-footprint analysis, adds the following:[55]

> In short, the net benefits of many transgenetics, even to producers, are by no means clear and their widespread use poses a range of threats to food (quite apart from any possible risk associated with consuming genetically engineered food).

Both sides of the debate lay claim to the role of advocates for sustainable development. Those arguing for biotechnology claim that GMOs can contribute to environmental protection by limiting the reliance on pesticides and herbicides and by reducing the need for expanding agricultural activities into natural, wild habitat while simultaneously meeting essential human needs. Those for strict regulation of biotechnology have rejected these claims vigorously by pointing out risks to biodiversity attendant to the use of modern biotechnology.

A claim by proponents that has not been subject to the same level of vigorous scrutiny is the claim that GMOs could contribute to the alleviation of hunger. Some commentators have, however, showed this claim to be misleading.[56] These commentators note that hunger in the developing world is not caused by food shortages but rather by inequity, politics and poverty.[57] Jabara points out that the problem of hunger throughout the world is caused not by 'shortages in food production – it is a problem of distribution'.[58]

The importance of the North-South divide in any question of sustainable development requires that the issues relating to the impact of GMOs on the South be brought to the surface. Colin Tudge, author of *So Shall We Reap*, on the state of world food, had an article on GMOs published in the *Mail and Guardian* (South Africa). In the article Tudge argued that GMOs would represent excellent achievements only if 'the world had agricultural policies designed for the benefit of humankind'.[59] According to Tudge, however, the world is locked in the 'mantra embraced by the World Bank, the International Monetary Fund ...' of making profit.[60] He argues that

54 Nanda & Pring (n 1 above) 359.
55 WE Rees 'The eco-footprint of agriculture: A far-from-(thermodynamic)-equilibrium interpretation' unpublished paper (on file with author).
56 Rees (n 55 above) 356; Jabara (n 4 above) 144. See especially Kolehmainen (n 19 above).
57 As above.
58 Jabara (n 4 above) 144; See also C Tudge 'Farming is not just a business' in *The Mail and Guardian (South Africa)* 2004 21-27 May 2004 available at http://www.mg..co.za (accessed on 30 July 2004); see also Kolehmainen (n 19 above) 286.
59 Tudge (n 58 above).
60 As above.

unfortunately for the world, agriculture is also a business and like all other businesses 'must seek to maximise profit'.[61] The argument he makes is that the increase in yield is important, not to feed the hungry, but to make profit.[62]

Tudge's article reminds one that in addition to the promotion of environmental and social values, economic growth-related issues are also relevant to the concept of sustainable development. If one considers the claim that biotechnology can increase agricultural yield then it becomes apparent that attempts to restrict the trade of GMOs will mean economic losses for those farmers (and their states' economies) dependant upon GMOs. As Jabara points out, European resistance to GMOs crops has 'cost American farmers millions of dollars in lost exports'.[63]

A second economic factor to bear in mind when considering GMOs is food security.[64] Related to the problem of food security problem is the concern of farmers with their lack of autonomy attendant to the extended use of biotechnology in agriculture.[65] Biotechnology companies that develop GMOs and stand to lose the most from strict regulation of GMOs are, for obvious business reasons, registering patents over the GMOs developed by them.[66] It has been noted that patenting essentially prohibits farmers from legitimately using seed from the previous year's stock.[67] In particular, GM companies incorporate into their seeds a technology referred to as the 'terminator'.[68] This technology essentially sterilises GMO plants, thus preventing farmers from obtaining seeds from previous year's crops.[69]

Given that thirteen 'companies own 80 per cent of the GM crop patents' this process of patenting GMOs and using technology to sterilise GMO plants has the potential to create an agricultural mono-

61 As above.

62 As above. See also Stoll (n 8 above) 100 who states that the movement of LMOs 'take place primarily for commercial reasons'. See also generally Friends of the Earth International *Who benefits from GM crops* (n 48 above).

63 Jabara (n 4 above) 139.

64 See Nanda & Pring (n 1 above) 357.

65 M Chong 'Rhetoric and reality: The case of the golden rice in Thailand' (2002) available at http://wwweinnadi.cornell.edu/southasia/workshop/pdf/golden_rice.pdf (accessed on 22 September 2005)

66 As above. See also Jabara (n 4 above) 139. See also generally Kolehmainen (n 19 above) 282.

67 Jabara (n 4 above) 140.

68 See for discussion, J Yoder 'Genetically modified grain' available http://www.goshen.edu/bio/Biol410/BSSpapers99/jeri.html (accessed 22 September 2005).

69 As above.

poly and consequently threaten rather than promote food security.[70] In this regard Tudge makes the following observation:[71]

> If the world embraces GM crops, all agriculture will be controlled by a few high tech companies and the governments to which they are loosely answerable. All hope of autonomy is wiped out at a stroke.

The above are dilemmas facing those charged with creating a global regulatory regime for biotechnology. It is these dilemmas and conflicts that will guide the analysis of the Protocol in section 4 of the chapter. Given these dilemmas, conflicts and unresolved scientific issues, the question in this chapter relates to the kinds of compromises and trade-offs that are made in the regime on biodiversity. In the next section I briefly set out the drafting history and the text of the Protocol.

3. Biosafety under the biodiversity regime

3.1 The Biodiversity Convention

The Biodiversity Convention was adopted at the 1992 UN Conference on Environment and Development as part of the Rio instruments. As with the United Nations Framework Convention on Climate Change[72] considered in the previous chapter, it is a typical framework, setting out broad principles as well as the institutional structure of the regime. The Convention's objectives are three-fold: (i) the conservation of biological diversity; (ii) sustainable use of the components of biodiversity; (iii) the fair and equitable sharing of the benefits arising out of the benefits of the utilisation of genetic resources.[73] In addition to the objectives set out above, the Convention also declares itself to be based on the principle of the sovereign right of states to exploit their natural resources pursuant to their own environmental policies as limited by their responsibility to ensure that activities within their jurisdiction or control do not cause environmental harm beyond their jurisdiction.[74] Other broad principles in the Convention include the principle of co-operation 'for the conservation and sustainable use' of biodiversity,[75] as well as *in-*

70 See Nanda & Pring (n 1 above) 357. The Friends of the Earth report cited above suggests that three companies – Monsanto, Syngeta and Bayer 'are responsible for virtually all of the commercially released GM crops in the world today'. See Friends of the Earth *Who benefits from GM crops* (n 48 above) para 1.2. See also Yoder (n 68 above) who reminds us that '15 - 20% of the world's food is grown by farmers who cannot afford to buy seeds every year'.

71 Tudge (n 58 above).

72 The United Nations Framework Convention on Climate Change (1992) reprinted in Cullet & Gowlland-Gualtieri (n 5 above) 124.

73 Art 1 Convention on Biological Diversity.

74 Art 3 Convention on Biological Diversity.

75 Art 5 Convention on Biological Diversity.

situ[76] and *ex-situ*[77] conservation. In the light of the effects, positive or negative (noted in section 2 of this chapter) that modern biotechnology can have on biodiversity, it was appropriate that the regime on biodiversity should in some way regulate biotechnology to meet the stated purposes.

The Biodiversity regime is characteristic of modern multilateral environmental agreements in the sense that it is developed incrementally. Thus these regimes have a framework treaty which provides basic principles and objectives. The idea is that these basic principles and objectives will be the foundation upon which 'harder' obligations will be built.[78] The Convention on Biological Diversity is the framework Convention for the Biodiversity regime. The Protocol builds upon the Convention by providing 'harder' and more specific norms and procedures on the transboundary movement of genetically modified organisms.

During the negotiations on the drafting of the Biodiversity Convention, Malaysia and other developing countries called for a prior informed consent procedure to be instituted to regulate the transboundary movement of GMOs.[79] However, this suggestion received criticism, primarily from the North. As a compromise article 19, providing for the future elaboration of an agreement on living modified organisms (LMOs), was included in the Convention. In addition to article 19, other provisions affecting biotechnology include articles 15 and 16. Article 15 is concerned with access to genetic resources, which is vital for the development of biotechnology, while article 16 is concerned with the transfer of technology, which would include technology for the modification of biological resources.

Article 15 begins by recognising, in accordance with the principle of sovereignty over natural resources, that 'the authority to determine access to genetic resources rests with the' governments

76 Art 8 Convention on Biological Diversity.

77 Art 9 Convention on Biological Diversity.

78 Although the Biodiversity Convention, as a convention, would traditionally be referred to as a 'hard instrument', there is something to be said for the view the provisions of such framework conventions are, nevertheless, 'soft'. Thus a distinction between soft and hard law can be made not only with reference to the form, eg whether an instrument is a convention or a resolution, but also with reference to the strength or concreteness of the obligations undertaken. It is thus conceivable that formally 'hard' instruments can contain 'soft' norms. See, for a related analysis of 'hard' and 'soft' law, D Shelton 'Introduction' in D Shelton (ed) *Commitment and compliance: The role of non-binding norms in the international legal system* (2000) 10 *et seq*.

79 A Gupta 'Governing trade in genetically modified organisms' (2000) 42 *Environment* 23 24. This call for prior informed consent in the Biodiversity Convention arose from a fear on the part of developing states that GMOs could be transported into their territories where they would have neither the capacity nor the regulations to deal with potential hazards posed by such GMOs.

of the state in which the resources are to be found.[80] The Convention provides that state parties are to 'endeavour to create conditions to facilitate access to genetic resources'.[81] However, such access is supposed to be 'for environmentally sound uses'. The Convention further provides that access is to be granted on 'mutually agreed terms'[82] and subject to 'prior informed consent'.[83] Importantly, the Convention requires the sharing 'in a fair and equitable way' of the benefits of access to genetic resources with the state providing the resource.[84]

Article 16, concerned with the transfer of technology, provides that 'technology includes biotechnology'.[85] In terms of this provision, developed state parties are to provide for the transfer of technologies to other developing state parties.[86] The transfer of technologies is to take place 'under fair and most favourable terms'.[87] Needless to say, this provision on the transfer of technologies is, as with the equivalent provision in the Climate Change Convention, in keeping with common but differentiated responsibilities as discussed in chapter 3. Again, similar to the UNFCCC, the Biodiversity Convention also provides for the transfer of financial resources 'in respect of those national activities which are intended to achieve the objectives' of the Convention.[88] In this context, developed countries are to provide 'new and additional' finances to help developing countries 'meet the agreed full incremental costs' for measures under the Convention.[89] The phrase 'incremental costs' limits the financing to costs that would not have otherwise been incurred by the developing country.[90] As in the Climate Change Convention, the Biodiversity Convention makes provision for financial resources, a condition for developing countries to fulfil their commitments under the Convention.[91]

While articles 15 and 16 relate to issues affecting biotechnology. Article 19 lays the foundation for the Protocol. Article 19(3) provides as follows:[92]

80 Art 15(1) Convention on Biological Diversity
81 Art 15(2) Convention on Biological Diversity
82 Art 15(4) Convention on Biological Diversity.
83 Art 15(5) Convention on Biological Diversity.
84 Art 15(7) Convention on Biological Diversity.
85 Art 16(1) Convention on Biological Diversity.
86 As above.
87 Art 16(2) Convention on Biological Diversity.
88 Art 20(1) Convention on Biological Diversity.
89 Art 20(2) Convention on Biological Diversity.
90 This phrase, along with its nuances and complexities, is explored in more depth in the chapter on the Global Environment Facility (ch 6).
91 Art 20(4) of the Convention on Biological Diversity provides as follows: 'The extent to which developing country Parties will effectively implement their commitments under this Convention will depend on the effective implementation by developed country Parties of their commitments under this Convention related to financial resources and transfer of technology'.
92 Art 19(3) Convention on Biological Diversity.

> The parties shall consider the need for and modalities of a protocol setting out appropriate procedures, including, in particular, advance informed agreement, in the field of the safe transfer, handling and use of any living modified organism resulting from biotechnology that may have adverse effect on the conservation and sustainable use of biological diversity.

Article 19(3) was, in a way, a promise to developing countries that although not adequately dealt with, their cries for protection against the potential adverse effects of GMOs had been heard by the world. At the second COP to the Biodiversity Convention the parties agreed to establish an *ad hoc* Working Group on Biosafety with the mandate to develop a Protocol. The Protocol was intended to make true the promise of article 19(3) of the Convention by providing a legally binding instrument to deal with the fears related to the transboundary movement of genetically modified organisms.

3.2 Key Provisions of the Protocol

The plan was to have a Protocol ready for adoption by the extraordinary COP meeting held at Cartagena, Colombia, in 1999. However, by the end of that meeting it was clear that reaching an agreement on some of the contentious issues was not going to be an easy task. There remained sharp differences between the various groupings involved in the negotiation of the Protocol.

The literature on the negotiation process identifies five separate alliances.[93] A prominent group, called the Miami group, comprised six agricultural exporting countries namely the United States, Australia, Canada, Argentina, Chile and Uruguay. Another prominent group in the negotiation process was the European Union. The Compromise group comprises mostly OECD countries that are not agricultural exporters and not part of the European Union such as Japan, Mexico, South Korea, Norway and Singapore. The Central European countries also formed a negotiation block. The developing countries, excluding developing countries in the Miami group, also formed a negotiation block, the Like-Minded group. Of these alliances the Like-Minded group, the Miami group and the European Union can be singled out as the most prominent participants at the negotiations.

93 See especially C Bail *et al* (eds) *The Cartagena Protocol on Biosafety: Reconciling trade in biotechnology with environment and development* (2002) which is a collection of essays from people who were intimately involved in the negotiations leading to the adoption of the Protocol.

The issues dividing these groups related to the scope of the Protocol, the use of the Advanced Informed Agreement (AIA) Procedure, the inclusion of the precautionary principle in the Protocol and the relationship of the Protocol to the WTO agreements.[94] In general, the Miami group sought a limited and weak Protocol which would ensure that the free trade system was unaffected, while the other groups, in particular the European Union and the Like-Minded group, sought a stronger Protocol.[95] In the first place, the Miami group argued that the scope of the Protocol and the scope of the AIA should be limited. The Like-Minded group, on the other hand, sought to widen the scope of the Protocol and the AIA procedure under the Protocol. Similarly, it was the Miami group that opposed the inclusion of the precautionary principle while the European Union sought the inclusion of the precautionary principle as part of the decision-making process. Finally, the Miami group sought a clear provision expressing the supremacy of the WTO in case of conflict. In the next subsection look at the content of the Protocol with specific reference to these issues.

The following subsection consists of a brief descriptive analysis of the provisions included in the Cartagena Protocol. In it I will describe the scope of the Protocol and its various procedures, decision-making under the Protocol, the relationship between the agreement and the WTO agreements, as well as other provisions in the agreement relevant to sustainable development, such as the financial mechanisms. Bearing in mind the various dilemmas and conflicts faced by states in the negotiation of the Protocol, the key provisions of the Protocol described in this section will be evaluated in terms of the variations of sustainable development developed in chapter 3.

3.2.1 Scope of the Protocol and AIA procedure

With regards to the scope of the agreement, the Protocol declares itself to be applicable to the:[96]

> transboundary movement, transit, handling and use of all Living Modified Organism that may have adverse effects on the conservation and sustainable use of biological diversity, taking also into account risks to human health.

From this article two points can be made. The first point is that article 4 suggests that the Protocol is more of a trade agreement than an environmental agreement. While it may be said that the main purpose

94 For details regarding the arguments of the various groups on these contentious issues, see generally Tudge (n 58 above). See also SW Burgiel 'The Cartagena Protocol on Biosafety: Taking steps from negotiation to implementation' (2002) 11 *RECIEL* 53.

95 Burgiel (n 94 above) 55.

96 Art 4 Cartagena Protocol.

of the agreement is the preservation of biodiversity, an environmental goal, the tool used to deal with the specific environmental issue is the regulation of trade in specific organisms that may harm biodiversity, that is LMOs. Any living modified organism not potentially destined for transboundary movement is not subject to the Protocol.[97] In this respect the Protocol does not go as far as an IUCN resolution calling for a 'moratorium on further environmental release of GMOs'.[98] Moreover, the Protocol is different from, for example, the International Treaty on Plant Genetic Resources for Food and Agriculture, which is concerned with facilitating access to genetic resources as well as benefit-sharing from the use of such resources rather than the processes necessary for trade in any genetic resources.[99] The Protocol is concerned primarily with requirements for trade in certain LMOs.

The second point worth making is that the applicability of the Protocol is limited to LMOs that 'may have adverse effect on ... biodiversity'. Thus, while 'risks to human health' are to be taken into consideration, the primary objective is biodiversity preservation.[100] Such an interpretation would be consistent with article 19 of the Biodiversity Convention, which can be said to be the basis for the Protocol. Article 19 of the CBD requires the parties to the Convention to adopt a Protocol on LMOs that 'may have adverse effects on the conservation and sustainable use of biological diversity'. The provision does not include any reference to human health considerations.[101] This secondary nature of human health to the regulation of GMOs is confirmed by article 7(4) of the Protocol which excludes covered LMOs that are 'not likely to have adverse effects' on

97 See, eg, art 18 Cartagena Protocol, dealing with handling and packaging. It makes it clear that this applies to LMOs subject to the transboundary movement or LMOs that will, at some point, be destined to such movement.

98 Res 3.007, Moratorium on the Further Release of Genetically Modified Organisms, adopted at the 2004 IUCN World Conservation Congress, Bangkok, Thailand (on file with author).

99 International Treaty on Plant Genetic Resources for Food and Agriculture (2001) in Cullet & Gowlland-Gualtieri (n 5 above). For discussion on the relationship between the Biodiversity Convention and the International Treaty on Plant Resource, see A van Hahn 'Implementation and further development of the Biodiversity Convention: Access to genetic resources, benefit sharing and traditional knowledge of indigenous and local communities' (2003) 63 *Heidelberg Journal of International Law* 295 307 *et seq*.

100 Similarly, art 16(2) of the Cartagena Protocol provides that the measures based on risk assessment are to be imposed to prevent adverse effects on LMOs 'on the conservation and sustainable use of biological diversity, taking also into account risks to human health'. See also art 15(1) Cartagena Protocol.

101 It is also notable that the current text containing the phrase 'taking also into account human health' was proposed by the EU which favoured the exclusion of LMOs identified as unlikely to have adverse effects on biodiversity. See UNEP: Secretariat of the Biodiversity Convention *Cartagena Protocol on Biosafety: A record of the negotiations* (2003) available at http://wwwbiodiv.org/doc/publications/bs-brochure-03-en.pdf (accessed 5 February 2006).

the biodiversity from the AIA procedure.[102] Similarly, article 7(2) excludes from the scope of the AIA procedure, LMOs that are intended for use as food, feed or for processing (LMO-FFPs). LMO-FFPs and LMOs not likely to have an adverse effect on biodiversity will be governed by a less stringent procedure. Both points made here serve to indicate the limited nature of the Protocol. It is also worth mentioning that the literature shows that the group seeking to limit the scope of the Protocol was consistently the Miami group.[103] Moreover, the Protocol excludes from its scope the transboundary movement of genetically modified 'pharmaceuticals for humans that are addressed' by other international agreements.[104]

The Protocol's primary tool for regulating trade in LMOs covered by the scope of the agreement is the advanced informed agreement (AIA) procedure. Under the AIA of the Protocol the state of export has the duty to notify (or require the exporter to notify) in writing the state of import prior to the intentional transboundary movement of LMOs.[105] Within 90 days of the receipt of the notification, the state of import is obliged to acknowledge receipt in writing.[106] The written acknowledgment of receipt is to state, *inter alia,* whether the import can go ahead in terms of the regulatory framework established in the state of import.[107] Within 270 days of the receipt of notification the state of import must inform the state of export and the Biosafety Clearing-House[108] of its decision to allow the import, with or without conditions, prohibit the import, request additional information or extend the specified time periods.[109] The state of import is further obliged to give reasons for its decision unless the decision is an unconditional approval of the import.[110] What is unclear under the Protocol is the consequences upon the failure of the state of import to respond to the notification. Article 10(5) of the Protocol provides that failure on the part of the state of import 'to communicate its decision within two hundred and seventy days' is not to be interpreted

102 According to the Protocol, the COP serving as the Meeting of Parties (COP/MOP) may make a determination that specific covered LMOs are not likely to have an adverse effect on biodiversity. Such LMOs will then not be subject to the AIA procedure.

103 See generally essays in Bail *et al* (n 93 above).

104 Art 5 Cartagena Protocol.

105 Art 8(1) Cartagena Protocol. The notification required in terms of this provision should contain, at least, the information contained in Annex I.

106 Art 9(1) Cartagena Protocol.

107 Art 9(2) Cartagena Protocol. In addition, the state of import can inform state of export that it can go ahead with the shipment either after it has given written consent for shipments or after, at least 90 days, without subsequent consent. Art 10(2) Cartagena Protocol.

108 The Biosafety Clearing-house is an institution established in article 20 of the Protocol to operate as part of the clearing-house in the Biodiversity Convention, with the aim of facilitating the exchange of information and assisting the parties in the implementation of the Protocol. See art 20(1) of the Protocol.

109 Art 10(3) Cartagena Protocol.

110 Art 10(4) Cartagena Protocol.

as 'consent to an intentional transboundary movement'. This provision is very ambiguous. It is not clear, for example, what the implications of a failure to respond for a period much longer than 270 days would be. It seems, however, that this provision cannot be interpreted as implying that failure to respond implies rejection of the transboundary movement.[111] The Basel Convention on Transboundary Movement of Hazardous Waste, in contrast, makes it clear that in the absence of consent, transboundary movement may not take place.[112]

The AIA described above is limited to the first transboundary movement of covered LMOs destined 'for intentional introduction into the environment of' state of import.[113] LMOs destined for 'intentional introduction into the environment' do not include LMOs that are intended to be used as food or feed, or for processing.[114]

The Protocol establishes a different procedure to be applicable to LMOs intended for use as food or feed, or for processing (LMO-FFPs). Under article 11 of the Protocol, once a Party makes a final decision regarding domestic use of an LMO 'that may be subject to transboundary movement' for use as food, feed or for processing, then such a party must inform the parties through the Biosafety Clearing-House.[115] The notification of other parties through the Clearing-House must include relevant information on the LMO-FFP concerned.[116] Other parties must then 'take a decision' under their own domestic regulatory framework on the import of such LMOs destined for food, feed or processing.[117] Where a state (in particular developing states and states with economies in transition) does not have a regulatory framework for LMO-FFPs such a state can declare, through the Clearing-House, that its decision on whether or not

111 See eg Stoll (n 8 above) 91 who comments on the provision: 'The Biosafety Protocol ... refrains from stating an unequivocal prohibition of export' in cases where consent has not been given. See, however, E Schoonejans 'Advance informed agreement procedure' in Bail *et al* (n 93 above) 313 who provides the following analysis of article 10(5) of the Protocol: 'Some may argue that the language '... shall not imply consent ...' in article 10(5) does not necessarily mean 'does imply refusal' but because the parallel provision in article 11(7) says '... shall not imply its consent or refusal', the omission of the word 'refusal' in articles 9(4) and 10(5) at least leads to the impossibility of interpreting that lack of response in Articles 9(4) or 10(5) as 'shall not imply refusal'.

112 Art 4(1)(c) of the Basel Convention on the Control of Transboundary Movement of Hazardous Wastes and their Disposal which provides that 'Parties shall prohibit or shall not permit the export of hazardous wastes and other wastes if the state of import does not consent in writing to the specific import, in the case where that state of import has not prohibited the import of such wastes'.

113 Art 7(1) Cartagena Protocol.

114 Art 7(2) Cartagena Protocol.

115 Art 11(1) Cartagena Protocol.

116 As above. Annex II details the information to be included.

117 Art 11(2) Cartagena Protocol.

import of LMO-FFPs will be taken within a period of 170 days after a risk assessment.[118]

The Protocol also excludes from the scope of the AIA procedure LMOs in transit or LMOs destined for contained use.[119] Contained use is defined in the Protocol as 'any operation within a facility' involving LMOs controlled by measures that 'limit their contact with, and their impact on' the environment.[120] This would exclude from the scope of the AIA procedure, for example, LMOs exported for research purposes. It is not clear whether such LMOs are then to be regulated under article 11 procedure or not. Article 11, by its own terms, only applies to LMO-FFPs. Whatever the case, this provision further limits the reach of the Protocol.

Clearly, the article 11 procedure is less stringent than the AIA procedure.[121] First, under the AIA procedure the state of export informs the specific state of import of its intention to export LMOs, whereas there is no direct notification to state of import in terms of article 11. The article 11 procedure described above essentially has the effect of placing the burden to act on the state of import which will, in most instances, be a developing country.[122] The relative weakness of the article 11 procedure is also illustrated by the information that must be provided in terms of article 11.[123] The information that has to be provided under the latter procedure, contained in Annex I, is less stringent than the information required under the AIA procedure, contained in Annex I.[124] In particular, Annex II, listing the information required for an article 11 procedure, does not include the following information required under Annex I for the AIA procedure:

(i) a description of the nucleic acid or the modification introduced, the technique used, and the resulting characteristic of the LMO;

118 Art 11(6) Cartagena Protocol.

119 Art 6 Cartagena Protocol.

120 Art 3 Cartagena Protocol.

121 Schoonejans (n 111 above) 298 describes the procedure as 'less detailed'.

122 See Schnier (n 12 above) 410 and Oliva (n 8 above) 25. Gupta says that the article 11 is 'far from a transaction-based notification and consent procedure'. He further notes that this procedure 'leaves the responsibility for initiating action to prevent harm by LMO-commodities on importing countries'. Gupta (n 79 above) 29.

123 See art 11 Cartagena Protocol.

124 The information required under the AIA procedure contained in Annex I of the Protocol is as follows: Name and contact details of exporter, name and contact details of importer, name and identity of LMO including domestic classification, intended dates of the transboundary movement, taxonomic status, common name and characteristic of recipient organism, centres of origin and centres of genetic diversity of organism, description of nucleic acid or the modification introduced, the technique used and the resulting characteristic of LMO, intended use of LMO, quality of volume to be transferred, a previous risk assessment, suggested methods of safe handling, regulatory status of LMO within state of export, result and purpose of any notification by the exporter to other states, and a declaration that the information provided is correct.

(ii) quantity or volume of the LMO to be transferred;
(iii) regulatory status of the LMO in state of export; and
(iv) the result and purpose of any notification by state of export to other states regarding the LMO.

In addition to the differences in the procedures required to obtain consent for shipments of LMOs, the Protocol also creates different labelling requirements for LMO-FFPs and LMOs intended for intentional introduction into the environment. In the case of the transboundary movement of LMO-FFPs, the documentation must state that the shipment 'may contain' LMOs and that the shipment is not intended for intentional introduction into the environment.[125] On the other hand, documentation accompanying LMOs subject to the AIA procedure must clearly identify such shipments as LMOs and must specify, *inter alia*, the identity and relevant traits as well as requirements for safe handling of the LMOs in question.[126] The labelling requirements contained in article 18(2) are a compromise between the EU and Miami group.[127] The Miami group had sought to have the labelling requirements applicable only to LMOs subject to the AIA procedure while the EU sought to have the detailed information included in the labelling requirement for LMO-FFPs.

To summarise, it can be said that the Protocol is limited in its scope of application both in terms of the LMOs to which it applies and in terms of the fact that it really only applies to *trade* in LMOs and does not seek to regulate other aspects of LMOs. In addition to its limited scope of application, the Protocol's main regulatory procedure, the AIA procedure, as well as the stringent labelling requirements, are limited only to LMOs that are destined for intentional introduction to the environment. On the other hand, it is also noted that, although not as strict as the regulations for LMOs intended for introduction into the environment, there is nevertheless regulation of trade in LMO FFPs. In this sense the Biosafety Protocol, by walking this tightrope, approximates a balancing act in its approach to biotechnology.

3.2.2 Decision-making: Precaution and socio-economic factors

Another contentious issue in the Biosafety Protocol is the decision-making procedure. There had been question marks posed about whether the precautionary approach is appropriate for the regulation of biotechnology and also about the kind of action the precautionary approach would require in the context of biotechnology. In criticising

125 Art 18(2)(a) Cartagena Protocol.
126 Art 18(2)(c) Cartagena Protocol.
127 For details of the proposals and arguments on labelling, see Tracy (n 2 above) 144 *et seq*. See also Nanda & Pring (n 1 above) 389.

the application of the precautionary approach to biotechnology, Adler makes the following observation:[128]

> The problem is that by focusing on one set of risks – those posed by the introduction of new technologies with somewhat uncertain effects – the precautionary principle turns a blind eye to the harms that occur, or are made worse, due to a lack of technological development.

The position of the Miami group regarding the precautionary approach had been that there should be a simple reference to the precautionary approach. However, the Miami group was against any attempt to state the approach as an objective of the Protocol and also sought to block any inclusion of the precautionary approach in the decision-making procedure.[129] The Protocol, however, does include the precautionary approach as an objective.[130] More importantly, the Protocol includes the precautionary approach in both the decision-making procedures for transboundary movement of LMOs covered by the AIA procedure and that required for LMO-FFPs. The Protocol provides as follows:[131]

> Lack of scientific certainty due to insufficient relevant scientific information and knowledge regarding the extent of the potential adverse effects of a living modified organism on the conservation and sustainable use of biological diversity in the Party of import, taking also into account risks to human health, shall not prevent that Party from taking a decision, as appropriate, with regard to the import of the living modified organism in question ... in order to avoid or minimise such potential adverse effects.

In light of the scientific uncertainty apparent in biotechnology, the precautionary principle allows individual states a margin to make determinations about the level of risk that they are willing to take. An important point in this regard, which plays a key role in the analysis in section 4 of the chapter, is that the inclusion of the precautionary principle has the *potential* to disrupt trade in LMOs in a major way.

A second bone of contention relating to decision-making was the question whether, in making decisions under the Protocol, factors other than scientific factors, in particular socio-economic factors, should be taken into account. Needless to say, the Miami group sought to have an agreement that required decision-making to be based on

128 Adler (n 3 above) 195. Adler's remarks reflect what can be termed an economic approach to precaution. See in this respect, A Trouwborst *The Precautionary rights and duties of states* (2006) 28, who states that in economic perspectives on risk 'both negative *and* positive consequences are integrated into the analysis' (emphasis original). See also Guruswamy (n 9 above) 483, where she focuses on the indeterminacy and ambiguity of the precautionary principle.

129 Nanda & Pring (n 1 above) 390.

130 Art 1 of the Cartagena Protocol reads, in part, as follows: 'In accordance with the precautionary approach ... the objective of this Protocol is to contribute to ensuring an adequate level of protection' against potential harm from modern biotechnology. Moreover, the fourth paragraph of the preamble reaffirms the precautionary approach contained in Principle 15 of the Rio Declaration.

131 Art 10(6) Cartagena Protocol. See also art 11(8) Cartagena Protocol.

sound scientific knowledge, while the Like-Minded group argued for a Protocol that would entitle decision-makers to base decisions not only on scientific considerations, but also on socio-economic considerations. Including socio-economic considerations as factors for decision-making would allow the state of import a wider discretion in making decisions about the import of LMOs and, consequently, would act as a potential barrier to trade. By limiting the decision-making factors to science, the discretion of the state of import is significantly reduced. Reducing the discretion of the state import in turn reduces the potential impact on free trade. The Protocol, as a compromise, distinguishes two procedures, namely, risk assessment and risk management. The relationship of risk management to risk assessment has been described as follows:[132]

> Risk assessment offers a quantitative assessment of risk based on the best available science, but the decision as to whether, or to what extent, GMOs should be regulated is a policy judgment made by risk managers.

Risk assessment is to be 'carried out in a scientifically sound manner ... and taking into account recognised risk assessment techniques'.[133] Article 16 of the Protocol provides for the management of risks established under the risk assessment procedure of article 15. Although article 16 does not mention socio-economic factors, the Protocol does allow states to take socio-economic considerations into account. Article 26 provides that states, when making decisions, 'may take into account, consistent with their international obligations, socio-economic considerations arising from the impact of living modified organisms on the conservation and sustainable use of biological diversity'.[134]

The importance of this for the relationship to the free trade regime is obvious. In making decisions on risk management, states could base decisions on reasons that are viewed as protectionist, such as the protection of local agriculture (a socio-economic concern). Thus, Oliva notes that while the kinds of socio-economic considerations that can be taken on board are unclear it:[135]

> is conceivable that a country could ban imports of seeds derived from biotechnology due to consumer concerns ('social' considerations), or because of the consequences to local farmers (an 'economic' consideration).

132 Guruswamy (n 9 above) 481.

133 Art 15(1) Cartagena Protocol.

134 Art 26(1) Cartagena Protocol. What is interesting, however, is that art 10(1) of the Protocol provides that the decisions taken by a state of import 'shall be in accordance with art 15'. Article 10 does not refer to art 26 as a legitimate basis for the decision of the state of import.

135 Oliva (n 8 above) 26. Whether reliance on socio-economic considerations is narrowed by the phrase 'consistent with international obligations' is discussed in the analysis of art 26 below (para 4.3).

Again, in this area the Protocol has had to deal with the three apparently conflicting concerns in decision-making relating to GMOs. The Protocol has had to find some kind of balance between the need for reliance on available scientific information versus the need for precaution, on the one hand, and the reliance on scientific assessment methods versus the need to consider socio-economic factors on the other. The protocol allows parties, in making decisions, to take into account a variety of factors including scientific assessments, precaution and socio-economic considerations.

Moreover, the Protocol includes procedures for the review of decisions taken in terms of the decision-making procedures described above.[136] Article 12(1) allows a state of import to 'review and change a decision' it took relating to the import of LMOs 'in light of new scientific information'. In such a case, the state of import has to inform previously notified states as well as the Biosafety Clearing-House of the changed decision. In terms of this provision, the state of import has to provide reasons for its change of decision (presumably this applies especially where the change is from allowing to refuse the import of LMOs). Similarly, the state of export may request the state of import to review its decisions where there has either been a change of circumstances that may affect the decision or where additional scientific or technical information having a bearing on the decision has become available.[137] In such a case the state of import is obliged to respond within 90 days, giving reasons.[138]

Two points are worth noting about the provisions on the review of decisions. First, the provisions imply a need for continued assessment of the scientific information and other factors having a bearing on the impact of LMOs on biodiversity. Second, the provision places a burden of argument on the state of import. Article 12(1), for example, provides that the state of import 'shall set out reasons for its decisions'. Similarly, where the request is made by the state of export for a review of decisions in terms of article 12(2), the state of import has to respond in writing, setting out 'reasons for its decision'.[139] Obviously, the decision of the state of import (whether in terms of article 12(1) or 12(3)) will be uncontested unless it amounts to a refusal to allow the import of LMOs. Thus, by placing the burden of argument on the state of import, the Protocol, essentially, requires that refusals for the import of LMOs be justified.

The placing of the burden of arguments on states wishing to prohibit import of LMOs is evident in the AIA procedure of the Protocol as well. In fact, article 10 makes it clear that the need for

136 See art 12 Cartagena Protocol.
137 Art 12(2) Cartagena Protocol.
138 Art 12(3) Cartagena Protocol.
139 Art 12(3) Cartagena Protocol.

justification arises where a state of import refuses the import of LMOs. Article 10(4) provides as follows: 'Except in a case in which consent is unconditional, a decision under paragraph 3 above, shall set out the reasons on which it is based'.

Thus, the Protocol places the burden of argument on those seeking to prohibit import of LMOs. In most instances this may turn out to be developing countries which lack the capacity to sufficiently gather and evaluate scientific information relating to the risks posed by LMOs on biodiversity. In this respect it is interesting to note that the provisions of the Protocol relating to risk-management do not take into account this probable lack of capacity.[140] What the Protocol does do is to provide that the costs of the risk assessment 'shall be borne by the notifier'.[141] However, given that risk assessment is but one factor to be considered, the question of capacity remains.

Moreover, it is not clear whether placing the financial costs of the risk assessment on the exporter implies, at the same time, that the exporter has a degree of influence on the risk assessment process, including the identity of the assessor and the risk assessment techniques. Furthermore, all this raises the question of who has the knowledge on the relevant LMO. The information certainly does not lie with the importing state. The information lies with the exporter (or the developer of the technology) who has an interest in having the export approved. It is this exporter who will have the choice of the kind of information to transmit for the purposes of risk assessment, as well as the way in which to present this information. This will make it very difficult for developing state parties to make a decision to object to the import of LMOs.

3.2.3 Relationship of the Protocol to WTO Agreements

In addition to the scope and decision-making procedures, a third area of conflict is the relationship between the Protocol and the WTO agreements.[142] While WTO agreements aim at increasing free trade,

140 See art 16 of the Protocol. Although article 22 deals with capacity building, the provision in no way sheds light on how the lack of capacity influences risk management.

141 Art 15(3) of the Protocol.

142 For an analysis of the various positions taken at the negotiations see S Safrin 'The relationship with other agreements: Much ado about a savings clause' in Bail *et al* (n 93 above) 438 *et seq*.

the Cartagena Protocol, through the AIA procedure, the inclusion of precautionary principle and by allowing socio-economic factors in decision-making creates potential trade barriers.[143] As I mentioned earlier, I have no intention of undertaking an analysis to determine whether the Protocol is compatible with the WTO agreement. Such an analysis will not add any value to the central question posed in the study.[144] What is relevant to the theme of the study, however, is they way in which the Protocol has dealt with the potential conflict.

The Protocol 'deals' with the potential conflict between the WTO agreements and the Protocol by including very strange language in the preamble. The tenth paragraph of the preamble emphasises that the Protocol 'shall not be interpreted as implying a change in the rights and obligations of a Party under any existing international agreements' (the savings clause). The implication of this provision is, of course, that WTO agreements should take precedence over the Protocol. However, this recital is immediately qualified in the eleventh recital of the preamble which provides that the 'above recital is not intended to subordinate this Protocol to other international agreements' (the no-subordination clause). The latter provision appears to nullify the former. These very curious preambular provisions have been described as making 'a travesty of international law'.[145] Guruswamy says of the provisions relating to the relationship between the Protocol and other (trade) agreements:[146]

> If, as it is abundantly clear, the parties to the Biosafety Protocol were unable to agree on the priority or precedence of the Biosafety Protocol over other trade treaties, they ought to have recognised their

143 The United States made a request for the establishment of panel to settle the dispute pertaining to the European Union's moratorium on the approval of biotech products. See *EC – Measures Affecting the Approval and Marketing of Biotech Products* WT/DS291/23 8 August 2003, available at http://www.wto.org (accessed 15 January 2004). The panel reached a decision in 2006. The leaked interim report of the Panel in *EC-Measures Affecting the Approval and Marketing of Biotech Products* is available at http://www.foei.org/media/2006/WTO report descriptive.pdf and http://www.foei.org/media/2006/WTO report findings.pdf (accessed 8 August 2006).

144 See n 7 above for literature analysing the compatibility of the Protocol with the WTO agreements.

145 Guruswamy (n 9 above) 491. Incidentally, the FAO International Treaty on Plant Genetic Resources for Food and Agriculture contains a similar recital: '*Affirming* that nothing in this treaty shall be interpreted as implying in any way a change in the rights and obligations of the Contracting Parties under other international agreements; *Understanding* that the above recital is not intended to create a hierarchy between this Treaty and other international agreements'. The preamble of the FAO treaty has not caused much furore, probably because the agreement more than likely envisaged by the recitals is the Biodiversity Convention which is consistent with the FAO treaty.

146 Safrin (n 142 above). She goes on to say the Protocol is 'a corrupted treaty that adopts the impossible and absurd position of both affirming and rejecting earlier obligations'.

disagreement during the negotiation process, but refrained from using the Protocol to publicise their differences.

Whether these two preambular recitals simply cancel each other out as suggested by Guruswamy is unclear.[147] What is clear, however, is that these recitals will be very important for the interpretation of the Protocol in the case of irreconcilable conflict with any WTO agreements. If the no-subordination recital is given preference, the effect is that in the case of irreconcilable conflict the Protocol will be given effect to. This will reinforce the potential barriers to trade created by the decision-making process and, to a lesser extent, the AIA process under the Protocol. However, if the effect of the two recitals together is to reinforce the savings clause, then the effect would be to strip away the discretion of the state of import in the decision-making process and, consequently, to reinforce free trade ideals. In that sense, the preamble, as an interpretative tool for the Protocol, is critical.

A further indication of the relationship between the Protocol and WTO agreements may, arguably, be deduced from article 26 which allows states to, 'consistent with their international obligations', take socio-economic considerations into account. This provision equally raises the question whether the rights of the state of import are made subject to legal obligations imposed by WTO agreements. Again, such an interpretation of article 26 would have the effect of reducing the discretion of the state of import in the decision-making procedures and, consequently, reinforce free trade rights.

The three areas of contention discussed above, namely, the scope of the Protocol, questions surrounding decision-making and the relationship between the Protocol and the WTO will be analysed in terms of the three variations of sustainable development. However, in addition to these issues the Protocol does contain other provisions that are relevant for the consideration of any question relating to sustainable development, and therefore, deserve mention.

3.2.4 Provisions giving effect to intragenerational equity

As with other MEAs, including both climate change treaties, the Biodiversity Convention and the Protocol make provision for the transfer of financial resources from developed to developing countries.[148] The provisions for financial transfer under the Protocol are linked to equivalent provisions of the Convention. The Protocol provides, for example, that in implementing the provisions on financial resources transfer, 'the Parties shall take into account the

147 See also Schnier (n 12 above) 414, who describes the issue as 'unresolved'.
148 Art 28 Cartagena Protocol.

provisions of article 20 of the Convention'.[149] This means that the qualifiers applicable to finance transfers under the Convention, such as that the financing should be 'new and additional' and be for 'agreed full incremental costs', are equally applicable to financing under the Protocol.[150] In the context of the provision on financial resources, the Protocol also provides that the 'needs of developing countries', especially the 'least developed and the small island developing states' should be taken into account in efforts that relate to capacity-building.[151]

Given the nature of the obligations imposed by the Protocol and, in particular, the need for decision-making based on, *inter alia,* sound science, capacity-building is crucial for the full implementation of the Protocol. The Protocol, thus, has very detailed provisions on capacity-building.[152] The Protocol provides that parties should co-operate 'in the development and/or strengthening of human resources and institutional capacity' relating to biosafety for the 'effective implementation of' the Protocol.[153] Article 22 further provides for the transfer of 'financial resources and access to and transfer of technology and know-how' in accordance with the provisions of the Biodiversity Convention.[154] The Protocol does not provide for benefit sharing in the way envisioned under article 15 of the Convention.

Article 22, while capable of incorporating the access to genetic resources and benefit sharing provisions under the Convention, appears to be contextually limited to 'scientific and technical training in the proper and safe management of biotechnology' and the 'enhancement of technological and institutional capacities in biosafety'.[155] The provisions of the Protocol on capacity building are linked to financial transfers through article 28(3), which provides that in the context of article 22, the Conference of the Parties serving as the Meeting of the Parties (COP/MOP) should take into account the need for financial resources.

149 Art 28(1) Cartagena Protocol. The provisions of the Biodiversity Convention on financial transfers are discussed in para 3.1 of this ch.

150 See art 20 of the Convention. See also for discussion of 'new and additional' and 'full incremental costs' ch 7 below on the Global Environment Facility.

151 Art 28(4) Cartagena Protocol.

152 See generally art 22 Cartagena Protocol.

153 Art 22(2) Cartagena Protocol

154 Art 22(2) Cartagena Protocol.

155 Art 22(2) Cartagena Protocol. Compare this with art 16(1) of the Convention providing for the transfer of technology which 'includes biotechnology'.

4. Analysis — Establishing the central value in the Protocol

4.1 General

In this section I attempt to categorise the biodiversity regime, especially the Protocol, under one of the variations of sustainable development identified in Part B of the study. This requires that, using the various provisions of the Convention and the Protocol described above, the compromises and trade-offs reflected in the instruments are identified. Does the regime, when seen as a whole, appear to favour economic interests over environmental and social interests? Does the text of the instruments reflect environmental interests as the overarching objective? Does the regime favour social considerations? Are there any indications, when judging the Protocol holistically and taking into account the various conflicts and dilemmas identified above, that the Protocol attaches more importance to social, economic or environmental needs? I will assess the Protocol by looking at three key areas of the Protocol, namely, the scope of the Protocol (including the scope of the AIA procedure), the decision-making procedures and the relationship with other agreements (most notably the WTO). In addition, the various provisions of the Convention considered in paragraph 3.1 of this chapter are factored into the analysis.

In considering the various compromises and trade-offs represented in the Protocol, several points must be kept in mind. First, the issues are in many ways related. For example, the various arguments and positions adopted during the negotiations on the precautionary principle were inextricably linked to questions about the relationship between the WTO and the Protocol.[156] The same applies to arguments pertaining to the role of socio-economic considerations in decision-making. Second, an important point to keep in mind is the lack of scientific certainty regarding the nature and extent of the impact of GMOs on both the environment and human health. A third point, related to the second, is that, given the complexity of the GMO debate, difficulty arises in assigning a particular decision by drafters of the Protocol as reflecting one or other of the three values of sustainable development. In other words, the fact that proponents of GMOs assert that GMOs are beneficial to biodiversity while opponents assert that GMOs are harmful to biodiversity, makes the proposed analysis rather difficult. The same position applies to the claim made by proponents of GMOs regarding the potential of GMOs to be a solution to the world's food crisis. This

156 See the various accounts in Bail *et al* (n 93 above).

means that some of these claims and counterclaims have to be approached with caution.

4.2 The Scope of the Protocol

With regards to the scope of the Protocol, including the Protocol's main regulatory tool, the AIA procedure, a few points were noted above. The scope of the Protocol itself, is limited in three important ways. First, the Protocol does not apply to 'pharmaceuticals for humans' that are addressed by other agreements. Second, the Protocol primarily seeks to regulate LMOs that could have an impact on biodiversity while the role of human health is seen as secondary to the regulation LMOs. Thirdly, the operative provisions of the Protocol, with the exception of information sharing obligations, apply primarily to LMOs that are being traded or that are likely to be traded in the future.

The rationale for excluding pharmaceuticals for humans was that such pharmaceuticals were, in any event, covered by other agreements. [157] This is curious for two reasons. First, many LMOs covered by the Protocol are covered by other agreements, notably the WTO agreements and also the FAO International Treaty on Plant Genetic Resources for Food and Agriculture.[158] Second, it is unclear which agreements cover pharmaceuticals for human use. Marquard notes that, during the negotiations, the Like-Minded group raised several concerns regarding the exclusion of pharmaceuticals for humans.[159] One of those concerns was whether LMOs were really adequately covered elsewhere. She notes that the concerns of the Like-Minded group were allayed when:[160]

> details were circulated of the WHO Certification Scheme on the Quality of Pharmaceutical Products Moving in International Commerce. Under this scheme, a prospective party of import may ask for additional information, which could include an environmental assessment. If the party is not satisfied with the information it may refuse to accept a product.

It appears, from Marquard's account, that the 'agreement(s)' being referred to are the World Health Organisation's Certification Scheme. However, the Certification Scheme is not an agreement. The Scheme is a set of guidelines that WHO 'urges members to adopt and apply'.[161] It appears, further, that it was the pharmaceutical industry in North America and Europe that opposed the inclusion of

157 See H Marquard 'Scope' in Bail *et al* (n 93 above) 295.
158 See International Treaty on Plant Genetic Resources in Cullet and Gowlland-Gualtieri (n 5 above).
159 Marquard (n 157 above) 295.
160 As above.
161 See http://www.who.int/medicines/organization/qsm/activities/drugregul certification/certiguide.html (accessed 30 July 2004).

pharmaceuticals for humans in the Protocol.[162] This opposition, and consequent non-inclusion of pharmaceuticals for humans in the Protocol, can be explained in one of two ways. First, it may be that the inclusion of pharmaceuticals for humans in the Protocol would unduly hinder the movement of much-needed medicines.[163] From this perspective then, the restriction on the scope of the Protocol serves human needs. On the other hand, for the multi-billion dollar pharmaceutical industry, such inclusion might imply a loss of substantial revenue. Seen from that angle, the choice not to include pharmaceuticals for humans in the scope of the agreement appears to be a choice based on economic rather than health (social) concerns. It would be naïve to believe that profits are not the primary motivation for pharmaceutical companies in their arguments not to include pharmaceuticals in the scope of the Protocol. The various and well-publicised AIDS medication controversies where pharmaceuticals sought to prevent the manufacture and distribution of cheap AIDS drugs under the mantra of intellectual property (meaning loss profits) are excellent illustrations of this viewpoint.[164]

From the perspective of the limited objective and scope of the Protocol, however, the choice may appear somewhat defensible given that such pharmaceuticals are not destined for intentional release into the environment. After all, the Protocol is *primarily* limited to LMOs destined for intentional release into the environment.[165] While article 4 does mention 'risks to human health' the reference is couched in subsidiary terms. While Marquard is of the opinion that article 4 is *potentially* capable of meaning that the Protocol applies to LMOs that have a direct effect on human health even where such LMOs have no impact on biodiversity, the more correct interpretation

162 Marquard (n 157 above) 295.

163 As above.

164 See eg *Pharmaceutical Manufactures Association and Other v The President of South Africa and Other* 1999 (4) SA 788 (T) where the Pharmaceutical Manufacture Association in South Africa, backed by forty international pharmaceutical companies instituted a lawsuit against the South African government challenging a law that allowed the importation and distribution of AIDS drugs without the consent of the patent holder. See also H Kihl *Trips and AIDS in South Africa: New actors in international relations – Weighing patents, pills and patients* (2002) available at http://departments.oxy.edu/dwa/papers/103.pdf (accessed 7 August 2003). For other accounts see D Barker & J Mander 'The invisible government: The World Trade Organization: A global government for the new millennium? A primer' 1999 *The International Forum on Globalization* 1; M Cohn 'The World Trade Organization: Elevating property interests above human rights' (2001) 30 *Georgia Journal of International and Comparative Law* 427 436. See also 'US drops Brazil Case' available at http://news.bbc.co.uk/1/hi/business/1407472.st, (accessed 7 August 2003).

165 See art 4 of the Protocol. The argument advanced by Canada before the WTO panel on the relevance of the Cartagena Protocol is consistent with this viewpoint. In that case, Canada argued that as the Protocol is 'concerned the impact of LMOs on biodiversity, even under the European Community's theory, the *Protocol* is of no relevance to the risk assessment of biotech products for food use ...' See *EC-Measures Affecting the Approval and Marketing of Biotech Products* (n 143 above) at para 7.61.

would seem to be that, under article 4, the Protocol will apply to LMOs impacting on human health as a secondary effect flowing from an impact on biodiversity.[166] Accepting the possibility that the Protocol can apply to LMOs having no impact on biodiversity does not seem to be consistent with the subsidiary language used to refer to risks to human health throughout the Protocol.[167] To be fair to Marquard, she does not argue that under article 4, the Protocol applies to LMOs having no direct impact on biodiversity. She merely states the possibility that the provision could be interpreted in that way. From a sustainable development standpoint the inclusion of *secondary* impacts, serves to emphasise the interrelated nature of environmental and human health problems, which, after all, is what sustainable development is about.

However, for the purposes of the analysis, the exclusion of pharmaceuticals suggests that, in the hierarchy of values, social needs were not considered to be as important as environmental and economic needs. Environmental concerns, in the form of biodiversity, are represented while social concerns, in the form of risks to human health, are considered in the context of biodiversity loss. Certainly, given the general structure of the Protocol and the secondary nature of social concerns in the regulation of trade in LMOs, there is no reason why pharmaceuticals could not have been dealt with under article 11 as other LMOs not destined for release into the environment. What this illustrates is the trumping of social concerns (for economic reasons) by limiting their relevance to cases also involving biodiversity impacts.

In addition to the exclusion of pharmaceuticals for humans and limitation to LMOs that will have an impact on biodiversity, the

166 See discussion in Marquard (n 157 above) 295.

167 See in addition to the provisions of the Protocol cited, Annex III. Para 8(a) of Annex III similarly contains the phrase 'taking also into account risks to human health'. Moreover, para 9, which catalogues points to consider in the risk assessment, includes factors that suggest that the primary aim of the risk assessment is the determination of the impact of LMOs on biodiversity. The clearest example of this is reference to the receiving environment. This view of the interpretation of these articles is buttressed by the approaches to risk assessment in practice. According to the South African Biosafety National Focal Point, South Africa, while supporting the view that human health is equally important, treats risk assessment issues related to human health not affecting biodiversity in terms of the WHO Guidelines on Food Safety and not the Protocol. See e-mail discussion with Dr J Jaftha, contact person for the South African National Focal Point (on file with author). Similarly, according to Dr G Ridley of the National Focal Point in New Zealand, to import LMOs into New Zealand, it is not sufficient that all the requirements of the Biosafety Protocol are met. In addition, and apparently more importantly, the import must comply with the Hazardous Substances and New Organisms Act of 1996. What is interesting is that the purpose of the Act is to 'protect the environment, and the health and safety of people and communities'. The wording of that section, in contrast with the wording of Protocol, makes it clear that human health and biodiversity issues are treated as equal in importance. See e-mail discussion with Dr G Ridley (on file with author).

Protocol is also limited to LMOs that are destined to be subject to transboundary movement (or at least have the potential to be subject to such movement). This leaves out of the ambit of the Protocol many issues pertaining to biotechnology. For example, the Protocol does not impose any obligations (hard or soft) on the production of LMOs. This may well be defensible, from an economic point of view, as an understandable choice given the scientific uncertainty relating to the (long-term) risks and benefits of modern biotechnology. However the limitation of the scope of the Protocol to LMOs destined to be subject to transboundary movement also serves as a limitation of the environmental objectives set out in the Protocol.

The significant distinction in the processes relating to, on the one hand, LMOs destined for intentional introduction into the environment and, on the other, LMO-FFPs, serves further to compromise the objectives of the Protocol. The former are subject to the AIA procedure while the latter are subject to an alternative, less stringent, procedure. It has to be remembered that initially it was developing countries (more likely to be a state of import) which pushed for a Protocol because of a lack of domestic regulatory frameworks to adequately make decisions and deal with LMOs. The distinction between LMOs subject to the AIA procedure and LMO-FFPs may result in the transboundary movement of LMOs to states which would, had the AIA procedure applied, not consented to such transboundary movement. The lack of a domestic regulatory framework coupled with the lack of capacity, including human resource capacity, limits the effectiveness of the Protocol with regards LMO-FFPs by placing the responsibility to prevent harm from LMOs on the states least able to do so.[168]

What is further interesting is the kinds of information and documentation required under the respective procedures. LMOs subject to the AIA procedure, under articles 8 - 10, must undergo detailed environmental scrutiny.[169] The kinds of documentation required for the shipment of the respective LMOs are also different. The shipment of LMOs destined for intentional introduction into the environment are required to be accompanied by documentation containing specified information as set out in article 18(2) of the Protocol. The said document must clearly identify the organism being shipped as LMOs and must specify the identity and relevant characteristics of the said LMOs.[170] On the other hand, documents accompanying shipments of LMO-FFPs need only indicate that such shipments *may contain* LMOs. There is no requirement that the documentation accompanying LMO-FFPs must specify the identity and relevant characteristics.

168 Gupta (n 79 above) 29.
169 J Bodegard 'Documentation' in Bail *et al* (n 93 above) 338.
170 See art 18(2)(c) of the Protocol.

Article 18(2)(c) is a compromise between the position adopted by the EU and the position adopted by the Miami group. The European Union proposed that LMO-FFPs should be clearly identified in the documentation accompanying shipment as LMOs while the Miami group argued against any documentation requirement for the shipment of LMO-FFPs.[171] The Miami group was not willing to accept any procedure 'that would add further costs to agricultural production'.[172] According to the Miami group, the cumbersome nature and costliness of any labelling requirements stemmed from the fact that, in bulk shipments of grain, grain from many different sources is mixed.[173] This economic interest was pitted against consumer interest to know the content of the product they are purchasing. Consumers want to know what is contained in their products for a variety of reasons including ethical, preference and health reasons.[174] Again, the choice here appears to be economic interests over social interests. A consideration that has to be factored into the trade-off made is that LMO-FFPs are, by definition, not destined for intentional introduction to the environment. Accepting, as I argued above, that the legal regime established by the Protocol applies principally to LMOs destined for intentional introduction to the environment, the choice makes sense. However, accepting the latter further emphasises that the Protocol intends to protect the environment from the risks of biotechnology while direct human interests (not secondary or flowing from impacts on biodiversity) are not a primary consideration.

The debates surrounding the breadth of the scope of the Protocol and the AIA procedure illustrate some conflict between the need to trade, an economic growth concern and the need to prevent possible harm to the environment by the release of LMOs. In this area the Protocol strikes a delicate balance between the various interests. On the one hand, the Protocol does not, as environmentalists would have wished, call for a moratorium on the release of LMOs into the environment.[175] Instead, the Protocol is limited to the regulation of trade in LMOs. Moreover, the LMOs that are made subject to the Protocol are also limited. In this sense the Protocol appears to favour economic interests associated with LMOs. On the other hand, the Protocol, by introducing the AIA procedure, does place some hurdles to be cleared before trade in LMOs can go ahead. To be true, this

171 See Bodegard (n 169 above) 341.

172 As above. See also Tracy (n 2 above) 146.

173 Nanda & Pring (n 1 above) 389.

174 See generally J Halloran & M Hansen 'Why we need labelling of genetically engineered food' available at http://www.consumersinternational.org/documents_asp/ViewADcoment.asp?regid=135&ID=5838&categoryid=langid=1 (accessed on 3 August 2004).

175 See IUCN Res.3.007 of the Bangkok Conference calling for a moratorium. Since then various NGOs have called on the IUCN to ensure compliance with the moratorium.

procedure does not apply to trade in all LMOs and some LMOs are governed by a less stringent procedure in article 11. Nevertheless, what is evident in the discussion on the scope of the Protocol is that there is a series of trade-offs between environmental considerations and economic considerations.

4.3 Decision-making: Precaution and Socio-Economic Factors

The second area open for analysis is the decision-making procedures under the Protocol. In particular, the use of the precautionary approach and the use of socio-economic factors in the Protocol as part of the decision-making process under the Protocol were contentious issues in the negotiations. These questions of decision-making that could influence the free trade of LMOs became extremely important in the negotiation of the Protocol.

The precautionary approach is reflected in two distinct ways in the Cartagena Protocol. In the first place the adoption of the Protocol itself reflects a precautionary approach given that, while the immediate benefits of biotechnology are patent, there is a lack of scientific certainty regarding the risks.[176] This is an important factor which has to impact on the analysis of other aspects of the Protocol, including the scope of the Protocol. By putting into place a regulatory framework to allow states to prevent the *potential* harm to the environment at the economic cost to major industries and in the face of the scientific uncertainty existing with regard to biotechnology, the very adoption of the Protocol may indicate the premium that the international community places on the environment (at least in the context of biodiversity).

The Protocol, in addition to itself being a reflection of precaution, contains four references to precaution. Both the preamble and article 1 (objective) of the Protocol make references to principle 15 of the Rio Declaration.[177] In a sense the latter references (preamble and article 1) confirm that the Protocol is *itself* a product of precaution. The operative references to the precautionary principle can be found in articles 10(6) and 11(8) of the Protocol dealing with decision-

[176] R Mackenzie & P Sands 'Prospects for international environmental law' in Bail *et al* (n 93 above) 461. The authors state that the Protocol 'could to some extent be characterised as an inherently precautionary instrument – in so far as there remains a lack of scientific consensus as to the likelihood or magnitude of risks to the environment or human health posed by the release of LMOs into the environment'.

[177] Principle 15 of the Rio Declaration on the Environment and Development provides as follows: 'In order to protect the environment, the precautionary approach shall be widely applied by States according to their capabilities. Where there are threats of serious or irreversible damage, lack of full scientific certainty shall not be used as a reason for postponing cost-effective measures to prevent environmental damage'.

making in relation to LMOs, subject to the AIA procedure and LMO-FFPs respectively.

In deciding whether or not to allow, in accordance with the decision-making procedures set in the Protocol, the import of LMOs, the state of import must base such a decision on risk assessment.[178] Such a risk assessment has to 'be carried out in a scientifically sound manner'.[179] Thus, as a starting point, the text of the Protocol adopts scientific risk assessment.[180] The implication of this provision on its own is that a state of import cannot, without scientific evidence about the risks posed by the LMOs to the environment, refuse the import into its territory of the LMOs concerned. The problem is that the environment is too complex for decisions to be based purely on science and scientific decision-making cannot provide a clear answer of long-term environmental impacts.[181] This is particularly true in the case of biotechnology where the long-term effects of GMOs on the environment and human populations remain unknown.[182] As was made clear in the discussion on the precautionary principle in paragraph 2.1 of chapter 3, this is where the role of the precautionary approach comes in; to deal with the inherent inability of science to determine the long-term risks to the environment of human conduct with a degree of certainty. Thus, the role of articles 10(6) and 11(8) is to address the inadequacy of risk assessment based purely on science to assess the potential risks posed by LMOs. Under these articles states are given the discretion to prohibit import of LMOs where the import of such LMOs creates the potential for significant environmental harm.

Although the inclusion of the precautionary principle *can* indicate a compromise in favour of the environment, as cautioned in chapter 3, not all formulations of the precautionary principle indicate an inclination towards the protection of the environment. For example, some formulations of the precautionary approach subject pre-cautionary action to economic feasibility (sometimes euphemistically referred to as 'cost-effectiveness').[183] Thus, while the mere inclusion of the principle in the Protocol should serve as a *provisional* indication of the kinds of compromises made, it is important to consider the formulation of the principle in the Protocol.

178 See art 10(1) of the Protocol. See also art 11(6) of the Protocol.
179 Art 15(1) of the Protocol.
180 Tudge (n 58 above) 30.
181 See Oliva (n 8 above) 24.
182 See generally Nanda & Pring (n 1 above) 357, 359.
183 See eg the formulation of the precautionary principle in the Rio Declaration cited above. For various formulations of the precautionary principle see D Freestone & E Hey 'Origins and development of the precautionary principle' in D Freestone & E Hey (eds) *The precautionary principle and international law: The challenge of implementation* (1996).

One of the essential elements triggering the precautionary principle is the potential for some kind of environmental harm.[184] What degree of potential harm is sought under the Protocol to bring into play the possibility of precautionary action? Must there be a threat of serious harm? Must the threatened harm be irreversible? Whereas the Rio formulation of the precautionary principle (upon which the adoption of the Protocol is predicated) refers to 'threats of serious or irreversible damage' to the environment as a qualitative threshold for invoking the precautionary principle, the Protocol simply refers to 'potential adverse effects'. Such a formulation implies that the state of import need not show that the threatened harm is of a certain degree of seriousness. [185] This would appear to allow the state of import to determine for itself the level of risk it would open its territory to. Put differently, the formulation in the Protocol arguably allows a wider discretion for the state of import to take precautionary measures than, for example, a formulation similar to that in Principle 15 of the Rio Declaration. This opens up the possibility of states taking action, for example, prohibiting import of LMOs, even where there is no proof that the risk attendant to the release of such LMOs would be 'serious or irreversible'. The other side of the coin, of course, is that such a choice also makes it easier for states to use precaution as an excuse for the restriction of trade. Given that, in chapter 3, I suggested that free trade represented the economic growth value, this choice of words may indicate a willingness to compromise economic values in favour of environmental values.[186]

While Oliva concedes the significance of the precautionary principle in the Protocol, she does caution that the reach of the principle may be limited due to the fact that articles 10(6) and 11(8) require the scientific uncertainty to be 'due to insufficient relevant scientific information and knowledge' pertaining to the extent of the

184 See Oliva (n 8 above) 24.

185 See Trouwborst (n 128 above) 45, who provides a list of many other instruments formulating the precautionary principle without including a threshold, and suggests that such formulations 'certainly implies that their drafters have meant for the precautionary principle's scope of application to be as broad as possible'. He is, however, quick to point out, at 47, that to understand these instruments as implying 'that *all* potential damage to the environment, however insignificant, to be forestalled or reduced' represents a 'utopian scheme' (emphasis original). See generally for discussion of threshold L Graff 'The precautionary principle' in Bail *et al* (n 93 above) 417 *et seq*. Of course the SPS agreement of the WTO contains a similar wording and the Appellate Body in *EC Measures Concerning Meat and Meat Products (Hormones)* AB-1997-4 still precludes the reliance on precaution by the EU. See for discussion D Tladi 'Can the wolf protect the lamb? Free trade regimes as instruments towards sustainable development' (2002) 27 *South African Yearbook of International Law* 149.

186 See Adler (n 3 above) who suggests that the precautionary principle (along with the inclusion of socio-economic considerations) as a tool in the decision-making process adopted in the Protocol could 'permit member nations to block importation due to unfounded environmental scares or special interest pressures'.

potential effects.[187] Thus, while the threshold of the extent of potential harm is low, the qualification implies that there must be some initial information that the specific LMOs pose a risk.[188] This is certainly true, but does not justify the conclusion that under the formulation the 'burden of proof is on those who wish to show some adverse impact'.[189] The nature of the precautionary principle is that those who wish to base action on the precautionary principle must show, *prima facie*, that there is *potential* for harm.[190] Under articles 10(6) and 11(8) the state of import need not necessarily show that the potential harm is 'serious or irreversible'. Once the *prima facie* information is presented, the burden of argument would rest on anyone wishing to prevent the precautionary action. What articles 10(6) and 11(8) do not tell us is what the likelihood of the risk materialising must be before precautionary actions are permitted. It seems reasonable to argue, given the object and purpose of the Protocol, that article 10(6) and 11(8) cannot be interpreted as requiring a high likelihood of the risk materialising.

Further, unlike typical formulations of the precautionary principle, the possibility of prohibiting import of LMOs for precautionary reasons is not made subject to economic considerations (referred to as 'cost-effectiveness'). It would be hard to argue that, in as far as the inclusion of the precautionary principle is concerned, the Protocol does not rank environmental protection as a central concern of the Protocol. As far as the formulation of these provisions is concerned, environmental integrity seems to trump economic considerations.

In addition to the inclusion of the precautionary principle as a decision-making tool for states of import, the Protocol further allows socio-economic factors to be taken into consideration when making decisions. Needless to say, this will be viewed as a further tool that will enable states to place, whether legitimately or not, barriers to trade, particularly from those states with a thriving biotechnology industry. The Like-Minded states, on the other hand, primarily importers of LMOs, were concerned about the socio-economic impact of LMOs.[191] Article 26 thus allows states of import to take socio-economic considerations into account when making decisions about the import of LMOs.

In terms of article 26, states could prohibit the import of LMOs under the Protocol due to, *inter alia*, consumer concerns about health or for fear that the import of LMOs could harm local farmers.[192]

187 Oliva (n 8 above) 26
188 As above.
189 As above.
190 See discussion in ch 3.
191 RH Khwaja 'Socio-economic considerations' in Bail *et al* (n 93 above) 362
192 Oliva (n 8 above) 26.

Khwaja, for example, opines that during the negotiations for the Protocol, African states were concerned that introduction of transgenic crops could lead to the displacement of traditional varieties with negative impact on the livelihood of farmers.[193] There are also fears that biotechnology could result in the replacement of crops such as sugar, cocoa, tobacco and coconut oil, which form the economic backbone of many African states. The replacement of the said crops would not only harm the livelihoods of farmers and the economies of the states, but would have disastrous social consequences.[194] Nevertheless Oliva does caution that the kinds of socio-economic considerations that can be taken into account will be narrowed by the requirement in the *caveat* that these factors must be consistent with the state's international obligations.[195] She argues, therefore, that trade and economic integration agreements would serve to limit the possibility of relying on socio-economic considerations.[196]

I interpret the phrase 'consistent with their international obligations' differently. It seems to me that the inclusion of the phrase, rather than limit the socio-economic considerations, serves to emphasise or legitimise the importance of taking them into consideration. After all, there are international obligations on states to progressively realise various socio-economic rights of those subject to their jurisdiction.[197] Various rights in international human rights law instruments such as the International Covenant on Economic, Social and Cultural Rights and the African Charter on Human and Peoples' Rights would serve to, in the context of article 26, widen the state of import's discretion in the decision-making process.[198] The argument is not that the obligations imposed in the WTO are to be ignored, only that we have to guard against viewing the WTO as the only source of international obligations. Thus, in interpreting the effect of the phrase 'consistent with their international obligations'

193 Khwaja (n 191 above) 362.

194 As above.

195 As above.

196 As above.

197 See eg the various rights in the International Covenant on Economic, Social and Cultural Rights (1961) reproduced in I Brownlie (ed) *Basic documents in international law* 5th Edition, (2002) at 197. See also a catalogue of socio-economic rights in the 1986 African Charter on Human and Peoples Rights reproduced in L Mashava (ed) *Economic and social rights series Vol 7: A compilation of essential documents* (2000).

198 See eg art 12 and art 11 of the International Covenant on Economic, Social and Cultural Rights which provide for the right to health and the right to food respectively. See also art 16 of the African Charter on Human Peoples' Rights which provides for the right to health. In the context of art 14 of the International Covenant on Economic, Social and Cultural Rights, the Committee on Economic, Social and Cultural Rights eg has observed that health is 'indispensable to the exercise of other human rights'. See CESCR General Comment No. 14, *The right to the highest attainable standard of health,* reproduced in BG Ramcharan (ed) *Judicial protection of economic, social and cultural rights: Cases and materials* (2005).

on the discretion of the state of import's discretion in terms of article 26, all international law obligations and not only those flowing from the WTO must be considered.

The fact that I do not view the phrase 'consistent with their international obligations' as narrowing the kinds of socio-economic considerations to considerations that would be consistent with the free trade regime is not to say there are no limitations placed on the right of the state to consider socio-economic consideration. Article 26 limits the socio-economic considerations that can be taken into account to those 'arising from the impact of living modified organisms on the *conservation and sustainable use of biological diversity*' (emphasis added). In other words the socio-economic considerations must have some causal relationships with the LMOs' possible impact on the conservation of biological diversity. Thus a state would be entitled to rely on the impact of LMOs on the livelihoods of farmers if such impact was a result of the impact of LMOs on biodiversity. It would probably be more difficult to rely on article 26 to justify a prohibition on the import of LMOs based purely on hardships unrelated to biodiversity conservation that society would suffer. This means that it will probably be difficult to rely on article 26 for prohibiting imports of LMOs on the grounds of the various health risks such as antibiotic resistance and allergens in food. Thus, a state wishing to prohibit the import of LMOs for health reasons, for example, would have to argue that the health concerns arise from the impact of the LMOs on biodiversity. This interpretation of article 26 is consistent with the view taken above that the much-repeated phrase 'taking also into account human health', has the effect of making biodiversity the primary focus while placing social considerations as secondary concerns.

It is submitted that article 26 does three things that impact on the analysis in the chapter. First (and most obvious), article 26, by including socio-economic considerations into the decision-making process, acknowledges the relevance of human needs. Second, article 26, by limiting socio-economic considerations to those flowing from impacts on biodiversity, reminds us that while human needs are an important consideration, the primary concern in the Protocol is biodiversity. Socio-economic considerations are a subsidiary consideration in the scheme of the Protocol. The third point is, I think, more subtle and emphasises the complimentary relationships of environmental and social issues. While social issues that may be considered must flow from the impact of LMOs on biodiversity, this would cover many of the social considerations that developing states of import would want to take into account. Even if the primary concern of developing states (and their populations) is not environmental, these primary concerns are more than likely re-lated to the possible impact on the environment. Consider the issues of food security raised by Tudge[199] and Nanda and Pring.[200] Arguably, such a problem could arise, in the context of LMOs, from LMOs displacing traditional varieties of crops.[201] That means that food security concerns would qualify as socio-economic considerations 'arising from the impact of' LMOs on biodiversity conservation. However, there will still be some socio-economic ills resulting from the import of LMOs without any link to impact on biodiversity. As already mentioned, a typical example would be the creation of antibiotic resistance and allergens in foods thought to be safe. Such ills cannot, under article 26 of the Protocol, be considered. Again, as with the scope of the Protocol, the effect is to trump social concerns by limiting their relevance to cases involving impacts on biodiversity.

Both the provisions relating to the precautionary principle and the provision allowing the consideration of socio-economic factors essentially make it easier for states to place barriers on trade.[202] To the extent that free trade represents economic growth values in international law as suggested in chapter 2, the provisions on decision-making procedures in the Protocol seemingly sacrifice economic values for environmental integrity. The inclusion of the precautionary principle and, more to the point, the particularly strong formulation of the precautionary principle in articles 10(6) and 11(8), underscore the importance of environmental integrity under the Protocol. Similarly, allowing states to consider socio-economic impacts flowing from impacts of LMOs on biodiversity is also an indication of the importance of biodiversity. In an indirect way the importance attached to environmental integrity has the effect of furthering social goals, albeit as a secondary goal. This secondary effect is made more express in the wording of article 26, allowing socio-economic consideration, 'arising from the impact of' LMOs on biodiversity.

Although the decision-making procedures in the Protocol suggest an inclination towards environmental concerns, especially biodiversity, as central, the various provisions in the Protocol placing the burden of argument on the state wishing to prevent the import of LMOs must be seen as a compromise of environmental integrity in favour of economic considerations.[203] By placing the burden of argument on the state wishing to prevent the transboundary movement of LMOs, the Protocol creates a hurdle (albeit a low one) for the importing state relying on the decision-making procedures to ban import of (certain) LMOs.

199 Tudge (n 58 above).
200 Nanda &Pring (n 1 above) 357.
201 Khwaja (n 188 above) 362.
202 See also Mackenzie & Sands (n 176 above) 461 who say of the inclusion of the precautionary principle: 'At the very least, in our view, it indicates that the supremacy of international trade rules can no longer be presumed'.
203 See eg art 10(4) and also art 12 of the Protocol.

4.4 Relationship of the Protocol to WTO Agreements

Much has been said about the possible conflict between WTO instruments and the Cartagena Protocol. It does appear that the AIA procedure, the precautionary principle and the inclusion of socio-economic consideration have the potential to conflict with WTO instruments.[204] For the reasons explained earlier in the chapter, the question of the compatibility of the Protocol with the WTO is not central to the present analysis. What is relevant, however, is the manner in which the Protocol deals with the potential conflict.

The Protocol deals with the potential conflict by including recitals in the preamble. Obviously the preambular recitals do not, on their own, create rights and obligations that parties can seek to enforce. However, the recitals in the preamble are an important tool for contextual and purposive interpretation.[205] Much debate has surrounded the preambular recitals and only a few thoughts are given here. What is clear from the literature is that the preambular language has had the effect of sowing confusion.[206] In effect, the language puts into doubt the applicability of the position envisaged in article 30(3) of the Vienna Convention on the Law of Treaties, that the later treaty prevails.[207]

It is generally accepted that the tribunal most likely to adjudicate a dispute relating to the relationship between WTO agreements and the Protocol would be a WTO dispute-settlement body, including the Appellate Body. Given the manner in which the WTO dispute settlement bodies have to date dealt with environmental agreements it would seem unlikely that a WTO dispute settlement body would uphold the provisions of an environmental agreement at the expense

204 See literature cited in n 7 above.

205 See art 31(2) Vienna Convention on the Law of Treaties.

206 See eg Safrin (n 142 above) and M Alfonso 'The relationship with other agreements: An EU perspective' in Bail *et al* (n 93 above). See also Guruswamy (n 9 above) 493 *et seq*.

207 Art 30(3) of the Vienna Convention on the Law of Treaties provides as follows: 'When all parties to the earlier treaty are party also to the later treaty but the earlier treaty is not terminated or suspended ... the earlier treaty applies only to the extent that its provisions are compatible with those of the later treaty'.

of a WTO agreement.[208] To be true, the WTO bodies will uphold WTO agreements over other treaties such as the Protocol, mainly because of the terms of reference of WTO dispute settlement bodies. WTO dispute settlement bodies under the Dispute Settlement Understanding are to make their decisions based on WTO agreements and not other agreements.[209] It seems, therefore, that it is the terms of reference of the WTO bodies, and not the preambular language, that results in the subordination of the Protocol to the WTO agreements. Nevertheless, the effect of the confusion sowed by the preambular language may be to legitimise the subordination in the event of a decision by the WTO bodies.[210]

4.5 Intragenerational Equity

As is the case under the climate change regime, the primary manifestation of the common but differentiated responsibilities principle lies in the transfer of financial and technological resources. In both the Convention and the Protocol provision is made for the transfer of financial and technological resources. In addition the

208 A few words about the apparent sensitivity shown by WTO bodies to environmental consideration are warranted here. Assertions about the progress made by WTO bodies in this respect are based, largely on decisions made by the Appellate Body such as *US-Measures Concerning Import Prohibition of Certain Shrimp and Shrimp Products* AB-1998-4 (1999) 38 *ILM* 123. See eg M Matsushita *et al The World Trade Organization: The law, practice and policy* (2002). Although falling outside the scope of this study, a few cursory remarks about the perception that the WTO under the guidance of the Appellate Body has assumed a more environmentallly-sensitive approach are warranted. Such arguments have been put forward, for example, by NL Wallace-Bruce 'Global free trade and sustainable development: Two steps forward in the WTO?' (2002) 35 *Comparative and International Law Journal of Southern Africa* 236. However, these developments are little more than cosmetic. In Tladi (n 185 above), analysing the WTO Appellate Body decision in *EC-Measures Concerning Meat and Meat Products (Hormones)*, available at http://www.wto.org/wto/dispute/distab.htm (accessed on 5 January 2002), I made the argument that while in the past environmental regulations were defeated on account of not meeting the first tier of the test under article XX of the GATT, the new and improved test makes it possible to meet the first tier but impossible to meet the second tier. More importantly, while proponents of the WTO correctly point to the *EC-Measures Affecting Asbestos and Asbestos-containing Products* (AB – 2000 - 11) as a clear case of victory for environment/ health concerns, it is difficult to identify any other such case. The recent WTO panel decision in *EC-Measures Affecting Biotech Products* (above) n 145 appears to continue this trend (at para 8.64).

209 Art 7 of the Understanding on Rules and Procedures Governing the Settlement of Disputes (1993) in (1994) 33 *ILM* 112 provides that the panels are to 'examine, in light of the relevant provisions in [the covered agreement cited by the parties to the dispute], the matter referred to the DSB'.

210 It is worth mentioning, in this respect, that both the United States and Canada relied on the savings clause in their arguments to exclude the relevance of the Protocol in a recent WTO dispute. See *EC-Measures Affecting Biotech Products* (above) n 143 at paras 7.59 and 7.61. Similarly, in considering the relationship between the precautionary principle and the Sanitary and Phytosanitary Measures Agreement, the Appellate Body in *Beef Hormones* (above) n 208 emphasised that the precautionary principle could not, in the absence of 'a clear textual directive to that effect' relieve a panel from applying the terms of the Agreement'.

Protocol also makes provision for co-operation of the parties in capacity-building relating to biosafety in developing countries. These provisions relating to the transfer of technological and financial resources, as suggested in chapter 3 of the study and in the literature on common but differentiated responsibilities, are based on equitable principles taking into account the disadvantaged situation of developing countries. The operation of the financial transfer provisions has been delegated to the Global Environment Facility (GEF), and will be considered in chapter 7 on the GEF.

For the purposes of this chapter, however, it is a different manifestation of the intragenerational equity that calls for closer scrutiny. The biodiversity instruments include some provisions relating to access to genetic resources and benefit sharing.[211] Genetic resources, as mentioned in paragraph 3.1 above, are crucial for biotechnology.[212] Thus, equitable sharing rules of benefits from genetic resources, particularly where these have been obtained by developed countries (or multinational corporations) from developing countries, will have to promote intragenerational equity. Benefit sharing, as a mechanism taking into account the development needs of economically poorer countries, is a distributive justice mechanism and, consequently, suggests a social inclination. Nevertheless, there are trade-offs and compromises that militate against this inclination.

The Convention's provisions relating to access to genetic resources and benefit sharing strikes a delicate balance between, on the one hand, the needs of developed states (and specifically entities from developed states) to gain access to biological resources found in developed countries, and, on the other hand, developing countries' claim for benefits derived from using biological resources accessed in their territories. The sovereignty 'over genetic resources' and flowing from that 'the authority to determine access to genetic resources', proclaimed in article 15(1) of the Convention, becomes somewhat limited in article 15(2) which provides that states are not to 'impose restrictions [on access to genetic resources] that run counter to the objectives' of the Convention. This give-and-take, of course, highlights the extent to which compromises and trade-offs take place in negotiations on instruments relating to sustainable development.

The give-and-take evident in the provisions on access to genetic resources does not end there. Quite literally in a trade-off, the access

211 On the equity roots of the access and benefit sharing concept see TR Young 'An implementation perspective on international law of genetic resources: incentive, consistency and effective operation' (2004) 15 *Yearbook of International Law Environmental Law* 3 11 *et seq.*

212 As above 47.

provisions are accompanied, in the Convention, by provisions on benefit sharing.[213] Article 15(6) of the Convention makes it clear that states having access to genetic resources in other states are to share, with the host state, 'in a fair and equitable way the results of research' as well as the 'benefits arising from the commercial' uses of the resources. In addition, article 16 is dedicated to the transfer of technology, which by the terms of the Convention includes biotechnology, to developing countries.[214] Thus, developed countries obtain their prize, namely access to genetic resources found mainly in developing countries, while developing countries also get their prize, the benefits from the development of such resources from financially and technologically advanced developed countries.[215]

A further point to be made is that the access and benefit sharing provisions in the Convention are couched in rather soft language. For example, article 15(2) on access to genetic resources provides that states 'shall endeavour to create conditions to facilitate access'. Moreover, the Convention makes it clear that access is to be granted on 'mutually agreed terms', implying that the state wanting access does not have a right to access.[216] Similarly, the Convention provides that access is to be subject to 'prior informed consent'.[217] However, it is to be noted that the duty imposed by the Convention to a fairly and equitably share in the benefits arising from the access to genetic resources can only be relied upon if access has, in fact, been granted.

Thus, the provisions on access to genetic resources and benefit sharing in the Convention, and indeed also in the FAO Treaty on Plant Genetic Resources, create a transaction-based approach where one party grants access to the resources and another party compensates, either through technology or finances or both.[218] The transaction-based approach is equally apparent when one considers the work done thus far by the Ad Hoc Open-Ended Working Group on Access and Benefit-sharing established by the COP to the Biodiversity Convention.[219] The draft text provided at the eighth meeting of the

213 See art 15(7) of the Convention

214 See especially art 16(1) of the Convention on Biodiversity which provides that 'technology includes biotechnology'.

215 The complexities in negotiating such a give-and-take regime for access and benefit sharing of genetic resources are described by M Dross & F Wolff 'Do we need a new access and benefit sharing instrument?' (2004) 15 *Yearbook of International Environmental Law* 95 110 *et seq*.

216 See art 15(4) of the Convention on Biodiversity.

217 See art 15(5) of the Convention on Biodiversity.

218 The FAO Treaty essentially institutionalises access to genetic resources and benefit sharing through the multilateral system of access and benefit sharing. See Part IV of the FAO Treaty on Plant Genetic Resources.

219 See Decision VII/19 of the Seventh Meeting of the Conference of the Parties to the Biodiversity Convention.

conference provided for access to genetic resources 'dependent upon' benefit sharing arrangements.[220]

The transaction-based approach reflected in the access to resources and benefit sharing provisions, while illustrating the point that sustainable development is concerned with trade-offs and compromises, also suggests something more fundamental for this study. By suggesting a contractarian model, this approach essentially commercialises genetic resources. In a sense, this approach may represent the kind of common but differentiated responsibilities approach referred to by Stone as *'rationale bargaining CDR'*.[221] According to Stone this kind of common but differentiated responsibilities approach should be 'welcomed as natural outcomes of mutually beneficial negotiations'.[222] There is an eerie synergy between this notion of common but differentiated responsibilities and Petersmann's theory of equal liberty rights such as freedom of contract.[223] In paragraph 3.3 of chapter 3, considering this kind of approach to human rights, I suggested that such an approach, in and of itself, cannot bring about the kind of equitable outcome envisaged by intragenerational equity.[224] This commercialisation of genetic resources, again, interferes with the social inclination of benefit sharing and may suggest an economic-centred approach consistent with an economic growth variation of sustainable development.

5. Concluding remarks

The problem and debate on genetic modification are complex. The complexity of the problem, however, is matched by the complexity of the solutions offered in the Protocol. The Protocol offers, as a

220 See Annex to Decision VIII/4 of the Eighth Meeting of the Conference of the Parties to the Biodiversity Convention. The phrase 'dependent upon', in the draft text, is bracketed with 'related to' being the alternative phrase. It is perhaps appropriate to mention at this point that the Open-Ended Informal Consultative Process on Oceans and the Law of the Sea established by the United Nations General Assembly is also considering the possibility of benefit sharing regime for genetic resources beyond areas of national jurisdiction. See eg United Nations GA/ 61/65 Report of the Ad Hoc Open-ended Informal Working to Study Issues Relating to the Conservation and Sustainable Use of Marine Biological Diversity Beyond Areas of National Jurisdiction.

221 See CD Stone 'Common but differentiated responsibilities in international law' (2004) 98 *American Journal of International Law* 276 283 *et seq.*

222 As above.

223 EU Petersmann 'Time for a United Nations 'global compact' for integrating human rights into the law of the World Trade Organization: Lessons from European integration' (2002) 13 *European Journal of International Law* 621. Petersmann's article is considered in para 3.3 of ch 3.

224 This conclusion is confirmed by Stone's illustration of this rationale bargaining common but differentiated using two adjacent coastal states jointly exploiting a stock of fish. He correctly observes that the kind of outcome will depend largely on negotiating skills and that the outcome may be more advantageous to the richer state, Stone (n 221 above) 284.

solution to the impasse surrounding GMOs, a myriad of trade-offs and compromises. The golden thread of this myriad of compromises and trade-offs appears to be the tug of war between free trade, representing economic interests, and the precautionary approach, representing interests of environmental protection from potential negative impacts of GMOs.

The limited scope of the Protocol itself, both in terms of its aims and the LMOs to which it applies, on the one hand, as well as the limited applicability of the AIA procedure, on the other, are all decisions that suggest compromising environmental concerns in favour of economic concerns. This conclusion is somewhat off-set by the fact that the AIA procedure, albeit not applicable to all LMOs, will create hurdles for trade in LMOs. Moreover, the decision-making procedures under the Protocol seem, on the whole, to reflect a compromise of trade concerns in favour of environmental concerns. While the provisions on decision-making proclaim that risk assessment should be based on sound science — a provision certainly limiting the ability of importing states to prohibit imports of LMOs — the Protocol then goes on to allow states of imports to base their decisions on precautionary reasons and socio-economic considerations. However, to this compromise is added yet another trade-off in that the state of import is saddled with the burden of arguments in this decision-making process. This, yet again, illustrates a give and take between environmental and economic considerations.

What is clear, however, is that social considerations do not play much of a role in these myriad of trade-offs and compromises in comparison to environmental and economic considerations. The point should not be overstated, however, because, as noted above, social considerations, such as health, are given some role, albeit a subsidiary role in that they should flow from environmental impacts. This applies both with respect to the scope of the agreement and the decision-making procedures. In both cases the text of the agreement suggests that social consideration must, in some way, be linked to biodiversity concerns. As noted in the analysis, this suggests a subtle, yet effective way of trumping social considerations by limiting the relevance of social factors to cases where there is, simultaneously, an impact on biodiversity.

As argued above, the inclusion of the preambular recitals on the relationship between the Protocol and other agreements, by interfering with the position in the Vienna Convention on conflicting treaties, has the effect of legitimising the subordination of the Protocol to the WTO — and in that way favouring economic interests over environmental (and social) interests. This trumping of social and environmental concerns effectively disturbs the delicate balance struck between environmental and economic concerns in the Protocol and, thus, tilts the scales towards economic interests. Furthermore, the provisions on access to genetic resources and benefit sharing, through the commercialisation of genetic resources, serve to suggest an economic-growth approach to the benefit sharing mechanism. Nevertheless, the Protocol does illustrate a delicate balance between environmental and economic considerations, with economic interests the main consideration. The biosafety regime can thus be described as reflecting an economic growth-centred variation of sustainable development with a strong concern for environmental issues.

The analysis of the biosafety regime above, in addition to suggesting the variation of sustainable development reflected in the instruments, also serves to confirm the centrality of trade-offs and compromises in sustainable development. These trade-offs run throughout the regime. On the one hand, the Protocol places economic concerns at the centre by limiting the scope of the Protocol. On the other hand, however, economic concerns are compromised for environmental concerns in the AIA procedure. Furthermore, the decision-making procedures in the Protocol suggest an inclination towards environmental and social concerns at the expense of trade or economic concerns. However, an important trade-off, the preambular citations, suggests an inclination towards economic growth. These trade-offs and compromises are equally reflected, as discussed above, in the provisions on access to genetic resources and benefit sharing.

7

The Global Environment Facility: Institutional Structure, Operations and Policies

1. Introduction

In this chapter the focus falls on the Global Environment Facility (the GEF). In particular, I try to determine the contribution that the GEF has made to the normative development of the principle of sustainable development. As in the previous two chapters, the enquiry into the contribution of the GEF to sustainable development is made with reference to another enquiry, namely, what variation of sustainable development best reflects the GEF.

The factors considered and questions asked in this chapter are, for that reason, similar to those that were asked in the chapters on the climate change and the biodiversity regimes. Thus, in this chapter I consider the kinds of compromises and trade-offs that are made in the GEF between the economic, environmental and social values. Which of these values in the GEF is afforded a central position? Which value triumphs in cases of conflict? Are environmental values favoured over social and economic concerns? Are there indications that socio-economic considerations trump environmental and/or economic considerations? Does the GEF display characteristics that reflect the of one or other variation of sustainable development? Yet again, in attempting to situtate the GEF within one of the variations of sustainable development, I will be guided by the same considerations expounded in chapter 3.

While the questions asked in this chapter are similar to those asked in previous chapters, the chapter on the GEF comes with a different set of challenges and, accordingly, the approach to the enquiry is somewhat different. In some sense the discussion of GEF could easily be integrated into the other chapters in Part B. No account of either the international climate change or biodiversity regimes is complete without some discussion of GEF. As the financial mechanisms of the United Nations Framework Convention on Climate Change, the Kyoto Protocol to the Climate Change Convention, the Biodiversity Convention and the Cartagena Protocol on Biosafety, the GEF has had a huge impact on the international policy relating to climate change and biodiversity.[1] A further factor complicating the discussion of the GEF is the innovative institutional structure created by the GEF. The discussion in this chapter is mindful of these challenges.

To address the first challenge, in discussing the GEF, the focus will fall primarily on GEF activities and policies impacting on those regimes already discussed – the climate change and biodiversity regime in particular. In addressing the second challenge, while maintaining the substantive and normative flavour of the study, the analysis here is undertaken against the background of this innovative yet complex institutional structure.

I begin the chapter with a background discussion of the GEF. In the discussion I consider, in addition to the various challenges facing the GEF, the creation of the GEF. In section 3 of the chapter I give a brief descriptive analysis of some of the policy instruments adopted by the GEF. In particular I consider various conflicts arising from the institutional framework of the GEF and the ambivalence in the funding policies of the GEF. The ambivalence in funding policy will be used to evaluate the normative contribution of the GEF to sustainable development.

2. Background to the GEF: Creation and institutional make-up

2.1 Background: Establishing the Pilot Phase

One way of expressing the principle of intra-generational equity is through the common but differentiated responsibilities principle. The common but differentiated responsibilities principle is a lynchpin of major modern, global environmental regimes.[2] Indeed it is a lynchpin of the principle of sustainable development. The principle of common but differentiated responsibilities certainly forms an integral part of the multilateral environmental agreements (MEAs) discussed in chapters 5 and 6. The Kyoto Protocol, for example, sets targets for the reduction of greenhouse gas emission by developed states (Annex

1 The United Nations Framework Convention on Climate Change (1992) 31 *ILM* 851; Kyoto Protocol to the United Nations Framework Convention on Climate Change (1998) 37 *ILM* 22 available at http://unfccc.int/resource/docs/convkp/kpeng.pdf (accessed 19 February 2002) (1997). The text of the Protocol is reproduced in P Cullet & A Gowlland-Gualtieri (eds) *Key materials in international environmental law* (2004); 1992 Convention on Biological Diversity (1992) 31 *ILM* 818; Cartagena Protocol on Biosafety to the Convention on Biodiversity (2000), available at http://www.untreaty.org/English/notpubl/27-8a-eng.htm (accessed 20 April 2004).

2 See for discussion para 2.2 of ch 3. See also para 3.1 of ch 5 and para 3.2.4 of ch 6.

I) but does not do the same for developing states.[3] An important expression of the common but differentiated responsibilities principle in MEAs is the transfer of financial resources from developed to developing countries to meet the costs associated with the relevant MEAs.[4] In the context of financial transfers in MEAs, the question as to how transfers were to take place arose. Was a new institution to be created as a financial mechanism? Was there to be more than one institution? It was in this context that the GEF was mooted.

A brief historical sketch of the creation of the GEF will shed light on some of the issues, challenges and conflicts facing the GEF. The literature, especially legal literature on the GEF, has tended to focus chiefly on institutional and structural issues pertaining to the GEF.[5] The focus in this study is, of course, on normative aspects of sustainable development and that theme is continued in this chapter. Nevertheless, the institutional and structural dilemmas identified by the literature are described. The brief description of these issues is critical for an understanding of how this innovatively designed institution operates. To understand the GEF's understanding of 'incremental cost' and 'global environmental benefit', for example, requires an understanding of the relationship between the Fund and the Conference of the Parties (COPs) of the conventions to which it serves as the financial mechanism.

Further, the institutional structure of the GEF would be crucial to understanding how the GEF might (or might not) be able to deal with conflicts between the potentially-competing interests of different treaty regimes or conflicts with different institutions associated with the GEF. Nevertheless, given the focus of this study on normative issues, I canvass these structural issues only in broad descriptive terms, and always with a view to providing a context for the contribution made by the GEF to the normative aspects of sustainable development.

3 See generally discussion in ch 5 above. See also J Werksman 'Consolidating governance of the global commons: Insights from the Global Environment Facility' (1995) 6 *Yearbook of International Environmental Law* 27 47 where he gives substantive expressions of the common but differentiated principle found in treaties.

4 See eg art 28 of the Cartagena Protocol on Biosafety to the Convention on Biodiversity; art 21 of the Biodiversity Convention; art 11 of the United Nations Framework Convention on Climate Change; art 11 of the Kyoto Protocol to the UN Framework Convention on Climate Change.

5 See eg Werksman (n 3 above); see also J Werksman 'Consolidating global environmental governance: New lessons from the GEF?' available at www.yale.edu/gegdialogue/docs/dialogue/oct03/papers/werksman%20GEF.pdf (accessed June 2003); H Sjöberg 'The Global Environment Facility' in J Werksman (ed) *Greening international institutions* (1996). See also E Hey 'Sustainable development, normative development and the legitimacy of decision making' (2003) 34 *Netherlands Yearbook of International Law* 3 especially 32 *et seq*.

Unsurprisingly, the need for a financial mechanism formed a logical part of the progressive development of the concept of sustainable development. Given that the 1972 Stockholm Conference is viewed as a critical point in the evolution of sustainable development by recognising the global nature of the environmental and developmental crisis, it comes as no surprise that the 1980s were characterised by a great concern for the global environment. Further, given that the same conference recognised the connection between the environmental crisis and developmental issues, it came as no surprise that in the 1980s questions around funding for environmental concerns in developing countries began to surface. In 1987 the Brundtland Commission asserted a need for a 'significant increase in financial support' to developing countries for environmental purposes.[6] Following on the heels of the call for increased financial support from the Brundtland report, in 1989 France proposed that the World Bank consider the possibility of establishing a program for funding environmental projects in developing countries.[7] After a series of bilateral negotiations, the World Bank in November 1990 arranged a meeting with 24 participants, a third of which were developing countries, in November 1990.[8] At this meeting the parties thrashed out an agreement for the creation of a facility to fund environmental programmes in developing countries.[9]

In 1991, putting into effect earlier negotiations, the World Bank Board of Directors created, by resolution, the GEF (GEF Pilot) as a three-year pilot programme to provide funding to developing countries.[10] Under the resolution the GEF would fund projects in developing countries in four focal areas, namely, climate change, ozone depletion, biodiversity and international waters pollution.[11] An important aspect of the GEF was that the funding was to be for projects providing global environmental benefits. Thus, although the funding would be provided to developing countries, for projects in developing countries, the benefits would accrue to the world as a whole.[12] Consequently, the GEF was not to be regarded as charity or development assistance from the North to the South. The notion that funding for the GEF was not to be seen as official development assistance further underscored the idea pushed by developing countries that the funding from the GEF had to be in addition to

6 World Commission on Environment and Development *Our Common Future* (1987) 336.

7 Sjöberg (n 5 above) 150. For discussion of other proposals, see L Boisson de Chazournes 'The Global Environment Facility galaxy: On linkages among institutions' (1999) 3 *Max Planck Yearbook of United Nations Law* 243 245.

8 Sjöberg (n 5 above) 151.

9 As above.

10 See World Bank Resolution Establishing the Pilot Phase GEF, Res No 91-5 (1991) 30 *ILM* 1735 at 1758.

11 Werksman (n 3 above) 48.

12 Sjöberg (n 5 above) 151.

existing development assistance.[13] In her work Sjöberg considers the rationale for additionality. She notes that it was important for developing countries, so as not to divert funding from national priorities. Over and above the concerns of developing countries, from an environment perspective, GEF funding had to be additional to efforts by development agencies to integrate environmental concerns into their mainstream activities.[14] Thus, funding from the GEF was not to be seen as an excuse for not providing official development assistance and for not integrating environmental concerns into mainstream activities.[15] In this sense the GEF Pilot experiment was a rather innovative institution.

Institutionally the GEF was also innovative. The GEF Pilot, created by a World Bank resolution, established a loose network of legal and institutional relationships.[16] In other words, rather than create a new legal institution, the designers of the GEF Pilot sought to rely on existing institutions. In particular, the GEF Pilot relied on the institutional expertise of the UNDP, UNEP and the World Bank as implementing agencies. The loose network of relationships characterising the GEF Pilot was given effect to by an interagency agreement between the implementing agencies.[17] The resolution adopted by the World Bank in 1991 created a trust fund (GEF Pilot Trust Fund). Although the GEF Pilot was based on a loose network of relationships, that the Bank played a dominant role was beyond question.[18] Under the GEF Pilot the Bank administered the GEF and exercised decision-making powers.[19] It was the Bank that prepared the work programme, allocated resources to the implementing agencies and entered into individual funding agreements with recipient countries.[20] Although the Bank had to report to the donors of the Fund every two years, the role of the donors was merely advisory.[21] Nevertheless, donor countries were able to exert

13 As above.

14 See also GEF *Incremental costs* at para 6 which states the following: 'Financing the incremental costs from new and additional sources, ensures two desirable objectives. First, these scarce funds will be dedicated to achieving global environmental benefits rather than to achieving development and local environmental benefits ... Second, and equally importantly, eligible countries need not divert scarce development finance to achieve global objectives and need not give up their national development goals to do so'. GEF/C.7/Inf.5.

15 As above.

16 Werksman (n 3 above) 49.

17 Procedural Arrangements among the International Bank for Reconstruction and Development, United Nations Environment Programme and the United Nations Development Programme for Operational Co-operation Under the GEF, Annexure C to Res 91-5 establishing the Pilot Phase GEF.

18 See generally Hey (n 5 above) 32 and Werksman (n 3 above) 49.

19 Hey (n 5 above) 32.

20 Werksman (n 3 above) 49. To emphasise the Bank's dominance in GEF I structure, Werksman notes that the resolution creating GEF Pilot 'places the facility securely in the legal control of the Bank'.

21 Hey (n 5 above) 32.

substantial influence, indirectly, through their control of the World Bank.[22]

The control exercised by the World Bank over the GEF, coupled with the control exercised by developed countries over the World Bank, caused some suspicion from certain quarters with regards to the governance structure of the GEF Pilot.[23] The World Bank had come under severe criticism for the effect that its programmes have had on people in developing countries. Michel Chossudovsky, for example, has argued that Bank policies have been responsible for the impoverishment of 'hundreds of millions of people'.[24] It is thus not surprising that developing countries overwhelmingly rejected the GEF Pilot as the operator of the financial mechanism of the UNFCCC and the Biodiversity Convention. In addition to criticism relating to the impact of its policies on developing countries, during the 1990s the Bank, more generally, was also the subject of severe criticism for the environmental impact that some of its projects had.[25] Although the World Bank adopted environmental and social policies in response to both internal and external criticisms, the projects financed by the Bank continued to be dogged by controversy.[26] All this suggested that the GEF, especially as regards its institutional structure, had to be restructured if it was going to survive.

22 Under the Bank's Articles of Agreements members have, in addition to normal votes, 'one additional vote for each share of stock held'. Given that it is the donor (developed) countries that hold controlling shares, it is the latter that make the decisions in Bank. See art V S 3(a) of the International Bank for Reconstruction and Development, Articles of Agreement, in IFI Shihata *The World Bank in a changing world: Selected essays* (compiled and edited by F Tschofen & AR Parra) (1991).

23 Werksman (n 3 above) 50 *et seq*. See also Sjöberg (n 5 above) 153 *et seq*.

24 M Chossudovsky *The globalisation of poverty: The impacts of IMF and World Bank reforms* (1997) 34; See also World Bank *Adjustment lending: An evaluation of ten years of experience* (1988).

25 Arguably, the most scathing criticism comes from B Rich *Mortgaging the earth: The World Bank, environmental impoverishment and the crisis of development* (1994). In his book, Rich gives an account of the environmental destruction and human suffering caused by Bank-financed projects. The book has been described by Hourde as '[u]nabashed advocacy. Therein lies its beauty and its flaw. The beauty is the wrenching emotion evident in the description of the disadvantaged people's lives in the name of development .... The flaw is that this emotion is too often worn on the author's sleeve and draped in hyperbole ...' See L Hourde 'Mortgaging the earth: The World Bank, environmental impoverishment and the crisis of development' 1995 *George Washington International Law Review* 721. For other accounts of the impact of World Bank projects see K Horta 'Boundaries in the field of human rights: Rhetoric and reality: human rights and the World Bank' (2002) 15 *Harvard Human Rights Journal* 227; G Hernandez Uriz 'To lend or not to lend: Oil, human rights, and the World Bank's internal contradictions' (2001) 14 *Harvard Human Rights Journal* 197 197; G Handl 'The legal mandate of the multilateral development banks as agents for change towards sustainable development' (1998) 92 *American Journal of International Law* 642; J Werksman 'Greening Bretton Woods' in P Sands (ed) *Greening international law* (1993).

26 See for discussion B Rich 'Still waiting: The failure of reform at the World Bank' in CR Goddard *et al* (eds) *International political economy* 2nd ed (2003); Uriz (n 25 above); Horta (n 25 above).

2.2 Towards the Restructured GEF

UNCED was critical to the restructuring of the GEF.[27] In events leading up to UNCED, developing countries called for funds separate from the Bank to be made available for the purposes of funding costs associated with complying with international environmental obligations. Under such a suggestion the approach to the financial arrangements of the Montreal Protocol on Substances that Deplete the Ozone Layer could serve as model.[28] The Montreal Protocol has its own financial mechanism, the Montreal Protocol Multilateral Fund, created in terms of the 1990 London Amendment to the Montreal Protocol.[29] While such a model was attractive for developing countries, donor countries, predictably, were concerned that such an arrangement would lead to a proliferation of institutions, and more importantly, lead to 'increased demand for resources over which they would have less control'.[30] As a compromise the parties negotiating the Climate Change Convention and the Biodiversity Convention accepted the GEF as the financial mechanism for the two MEAs adopted at UNCED, initially on an interim basis, subject to the restructuring of the GEF.[31] In this respect the Climate Change Convention provides that the GEF:[32]

> shall be the international entity entrusted with the operation of the financial mechanism referred to in article 11 on an interim basis. In this connection the Global Environment Facility should be appropriately restructured ...

In particular, the Climate Change Convention provides that the COP and the entity entrusted with the operation of the financial mechanism must reach agreement on modalities to ensure that the entity acts 'in accordance with the policies, programme priorities and eligibility criteria established by the' COP.[33] The Biodiversity Convention, in a similarly suspicious tone, provides that the financial mechanism adopted by the COP 'shall function under the authority and guidance of, and be accountable to the' COP.[34] Further, the

27 See, amongst others, Boisson de Chazournes (n 7 above) 251.
28 See 1987 Montreal Protocol on Substances that Deplete the Ozone Layer (as amended) reproduced in Cullet & Gowlland-Gualtieri (n 1 above).
29 See art 10 of the Montreal Protocol.
30 Werksman (n 3 above) 52.
31 The COP to the UNFCCC, for example, decided that 'the restructured GEF shall continue, on an interim basis, to be the international entity entrusted with operation of the financial mechanism referred to in article 11 of the Convention'. See Dec 9/CP.1, FCCC/CP/1995/7/Add. 1. As with all other decisions of the UNFCCC COP, the decision is available at http://unfccc.int (accessed 10 November 2004).
32 Art 21(3) UNFCCC. The Biodiversity Convention contains a similar provision, in art 39(1): 'Provided that it has been fully restructured, the Global Environment Facility ... shall be the institutional structure referred to in article 21 on an interim basis ...'
33 Art 11(3)(a) UNFCCC.
34 Art 21(1) Biodiversity Convention.

convention provides that the COP shall, for the purposes of meeting the objectives of the convention, 'determine the policy, strategy and eligibility criteria relating to' access to resources of the mechanism. Thus, both conventions require, as a condition for the GEF acting as financial mechanism, the right to determine the funding policies of the GEF in respect of funding associated with the respective conventions.[35]

The conventions also require that the governance structure of the GEF allow for the equitable representation of developing countries. The Climate Change Convention provides, in that context, that the financial mechanism 'shall have an equitable and balanced representation of all Parties within a transparent system of governance'.[36] The Biodiversity Convention, for its part, provides that the mechanism 'shall operate within a democratic and transparent system of governance'.[37] A key element in the demand of the conventions was, thus, that the GEF be more representative and accountable to the COPs.[38]

2.3 Restructured GEF: Institutional Structure

After much negotiation the restructured GEF came into being in terms of the Instrument for the Establishment of the Restructured GEF.[39] To give effect to the instrument, the three implementation agencies, the World Bank, UNDP and UNEP, adopted three parallel resolutions. It is this restructured GEF that is the focus of this chapter. As with the pilot phase GEF, the restructured GEF has at its core a trust fund established by the Bank's Board of Directors.[40] Structurally, the GEF Instrument creates three bodies.[41] First, the Instrument creates the Assembly, which consists of representatives of all participants.[42] The duties of the Assembly include review of the general policies of the GEF, evaluation of the operation of the GEF on the basis of reports submitted by the Council and the consideration for approval of amendments to the Instruments on the basis of recommendations by the Council.[43] The Assembly meets once every three years.[44] The

35 On the legal nature of the requirement set by these conventions for the restructuring of the GEF see Werksman (n 3 above) 53.
36 Art 11(2) UNFCCC.
37 Art 21(1) Biodiversity Convention.
38 Werksman (n 3 above) 54.
39 The Instrument for the Establishment of the Restructured Global Environment Facility, as with all other official GEF documentation referred to in this chapter, can be accessed at http://www.gefweb.org (accessed 10 September 2004).
40 Para 8 GEF Instrument.
41 Para 11 GEF Instrument.
42 Para 13 GEF Instrument. According to the GEF website, as at 15 November 2005, GEF participants numbered 176, consisting of states from developed and developing states as well as states with economies in transition.
43 Para 14 GEF Instrument.
44 Para 13 GEF Instrument.

second body, the Council is perhaps the most important.[45] The Council consists of 32 members 'representing constituency groupings formulated and distributed taking into account the need for balanced and equitable representation' of participants.[46] In accordance with this equitable representation system there are 16 members from developing countries, 14 members from developed countries and two members from countries with economies in transition.[47] The main responsibility of the Council is to develop, adopt and evaluate the operation, policies and programs for GEF-financed activities. In principle, the decisions of the Council are to be taken by consensus.[48] However, where consensus is not possible the Instrument adopts a double-weighted majority as a decision-making tool where there is a requirement of 60 per cent majority of the total number of participants in addition to 60 per cent majority of total contributions.[49] This important provision alleviated concerns of developed and developing countries by ensuring that both recipient and donor countries exercised a level of control in the Council.[50]

The third body established by the GEF is the secretariat.[51] The secretariat, although functionally independent, is housed at the headquarters of the World Bank. It is responsible for the day-to-day running and administration of the GEF.[52] To emphasise its functional independence from the Bank, the Instrument provides that the secretariat's CEO shall be accountable to the GEF Council and not the Bank, as was the case under the Pilot phase.[53] As under the GEF Pilot the implementing agencies are the UNDP, UNEP and the World Bank.[54] The implementing agencies are also said to be accountable to the Council.[55] The structure and functions of these bodies are illustrative of conflicting interests between various constituencies. These conflicting interests and their representation in the structure of these bodies are discussed, albeit briefly, below.

A further aspect of the institutional structure to consider is the relationship between the GEF and the COPs of the conventions to which the GEF serves as financial mechanism.[56] As mentioned in paragraph 2.2 above, the Climate Change Convention and the

45 PH Sand 'The potential impact of the Global Environment Facility of the World Bank, UNDP and UNEP' in R Wolfrum (ed) *Enforcing environmental standards: Economic mechanisms as viable means?* (1996) 484 where the Council is described as the 'main governing body of the new GEF'.
46 Para 16 GEF Instrument.
47 As above.
48 Para 25(b) GEF Instrument.
49 Para 25(c) GEF Instrument.
50 See Boisson de Chazournes (n 7 above) 260 *et seq*.
51 Para 21 GEF Instrument.
52 As above.
53 As above.
54 Para 22 GEF Instrument.
55 As above.
56 For the relevant instrument see para 3.1 below.

Biodiversity Convention accepted the GEF as the financial mechanism on condition that GEF was accountable to the COPs of the conventions. The Instrument, in this context, provides that the use of GEF resources 'shall be in conformity with the policies, program priorities' decided by the COPs. To facilitate the relationship between the GEF and the COPs, the Instrument also provides for the conclusion of a co-operative arrangement or agreements with the COPs.

2.4 The Restructured GEF: An Institution *Sui Generis*

The institutional structure and character of the GEF are responsive to the conflicting interests represented in the negotiations leading to the adoption of a restructured GEF. These institutional issues and conflicts are discussed and analysed in greater depth elsewhere.[57] All that I try to do here is to set out these institutional issues with the aim of contextualising the related normative aspects of sustainable development. Unsurprisingly, the North-South divide is central to the institutional structures resulting from the negotiations of the GEF restructuring.

One aspect that developing countries felt strongly about was the dominant role that the World Bank played in GEF Pilot.[58] One must remember that the GEF Pilot was created by the Bank and the Bank exercised decision-making powers. Under the resolution establishing the GEF Pilot, the Bank had the authority to 'administer the Facility in accordance with ... the Bank's Articles of Agreement'.[59] While many of the developing countries would have preferred to see the restructured GEF, at the least as autonomous from the Bank, or, at best, each MEA having its own separate fund, developed countries opposed this for fear that such a move would lead to a proliferation of financial mechanisms with the consequence of increased demand for resources and decreased control over such resources.[60] The compromise was the creation of an instrument *sui generis*.[61]

This *sui generis* character of the restructured GEF has resulted in questions over the legal nature of the GEF.[62] The complexity of the

57 See eg Werksman (n 3 above); Hey (n 5 above); Sjöberg (n 5 above) and to a lesser extent Sand (n 45 above).

58 See Sand (n 45 above) 482. See also AS Miller 'The Global Environment Facility and the search for financial strategies to foster sustainable development' (2000) 24 *Vermont Law Review* 1229 1235.

59 Werksman (n 3 above) 50.

60 Werksman (n 3 above) 52. See also Miller (n 58 above) 1235.

61 See for this characterisation of the GEF Instrument, see Boisson de Chazournes (n 7 above) 254. Similarly, Werksman (n 3 above) 56 notes, regarding the compromise, that the 'result achieved, after extensive and often bitter negotiations, was another curious compromise that leaves the GEF's legal character in doubt'.

62 As above.

legal arrangement becomes apparent when one considers Werksman's article on the institutional and structural aspects of the GEF. On the one hand Werksman emphasises that at the core of the GEF mechanism is a trust fund '*established*' by the Bank's Board of Directors.[63] He then asserts that this suggests that the GEF 'remains legally tied most closely to the Bank'.[64] Not long after that, however, Werksman adds the following:[65]

> Despite the Instrument's carefully chosen words, the GEF has accrued many of the outward characteristics of an independent institution. It has an intergovernmental council capable of taking decisions that direct the utilisation of GEF funds, and has the authority to hold accountable other international organisations, UNEP, UNDP and the World Bank, for their GEF financed activities (footnotes omitted).

In her analysis of the legal nature of the GEF, Boisson de Chazournes, takes an equally (if not more) nuanced view. Her analysis hinges on what she terms the two-stage process characteristic of the GEF. This two-stage process is apparent in the way in which the GEF was created, the procedure for the amendment and termination and the procedure for the approval of agreements or arrangements with COPs of the relevant MEAs.[66] With regards to the creation of the GEF, the first stage was the agreement by the states represented at the negotiations of the Instrument while the second stage was the adoption of the Instrument by the three implementing agencies.[67] Interestingly, of the three institutions, only the Bank, as a fully fledged international organisation in contrast with the UNDP and UNEP which are only programmes of the UN, has the capacity to create a new institution.[68] While the initial approval of the states cannot be said to have been an agreement creating an international organisation, it cannot be said to be without legal consequence. Boisson de Chazournes postulates that the approval by the states 'constituted a preliminary condition to the decision' of the implementing agencies creating the GEF.[69] The same applies to a decision to amend or terminate the GEF. First, the Assembly, upon recommendation by the Council (made up of states), makes the decision by consensus but the decision only becomes effective after it has been adopted by the implementing agencies (the second stage).[70] The point here is to highlight the ambivalence surrounding the GEF

63 Werksman (n 3 above) 57 (emphasis original).
64 As above.
65 As above.
66 Boisson de Chazournes (n 7 above) 255 *et seq.*
67 As above.
68 As above; see also Hey (n 5 above) 33 who says the following on the creation of the GEF: 'The GEF in its present form was *de facto* established on the basis of an agreement reached between the states and three identical decisions taken by the implementing agencies, however, *de jure*, it was established by the World Bank, it being the only one of the three implementing agencies that has the competence to establish new institutions'.
69 See Boisson de Chazournes (n 7 above) 255.

structure. On the one hand, the GEF acting through the Council makes decisions. On the other hand, these decisions only acquire legal effect after adoption by the implementing agencies.

The legal status of the GEF becomes important when one considers the legal nature of the agreements or arrangements concluded with COPs of the relevant MEAs. The GEF Instrument entitles the Council to 'consider and approve co-operative agreements or arrangements' with COPs to the MEAs for which the Facility operates as financial mechanism.[71] This *could* be used to support an argument that the GEF does have *some* international legal personality. However, Boisson de Chazournes is quick to point out that this right to conclude agreements is qualified in Annex B to the Instrument on the Role and Fiduciary Responsibility of the Trustee of the GEF Trust which provides that on the request of the 'Council the Trustee will, for the purposes of paragraph 27 of the Instrument, formalise the arrangements' concluded with the COPs. Boisson de Chazournes suggests that this procedure for external relations conforms to the two-stage process characterising the GEF.[72] All this serves to demonstrate the uncertainty surrounding the legal nature of the GEF. Commentators, nonetheless, seem to agree that while the GEF does not posses a distinct legal personality under international law, it does enjoy a large degree of functional autonomy.[73]

3. The GEF operation and policies

3.1 Policies and Objectives in the GEF Instrument

The purpose of the GEF is described in the GEF Instrument, as the provision of 'new and additional grant and concessional funding to meet agreed incremental costs of measures to achieve agreed global

70 Para 34 of the Instrument. See for discussion Boisson de Chazournes (n 7 above) 256.

71 Para 27 of the Instrument.

72 Para 27 arrangements entered into by the GEF and the COPs, known as Memoranda of Understanding, have not been formalised by the Bank in its capacity as the Trustee. For this reason they are probably not to be regarded as legally binding. See R Churchill & G Ulfstein 'Autonomous institutional arrangements in multilateral environmental agreements: A little noticed phenomenon in international law' (2000) 94 *American Journal of International Law* 623 651.

73 Boisson de Chazournes (n 7 above) 258. See also Werksman (n 3 above) 57. Elsewhere, however, Werksman (n 5 above) 6 states, categorically, that the 'GEF is not an autonomous institution'. In fairness this statement appears to relate solely to the capacity to enter into agreements. See also S Boehmer-Christiansen 'Investing against climate change: Why failure remains possible' (2002) 11 *Environmental Politics* 1 8 who describes the GEF as 'housed inside the Bank remains legally part of it'. Although the sentence from which the latter quotation is taken is preceded by a reference to the Pilot Phase GEF, the author does not seem to view the two versions of the GEF as different. See also Hey (n 5 above) 33.

environmental benefits' in six focal areas, namely, biodiversity, climate change, international waters, land degradation (primarily desertification and deforestation), ozone layer depletion and persistent organic pollutants.[74] It has to be mentioned that the GEF is not the only source of finance for sustainable development in these areas. In the area of climate change, for example, the World Bank is involved in several other funds, additional to its involvement in the GEF, related to carbon financing.[75] Examples of such other funds include the Prototype Carbon Fund, considered in paragraph 4.4 of chapter 5, the Netherlands Clean Development Facility within the Bank, established by the Dutch Ministry of Housing, Spatial Planning and the Environment as well as an Italian Carbon Fund established by the Italian Ministry for the Environment and Territory, also within the Bank.[76] In addition to these the Bank has also established two specialised funds for operation in the poorest countries, namely, the Community Development Carbon Fund and the BioCarbon Fund.[77]

From the purpose of the GEF three elements can be isolated. First, the funding from the GEF will be new and additional. The addition of this element was in response to fears from developing countries that the GEF should not be used to impose 'green conditionalities' on the development process.[78] Sjöberg asserts that the requirement that GEF funding be 'new and additional' has, itself, two components.[79] In the first place, GEF funding had to be additional to regular development assistance so that it could not be used as an excuse to reduce existing development assistance. Second, it had to

74 Para 2 GEF Instrument. The early literature on the restructured GEF, eg Boisson de Chazournes (n 7 above), Werksman (n 3 above), Sjöberg (n 5 above), does not include land degradation and persistent organic pollutants in the focal areas. Land degradation and persistent organic pollutants were added in an amendment to the instrument in 2002. See Beijing Declaration adopted at the Second GEF Assembly, 18 October 2002, which expanded the mandate of the GEF to include these two areas as focal areas. The Declaration further expanded the role of the GEF by confirming that the GEF will act as financial mechanism to the United Nations Convention to Combat Desertification in those Countries Experiencing Serious Drought and/ or Desertification in Cullet & Gowlland-Gualtieri (n 1 above). The Beijing Declaration is available at http://web8.epnet.com (accessed 15 September 2004). Para 3 makes allowances for the funding of other relevant activities under Agenda 21 'insofar as they achieve global environmental benefits by protecting the global environment in the focal areas'. In August 2006, in Cape Town, South Africa, the GEF approved a US$3.13 billion replenishment to meet these purposes.

75 See generally D Freestone 'The UNFCCC, the Kyoto Protocol and the Kyoto mechanisms: General issues' in D Freestone and C Streck (eds) *Legal aspects of implementing the Kyoto Protocol mechanisms* (2005) 17 *et seq*. See D Freestone *et al* 'World Bank' (2003) 14 *Yearbook of International Environmental Law* 774 783 *et seq*.

76 As above. The Dutch Facility is geared to the purchase of 21 million tons of emissions reduction units. The Italian government has pledged an initial US$15 million for its Fund.

77 As above. The anticipated size of the Community Development Carbon Fund and the BioCarbon Fund is US$100 million each.

78 Sjöberg (n 5 above) 151. See also Miller (n 58 above) 1234.

79 Sjöberg (n 5 above) 151.

be additional to efforts by developmental institutions to integrate environmental considerations into mainstream practices, so that it could not be used as an excuse for not integrating environmental concerns into their regular activities. More than anything, the first element, that funding be 'new and additional', is a call to other institutions and forums (and developed states in particular) not to reduce development finance on account of GEF funding; it is thus not directed to the GEF.

The second element, that GEF funding be directed at incremental costs, implies that GEF funding would only be allocated for cost exceeding those that would, in any event, have been incurred by the recipient developing countries. In one sense, the second element represents the other side of the 'new and additional' element in that, inasmuch as GEF funding could not be used as a justification for reducing development funding, GEF funding could not be used to increase development funding.[80] Moreover, the incremental costs element implies that even in cases of environmental projects, GEF will not fund costs that the recipient country would have incurred 'pursuant to national environmental protection policies'.[81] The third element, that the GEF will fund 'measures to achieve agreed global environmental benefits', is of course, directly related to the second element. The presumption here (which, admittedly, will not be true in all cases) is that developing countries will, in any event, incur costs for developmental activities and environmental measures with strictly national benefits.[82] The GEF will not fund such costs.

In partial fulfilment of its purposes under paragraph 2, the GEF also serves as the financial mechanism for the Climate Change Convention and the Convention on Biodiversity.[83] In addition to these, the GEF serves as financial mechanism for the Kyoto Protocol and the Cartagena Protocol. Indeed, Werksman suggests that the operation of the financial mechanism of the climate change and biodiversity regimes is the primary function of the GEF.[84] The fulfilment of this objective has to be carried out 'in accordance with the cooperative agreement or arrangements' concluded with the COPs of the respective MEAs.[85] In this respect paragraph 26 of the Instrument provides that the use of GEF funds for purposes of meeting the

80 As above.
81 Boisson de Chazournes (n 7 above) 249.
82 Sjöberg (n 5 above) 151.
83 Para 6 GEF Instrument. The facility also serves as the financial mechanism for the Stockholm Convention on Persistent Organic Pollutants and the United Nations Convention to Combat Desertification.
84 Werksman (2003) (n 5 above). Confirming this view, OPS 3 states that the 'Biodiversity and Climate Change focal areas together account for the overwhelming majority of the GEF project portfolio in terms of funding, representing 70 percent of the overall GEF funds committed from 1991 through March 2005' 13.
85 Para 6 GEF Instrument.

objectives of the conventions to which the GEF serves as financial mechanism 'shall be in conformity with the policies, program priorities and eligibility criteria' of the relevant regime.[86]

Questions about the institutional relationship between the COP, the MEAs and the GEF have been canvassed by several authors.[87] However, these institutional issues and questions have important consequences for the normative development of the principle of sustainable development. What impact, if any, does this uncertainty about the legal status of the GEF have on the kinds of compromises and trade-offs that are made? In chapters 5 and 6 I considered the climate change regime (Kyoto Protocol in particular) and the biodiversity regime (Cartagena Protocol in particular). What kind of influences on GEF policies do these regimes and institutions exert? Is there an indication that one value is supported over others as a result of the influences from the various regimes? As tools of analysis, and to answer these questions, I focus on aspects of GEF policies discussed above, namely, that funding must be 'new and additional', towards 'incremental costs', and related to projects with 'global environmental benefits'. In the analysis I ask how these elements are interpreted by the GEF. What are the differences between how the GEF interprets these elements and how the COPs to the Climate Change and Biodiversity conventions interpret the same elements? More to the point, does the interpretation signify an inclination either to environmental, economic or social concerns?

The conceptualisation of sustainable development suggested in chapter 3 rests on compromises and trade-offs in the case of conflict. To this end, I adopt two sources of conflict in the analysis as themes for consideration of the requirement that the funding from the GEF must be towards 'incremental costs' and for projects related to 'global environmental benefits'. First, I consider the differences between the approach of the GEF to these requirements, on the one hand, and the approach of the COP to the same requirements. This tension, of course, is heightened by the fact that the GEF instrument, while setting down these requirements, simultaneously requires that the funding of the GEF be 'in conformity with the policies, programme priorities and eligibility criteria established' by the COPs.[88] The second theme relates to the tension represented by paragraph 2, which sets out the requirements for incremental costs and global environmental benefits, on the one hand, and, on the other hand, paragraph 4, which provides that the GEF should fund programmes 'based on national priorities'. On the basis of the above analysis, and in particular the kinds of compromises and trade-offs resulting from

86 See also para 27 of the GEF Instrument. See also art 11(3) of the Kyoto Protocol.

87 See eg Werksman (n 3 above); Boisson de Chazournes (n 7 above); Sand (n 45 above); Sjöberg (n 5 above).

88 See para 26 of the GEF Instrument.

the conflicts, I suggest the variation of sustainable development favoured by the GEF.

3.2 Eligibility for GEF Funding: 'Incremental Costs' and 'Global Environmental Benefits'

As stated above, in considering the policies of the the GEF, the focus will fall on the climate change and biodiversity regimes. With this in mind, I enquire as to the what kinds of climate change and biodiversity projects eligible for GEF funding. Are there differences between the criteria applied by the GEF, on the one hand, and the policies of the COPs to the climate change and the biodiversity instruments, on the other? In particular, how do the COPs to these conventions interpret the GEF Instrument objectives of GEF funding for 'incremental costs' with 'global environmental benefits'? How responsive is the GEF to COPs interpretations of these objectives?

3.2.1 COP and GEF approach to incremental costs

The first point that has to be considered is the requirement that GEF funding be available only for 'incremental costs'. This requirement can be found at several places in GEF documents.[89] What is interesting is that the MEAs place relatively less reliance on the notion of incremental costs. Although the Biodiversity Convention does provide that funding must be to meet 'the agreed full incremental costs' it does appear that the practice of the COP to the Biodiversity Convention is to require all biodiversity projects to be funded.[90] The same approach is evident in the Climate Change Convention.[91]

89 See eg paras 2 and 3 of the GEF Instrument. See also GEF *Operational strategy of the Global Environment Facility,* available at www.gefweb.org (accessed 30 August 2004) and GEF *Second overall performance study of the GEF* (2001) at 4 GEF/C.18/7. At the time of initial writing of this chapter (November 2004) only OPS 2 had been produced. However, OPS 3 was completed shortly thereafter, in June 2005, and the important findings with regards the canvassed issues have been incorporated. See GEF *Third overall performance study of the GEF* (2005).

90 See art 20 of the Biodiversity Convention. For the view that practice of the COP requires all biodiversity projects to be funded, see R Lake 'Finance for the global environment: The effectiveness of the GEF as the financial mechanism to the Convention on Biological Diversity' (1998) 7 *Review European Community and International Environmental Law* 68 71.

91 Art 4(3) of the UNFCCC, for example, provides that developed countries 'shall provide new and additional financial resources to meet the *agreed full costs* incurred by developing countries'. Of course art 11 of the Kyoto Protocol does refer to 'agreed full incremental costs'. See also art 11(2)(a) of the Kyoto Protocol.

Although the COP to the UNFCCC has referred to 'agreed full incremental costs', this has been couched in cautious and guarded language.[92] This raises many questions about the application of the 'incremental costs' requirement by the GEF, given the ambivalence of the climate change and biodiversity regimes' attitude towards the requirement.

What is clear, however, is that the 'incremental cost' requirement, in one sense at least, limits eligibility to purely environmental projects and excludes development funding from the ambit of GEF activities. It is in this sense that the 'incremental costs' requirement represents the other side of the 'global environmental benefits' coin. To this extent this limitation will be examined under the 'global environmental benefits' element of the GEF eligibility requirement.

The 'incremental costs' element, however, clearly has an extended function. Implicit in the notion of 'incremental costs' is the idea that, even where a project is an environmental project and not a developmental project, the GEF should only fund the portion of the costs that would not have been, in any event, incurred by the recipient developing country. Incremental costs, in this sense, could mean that in a project with 'global environmental benefits', the recipient country would incur the costs (or equivalent thereof) for achieving *any national benefit derived from the project*. However, an equally plausible alternative interpretation could be that the recipient would only be responsible for a portion of the costs of achieving national benefit where the project had a *separate national component* from which no global environmental benefits would accrue. Clearly, the first approach is more restrictive as it would imply greater costs to developing countries for even *incidental* benefits flowing from a project.[93]

The question, then, is which approach was adopted by the GEF and in what way does this tie in with the COPs' reluctance to require the funds to be 'incremental'. The Council has defined the phrase 'incremental costs' as follows:[94]

> The costs of GEF eligible activity should be compared to that of an activity it replaces or makes redundant. The difference between the two costs – the expenditure on the GEF supported activity and the costs saving on the replacement or redundant activity – is the incremental

92 At COP I, on the initial guidance to the GEF on the funding eligibility, the COP stated that priority 'should be given to funding of agreed full costs (or agreed full incremental costs, as appropriate)'. In the same decision the COP stated that the 'application of the full agreed incremental costs should be flexible, pragmatic and on a case-by-case basis'. Dec 11/CP.1 in FCCC/CP/1995/7/Add.1.

93 For example of how this might work, see the China Methane Recovery Project discussed (n 97 below).

94 See GEF *Incremental costs*, para 10.

> cost. It is a measure of the future economic burden on the country that would result in its choosing the GEF supported activity in preference to one that would have been sufficient in the national interest.

A purely textual reading of this definition does not it make it clear which of the two alternative interpretations it supports. However, a contextual interpretation of the document, taking into account examples offered of what would constitute incremental costs, suggests that the GEF Council has in mind the first, more restrictive interpretation:[95]

> A simple example of an action that incurs an incremental cost in order to realise global environmental benefits is the use of advanced solar energy technology in a situation where a less costly coal-fired power generator with pollution would have been sufficient to generate the electric power needed for development, while meeting reasonable environmental standards ... the incremental cost is associated with the global environmental benefit of reduction in greenhouse gases.

Thus, in such cases there is a suggestion that, to get the incremental costs, the costs of the less costly coal-fired power generator should be deducted from the costs of the advanced solar energy technology. Thus, as in the first interpretation, the cost of achieving *any national benefit*, even if not flowing from separate national component of a project, will be for the account of the recipient developing country in question. It has to be emphasised, however, that what the GEF refers to here is the 'cost of achieving' the benefit and not the benefit itself. In other words, where a state would not have engaged in an activity the GEF would fund the full costs because the full costs would have been incremental. This is so even if the recipient developing country acquires a purely national benefit. The GEF emphasises that any grants are to be for the full 'incremental costs [as defined and described] and not for any lesser amount' reached by deducting 'any domestic benefit or the share of the global benefit that the country enjoys'.[96]

In addition to the complex distinction the GEF makes between 'the benefit' and 'costs of achieving the benefit', the GEF has also responded to the MEAs COPs' call for a relaxation of the 'incremental costs' requirement. An example of the GEF's approach to incremental costs can be discerned from the GEF's comments on the methane recovery project in China.[97] The aim of the project was to recover methane from existing and planned landfills in order to generate electricity for the country and, in the process, reduce the emission of methane into the earth's atmosphere. The GEF identified four

95 GEF *Incremental costs*, para 4.
96 As above, para 30.
97 See China: Promoting Methane Recovery and Utilisation from Mixed Municipal Refuse (GEF CEO Approved project). Project documents available at http://www.gefweb.org (accessed 25 October 2004).

domestic benefits, in addition to the global environmental benefit from the decrease in pollution from the use of fossil fuels, flowing from the project, namely, removal of health hazards, improved technologies and communications, likely involvement of private entrepreneurs in future methane recovery and the direct domestic benefit from the sale of electricity and revenue collection. The only domestic benefit that GEF found not to be incremental was the revenues from the sale of the electricity valued at US$5.10 million, the total cost of the project being US$19.57 million. Thus, in this example, costs associated with other domestic benefits that are closely related to the global environmental benefit are treated as incremental and thus qualify for GEF funding. It is interesting that, consistent with the fine distinction between national benefits and the costs of achieving national benefits, the GEF project document noted that, although the project would produce in addition to global benefits, significant national benefit, it was unlikely to be included in China's development portfolio without GEF funding and therefore constituted incremental cost.[98]

In addition, the GEF Council accepted the call of UNFCCC that agreed full costs, not incremental, have to be paid in certain instances.[99] There appears, nevertheless, to be some lingering uncertainty over the meaning of 'incremental costs'.[100] Some of the ambiguities relating to the notion of 'incremental costs' become pronounced when one flips the coin over and examines what is meant by 'global environmental benefits'.

3.2.2 COP and GEF approach to global environmental benefits

Even with the uncertainty surrounding the interpretation of the notion of 'incremental costs', there is little ambivalence about the acceptance of the notion as a guiding principle.[101] There does, however, appear to be at least some ambivalence about the acceptance of the 'global environmental benefits' element as a guiding principle. Certainly, some developing countries, according to

98 As above, para 33.

99 Para 19 GEF *Incremental costs*.

100 See GEF *Second overall performance study* paras 243-251. At para 245 eg the study found that there was 'considerable lack of clarity on [incremental costs and global benefits] even among IA field office staff'. See also UNFCCC COP 'Initial guidance on policies, programme priorities and eligibility criteria to the operating entity of the financial mechanism' FCCC/CP/1995/7/Add.1 dec. 11/CP.1, June 6, 1995, attached as Annex Appendix A to GEF 'Climate change' in *Operational strategy* which asserts that the 'various issues of incremental costs are complex and difficult and further discussion on the subject is therefore needed'.

101 In this respect the Second overall performance study found that country participants 'did not question the principle of GEF financing agreed costs associated with meeting obligations of the conventions. Rather they raised issues about how this has been operationalised ...' GEF *The second overall performance study* 65 para 246.

the *Second Overall Performance Study*, 'questioned the priority of global environmental benefits over national environmental benefits', notably poverty alleviation.[102] Even large parts of the *Third Overall Performance Study* are dedicated to issues surrounding global environmental benefits.[103] It is interesting to note the requirements set out in the Kyoto Protocol for the provision of financial resources to developing countries. Article 11 requires the provision of 'new and additional resources' to meet the 'agreed full incremental costs' of existing commitments under article 4 of the UNFCCC. The requirement in article 11 of Kyoto is nowhere linked to the element of 'global environmental benefit'.[104] By the same token the guidance of the COP to the UNFCCC makes no mention of 'global environmental benefits'.[105] The same approach is evident in the biodiversity regime. Article 20 of the Biodiversity Convention, while containing the requirement of 'incremental costs', does not contain the requirement that the funding must be for global environmental benefits.[106]

In the context of climate change the UNFCCC COP was concerned that the 'global environmental benefit' requirement might preclude GEF funding for activities aimed at helping developing countries to adapt to the impact of global climate change which, as described in chapter 5, is central to the climate change regime.[107] According to the COP to the UNFCCC the GEF should fund the 'agreed full cost of relevant adaptation activities' in accordance with article 12 of the Convention.[108] Adaptation measures do not, at least not in any obvious way, have global environmental benefits.[109] They are meant to assist a state with coping with the consequences of climate change. In that sense such measures are, essentially, for the benefit of the particular state (or possibly region). This presents a real dilemma for the GEF.

The GEF instrument makes it clear that funding is to be for measures with 'global environmental benefits'.[110] The Instrument also requires that in the area of climate change the GEF shall function 'under the guidance of, and be accountable to the COP which shall

102 GEF *Second overall performance study* 66.

103 This is particularly, though not exclusively, true in relation to the land degradation focal area. See GEF *Third overall performance study* 61 *et seq*.

104 See art 11 of the Kyoto Protocol to the UNFCCC.

105 See Dec 11/CP.1 FCCC/CP/1995/7/Add.1.

106 See art 20 of the Convention on Biological Diversity. For its part the Cartagena Protocol on Biosafety to the Convention on Biological Diversity refers to art 20 of the CBD.

107 Werksman (2003) (n 5 above) 9.

108 See Dec 1/CP. 10 FCCC/CP/2004/10/Add.1. See on the arguments from the Pacific region GEF *Third overall performance study* 39.

109 This view is confirmed in OPS 3 which states as follows: '... adaptation will be a complicated new programme area because adaptation issues are typically local; thus the calculation of global environmental benefits and incremental costs will be difficult'. See GEF *Third overall performance study* 39.

110 See para 2 of the GEF Instrument.

decide on' funding and eligibility criteria.[111] By funding adaptation measures the GEF will not be acting consistently with the GEF Instrument's call to fund programs, projects and activities with global environmental benefits. On the other hand, by not funding such activities the GEF will be acting contrary to its obligation to use the resources of the GEF 'in conformity with the policies, program priorities and eligibility criteria decided by the Conference of Parties'.[112] Faced with this dilemma the GEF decided to follow COP guidelines and fund adaptation measures. The GEF decided that it will, to begin with and in accordance with COP guidelines, meet the 'full agreed costs' of Stage I adaptation measures.[113] Adaptation measures have increasingly become important and the Third Overall Performance Study (OPS 3) notes that many developing countries regard adaptation measures as more important than mitigation.[114] The GEF has already approved several adaptation projects.[115]

In the context of the biodiversity regime the 'global environmental benefits' requirement is not without its difficulties. One problem that arises here is that of benefit sharing of genetic resources. The global environmental benefits of activities leading to sustainable use and benefit sharing of biological resources are not immediately apparent.[116] However, article 15 of the Biodiversity Convention makes provision for benefit sharing.[117] Moreover, the COP to the Biodiversity Convention has made it clear that benefit sharing should be an integral part of the GEF funding.[118] Werksman, in considering the *Second Overall Performance Study,* finds that the area is controversial because it would imply the 'intervention of international law and institutions into what might otherwise be a

111 Para 6 GEF Instrument. See also para 2 of the Memorandum of Understanding Between the Conference of the Parties to the United Nations Framework of Convention on Climate Change and the Council of the Global Environment Facility which provides that the COP will 'decide on policies, programme priorities and eligibility criteria'. The MOU is attached as an annex to FCCC/CP/1996/15/Add.1.

112 Para 26 GEF Instrument.

113 GEF *Operational strategy*. Stage I adaptation measure are described by the COP as planning, which includes studies of possible impacts of climate change, identification of policy options for adaptation and appropriate capacity building. According to the *Operational strategy* GEF funding for Stage II adaptation measures will be 'dependant on COP guidance'.

114 GEF *Third overall performance study* 39.

115 See eg The Democratic Republic of Congo: National action plan for adaptation to climate change (GEF CEO approved); Lesotho: National adaptation program of action (GEF CEO approved); Maldives: National adaptation plan of action (GEF CEO approved). See also on global level assessment of impacts and adaptation to climate change in multi regions and sectors. Documents and information relating to these and other projects are available at http://www.gefonline.org/projectList.cfm (accessed 20 December 2004).

116 GEF *Second overall performance study* 52. See also Werksman (n 3 above) 10.

117 See, especially art 15(7) of the Convention on Biodiversity. The importance and implications of benefit sharing in connection with access to genetic resources are considered in chapter 6.

118 See eg decision V/13 of the CBB COP 'Further guidance to the financial mechanism' UNEP/CBD/COP/5/23.

largely commercial relationship in order to ensure 'fair and equitable' sharing of benefits'.[119]

Surely this should not be a difficulty in the context of GEF funding. The call by the COP to the Biodiversity Convention for a stronger portfolio in this area does not amount to a call to the GEF to *create* legal rules that would result in the interference of such commercial relations. It seems to me that, given the explicit inclusion of benefit sharing in the Biodiversity Convention, the notion of benefit sharing has already entered the arena of international law.[120] Moreover, benefit sharing is given further recognition in the FAO International Treaty on Plant Genetic Resources for Food and Agriculture.[121] It may be argued that benefit sharing as a concept in international law already flows from the principle of sustainable development. What the GEF is merely called upon to do is to contribute to the *realisation* of the objective by funding activities in this area. The real issue, however, is captured in the *Second Overall Performance Study*. The study, without providing an explanation, alludes to the problem in the context of differences in the definition of 'global environmental benefits'.[122] Although benefit sharing forms part of the aims and objectives of the Biodiversity Convention, a strict reading of the notion of 'global environmental benefit' would render benefit sharing activities outside the scope of the GEF. Moreover, to the extent that benefit sharing results in benefits, these are probably *more* 'developmental' than environmental. Benefit sharing can be described as yet another embodiment of the principle of intragenerational equity.[123] It is undeniably meant to recognise the special position of communities in the developing world. This is not to say that benefit sharing can yield *no* environmental benefits. Only that such environmental benefits are, at best, indirect. To the extent that benefit sharing does not *yield* environmental benefits, whatever benefits it may yield are probably also not global. The benefits are for developing countries and, more specifically, the recipient developing country (recipient of GEF funding). Again, that is not to say that there can be no global benefits, but that such benefits are likely to be indirect.

119 Werksman (2003) (n 5 above) 10.

120 Art 1 of the Biodiversity Convention provides as follows: 'The objectives of this Convention to be pursued in accordance with its relevant provisions, are the conservation of biological diversity, the sustainable utilisation of its components and *the fair and equitable sharing of the benefits arising out of the utilisation of genetic resources*, including by appropriate access to genetic resources and by appropriate transfer of relevant technologies, taking into account rights over those resources and technologies, and by funding' (emphasis added).

121 International Treaty on Plant Genetic Resources for Food and Agriculture (2001) reproduced in Cullet & Gowlland-Gualtieri (n 1 above).

122 GEF *Second overall performance study* 52. OPS 3 simply noted that benefit sharing had received the least GEF attention of the all biodiversity objectives. See GEF *Third overall performance study* 23.

123 See for discussion para 4.5 of ch 6.

As mentioned earlier, the tension caused by the GEF's requirement that funding be for 'global environmental benefit' and the COPs' requirement that a broad spectrum of projects be funded, including those that potentially do not have a global environmental benefit, was a theme running through OPS 3. For example, the report states that one of the challenges confronting the GEF will be to find a 'mutually beneficial balance of trade-offs between global environmental benefits and sustainable livelihoods while not diverting from the GEF core mandate to protect the global environment'.[124]

Although the analysis of the GEF in this chapter relies primarily on the climate change and biodiversity regimes, as regimes considered in Part B, the complexity of the global environmental benefit requirement becomes particularly enhanced in the land degradation focal area. The portfolio of the GEF in the land degradation focal area is guided, principally, by the United Nations Convention on Desertification. The objectives of the Desertification Convention are to 'combat desertification and mitigate the effects of drought in countries experiencing' serious drought and/or desertification.[125] These objectives are not, strictly speaking, for the benefit of the global environment.[126] To justify funding programmes under the land degradation focal area in light of the global environment benefit requirement is thus particularly daunting.

Of course, land degradation does affect regimes that directly benefit the global environment, such as climate change and biodiversity. Obviously, land degradation affects species habitats and consequently biodiversity as well as climate change through the reduction of sinks. However, this cannot be a justification for funding activities aimed at combating land degradation as such activities could easily be funded under the biodiversity and climate change regimes respectively, as was the case prior to the introduction of the land degradation focal area in terms of the Beijing Declaration. The inclusion of the land degradation portfolio means that land degradation activities are funded in their own right and not for some benefits that they may produce for objectives in other focal areas. Recognising the difficulty of explaining the global environmental benefits under the land degradation focal area, OPS 3 simply states: 'Because the United Nations Convention to Combat Desertification has been agreed upon by the international community the priorities outlined in the Convention are recognised as global priorities'.[127]

124 GEF *Third overall performance study* 65.

125 Art 2(1) Desertification Convention.

126 Indeed it was for this reason that, while it may have been attractive to consider the Desertification Convention, the Desertification Convention was not considered in Part B. To be fair, issues around land degradation do have an impact on the regimes considered globally beneficial such as the biodiversity and climate change regimes.

127 GEF *Third overall performance study* 61.

This is not a sufficient explanation. The acceptance of such an explanation would require accepting the idea that all objectives contained in all MEAs would qualify as bringing forth global environmental benefit. It would essentially turn the eligibility requirement of the GEF into 'incremental costs' for objectives agreed upon in international environmental agreements. It is submitted that the answer for the tension between the GEF's requirement for 'global environmental benefit' and the MEA COPs' suspicion of the requirement is the second theme identified, namely, the interplay between paragraphs two and four of the GEF instrument.

3.2.3 Interplay between national priorities and global environmental benefits

In assessing the compatibility of the GEF's funding of activities that are unlikely to produce global environmental benefits such as adaptation measures, benefit sharing and land degradation, with the GEF's mandate to fund measures with global environmental benefits in terms of paragraph 2 of the Instrument, a different provision of the Instrument may prove useful. Paragraph 4 of the Instrument provides that the GEF:

> shall fund programs and projects which are country-driven and based on national priorities designed to support sustainable development and shall maintain sufficient flexibility to respond to changing circumstances in order to achieve its purposes.

Two aspects of paragraph 4 immediately become apparent. The first and obvious aspect is the emphasis on 'national priorities' and support for 'sustainable development'. For many poor countries the ability to adapt to climate change is a priority.[128] That is not to say that this call to 'national priorities' has the effect of nullifying the requirement that funding be limited to measures with global environmental benefit, but rather, that 'national priorities' become important tools in the interpretation of the notion of 'global environmental benefit'. This becomes more apparent, I think, when one considers that these national priorities are, in fact, made obligatory in the UNFCCC, an MEA designed to achieve global environmental benefits.[129] It is, at this point, worth mentioning that

128 In this regard the IPCC made the following observation: 'The ability of humans to adapt to and cope with climate change depends on such factors as wealth, technology, education, information, skills, infrastructure ... Least developed countries are, generally poorest in this regard. As a result they have lesser capacity to adapt and they are more vulnerable to climate changes, just as they are more vulnerable to other stresses'. IPCC *Climate change 2001: Impacts, adaptation, vulnerability* (2001) available at http://wwwgrida.no.climate/ipcc_tar/wg2/index.htm (accessed 19 February 2004). See also C Kemfert & R Tol 'Equity international trade and climate policy' (2002) 2 *International Environmental Agreements: Politics, Law and Economics* 23 23.

129 See in particular art 12 of the UNFCCC.

the COP to the Climate Change Convention has established two new funds, namely, the Least Developed Country Fund (LDCF) and the Special Climate Change Fund (SCCF), both of which are to be managed by the GEF.[130] Both these funds are designed to meet the special needs of developing countries and adaptation is to be a top priority.[131] Linked to this national priority emphasis is the invocation of sustainable development — that these GEF-funded national priorities must support sustainable development. What I find interesting about the invocation of sustainable development in the context of global environmental benefit flows from a reading of the Operational Strategy of the GEF.[132] In the first chapter, titled Policy Framework, the phrase 'sustainable development' is used several times. Almost every invocation of the phrase 'sustainable development' in that document is linked to national strategies and policies, in much the same way that it is used in paragraph 4, while comparative action at the international or global level is referred to as action with global environmental benefits.[133] This dichotomy is probably open to criticism because of its failure to acknowledge the international dimensions of sustainable development, but that is not the point here. The point here is that sustainable development, when used in this manner, may further be used to support the need for action that is not purely globally beneficial.

The second point that becomes apparent when considering paragraph 4 of the Instrument is the call to 'maintain sufficient flexibility' to enable the Facility to respond to changing circumstances. Thus, in interpreting 'global environmental benefit', and indeed 'incremental costs', the GEF must adopt a flexible approach. In this way projects that do not, strictly speaking, produce global environmental benefits, can still be funded. It seems that it was this call to maintain flexibility that is responsible for the GEF's willingness to fund activities that might, otherwise, not be considered to produce global environmental benefits.[134] However, the *Second Overall Performance Study*, commissioned by the GEF, found this reliance on 'operational flexibility and more freedom for case-by-case interpretation' to be inappropriate without explaining why.[135] In light

130 See for more information GEF Newsletter, *Talking points* vol 5 no 2 May 2005 3.

131 As above. See also GEF Newsletter, *Talking Points* vol 5 no 1 March 2005 4.

132 GEF *Operational strategy* (n 71 above).

133 Early on the document provides that 'GEF activities will be consistent with, and supportive of, the recipient countries' own actions for sustainable development'. Elsewhere the document states that actions 'by individual countries' to achieve sustainable development at the national level can be complemented and supplemented by other efforts aimed at securing global environmental benefits'. It is this last sentence that captures the dichotomy between sustainable development as an essentially domestic (probably also developing country) interest and environmental protection as a global (perhaps also developed country) interest most succinctly.

134 See also GEF *Second overall performance study* 66. See also Werksman (2003) (n 5 above) 10.

of the call in paragraph 4 for funding of activities reflecting national priorities as well the call for flexibility, it appears that this operational flexibility and case-by-case interpretation of the notion of global environmental benefit is not only appropriate, but also consistent with the GEF Instrument.

The issue of global environmental benefit and, indeed, incremental cost as requirements for GEF funding, goes to the heart of sustainable development discourse. It raises questions about the extent to which economic, social and environmental issues are, as called for in the Brundtland Commission report, one issue.[136] A strict reading of the global environmental benefits and incremental costs requirements would appear to exclude the possibility of funding for socio-economic concerns in developing countries. While the GEF has recognised the need to finance programmes and projects that 'address the underlying causes of global environmental deterioration, such as economic policy, social issues', it has also made it clear that 'efforts to achieve sustainable development at national level can be supplemented' by other means.[137] Nevertheless, it does seem clear from an overall reading of GEF documents in general, and the *Operations Strategy* in particular, that GEF funds are not to be utilised to finance socio-economic programmes. In the *Operational Strategy,* the comments on actions by individual countries to be supplemented by other efforts are, in the first place, preceded by a statement on the need to finance socio-economic projects. Second, these comments are made in the context of explaining the implications of incremental costs for global environmental benefits. This indicates that, even though the GEF recognises the need to finance socio-economic programmes, it remains constrained by its own mandate to finance only incremental costs of programmes with

135 GEF *Second overall performance study* 66.
136 WCED *Our common future* 4.
137 GEF *Operational strategy.*

global environmental benefits.[138]

4. GEF variation of sustainable development

It goes without saying that the central concern of the GEF is the global environment. The GEF was created to make funding available for projects with environmental benefits. In seeking to place the GEF within one of the variations of sustainable development, the question must be the extent to which other values have been integrated into GEF activities. In other words, to what extent have economic and/or social values and concerns influenced the activities and policies of the GEF? In pursuit of its primary objective of making finances available to meet the costs of activities capable of yielding global environmental benefits, whether the GEF has taken onboard social concerns of the developing countries that they serve. Using the discussion above I consider these questions. In particular, the tension represented in the two themes analysed above – on the one hand, the tension between COP and GEF approaches to global environmental benefit and incremental costs, and on the other hand, the tension between paragraph 2 and paragraph 4 of the GEF instrument – illustrates the conflict between environmental and social interests.

The GEF has had to, and indeed continues to, grapple with dilemmas flowing from the requirement that funding be for incremental costs associated with measures that can yield global environmental benefits. The effect of both these requirements, individually and taken together, is to make GEF funding strictly for environmental purposes on a global level. A project with purely developmental or national environmental benefits would not be eligible for GEF funding as such a project would not meet the global environmental benefit requirement. However, where a particular project falling within the mandate of the GEF has both global environmental and national developmental components, the GEF would, in terms of the incremental costs requirements, fund only

138 See also GEF *Second overall performance study* 36 which, when analysing the text in Operation Strategy under discussion, states that there 'has been considerable discussion within the GEF on this subject centering on what among the root causes is within the capacity and mandate of the GEF to address', thus implying that not all root causes of environmental degradation are within the mandate of the GEF to address. In respect of the tension between objectives of a regime and wider goals related to sustainable development, the ILA Committee on Sustainable Development, Second Draft Report (on file with author) states as follows: 'This tension is perhaps unsurprising; conflict between the objectives of a treaty and the more broader *(sic)* goal of sustainable development is, in most cases, inevitable. An unanswered and somewhat open-ended question is whether such treaties make a more effective contribution to sustainable development through simply focusing upon what they were initially established to do, or whether it does require a fundamental realignment in the light of the broader international context' (19).

incremental costs associated with the project. Similarly, where an eligible project has both a global environmental and national environmental component, the GEF would only fund the global environmental component. The costs funded by the GEF would be considered incremental. The above illustration of the impact of 'incremental costs' and 'global environmental benefits' should raise some serious questions about the role of sustainable development in the policies of the GEF.

I suggested in chapter 3 that the essence of sustainable development is integration. The notion of integration is predicated on the idea that there is an inextricable link between environmental, economic and social issues. In this context the Brundtland Commission referred to the interlocking crisis in which economic, environmental and social concerns can no longer be seen as separate but must be seen as one concern interwoven by a 'seamless net of cause and effect'.[139] However, the notions of incremental costs and global environmental benefits as restrictions on GEF funding *could* be taken to imply that these elements of the net can be, somehow, separated.

In fairness to the GEF, the interpretation of these concepts, made possible by the Instrument's call for 'sufficient flexibility',[140] has not been dogmatic. The methane recovery project in China illustrates this flexibility. Under an interpretation of 'incremental costs' where any national or social benefit is excluded from GEF funding, China would have been responsible for the value of the costs of removal of health hazards, improved technologies and communications, and the likely involvement of private entrepreneurs in future methane recovery.

Instead, under the project as approved, China will only be responsible for the costs associated with the direct benefit from the sale of electricity.

There has been a similar flexibility shown by the GEF to the interpretation of 'global environmental benefits'. Yet again, based on the GEF Instrument's call for flexibility, the GEF has decided to fund activities that appear, at the very least on the surface, to have no global environmental benefit. The GEF funds, both as a matter of policy[141] and practice,[142] measures for adaptation to climate change, even though the global environmental benefit of such projects is, to

139 WCED *Our common future* 5.
140 Para 4 GEF Instrument.

say the least, questionable.[143] Adaptation measures are critical to the needs of developing countries and, as suggested in chapter 5, the inclusion of adaptation measures in article 4 of the Framework Convention on Climate Change and article 10 of the Protocol cater for the social value of sustainable development. However, in paragraph 4.4 of chapter 5, I suggested that even social aspects of adaptation have been, as expressed in the climate change instruments, diluted by economic instruments in so far as adaptation is understood to include adaptation to 'the adverse effects of the implementation measures to respond to climate change'.[144] A careful reading of OPS 3 suggests that the GEF funding of adaptation measures has not, at least not yet, extended to measures to adapt to the economic impact of climate change regulation.[145]

Even though the GEF continues to be criticised for its weak portfolio on benefit sharing as defined by the Biodiversity Convention, including 'projects demonstrating the sharing of revenues from royalties, fees, etc, from exploitation of indigenous knowledge of biological resources', such weakness should not be laid solely at the door of the GEF.[146] The *Second Overall Performance Study* found that the weakness in GEF's benefit sharing portfolio may be a reflection of the COP to the Biodiversity Convention's failure to 'provide clear and precise guidelines' rather than unwillingness on the part of the GEF to fund such activities. The uncertainty of the GEF with regards to benefit sharing may be a reflection of the uncertainty in the Biodiversity Convention. In chapter 6 I suggested

141 See GEF *Operational strategy*.

142 The GEF has funded several climate change adaptation projects, including the Caribbean planning for adaptation to global climate change discussed in GEF *Second overall performance study*. See for other projects n 11 above. See also M Barbut, the Chief Executive Officer of the Global Environment Facility, at the GEF Assembly, in Cape Town, August 2006, commenting on the World Bank report, *Managing climate risks — Integrating adaptation into World Bank group*: 'Funding for adaptation to climate change is critical for adaptation. The best form of adaptation is mitigation. But we must deal with the climate change that the planet is already signed up to. I'm delighted that the Assembly has provided the opportunity to bring financing for adaptation forward in the environmental agenda...' in World Bank press release 'Development under Climate Threat', available at http://web.worldbank.org/WSITE/EXTERNAL/NEWS/0,,contentMDK:21035991~pagPK:343770~piPK:34424~theSitePK.4607.00.html (accessed 4 September 2006).

143 See Werksman (n 3 above) 9.

144 Art 4(10) UNFCCC. See also art 4(8) of the UNFCCC. See also art 3(14) of the Kyoto Protocol. For discussion see ch 5, para 4.

145 OPS 3 refers exclusively to adaptation to climate change measures. See eg GEF *Third overall performance study* 39. See also list of adaptation projects (n 110 above).

146 GEF *Second overall performance study* 31.

that there existed a number of compromises and trade-offs in the provisions on access to genetic resources and benefit sharing.[147] Moreover, as with adaptation measures in the climate change regime, economic influences are present in the Biodiversity Convention's provision on benefit sharing through, for example, the commercialisation of biological resources.[148] All these uncertainties flowing from the Convention would make it very difficult for the GEF to actively engage in direct benefit sharing funding. While the activities on benefit sharing have proved challenging for the GEF, the GEF has engaged in numerous projects having benefit sharing components, particularly capacity building projects.[149] An example of a typical capacity-building project with a benefit sharing com-ponent is the Conservation and Sustainable use of the Barrier Reef Complex in Belize designed to contribute towards to the operationalisation of the Coastal Management Act of Belize.[150] The benefit sharing component of the project, worth US$57 000 out of the total US$7.3 million, involves the development of legal regulatory capacities relating to biosprospecting agreements.[151]

While the text of the Instrument establishing the GEF requires only incremental costs of activities or measures with global environmental benefit to be funded, there is sufficient ambivalence to allow the GEF to fund projects and measures which, strictly speaking, will not yield global environmental benefit. In the first place there is paragraph 4 of the Instrument requiring the GEF to fund projects that are 'based on national priorities', 'designed to support [national] sustainable development' and, also to apply a 'degree of flexibility'.[152] The ambivalence flows, further, from the particular institutional arrangements created in the GEF, particularly as concerns the relationship between the GEF and the Conference of Parties to the MEAs to which the GEF serves as financial mechanism. On the one hand, the GEF, in making its decisions to fund a particular

147 See art 15 of the Biodiversity Convention.

148 See for discussion ch 6 above.

149 See email discussions with M Ramos and M Zimsky, GEF Program Managers. Examples of the kinds of project referred to by the GEF can be found in a report by the GEF to the fifth COP to the Biodiversity Convention entitled 'Activities of the Global Environment Facility in support of benefit sharing under the Convention on Biological Diversity' UNEP/CBD/COP 5/INF/17 (5 May 2000).

150 For further project details see http://www.gefonline.org/projectDetails.cfm7projID=592 (accessed on 25 August 2006).

151 See also the Central Asia Transboundary Biodiversity Project (Kazakhstan, Kyrgyz Republic and Uzbekistan), the project aim of which is to support the protection of vulnerable biodiversity. The benefit sharing component of the project involves the drafting of legislation for natural resource ownership. See http://www.gefonline.org/projectDetails.cfm7projID=110 (accessed on 25 August 2006).

152 Para 4 GEF Instrument. The word 'national' to qualify sustainable development is included here because it appears that in GEF texts the phrase sustainable development is associated with national endeavours while the phrase global environmental benefits is used to refer to equivalent endeavours at the international level.

project, must be faithful to the text of the Instrument, including the requirement to fund only incremental costs of projects with global environmental benefit. The latter implies the exclusion of social or developmental funding. On the other hand, however, the GEF is required by the very same Instrument to make decisions 'in conformity with the policies, programmes, priorities and eligibility criteria decided by the Conference of Parties' to the MEAs to which the GEF functions as financial mechanism. The guidance of the COPs to these MEAs has tended to require a broad spectrum of activities, including activities that will not readily yield global environmental benefits, to be eligible for funding.

The GEF has, at least for the time being, responded to the COP's call for broader funding. In this sense the GEF has, while funding projects with global environmental benefits, also been able to fund projects with increased social or developmental benefits. The need for integrating development projects into the GEF mandate, reminiscent of the Brundtland Commission's call for integration, is recognised by the *Second Overall Performance Study*:[153]

> The core of the GEF's overall mandate is to deliver global environmental benefits. Addressing the needs of the poor and the vulnerable though GEF-supported initiatives is one of the means towards achieving this end. Poverty-environment linkages are particularly strong in the focal areas of biodiversity and land degradation.

However, the very same flexibility that has enabled the GEF to fund *some* projects with national and/or developmental slants could be used, in future, to more restrictively apply the eligibility criteria of the GEF. While the GEF Instrument can be, and has been, interpreted in a flexible way to give effect to the wishes of COPs for funding of national priority projects, it is also legally possible to interpret the Instrument as prohibiting the funding of such projects. The point is that the ambivalence in the approach to developmental funding can be seen as a double-edged sword. While it allows the GEF flexibility to fund projects favoured by the COPs and containing some developmental aspects, it may in the future be used to prevent such funding.

However, in assessing the GEF's role it has to be remembered that the GEF is, essentially, a regime focused on the global environment. The contribution of the GEF to the normative development of sustainable development begins with global environmental benefits. The GEF has been able to integrate social concerns in two important ways. First, and as discussed in the preceding paragraphs, by following a flexible approach to the concepts of incremental costs and global environmental benefit, the GEF has been able to fund projects that will, arguably, not yield global environmental benefits. Second,

[153] GEF *Second overall performance study* 83.

the GEF requirement that funding be 'new and additional', although essentially directed at forums outside the GEF, reminds us that development funding should not be reduced on account of GEF funding.

It is too early to tell exactly how the coming into operation of the two protocols in the Climate change and Biodiversity regimes – the Kyoto Protocol and the Cartagena Protocol, respectively – will affect the delicate balance struck by the GEF. For example, the GEF is still undecided about how to approach carbon trading under the Kyoto Protocol.[154] In the analysis of these treaties in chapters 5 and 6 they were found to reflect different variations of sustainable development. The conclusion reached in chapter 6 was that the use of flexible mechanisms as a tool to mitigating climate change is indicative of an economic growth-centred variation of sustainable development. The way in which the entry into force of these protocols and subsequent GEF involvement affect the GEF remains, at this point, uncertain.

5. Conclusion

The GEF is an innovative institutional experiment. The complex institutional structure, which has received much attention in legal literature, impacts on the GEF's contribution to sustainable development. The interplay between the GEF Instrument, with its strong focus on 'global environmental benefits' and 'incremental costs', and the environmental regime's call upon the GEF to fund a diversity of projects including those which could not be said to produce global environmental benefits in a strict sense, flows from an aspect of this complex institutional system set up by the GEF instrument.

This interplay between, on the one hand, national priorities and global environmental benefits on the other, requires trade-offs and compromises between developmental concerns and global environmental concerns. To its credit, the GEF, by responding positively to the guidance of the COPs, has managed to maintain a flexibility that has allowed the GEF to integrate social concerns while not abandoning its primary role as financier for global environmental benefit. The GEF can therefore be said to be reflecting an environment-centred variation of sustainable development with a relatively strong social needs influence.

154 See generally GEF *Third overall performance study* 40 *et seq.*

FINAL CONCLUSION: SUSTAINABLE DEVELOPMENT: NEW LANGUAGE, SAME PARADIGM?

In this study the concept of sustainable development is conceptualised. The study was divided into two parts. The first part of the study, Part A, presented a framework within which various instruments were to be analysed. In the course of presenting this framework, a nuanced conceptualisation of sustainable development was offered. In addition, Part A served to illuminate the role that sustainable development is to play in international law. Part B consisted of an analysis of various instruments in light of the framework developed in Part A. In particular, Part B consisted of an analysis of specific environmental regimes and the mechanism tasked with effecting financial transfers under the relevant agreements. In particular the instruments analysed were the climate change regime, the biodiversity regime and the Global Environment Facility.

This final chapter serves three purposes. First, the chapter serves to tie these parts together into a coherent whole. Second, the purpose of this chapter is to evaluate, based on the preceding chapters of the study, the impact that sustainable development has had on international law. It aims, in that respect, to contribute to understanding whether sustainable development is achieving the lofty goals intended by its architects. Third, the chapter is intended to offer recommendations on how sustainable development can better serve the purposes for which it was developed.

1. Sustainable development: Implications for international law?

1.1 Three Variations of Sustainable Development

In chapter 3, having considered the main objections to sustainable development, namely, the indeterminacy objection – the idea that sustainable development is incapable of any determinable meaning – and the subordination objection – the idea that sustainable development has the effect of subordinating environmental imperatives to developmental concerns – I offered a nuanced conceptualisation of sustainable development. Under this nuanced conceptualisation of sustainable development there are three variations of sustainable development. These three variations are based on the *process of integrating* the three values of sustainable development, economic growth, social concerns and environmental protection.

In one variation, the economic growth-centred variation, economic growth concerns are central. In cases of conflict between economic growth concerns and the other values of sustainable development, economic growth concerns triumph. A second variation is the environment-centred variation of sustainable development. Under this variation it is the environment that is central and environmental concerns triumph in cases of conflict. A third variation is the social well-being-centred variation of sustainable development, where the needs of the poor are accorded a central position in the integration process. The conceptualisation of sustainable development offered here integrates intergenerational equity as well as intragenerational equity. However, as argued in section 3 of chapter 3, this more nuanced conceptualisation, by stripping sustainable development to its core, allows commentators to respond to the main objections to sustainable development. On a more practical level, such a nuanced conceptualisation can guide policy and lawmakers, in a more concrete way, as to what sustainable development requires.

In chapter 2, having considered the history and purpose of sustainable development, it was suggested that sustainable development is a reaction to the widespread environmental degradation and global poverty resulting from the economic growth paradigm. In that sense, sustainable development requires a paradigm shift from a economic concerns-dominated paradigm to a paradigm where social and environmental concerns are accorded a place of priority. That sustainable development was intended to have this transformative effect on international law is evidenced by a study of the evolution of the concept, starting from the early days in Founex and proceeding through to the conference in Johannesburg. Both environmental and social concerns played pivotal roles in each of the milestone events in the emergence of sustainable development. Moreover, these milestones seem to send out a message that the paradigm in which economic growth is pursued at the expense of environmental and social concerns is no longer acceptable.

Of course, the economic growth-variation of sustainable development is very similar to the pre-sustainable development economic paradigm to which sustainable development is a reaction. As with the prevalent paradigm, economic concerns are accorded a preferred position in the making of law and policy. However, the prevalent paradigm is not the same as the economic growth-centred variation of sustainable development. They are remarkably similar but they are not the same.

With the economic growth-variation of sustainable development, environmental and social concerns are to be integrated while with the prevailing economic paradigm there is no obligation to integrate social and environmental concerns. However, in this economic growth-variation of sustainable development, social and environmental concerns are integrated in such as way as to make them subordinate to economic concerns. Nevertheless, the economic growth-variation of sustainable development, by prioritising economic concerns over environmental and social concerns and thereby continuing the pattern of economic dominance, prevents sustainable development from achieving it's *raison de être*: the transformation of international law to a system that is sensitive to social as well as environmental concerns.

1.2 The Operation of Sustainable Development in International Law

While questions about the legal status of sustainable development in international law continue to arise, the reception into international law of the concept of sustainable development and related norms warrant and indeed requires, that the role of sustainable development in international law be scrutinised. What is sustainable development supposed to be accomplishing and what is sustainable development actually accomplishing in the area of international law?

In chapter 4, I sought to answer the first question. I suggested that the primary role of sustainable development in international law is to facilitate the paradigm shift referred to in chapter 2. In this context, the operation of sustainable development requires us to rethink legal rules and principles that promote the domination of economic concerns over social and environmental ones.

The role of sustainable development as a facilitator for the paradigm shift has important implications for the nature of sustainable development in international law. It will be remembered that the economic growth-centred variation has assumed the characteristics of the prevalent economic growth paradigm. Rules and principles of international law that reflect the economic growth-centred variation of sustainable development will have the effect of subordinating environmental and social concerns to economic concerns. This means that sustainable development, in that variation, will not fulfill its role as facilitating the paradigm shift required by international law. These rules, reflecting economic growth variations of sustainable development, also have to be rethought and, if necessary, challenged.

2. Sustainable development: The continued dominance of economic concerns

2.1 Patterns of Trumping

Using the framework established in Part A, various enviro-economic instruments were analysed in Part B. The purposes of the analysis was, to start with, an exercise designed to place the instruments within one or other of the variations of sustainable development – an exercise in associating a specific instrument or regime with a variation of sustainable development. Secondly, the analysis was meant to contribute towards an understanding of the role that sustainable development has played in the development of international law.

In Part B, both the climate change and biodiversity regimes were found to be reflecting an economic growth-centred variation of sustainable development, although in the biodiversity regime environmental considerations were also significantly influential in the design of the regime. In the climate change regime, to say that the target set for the reduction of greenhouse gases in the Kyoto Protocol is less than what would be environmentally required would be a gross understatement. As if that was not enough, the flexible mechanisms, in particular joint implementation, the clean development mechanism, the emissions trading and even the use of sinks, serve to further reduce the adequacy of the climate change instrument to effectively deal with the climate change problem. Again, that is not to say that the climate change regime does not take environmental and social concerns into account. Surely it does. The very conclusion of the agreements in light of the precautionary principle requiring some (uncomfortable) adjustments as well the various provisions giving effect to the common but differentiated principle, suggests that both environmental and social concerns played some role in the design of the regime. The problem relates to the manner and the extent to which environmental and social concerns are integrated. There is a clear sense that when push came to shove and hard choices had to be made, economic concerns triumphed over both environmental and social considerations.

The biodiversity regime similarly reflected an economic growth-centred variation of sustainable development. At the insistence of states wishing to protect free trade rights, the impact of the Biosafety Protocol was limited in several key respects. Although environmental considerations were influential, on the whole, judging from the trade-offs and compromises made in the design of the protocol, it is difficult not to reach the conclusion that economic considerations won the day. While the approach in the biodiversity regime reflected a greater deal of integration, the integration approach nevertheless reflected a bias in favour of economic concerns. What one discovers in analysing the biodiversity regime, and the Biosafety Protocol in particular, is a series of trade-offs between environmental concerns on the one hand, and economic concerns, on the other. The centrality of the precautionary principle, for example, reflects a compromise in favour of environmental concerns. However, the limited scope of the Protocol suggested a bias in favour of economic concerns. When seen together, as a whole, the series of compromises and trade-offs suggested an overall bias towards economic concerns. What was equally apparent in the analysis was that social issues were even more peripheral than environmental issues in the integration process. Both the climate change and biodiversity regimes – regimes of which the instruments can be traced back to the 1992 UN Conference on Environment and Development – reflect an economic growth-centred variation of sustainable development.

The analysis of the Global Environmental Facility revealed different conclusions. It appeared that environmental considerations were central. In addition there was an indication that the practice of the GEF showed sufficient flexibility to allow the increased influence of social concerns. The GEF's mandate is purely environmental. Yet the GEF was, through a flexible and pragmatic approach, able to integrate social concerns by embracing projects which were, technically, not for 'global environmental benefits'. What we see *emerging* in the Global Environment Facility is the possibility of meaningful integration of environmental and social concerns into the design of an international instrument. Of course, especially in the context of climate change, this point has to be considered against the background of the plethora of financing mechanisms within the World Bank's portfolio, such as the Prototype Carbon Fund, the Dutch and Italian Clean Development Facilities, the Community Development Carbon Fund and the BioCarbon Fund.

With the exception of the GEF, the other instruments considered in the study reflect an economic growth-centred variation of sustainable development. It will not be lost on the reader that much of the success in the integration of social concerns into GEF practice has been as a result of the insistence of the Conference of the Parties of the UNFCCC and the Biodiversity Convention, and yet the latter instruments reflect an economic growth-centred variation of sustainable development. The point being made here is that this integration happens in the context of the particular interactions within the GEF.[1] At least with regards the instruments considered in the study, economic concerns continue to dominate in international environmental law and policy-making. In essence then, to date sustainable development has represented a continuation of the prevalent economic paradigm and has not been able to achieve it's mandate as an agent for a change of paradigm in international law and policy-making. In the same vein and in trying to make sense of the World Trade Organisation's incorporation of sustainable development, the International Law Association Committee on International Law on Sustainable Development has stated as follows:[2]

> These views – whatever their validity – both begin and end from the same premise, namely that sustainable development can largely be accommodated within the current political and economic framework. Integration, thus becomes less about an idealistic imperative and is viewed, perhaps too critically, as more concerned with maintaining continuity of structures and systems.

What sustainable development has been able to do is to paint a picture of progress; a picture of integration in an international legal order where the plight of the poor and the state of the environment are of utmost importance, while the paradigm of economic

1 This point is discussed further in para 3 below.
2 ILA Committee on International Law on Sustainable Development, Second Report (on file with author) 8.

dominance continues unabated. The inability of sustainable development to impact significantly on the international law-making process can be attributed to both the indeterminacy and subordination objections to sustainable development. The indeterminacy of sustainable develop-ment has meant that, with the right jargon in place, law and policy makers can easily justify a variety of policies as supporting sustainable development, even when such policies reflect the ruling economic growth paradigm. After all, sustainable development can mean different things to different constituencies. The corollary of the latter, and reflecting the subordination objection, is that law and policy makers are able to put in place policies that subordinate environmental and social considerations to economic considerations and still be able to label them as sustainable development-based policies. What becomes apparent in the study of the GEF is that, whether by design or not, the express isolation of the values of sustainable development, especially social and environmental values, through concepts such as 'global environmental benefits', 'incremental costs', and 'national priorities', has contributed to a more meaningful integration of these values.

2.2 Methods of Trumping

In addition to showing that economic concerns have trumped social and environmental concerns, the study has shown how this trumping has occurred. With regards to how the trumping has occurred, two conclusions can be drawn. The first relates to the general hierarchy of the values of sustainable development. The second point relates to the technique of trumping.

With regards the first point, from the analysis of the enviro-economic instruments in Part B, it becomes apparent that there is a hierarchy of values in the integration process. While, as asserted in paragraph 2.1 of this chapter, economic concerns are accorded the key position, environmental concerns appear to occupy the secondary position while social concerns are accorded the position of least priority. While the relative position of social concerns *vis-à-vis* environmental concerns is less pronounced in the climate change regime, the position is much clearer in the biodiversity regime. In the biodiversity regime, particularly in the Cartagena Protocol, there is constant trade-offs taking place between environmental and economic concerns. Moreover, social concerns are made relevant only to the extent that they are connected to impacts on biodiversity. Further, in both the biodiversity and climate change regimes, the primary vehicle for social concerns, financial transfers, are, in a sense, outsourced to the GEF. The conclusion that social concerns occupy the least prominent position is strengthened by the fact that, in the GEF, environmental concerns are seen as primary with a degree of integration of social concerns.

As far as the second point is concerned, the trumping of environmental and social concerns takes place in a very subtle way. Within the climate change regime, environmental concerns have been trumped in a variety of ways. First, while emissions reduction targets have been set, by all accounts these targets have been set too low to have any significant impact on climate change. The argument advanced has been that these targets should only be seen as the beginning, implying that more stringent reduction targets will be set in the future. Second, the impact of these low emissions targets is further reduced by the provision for market mechanisms to ease the burden of emissions targets. Social concerns are equally trumped by economic concerns in subtle ways. First, on close inspection, the CDM which is put forward as a way to achieve sustainable development in developing countries, appears to be rather for the benefit of the investors than for the developing host country. The CDM, further, illustrates how social and environmental concerns are pitted against each other for the benefit of the economic concerns. The CDM, being presented as a means to promote social concerns in developing countries while at the same time having the effect of reducing the environmental integrity of the Kyoto Protocol, may encourage the impression that environmental concerns are being trumped by social concerns while, in fact, environmental concerns are being trumped by economic concerns. Similarly, as suggested in paragraph 4.4 of chapter 5 a closer inspection of other concepts in the regime which may, at face value, appear to be aligned to the social value (for example adaptation) reveals significant economic interests being served. As suggested in chapter 5, this implies an instrumentalisation of social concerns for the achievement of economic goals.

As stated earlier in this paragraph, there is a constant give-and-take between environmental and economic concerns in the biodiversity regime. However, what is clear in this give-and-take is that social concerns are trumped by economic concerns. Interestingly, the trumping of social concerns by economic concerns is effected by emphasising the relationship between social and environmental concerns. In the Protocol the social impacts of LMOs are not relevant unless they are related to biodiversity impacts. While this, correctly, illustrates the relationship between biodiversity and social concerns, it does have the effect of denying social concerns an independent or intrinsic value and thereby subordinating these concerns to both environmental and economic concerns. What is important to note is that this subordination essentially takes place for economic purposes. The commercialisation of benefit sharing in the biodiversity regime also illustrates how the trumping of social concerns can take place through the instrumentalisation of social concerns to promote essentially economic values. This is achieved primarily through the use of a contractarian access and benefit-sharing approach.

The above methods of trumping further serve to illustrate the point made in paragraph 2.1 about the importance of a more nuanced conceptualisation of sustainable development which not only accurately and expressly takes account of the values that sustainable development is supposed to integrate, but also, more consciously, identifies a hierarchy. If, indeed, an economic growth-centred variation of sustainable development is unacceptable given the purpose of sustainable development, then the kinds of compromises and trade-offs made in these instruments become difficult to justify. However, in an environment where sustainable development means different things to different constituencies, these compromises are more easily justified.

3. Is there any cause for hope?

The conclusion of this study is that the popularity of the economic growth-centred variation of sustainable development in instruments professing to give effect to sustainable development suggests that the economic growth-centred paradigm continues to dominate the international legal order while using the new, more fashionable language of sustainable development. Environmental and social considerations, in this paradigm, play second and third fiddles respectively.

Nevertheless, there is some cause for 'modest hope', even leaving aside the progress identified in the GEF.[3] The environmental agreements analysed in Part B were concluded in the face of *some* uncertainty. This is especially true of the Biosafety Protocol. Even the compromised environmental standards set in these instruments will result in economic costs in the pursuit of environmental (and, perhaps social) benefits. The Kyoto Protocol's emissions targets as well as the procedures for transboundary movement of modified organisms will result in costs to states and major corporations. This willingness to bear some economic costs for environmental and social benefit is, in itself, a cause for modest hope.

Although falling outside the scope of the study, some institutional observations are relevant. As observed in paragraph 2.1 of this chapter, the greatest contributor to the progress of the GEF has, as a

3 The phrase 'modest hope' is borrowed from B Ward 'Only one earth, Stockholm 1972' in N Cross (ed) *Evidence of hope: The search for sustainable development* (2003) 9: 'Here I will admit to what I call a modest hope: I would say that it is possible that our science and our wisdom are coming together and our faith and our reality are beginning to coincide. If Stockholm is the place where that begins, well, let us thank God that we were here when it started'.

matter of fact, been the Conference of the Parties to the Climate change and Biodiversity conventions, two regimes which have reflected an economic growth-centred variation of sustainable development. How this is possible requires separate and further study focusing on institutional aspects relating to sustainable development.[4] Nevertheless, it is a cause for 'modest hope' that regimes reflecting an economic growth-centred variation of sustainable development can, in other forums, have an influence leaning towards other concerns than economic.

This cause for modest hope is grounded in the fact that the economic growth-centred variation of sustainable development, even though still dominated by economic concerns, represents an approach based on integration. Thus, although economic concerns are still dominant, the economic growth-centred variation of sustainable development promotes the integration of both social and environmental concerns.

This is a start, but it is only a that! The understanding of sustainable development has to reflect its purpose: to transform the international order from a paradigm where economic concerns are central in the design of law, to a paradigm where the importance of environmental and social considerations permeates the design of international law. This cannot happen under conditions where sustainable development means different things to different people. Thus it is imperative that the international community acknowledges the different variations of sustainable and selects one variation to guide us into the future. If, indeed, the economic growth-centred variation of sustainable development is the preferred vehicle, then it is equally important that this be acknowledged in order to open up space for critique, engagement and justification.

4. Conclusion

For sustainable development to achieve the lofty goals for which it was created, to usher in a new paradigm in international law and

4 For an interesting an easily accessible text on some institutional issues impacting on sustainable development, see E Hey 'Sustainable development, normative development and the legitimacy of decision-making' (2003) 34 *Netherlands Yearbook of International Law* 3; see also R Churchill & G Ulfstein 'Autonomous institutional arrangements in multilateral environmental agreements: A little noticed phenomenon in international law' (2000) 94 *American Journal of International Law* 623. See also, in the context of human rights, K Arts *Integrating human rights into development co-operation: The case of the Lomé Convention* (2000) 372 where the author notes that many African Caribbean and Pacific states, as well as the members of the European Union, in addition to being in the Lomé arrangements are, at the same time, involved in different agreements and arrangements and may adopt different positions at different forums.

policy in which environmental and social concerns are treated as central and not peripheral, it is imperative that the indeterminacy and subordination objections to sustainable development are overcome. The nuanced framework, proposing three variations of sustainable development, would be a step in the right direction. However, this cannot be the end of the matter. It is important, once the need for a nuanced model is accepted, that a choice be made about which variation of sustainable development will secure the future of the planet and its inhabitants. A choice about the variation of sustainable development should then serve to restrict the acceptable design of international regimes by excluding designs that do not reflect the chosen variation of sustainable development.

What became clear in the study is that an economic growth-centred variation cannot form the basis for an acceptable approach to sustainable development. The economic growth-centred variation of sustainable development reinforces the old paradigm where, in the design of law and policy, economic concerns triumphed over both environmental and social concerns. This was clear from an analysis of instruments considered in this study. The result of the centrality of economic concerns in both the climate change and biosafety regimes has been reduced environmental integrity.

However, the elimination of the economic growth-centred variation of sustainable development as the preferred approach does not take us all the way. It begs the question of which variation should be adopted. Should the social well-being-centred variation be adopted? Should the environment-centred variation be adopted? Bosselmann makes an impassioned yet intellectual argument for what he terms a 'strong model' of sustainable development.[5] In Bosselmann's typology, a strong model of sustainable development can be equated with the environment-centred variation of sustainable development. This, he argues, is the only sustainable policy option since nature is overarching and everything else must be made subject to nature.

The environment-centred variation of sustainable development is very attractive in this age where there is an ever-present threat to our environment. Truth be told, our very survival on this planet is dependent on the environment from which we derive so much. However, the argument for an environment-centred variation is based on a misconception of the social well-being-centred variation of sustainable development. In general terms, as argued in chapter 3, there is no reason why a social well-being-centred variation of sustainable development does not qualify as strong sustainable

5 See K Bosselmann 'The concept of sustainable development' in K Bosselmann & D Grinlinton (eds) *Environmental law for sustainable societies* (2002). See for discussion, para 3.1 of chapter 3.

development. In specific terms the following three assertions can be made. First, and to be fair this is true of all three variations of sustainable development, the social well-being centred variation of sustainable development is based on integration and therefore environmental (and economic) concerns will, by definition, have to be incorporated. Second, it goes without saying that the major global environment problems facing the world arise from the over-exploitation of natural resources for industrial and economic growth-related activities and not from activities related to the meeting of basic social needs.

Third, and most importantly, the human needs that are to be accorded central position in this variation of sustainable development are not only those of the present generation. In keeping with the principle of intergenerational equity— an important theoretical pillar in sustainable development discourse — the needs of future (human) generations are similarly important in the integration process.

It was suggested, in chapter 3 of this study that the principle of intergenerational equity implies autonomy for future generations to determine for themselves what their needs are. The latter understanding of intergenerational equity would have the effect of requiring us, as the present generation, to protect jealously all aspects of nature, as the fulfilment of the needs of future generations may be dependent on those very aspects of nature that we may not find very useful. Thus, while a social well-being-centred variation of sustainable development places human needs at the centre, this implies great respect for nature as our destiny as a species is dependent entirely on nature.

The call made — for example in the Johannesburg Declaration on Sustainable Development — for a recognition that 'humans must be at the centre' of sustainable development is a call for a social well-being-centred variation of sustainable development. This call is consistent with the historical exposition of sustainable development from its early roots during the Stockholm process. It was the plight of the poorest and most vulnerable members of our human family that laid the seeds for the development of the concept. It should be the plight of the poorest and most vulnerable members of our human family that informs the understanding of this concept.

Bibliography

Adams, WM *Green development: Environment and sustainability in the third world* (Routledge, London, 1990)

Adelman, I & Ralston, K 'Institutions and economic linkages at village level in West Java, Indonesia' in de Janvry, A; Radwan, S; Sadoulet, E & Thorbecke, E (eds) *State, market and civil organizations: New theories, new practices and their implications for rural development* (Macmillan, London, 1995)

Adler, J 'More sorry than safe: Assessing the precautionary principle and the proposed international Biosafety Protoocol' (2000) 35 *Texas International Law Journal* 173

Adler, J 'The Cartagena Protocol and Biological Diversity: Biosafe or bio-sorry' (2000) 12 *Georgetown International Law Review* 761

Alfonso, M 'The relationship with other agreements: An EU perspective' in Bail, C; Falkner, R & Marquard, H (eds) *The Cartagena Protocol on Biosafety: Reconciling trade in biotechnology with environment and development* (Earthscan, London, 2002)

Alston, P 'Resisting the merger and acquisition of human rights by trade law: A reply to Petersmann' (2002) 13 *European Journal of International Law* 815

Arcas, RL 'Is the Kyoto Protocol an adequate environmental agreement to resolve the climate change problem' (2001) 18 *European Environmental Law Review* 282

Arts, K; Peters, P; Schrijver, N & Sluijs, van P 'Legal and institutional aspects' in Kuik, O; Peters, P & Schrijver, N (eds) *Joint implementation to curb climate change: Legal and economic aspects* (Kluwer, Dordrecht, 1994)

Arts, K *Integrating human rights into development co-operation: The case of the Lomé Convention* (Kluwer, The Hague, 2000)

Arts, K 'ACP-EU relations in a new era: The Cotonou Agreement' (2003) 40 *Common Market Law Review* 95

Ashe, JW 'The Financial Mechanism' in Bail, C; Falkner, R & Marquard, H (eds) *The Cartagena Protocol on Biosafety: Reconciling trade in biotechnology with environment and development* (Earthscan, London, 2002)

Bail, C; Falkner, R & Marquard, H (eds) *The Cartagena Protocol on Biosafety: Reconciling trade in biotechnology with environment and development* (Earthscan, London, 2002)

Barker, D & Mander, J 'The invisible government: The World Trade Organization: A global government for the new millennium? A primer' (1999) *The International Forum on Globalization* 1

Baumert, KA 'Participation of developing countries in the International Climate Change Regime: Lessons for the future' (2006) 38 *George Washington International Law Review* 363

Bermann, GA; Goebel, RJ; Davey, WJ & Fox, EM European Community law: Selected documents (Including European Union materials), 1998 edition (West Group, St Paul, 1997)

Birnie, PW & Boyle, AE *International law and the environment* (Clarendon Press, Oxford, 1996)

Blaunstein, AP & Flanz, GH *Constitutions of the countries of the world* (Oceana Publications, New York, 1993)

Bodegard, J 'Documentation' in Bail, C; Falkner, R & Marquard, H (eds) *The Cartagena Protocol on Biosafety: Reconciling trade in biotechnology with environment and development* (Earthscan, London, 2002)

Boehmer-Christiansen, S 'Investing against climate change: Why failure remains possible' (2002) 11 *Environmental Politics* 1

Bohm, P 'Improving cost effectiveness and facilitating participation of developing countries in international emissions trading' (2002) 2 *International Environmental Agreements: Politics, Law and Economics* 261

Boisson de Chazournes, L 'The Global Environment Facility galaxy: On linkages among institutions' (1999) 3 *Max Planck Yearbook of United Nations Law* 243

Boisson de Chazournes, L 'Policy guidance and compliance: The World Bank operational standards' in Shelton D (ed) *Commitment and compliance: The role of non-binding norms in the international legal system* (Oxford University Press, Oxford, 2000)

Bosselmann, K 'Justice and the environment: Building blocks for a theory on ecological justice' in Bosselmann, K & Richardson, B (eds) *Environmental justice and market mechanisms: Key challenges for environmental law and policy* (Kluwer, The Hague, 1999)

Bosselmann, K 'The concept of sustainable development' in Bosselmann, K & Grinlinton, D (eds) *Environmental law for sustainable societies* (New Zealand Centre for Environmental Law, Auckland, 2002)

Bosselmann, K 'Strong and weak sustainable development: Making the difference in the design of law', paper presented at the World Summit 2002: Environmental Law Foundations for Sustainable Development, University of Natal, Pietermaritzburg, South Africa

Bosselmann, K 'Human rights and the environment: A circular affair – The case for an ecological approach' (2003) unpublished draft manuscript, on file with author

Bothe, M 'The United Nations Framework Convention on Climate Change: An unprecedented multilevel regulatory challenge' (2003) 63 *Heidelberg Journal of International Law* 239

Boyle, A 'The role of international human rights law in the protection of the environment' in Boyle, A & Anderson, M (eds) *Human rights approaches to environmental protection* (Clarendon Press, London, 1996)

Boyle, A & Freestone, D 'Introduction' in Boyle, A & Freestone, D (ed) *International law and sustainable development* (Oxford University Press, New York, 1999)

Brack, D *International trade and the Montreal Protocol* (Earthscan, London, 1996)

Brack, D 'The shrimp-turtle case: Implications for multilateral environmental agreements - World Trade agreement debate' (1999) 10 *Yearbook of International Environmental Law* 13

Breidenich, C, Magraw, D, Rowley, A and Rubin, J 'The Kyoto Protocol to the United Nations Convention on Climate Change' (1998) 92 *American Journal of International Law* 315

Broches, A 'International legal aspects of the operations of the World Bank' (1959,III) 98 *Recueil des Cours Academie de Droit International* 297

Brown, DA *American heat: Ethical problems with the United States' response to global warming* (Rowman & Littlefield, Oxford, 2002)

Brown Weiss, E 'The planetary trust: Conservation and intergenerational equity' (1984) 11 *Ecology Law Quarterly* 494

Brown Weiss, E *In fairness to future generations: International law, common patrimony and intergenerational equity* (Transnational Publishers, New York, 1989)

Brown Weiss, E 'Our rights and obligations to future generations for the environment' (1990) 84 *American Journal of International Law* 198

Brown Weiss, E 'Introductory Note' (1992) 31 *International Legal Materials* 814

Brunnée, J 'The Kyoto Protocol: Testing grounds for compliance theories' (2003) 63 *Heidelberg Journal of International Law* 255

Bridgeman, NL 'World Bank reform in the "post policy" era' (2001) 13 *Georgetown International Law Review* 1013

Burchill, S & Linklater, A (eds) *Theories of international relations* (St Martins, New York, 1996)

Burgiel, SW 'The Cartagena Protocol on Biosafety: Taking steps from negotiation to implementation' (2002) 11 *RECIEL* 53

Cameron, J & Abouchar, J 'The status of the precautionary principle in international law' in Freestone, D & Hey, E (eds) *The precautionary principle and international law: The challenge of implementation* (Kluwer, The Hague, 1996)

Chong, M 'Rhetoric and reality: The case of the golden rice in Thailand' (2002) available at http://wwweinnadi.cornell.edu/southasia/workshop/pdfgolden_rice.pdf

Chossudovsky, M *The globalisation of poverty: The impacts of IMF and World Bank reforms* (Zed Books, London, 1997)

Chowdhury, SR; Denters, EMG & de Waart, PJIM (eds) *The right to development in international law* (Martinus Nijhoff, Dordrecht, 1992)

Churchill, R & Ulfstein, G 'Autonomous institutional arrangements in multilateral environmental agreements: A little noticed phenomenon in international law' (2000) 94 *American Journal of International Law* 623

Clausen, E 'Carping at Kyoto' (2002) 34 *George Washington International Law Review* 247

Codonier Segger, MC & Khalfan, A *Sustainable development law: Principles, practices and prospects* (Oxford University Press, New York, 2004)

Cohn, M 'The World Trade Organization: Elevating property interests above human rights' (2001) 30 *Georgia Journal of International and Comparative Law* 427

Cook, K 'Non-Parties' in Bail, C; Falkner, R & Marquard, H (eds) *The Cartagena Protocol on Biosafety: Reconciling trade in biotechnology with environment and development* (Earthscan, London, 2002)

Corino, C 'The Kyoto Protocol: Tradable emissions credits and compensatory solutions under the Bonn resolutions' (2001) 18 *European Environmental Law Review* 294

Crocker, DA 'Development ethics and globalization' (2003) 30 *Philosophical Topics* 9

Cullet, P & Gowlland-Gualtieri, A (eds) *Key materials in international environmental law* (Ashgate, Aldershot, 2004)

D'Amato, A 'Do we owe a duty to future generations to preserve the global environment?' (1990) 84 *American Journal of International Law* 190

D'Amato, A & Chopra, SK 'Whales: Their emerging right to life' (1991) 85 *American Journal of International Law* 21

Dross, M & Wolff, F 'Do we need a new access and benefit sharing regime?' (2004) 15 *Yearbook of International Environmental Law* 95

Drumbl, M 'Northern economic obligation, Southern moral entitlement, and international environmental governance' (2002) 27 *Columbia Journal of Environmental Law* 363

Dunoff, JL 'Institutional misfits: The GATT, the ICJ and trade-environment disputes' (1993/1994) 15 *Michigan Journal of International Law* 1043

Dworkin, R *Taking rights seriously* (Duckworth, London, 1977)

Eckersley, R *Environmentalism and political theory: Towards an ecocentric approach* (UCL Press, London, 1992)

Eichengreen, B & Kenen, PB 'Managing the world economy under the Bretton Woods system: An overview' in Kenen, PB (ed) *Managing the world economy: Fifty years after Bretton Woods* (Institute for International Economics, Washington DC, 1994)

Esty, DC *Greening the GATT: Trade, environment and the future* (Institute for International Economics, Washington DC, 1994)

Feris, LA & Tladi, D 'Environmental rights' in Brand, D & Heyns, C (eds) *Socio-economic rights in South Africa* (Pretoria University Law Publishers, Pretoria, 2005)

Flanz, GH *Constitutions of the countries of the world* (Oceana, New York, 2002)

Flanz, GH *Constitutions of the countries of the world* (Oceana, New York, 1999)

Franck, TM *Fairness in international law and institutions* (Oxford University Press, New York, 1995)

Freestone, D 'The precautionary principle' in Churchill, R & Freestone, D (eds) *International law and climate change* (Gordon and Trotman, Boston, 1991)

Freestone, D 'The United Nations Framework Convention on Climate Change, the Kyoto Protocol and the Kyoto mechanisms' in Freestone, D & Streck, C (eds) *Legal aspects of implementing the Kyoto mechanisms: Making Kyoto work* (Oxford, New York, 2005)

Freestone, D & Hey, E (eds) *The precautionary principle and international law: The challenges of implementation* (Kluwer, The Hague, 1996)

Freestone, D & Hey, E 'Origins and development of the precautionary principle' in Freestone, D & Hey, E (eds) *The precautionary principle and international law: The challenges of implementation* (Kluwer, The Hague, 1996)

Freestone, D 'Implementing precaution cautiously: The precautionary approach in the Straddling and Highly Migratory Fish Stocks Agreement' in Hey, E (ed) *Developments in international fisheries law* (Kluwer, The Hague, 1999)

Freestone, D 'International fisheries law since Rio: The continued rise of the precautionary principle' in Boyle, A & Freestone, D (eds) *International law and sustainable development* (Oxford Press, New York, 1999)

French, DA 'The role of the state and international organization in reconciling sustainable development and globalization' (2002) 2 *International Environmental Agreements: Politics, Law and Economics* 135

Friedmann, W 'The uses of "general principles" in the development of international law' (1963) 57 *American Journal of International* 279

Fuentes, X 'International law-making in the field of sustainable development: The unequal competition between development and the environment' (2002) 2 *International Environmental Agreements: Politics, Law and Economics* 109

Glasby, GP 'Sustainable development and the need for a new paradigm' (2002) 4 *Environment, Development and Sustainability* 333

Gillespie, A *International environmental law, policy and ethics* (Clarendon Press, New York, 1997)

Graff, L 'The precautionary principle' in Bail, C; Falkner, R & Marquard, H (eds) *The Cartagena Protocol on Biosafety: Reconciling trade in biotechnology with environment and development* (Earthscan, London, 2002)

Griffiths, M 'Biosafety Protocol' (1998) *Colorado Journal of International Environmental Law and Policy* 113

Grosko, B 'Genetic engineering and international law: Conflict or harmony? An analysis of the Biosafety Protocol, GATT and the WTO Sanitary and Phytosanitary Agreement' (2001) 20 *Virginia Environmental Law Journal* 295

Gumede, WL *Thabo Mbeki and the battle for the soul of the ANC* (Sebra Press, Cape Town, 2005)

Gundling, L 'Our responsibility to future generations' (1990) 84 *American Journal of International Law* 207

Gupta, A 'Governing trade in genetically modified organisms' (2000) 42 *Environment* 23

Guruswamy, LD 'Sustainable agriculture: Do GMOs imperil biosafety?' (2002) 9 *Indiana Journal of Global Legal Studies* 461

Haddad, B & Palmisano, J 'Market Darwinism vs market creationism: Adaptability and fairness in the design of greenhouse gas trading mechanisms' (2001) 1 *International Environmental Agreements: Politics, Law and Economics* 427

Hall, M 'Bush defends his rejection of pact on global warming' *USA Today* 1 April 2001, 2A

Halloran, J & Hansen, M 'Why we need labelling of genetically engineered food' available at http://www.consumersinternational.org/documents_asp/ViewADcoment.asp?regid=135&ID=5838&categoryid=langid=1

Handl, G 'Sustainable development: General rules versus specific obligations' in Lang, W (ed) *Sustainable development and international law* (Graham & Trotman, London,1995)

Handl, G 'The legal mandate of multilateral development banks as agents for change towards sustainable development' (1998) 92 *American Journal of International Law* 642

Handl, G 'Correspondence' (1999) 93 *American Journal of International Law* 625

Hayes, P & Kirk, S (eds) *The global greenhouse regime? Who pays?* (Earthscan, London, 1993)

Heavin, HD 'The Biosafety Protocol and the SPS Agreement: Conflicts and dispute resolution' (2003) 12 *Journal of Environmental Law and Practice* 373

Hey, E 'The climate change regime: An enviro-economic problem and international administrative law in the making' (2001) 1 *International Environmental Agreements: Politics, Law, and Economics* 75

Hey, E 'Sustainable development, normative development and the legitimacy of decision making' (2003) 34 *Netherlands Yearbook of International Law* 3

Heyns, CH & Van der Linde, M *Human rights law in Africa* (Martinus Nijhoff, Leiden, 2004)

Hohmann, H *Basic documents of international environmental law* (Graham and Trotman, London, 1992)

Horta, K 'Boundaries in the field of human rights: Rhetoric and reality: human rights and the World Bank' (2002) 15 *Harvard Human Rights Journal* 227

Houseman, R & Zaelke, D 'Trade, environment, and sustainable development: A primer' (1992) 15 *Hastings International and Comparative Law Review* 535

Hourde, L 'Mortgaging the earth: The World Bank, environmental impoverishment, and the crisis of development' 1995 *George Washington International Law Review* 721

Howse, R 'Human rights in the WTO: Whose rights, whose humanity? Comment on Petersmann' (2002) 13 *European Journal of International Law* 651

Hurrel, A & Kingsbury, B 'International politics of the environment: An introduction' in Hurrell, A & Kingsbury, B (eds) *The international politics of the environment: Actors, interests, and institutions* (Oxford University Press, New York, 1992)

Huq, S & Reid, H 'Benefit sharing under the Clean Development Mechanism' in Freestone, D & Streck, C (eds) *Legal aspects of implementing the Kyoto mechanisms: Making Kyoto work* (Oxford, New York, 2005)

ILA Report of the seventieth conference: New Delhi (London, 2002)

ILA Report of the seventy-first conference: Berlin (London, 2004)

ILA Committee on International Law on Sustainable Development Second Report (2006)

IMF Annual Report (1991)

IUCN, UNEP, WWF Caring for the earth: A strategy for sustainability (IUCN, Gland, 1990)

IPCC Climate change: The IPCC scientific assessment Houghton, JT; Jenkins, GJ & Ephraums, JJ (eds) (Cambridge University Press, Cambridge, 1990)

IPCC Climate change 2001: Impacts, adaptation, vulnerability (2001) available at http://www.grida.no/climate/ipcc_tar/wg2/index.htm

Jabara, K 'The Biosafety Protocol' (2001) 8 *University of Baltimore Journal of Environmental Law* 121

Johnson, H D 'Whose earth is it anyway?' (2002) 39 (3) *UN Chronicle* 8

Joyner, CC 'Burning international bridges, fuelling discontent: The United States and rejection of the Kyoto Protocol' (2002) 33 *Victoria University of Wellington Law Review* 27

Kerns, MP & Mingst, KA *International organizations: The politics and processes of global governance* (Rienner, London, 2004)

Keohane, RO *After hegemony: Co-operation and discord in the world political economy* (Princeton University Press, Princeton, 1984)

Kemfert, C & Tol, R 'Equity, international trade and climate policy' (2002) 2 *International Environmental Agreements: Politics, Law and Economics* 23

Khwaja, RH 'Socio-economic considerations' in Bail, C; Falkner, R & Marquard, H (eds) *The Cartagena Protocol on Biosafety: Reconciling trade in biotechnology with environment and development* (Earthscan, London, 2002)

Killick, T 'Low-income countries and the IMF - A case of structural incompatibility?' in Culpeper, R; Berry, A & Stewart, F (eds) *Global development fifty years after Bretton Woods* (St Martin's Press, New York, 1997)

Kiss, A 'The rights and interests of future generations and the precautionary principle' in Freestone, D & Hey, E (eds) *The precautionary principle and international law: The challenges of implementation* (Kluwer, The Hague, 1996)

Kiss, A & Shelton, D *International environmental law 2nd edition* (Transactional Publishers, New York, 2000)

Kolehmainen, S 'Genetically engineered agriculture: Precaution before profits: An overview of issues in genetically engineered food and crops' (2001) 20 *Virginia Environmental Law Journal* 261

Kohli, A 'Introduction' in Kohli, A; Moon, C & Sørensen, G (eds) *States, markets and just growth: Development in the twenty-first century* (United Nations University Press, Tokyo, 2003)

Kuik, O & Gupta, J 'Perspectives on Africa and the global debate on joint implementation' in Maya, RS & Gupta J (eds) *Joint implementation: Carbon colonies or business opportunities* (Southern Centre Climate Change Series, Harare, 1994)

Lashof, D and Fiedler, J 'Hot air - controlling the flow' available at http://www.climatenetwork.org/eco/4_Cop5_hot.html

Lilly, L *The mind of the dolphin: A non-human intelligence* (Doubleday and Company, New York, 1967)

Liu, SF 'The Koko incident: Developing international norms for the transboundary movement of hazardous wastes' (1992/1993) 8 *Journal of Natural Resources and Environmental Law* 121

Lomborg, B 'Global warming - are we doing the right thing?' available at http://image.gaurdian.co.uk/sys-files/Gaurdian/document/2001/08/14warming.pdf

Lopez, TM 'A look at climate change and the evolution of the Kyoto Protocol' (2003) 43 *Natural Resources Journal* 258

Lowe, V 'Sustainable development and unsustainable arguments' in Boyle, A & Freestone, D (eds) *International law and sustainable development* (Oxford University Press, New York, 1999)

Lowe, V 'The politics of law-making: Are the method and character of norm creation changing?' in Byers, M (ed) *The role of law in international politics: Essays in international relations and international law* (Oxford University Press, Oxford, 2000)

Mackenzie, R & Sands, P 'Prospects for international environmental law' in Bail, C; Falkner, R & Marquard, H (eds) *The Cartagena Protocol on Biosafety: Reconciling trade in biotechnology with environment and development* (Earthscan, London, 2002)

Mahar, DJ & Ducrot, CEJ *Land use zoning on tropical frontiers: Emerging lessons from the Brazilian Amazon* (Washington DC, Economic Development Institute of the World Bank 1998)

Malviya, RA 'Sustainable development and environment: Emerging trends and issues' (1996) 32 *Indian Journal of International Law* 57

Maluwa, T 'The African Union, the Southern African Development Community, and the New Partnership for Africa's Development: Some observations on

South Africa's contribution to international law-making an institution building in Africa, 1994-2004' (2004) 29 *South African Yearbook of International Law* 5

Mandela, N Address to World Economic Forum, January 1999, available at www.anc.org.za/ancdocs/history/mandela/1999/nm0129.htm

Mangu, AMB 'What future for human and peoples' rights under the African Union, New Partnership for Africa's Development, the African Peer-Review Mechanism and the African Court?' (2004) 29 *South African Yearbook of International Law* 136

Marahun, T 'A global energy strategy as a viable means for redressing climate change?' (2003) 63 *Heidelberg Journal of International Law* 281

Markandya, A; Halsnaes, K; Mason, P & Olhoff, A, 'A conceptual framework for analysing climate change in the context of sustainable development' in Markandya, A and Halsnaes, K (eds) *Climate change and sustainable development: Prospects for developing countries* (Earthscan, London, 2002)

Marquard, H 'Scope' in Bail, C; Falkner, R & Marquard, H (eds) *The Cartagena Protocol on Biosafety: Reconciling trade in biotechnology with environment and development* (Earthscan, London, 2002)

Mashava, L (ed) *Economic and social rights series (vol 7): A compilation of essential documents on the rights to water and environment* (Pretoria, 2000)

Matsui, Y 'Some aspects of the principle of "common but differentiated Responsibilities"' (2002) 2 *International Environmental Agreements: Politics, Law and Economics* 151

Matsushita, M; Schoenbaum, TJ & Mavroidis, PC The World Trade Organization: Law, practice and policy (Oxford University Press, New York, 2003)

Maybe, N; Hall, S; Smith, C & Gupta, S (eds) *Argument in the greenhouse: The international economics of controlling global warming* (Routledge, London, 1997)

Mayeda, G 'Where should Johanneburg take us? Ethical and legal approaches to sustainable development in the context of international law' (2004) 15 *Colorado Journal of International Law* 29

McCaffrey, S 'Biotechnology: Some issues of general international law' (2001) 14 *Transnational Lawyer* 91

Meijer, E & Werksman, J 'Keeping it clean - Safeguarding the environmental integrity of the Clean Development Mechanism' in Freestone, D and Streck, C (eds) *Legal aspects of implementing the Kyoto mechanisms: Making Kyoto work* (Oxford University Press, New York, 2005)

Menstrum, F 'Poverty reduction and sustainable development' (2003) 4 *Environment, Development and Sustainability* 41

Merrils, JG 'Environmental protection and human rights: Conceptual aspects' in Boyle, A & Anderson, M (eds) *Human rights approaches to environmental protection* (Clarendon Press, London, 1996)

Michaelowa, A & Tol, RSJ 'Outlook for the international climate policy - revolution or reform?' (2002) 2 *International Environmental Agreements: Politics, Law and Economics* 217

Mickelson, K 'North, South, international environmental law and international environmental lawyers' (2000) 11 *Yearbook of International Environmental Law* 52

Missfeldt, F 'Flexibility mechanisms: Which path to take after Kyoto?' (1998) 7 *Review of European Community and International Environmental Law* 128

Miller, AS 'The Global Environment Facility and the search for financial strategies to foster sustainable development' (2000) 24 *Vermont Law Review* 1229

Miller, MAL *The third world in global environmental politics* (Lynne Rienner Publishers, Boulder, 1995)

Moe, A 'Russian quota sales: Not just a lot of hot air' available at http://program.forskingradet.no/pretropol.hotair.php3

Moore, JB *The history and digest of the international tribunals to which the United States has been a party* (Washington, 1898)

Moore, M 'The multilateral trading system in support of Africa-led and Africa owned development' paper presented at Ecosoc, High Level Policy Dialgue, United Nations, July 2001 available at www.wto.org/spanish/news_s/spmm_s/spmm68_s.htm

Morgan-Foster, J 'The relationship of IMF structural adjustment programs to economic, social and cultural rights: The Argentine case revisited' (2003) 24 *Michigan Journal of International Law* 577

Mosley, P; Harrington, J & Toye, J *Aid and power: The World Bank and policy-based lending (vol I): Analysis and policy proposals* (Routledge, London, 1991)

Munro, RD & Lammers, JG (eds) *Environmental protection and sustainable development: Legal principles and recommendations* (Graham and Trotman, London, 1987)

Mugwanya, GW 'Global free trade *vis-à-vis* environmental regulation and sustainable development: Reinvigorating efforts towards a more integrated approach' (1999) 14 *Journal of Environmental Law* 40

Nanda, VP & Pring, G International environmental law and policy for the 21st century (Transnational Publishers, New York, 2003)

Nelson, P 'An African dimension to the Clean Development Mechanism: Finding a path to sustainable development in the energy sector' (2004) 32 *Denver Journal of International Law and Policy* 615

Ntambirweki, J 'The developing countries in the evolution of an international environmental law' (1991) 14 *Hastings International and Comparative Law Review* 906

Nollkaemper, A '"What you risk reveals what you value" and other dilemmas encountered in the legal assaults on risk' in Freestone, D & Hey, E (eds) *The precautionary principle and international law: The challenges of implementation* (Kluwer, The Hague, 1996)

Ochoa, C 'Advancing the language of human rights in a global economic order: An analysis of discourse' (2003) 23 *Boston College Third Law Journal* 57

O'Driscol, GP Jr & Hoskins, L 'Property rights: The key to economic development' in Schäfer, H & Raja, AV (eds) *Law and economic development* (Edward Elgar, Cheltenham, 2006)

Okafor, OC 'The status and effect of the right to development in contemporary international law: Towards a South-North "entente"' (1995) 7 *African Journal of International and Comparative Law* 865

Oliva, MJ 'The Cartagena Protocol: On Biosafety and the Agreement on Sanitary and Phytosanitary Measures: What will decisions on GMOs have to be based on' (2002) 13 *International Legal Perspectives* 22

Pan, J 'Emissions rights and their transferability: Equity concerns over climate mitigation' (2003) 3 *International Environmental Agreements: Politics, Law and Economics* 1

Pallemaerts, M 'From Stockholm to Rio: Back to the future?' in Sands, P (ed) *Greening international law* (New Press, London, 1993)

Pallemaerts, M 'Is multilateralism the future? Sustainable development or globalisation as a "comprehensive vision" of the future of humanity' (2003) 5 *Environment, Development and Sustainability* 275

Pallemaerts, M 'International law and sustainable development: Any progress in Johannesburg' (2003) 12 *Review of the European Community and International Environmental Law* 1

PCF Prototype Carbon Fund - Public private partnership: 2004 annual report (2004) available at http://www.prototypecarbonfund.org

PCF Board Fourth report on the implementation of the Prototype Carbon Fund and proposed amendments to the Instrument Establishing the Prototype Carbon Fund (2002) available at http://www.prototypecarbonfund.org

Petersmann, EU 'Time for a United Nations "global compact" for integrating human rights into the law of world wide organizations: Lesson from European integration' (2002) 13 *European Journal of International Law* 621

Pearson, CS *Economics and the global environment* (Cambridge University Press, Cambridge, 2000)

Pinzani, A 'Global justice as a moral issue: An interview with Thomas Pogge'(June 2005) 4 (1) *Ethic@ 1*

Pogge, TW 'Severe poverty as a human rights violation' available at http://www.etikk.no/globaljustice/

Porras, I 'The Rio Declaration: A new basis for international co-operation' in Sands, P (ed) *Greening international law* (New Press, London, 1993)

Prout, C 'Finance for developing countries: An essay' in Strange, S (ed) *International economic relations of the western world* (1959-1971) (vol II): *International monetary relations* (Oxford University Press, London, 1976)

Rakate, PTK 'The duty to prosecute and the status of amnesties for gross and systematic human rights violations in international law: Towards a balanced approach model' (unpublished doctoral thesis, University of South Africa, Pretoria, 2004)

Ramcharan, BG (ed) *Judicial protection of economic, social and cultural rights: Cases and materials* (Martinus Nijhoff, Leiden, 2005)

Rees, WE 'The eco-footprint of agriculture: A far-from-(thermodynamic)-equilibrium interpretation', (unpublished paper on file with author)

Rich, B *Mortgaging the earth: The World Bank, environmental impoverishment and the crisis of development* (Beacon Press, Boston, 1994)

Rich, B 'Still waiting: The failure of reform at the World Bank' in Goddard, CR; Cronin, P & Dash, KC (eds) *International political economy 2nd Edition* (Lynn Rienner Publishers, London, 2003)

Roessler, T 'The World Bank's lending policy and environmental standards' 2000 *North Carolina Journal of Law and Commercial Regulation* 105

Rose, A & Stevens, B 'An economic analysis of flexible permit trading in the Kyoto Protocol' (2001) 1 *International Environmental Agreements: Politics, Law and Economics* 219

Safrin, S 'Treaties in collision? The Biosafety Protocol and the World Trade Organization Agreements' (2002) 96 *American Journal of International Law* 606

Sahn, DE & Sarris, A 'The political economy of economic decline and reform in Africa: The role of the state, markets and civil institutions' in de Janvry, A; Radwan, S; Sadoulet, E & Thorbecke, E (eds) *State, market and civil organizations: New theories, new practices and their implications for rural development* (Macmillan, London,1995)

Sahn, DE; Dorosh, PA & Younger, SD *Structural adjustment reconsidered: Economic policy and poverty in Africa* (Cambridge University Press, Cambridge, 1997)

Salopek, P 'Shattered Sudan: Drilling for oil, hoping for peace' February 2003 *National Geographic* 30

Sand, PH 'The potential impact of the Global Environment Facility of the World Bank, UNDP and UNEP' in Wolfrum, R (ed) *Enforcing environmental standards: Economic mechanisms as viable means?* (Springer, Berlin, 1996)

Sands, P 'International law in the field of sustainable development: Emerging legal principles' in Lang, W (ed) *Sustainable development and international law* (Graham and Trotman, London, 1995)

Sands, P *Principles of international environmental law, vol I: Frameworks, standards and implementation* (Manchester University Press, Manchester, 1995)

Sands, P 'Sustainable development: Treaty, custom and the cross-fertilization of international law' in Boyle, A & Freestone, D (eds) *International law and sustainable development* (Oxford University Press, New York, 1999)

Sands, P 'Environmental protection in the twenty-first century: Sustainable development and international law' in Revesz, RL; Sands, P & Stewart, RB (eds) *Environmental law, the economy and sustainable development: The United States, the European Union and the international community* (Cambridge University Press, Cambridge, 2000)

Sands, P *Lawless world: America and the making and breaking of global rules, from FDR's Atlantic Charter to George W Bush's illegal war* (Viking Penguin, New York, 2005)

Schlemmer, EC 'Compliance with WTO obligations: Trade and the environment revisited' (2002) 27 *South African Yearbook of International Law* 272

Schnier, D 'Genetically modified organisms and the Cartagena Protocol' (2001) 12 *Fordham Environmental Law Journal* 377

Schoenbaum, S 'International trade and the protection of the environment: The continuing search for reconciliation' (1997) 91 *American Journal of International Law* 268

Schoonejans, E 'Advance informed agreement procedure' in Bail, C; Falkner, R & Marquard, H (eds) The Cartagena Protocol on Biosafety: Reconciling trade in Biotechnology with environment and development (Earthscan, London, 2002)

Schrijver, N 'De verankering en betekenis van duurzame ontwikkeling in het internationale recht' 2003 *Mededelingen van de Nederlandse Vereniging voor Internationaal Recht: Volkenrecht en Duurzame Ontwikkeling* 1

Schwartz, P & Randall, D 'An abrupt climate change scenario and its implications for the United States national security' (2003) (Report prepared for the Pentagon, on file with author)

Shelton, D 'Human rights, environmental rights, and the rights to the environment' (1991) 28 *Stanford Journal of International Law* 103

Shelton, D 'What happened in Rio to human rights?' (1992) 2 *Yearbook of International Environmental Law* 75

Shelton, D 'Environmental justice in a postmodern world' in Bosselmann, K & Richardson, B (eds) *Environmental justice and market mechanisms: Key challenges for environmental law and policy* (Kluwer, London, 1999)

Shelton, D 'Introduction' in Shelton, D (ed) *Commitment and compliance: The role of non-binding norms in the international legal system* (Oxford University Press, Oxford, 2000)

Shihata, IFI *The World Bank in a changing world: Selected essays of Ibrahim F Shihata* (Martinus Nijhof, Dordrecht, 1991)

Shihata, IFI *The World Bank Inspection Panel* (Oxford University Press, New York, 1994)

Shihata, IFI 'Correspondence' (1999) 93 *American Journal of International Law* 625

Shihata, IFI *et al The World Bank in a changing world: (vol III)* (M Nijhoff Publishers, Dordrecht, 2000

Sen, A 'Development thinking at the beginning of the 21st century' in Emmereji, L (ed) *Economic and social development in the XXI century* (Inter-American Development Bank, Washington, 1997)

Shaw, MN *International law (5th ed)* (Cambridge University Press, Cambridge, 2000)

Sjöberg, H 'The Global Environment Facility' in Werksman, J (ed) *Greening international institutions* (Earthscan, London,1996)

Smith, K; Swisher, J & Ahuja, D 'Who pays (to solve the problem and how much)?' in Hayes, P and Smith, K (eds) *The global greenhouse regime? Who pays?* (Earthscan, London, 1994)

Stiglitz, JE *Globalization and its discontents* (Norton and Company, New York, 2003)

Stoll, PT 'Controlling the risks of genetically modified organisms: The Cartagena Protocol on Biosafety and the SPS Agreement' (2001) 13 *Yearbook of International Environmental Law* 82

Stone, CD 'Common but differentiated responsibilities in international law' (2004) 98 *American Journal of International Law* 276

Strong, M *Where on earth are we going?* (Texere, New York, 2000)

Taylor, P *An ecological approach to international law: Responding to challenges of climate change* (Routledge, London, 1998)

Taylor, P 'Heads in the sand as the tide rises: Environmental ethics and the law on climate change' (2000/2001) 19 *Journal of Environmental Law* 247

Thoms, L 'A comparative analysis of international regimes on ozone and climate change with implications for regime design' (2003) 41 *Columbia Journal of Transnational Law* 795

Timoshenko, AS 'From Stockholm to Rio: The institutionalization of sustainable development' in Lang, W (ed) *Sustainable development and international law* (Graham and Trotman, London, 1994)

Tladi, D 'The quest to ban hazardous wastes import into Africa: First Bamako and now Basel' (2000) 33 *Comparative and International Law Journal of Southern Africa* 210

Tladi, D 'The Liability Protocol to the Basel Convention on Transboundary Movement of Hazardous Wastes: An overview' (2000) 7 *South African Journal of Environmental Law and Policy* 203

Tladi, D 'Of course for humans: A contextual defense of intergenerational equity' (2002) 9 *South African Journal of Environmental Law and Policy* 177

Tladi, D 'Can the wolf protect the lamb? Free trade regimes as instruments towards sustainable development' (2002) 27 *South African Yearbook of International Law* 149

Tladi, D 'Breathing constitutional values into the law of contract: Freedom of contract and the Constitution' (2002) 35 *De Jure* 306

Tladi, D 'One step forward, two steps back in the constitutionalisation of the common law: Afrox Health Care case' (2002) 17 *SA Public Law* 473

Tladi, D 'Strong sustainability, weak sustainability, intergenerational equity and international law: Using the Earth Charter to redirect the ethics debate' (2003) 28 *South African Yearbook of International Law* 200

Tladi, D 'Strong sustainable development, weak sustainable development and the Earth Charter: Towards a more nuanced framework of analysis' (2004) 11 *South African Journal of Environmental Law and Policy* 17

Tladi, D 'IMF conditionality, debt and poverty: Towards a "strong" anthropocentric model of sustainability' (2004) 16 *South African Mercantile Law Journal* 31

Tladi, D 'International law for sustainable development? Somber reflections on World Bank efforts' (2004) 29 *South African Yearbook of International Law* 164

Todaro, M *Economic development in the third world* (4th ed) (Longman, New York, 1989)

Trouwborst, A *Precautionary rights and duties of states* (Martinus Nijhoff, Leiden, 2006)

Tudge, C 'Farming is not just a business' in *The Mail and Guardian* (South Africa) 21-27 May 2004 available at http://www.mg..co.za

Rivera-Torres, O 'The Biosafety Protocol and the WTO' (2003) 26 *Boston College International and Comparative Law Review* 263

Tracy, L 'Does a genetically modified rose still smell as sweet? Labeling of genetically modified organisms under the Biosafety Protocol' (1999) 6 *Buffalo Environmental Law Journal* 129

UN Commission on Human Rights, Sub-Commission on the Promotion and Protection of Human Rights 'The realization of economic, social and cultural rights: Globalization and its impact on the full enjoyment of human rights' (preliminary report compiled by Oloka-Onyango, J & Udagama, D) E/CN4/Sub.2/2000/13 (on file with author)

UN Commission on Human Rights, Sub-Commission on Prevention of Discrimination and the Protection of Minorities, Human rights and the environment (1994) UN Doc E/CN.4/Sub.2/1994/9 in Boyle, A 'The role of international human rights law in the protection of the environment' in Boyle, A & Anderson, M (eds) *Human rights approaches to environmental protection* (London, 1996)

UNEP: Secretariat of the Biodiversity Convention Cartagena Protocol on Biosafety: A record of the negotiations (2003) available at http://wwwbiodiv.org/doc/publications/bs-brochure-03-en.pdf

Unknown Author 'The Johannesburg Summit test: What will change?' available at http://www.johannesburgsummit.org/html/whats_new/feature_story41.html

UNDP Human development report (New York, 1999)

Uriz, GH 'To lend or not to lend: Oil, human rights, and the World Bank's internal contradictions' (2001) 14 *Harvard Human Rights Journal* 197

Victor, DG *The collapse of the Kyoto Protocol and the struggle to slow global warming* (Princeton University Press, Princeton, 2001)

Von Hahn, A 'Implementation and further development of the Biodiversity Convention: Access to genetic resources, benefit sharing and traditional knowledge of indigenous and local communities' (2003) 63 *Heidelberg Journal of International Law* 295

Vyver, van der JD 'The criminalisation and prosecution of environmental malpractice in international law' (1998) 23 *South African Yearbook of International Law* 1

Wallace Bruce, NL 'Global free trade and sustainable development: Two steps forward in the WTO?' (2002) 35 *Comparative and International Law Journal* 236

Ward, B 'Only one earth, Stockholm 1972' in Cross, N (ed) *Evidence of hope: The search for sustainable development* (Earthscan, London, 2003)

Weeramantry, CG *Universalising international law* (Martinus Nijhoff, Leiden, 2004)

Weiszacker, von E 'Harmonizing environmental and developmental goals' (2002) 39 (3) *UN Chronicle* 12

Wemaere, M & Streck, C 'Legal ownership and nature of Kyoto units and EU allowances' in Freestone, D & Streck, C (eds) *Legal aspects of implementing the Kyoto mechanisms: Making Kyoto work* (Oxford, New York, 2005)

Werksman, J 'Greening Bretton Woods' in Sands, P (ed) *Greening international law* (New Press, New York, 1993)

Werksman, J 'Consolidating governance of the global commons: Insights from the Global Environment Facility' (1995) 6 *Yearbook of International Environmental Law* 27

Werksman, J 'Consolidating global environmental governance: New lessons from the GEF?' available at www.yale.edu/gegdialogue/docs/dialogue/oct03/papers/werksman%20GEF.pdf

Wiener, JB 'Global environmental regulation: Instrument choice in legal context' in Tietenberg, T (ed) Emissions trading programs: vol 1 (Ashgate, Aldershot, 2001) reprinted from (1999) 108 *Yale Law Journal* 677

Wirth, DA 'The sixth session (part two) and seventh session of the conference of the parties to the Framework Convention on Climate Change' (2002) 96 *American Journal of International Law* 648

Wolfensohn, J 'A new global balance: The challenge of leadership' speech delivered to the Board of Governors of the World Bank, September 2003, Dubai (on file with author)

World Bank *Adjustment lending: An evaluation of ten years' experience* (Washington DC, 1988)

World Bank *World development report* (New York, 2003)

World Commission on Environment and Development *Our common future* (Oxford University Press, Oxford, 1987)

Yamin, F; Burniaux, JM & Nentjes, A 'Kyoto mechanisms: Key issues for policy makers for COP 6' (2001) 1 *International Environmental Agreements: Politics, Law and Economics* 187

Yoder, J 'Genetically modified grain' available http://www.goshen.edu/bio/Biol410/BSSpapers99/jeri.html

Young, TR 'An implementation perspective on international law of genetic resources: Incentive, consistency and effective operation' (2004) 15 *Yearbook of International Environmental Law* 3

Permissions

All chapters in this book were first published in SDILAAKEEI, by Pretoria University Law Press (PULP) by Dire Tladi; hereby published with permission under the Creative Commons Attribution License or equivalent. Every chapter published in this book has been scrutinized by our experts. Their significance has been extensively debated. The topics covered herein carry significant information for a comprehensive understanding. They may even be implemented as practical applications or may be referred to as a beginning point for further studies.

We would like to thank the editorial team for lending their expertise to make the book truly unique. They have played a crucial role in the development of this book. Without their invaluable contributions this book wouldn't have been possible. They have made vital efforts to compile up to date information on the varied aspects of this subject to make this book a valuable addition to the collection of many professionals and students.

This book was conceptualized with the vision of imparting up-to-date and integrated information in this field. To ensure the same, a matchless editorial board was set up. Every individual on the board went through rigorous rounds of assessment to prove their worth. After which they invested a large part of their time researching and compiling the most relevant data for our readers.

The editorial board has been involved in producing this book since its inception. They have spent rigorous hours researching and exploring the diverse topics which have resulted in the successful publishing of this book. They have passed on their knowledge of decades through this book. To expedite this challenging task, the publisher supported the team at every step. A small team of assistant editors was also appointed to further simplify the editing procedure and attain best results for the readers.

Apart from the editorial board, the designing team has also invested a significant amount of their time in understanding the subject and creating the most relevant covers. They scrutinized every image to scout for the most suitable representation of the subject and create an appropriate cover for the book.

The publishing team has been an ardent support to the editorial, designing and production team. Their endless efforts to recruit the best for this project, has resulted in the accomplishment of this book. They are a veteran in the field of academics and their pool of knowledge is as vast as their experience in printing. Their expertise and guidance has proved useful at every step. Their uncompromising quality standards have made this book an exceptional effort. Their encouragement from time to time has been an inspiration for everyone.

The publisher and the editorial board hope that this book will prove to be a valuable piece of knowledge for students, practitioners and scholars across the globe.

Index

www.ingramcontent.com/pod-product-compliance
Lightning Source LLC
LaVergne TN
LVHW051048220926
848485LV00001BA/46
9781639891764